● 土木工程施工与管理前沿丛书

建设项目治理十讲

Ten Lectures on Construction Project Governance

沙凯逊　著

中国建筑工业出版社

图书在版编目（CIP）数据

建设项目治理十讲/沙凯逊著. —北京：中国建筑工业出版社，2017.11

（土木工程施工与管理前沿丛书）

ISBN 978-7-112-21043-5

Ⅰ.①建… Ⅱ.①沙… Ⅲ.①基本建设项目-项目管理 Ⅳ.①F284

中国版本图书馆CIP数据核字（2017）第180817号

本书结合我国建筑业改革发展的实际，坚持项目本位的立场，从新制度经济学的视角研究建设项目治理的相关问题，力求做到深入浅出、通俗易懂。

本书的结构可分为两部分。前面五讲主要介绍基本概念和方法，并在此基础上建立起整体分析框架。后面五讲涉及以下内容：(1) 基于委托代理的建设项目垂直治理研究；(2) 基于联盟博弈的建设项目水平治理研究；(3) 基于共同代理的针对项目经理的治理研究；(4) 建设项目治理中的非正式制度安排研究，涉及关系治理、建筑专业体制和行业自律；(5) 基于演化博弈的建筑交易体制的变迁机理研究。

本书可供高等学校工程管理专业和土木工程专业师生学习参考，也可供建设工程项目管理人员和政府建设管理部门阅读借鉴。

* * *

责任编辑：封 毅 毕凤鸣
责任设计：李志立
责任校对：焦 乐 张 颖

土木工程施工与管理前沿丛书
建设项目治理十讲
沙凯逊 著
*
中国建筑工业出版社出版、发行（北京海淀三里河路9号）
各地新华书店、建筑书店经销
北京红光制版公司制版
北京建筑工业印刷厂印刷
*
开本：787×1092毫米 1/16 印张：18½ 字数：390千字
2017年10月第一版 2017年10月第一次印刷
定价：**45.00**元
ISBN 978-7-112-21043-5
（30684）

目　录

组织间关系视角下的建设项目治理[*]
(代序)

摘要：从本质上看，建设项目属于企业间（inter-firm）项目的范畴，它不同于企业内（intra-firm）项目——前者可以视为市场中类似于企业的组织，后者则可以看作是科层组织中类似于市场的过程。为了更好地理解建设项目治理，本文把关注点从科层组织内的“项目—母组织”关系扩展到自组织对等结构中的“承包方—发包方”关系。首先识别项目有别于市场和企业的特征；区分项目的两种基本类型——Ⅰ型项目和Ⅱ型项目；然后研究治理的内涵，对管理与治理做出比较清晰的区隔。建设项目被概括为一种努力，它使法律上独立、具有不同战略目标和长远利益的项目参与者愿意为了共同的目标而在一起工作。划分出三个治理范畴——垂直治理、水平治理、针对项目经理的治理，并从博弈论的角度加以研究，为理解建设项目各种参与者之间的互动关系提供洞察力。问题的关键在于创造一个良好的制度环境，使人们有积极性做正确的事情。

关键词：项目治理；组织；制度；对等协调；建筑业

1 引 言

在社会经济的发展中，项目正发挥着日益重要的作用——它不仅提供产品、服务和基础设施，而且被用来在战略层面上改造组织的业务流程（Bjørkeng *et al.*，2009）。社会的“项目化”（projectification）倾向越来越强，商业环境已经更多地成为基于项目的经济（Lundin and Söderholm，1998；Turner and Keegan，2001）。然而，理论和实际工作者一直受到项目失灵的困扰。最近的一份报告指出，有37%的项目是失败的（PM Solutions，2011）。其他作者提供的数据甚至更高。例如，麦克马纳斯和伍德—哈珀（McManus and Wood—Harper，2014）的报告说，在IT行业，只有八分之一的项目可以视为完全成功的。在建筑业，项目失灵往往和严重的事故、人员死亡、房屋和桥梁的灾难性坍塌以及政商丑闻相伴随（Bologna and Nord，2000；Loosemore，2000；Piteroforte and Miller，2002；Sha，2004）。

---

[*] 本文的英文题目是 Understanding construction project governance：an inter-organizational perspective，2016 年 6 月发表在 *International Journal of Architecture, Engineering and Construction*，Vol. 5，No. 2，DOI：http：//dx. doi. org/10. 7492/IJAEC. 2016. 012，由作者本人翻译成中文。

面对频频发生的项目失灵，柯布（Cobb，1995）提出了一个悖论："我们知道项目为什么失灵，我们也知道如何去防止项目失灵，但是为什么它们依然失灵呢?"柯布悖论实际上指出了项目研究的困境。在很大程度上，与其说是项目失灵，不如说是项目理论的失灵。越来越多的理论和实际工作者认识到，项目管理的未来取决于它的理论；现在是发展更为宽泛和有效的理论基础以取代过时的理论基础的时候了（Koskela and Howell，2002）。因此，研究的视角已经从作为工具箱的"项目管理"（project management）扩展到作为战略手段的"多项目管理"（management of projects）（Morris，1997）；从纯技术理性（把项目视为理性的物件）扩展到社会—技术理性（把项目视为理性的行为者）（Ahern *et al.*，2014）。统计数据表明，有关项目治理的期刊论文数量在2005年出现大幅度增长，并在此后一直保持很高的水平，这说明治理已经成为项目研究领域的重要课题（Biesenthal and Wilden，2014）。

项目治理是一个多面性的复杂问题，因此很难通过单一的理论视角加以解析（Ahola *et al.*，2014）。有关项目治理的研究从经济学、组织理论、政治学、社会学和心理学，特别是从公司治理理论中汲取了许多养分。文献分析表明，委托代理理论、利益相关者理论和交易成本经济学这三个基本理论不仅支撑着一般的治理理论，而且比其他理论更加适合于项目治理的研究（Biesenthal and Wilden，2014；Ahola *et al.*，2014）。

人们从不同的角度出发，对项目治理做出了不同的定义：

- 对单一项目的风险进行管控的重要工具（Turner and Keegan，2001）；
- 对多个项目进行管理的一整套原则、结构和方法步骤（Crawford and Cooke—Davies，2009）；
- 项目的管理者、发起者（执行董事会）、所有者和其他利益相关者之间的一整套关系（Turner，2009）；
- 在基于项目的组织中，为组织流程、决策模型和项目管理工具提供框架的总体业务职能，它支持项目、项目群和项目组合的成功交付（PMI，2013）；
- 作为合作与反省的赋能者，帮助项目团队理解和应对各种利益相关者团体的基本策略（Biesenthal and Wilden，2014）；

如此等等，不一而足。值得指出的是，尽管定义各不相同，关于项目治理的基本观点却只有两种：（1）外在于特定项目的项目治理；（2）内在于特定项目的项目治理（Ahola *et al.*，2014）。前者着眼于组织内部的关系；后者所关注的则是组织之间的关系。

研究工作在不同的层次上通过不同的方式展开。在纵向上，项目治理被分为项目治理（对单个项目的治理）和对多项目的治理（对项目群和项目组合的集体治理）。前者主要考虑使"项目能够以正确的方式进行，以提供正确的产品，并保证产品能够带来预期收益"（Turner *et al.*，2010）。后者的视野超出了单个项目的范围（Williams *et al.*，2010），涉及使项目达到组织目标所需的价值体系、责任、过程和政策等内容

（Müller，2009）。除了这两个层次之外，项目管理办公室（PMO）被视为联系母组织（公司治理）和特定项目的治理的中间层次（Biesenthal and Wilden，2014）；治理性（governmentality）则被视为组织中整体的治理文化（Müller *et al*.，2014）。

在横向上，不同的研究取向往往以“二元体”的形式表现出来。例如，硬的方面 *vs*. 软的方面（Walker *et al*.，2008）；控制 *vs*. 参与（Toivonen and Toivonen，2014）；事前的规制机制 *vs*. 事后的规范与认识过程（Henisz *et al*. 2012）；内部过程 *vs*. 外部过程，以及灵活性 *vs*. 控制（这两个“二元体”共同构成了一个竞争价值框架）（Aubry *et al*.，2014）；利益相关者导向 *vs*. 股东导向，以及行为控制 *vs*. 结果控制（这两个“二元体”成为多项目治理的组织赋能者模型的两个坐标轴）（Müller and Lecoeuvre，2014）。此外，基于知识的方法专注于分布式的协调机制（Aubry *et al*.，2014）。基于系统工程的方法则重点考虑从“项目治理”到“系统治理”的转变（Locatelli *et al*.，2014）。

尽管取得了长足的进展，对项目治理的研究仍然处于十分初级的阶段，还有在理论和实践两方面作出贡献的巨大潜力（Pitsis *et al*.，2014）。文献分析表明，非项目管理类杂志和项目管理类杂志在讨论的话题和概念上都存在明显的差异。前者专注于治理的概念；而后者主要考虑项目管理方面的问题（Biesenthal and Wilden，2014），带有许多项目管理的“地方色彩”（Pitsis *et al*.，2014）。当前在多项目管理和项目治理领域占支配地位的标准和指南（Office of Government Commerce，2007；APM，2011；PMI，2013；DIN，2013）都是由一种理论框架支撑的，该框架把项目治理视为公司治理或企业（战略）层面上项目管理的一个子集（Too and Weaver，2014）。在这个框架内，“治理”只是“管理”话题中的一个概念（Biesenthal and Wilden，2014）。相当多的资料表明，有关项目治理的话语是建立在对项目管理话语本身表现的基础之上的（Ahola *et al*.，2014）。这一理论框架在处理基于项目的组织内部的关系时可能是有效的。然而，后面的分析将表明，它不适合于处理项目中的法律上独立的企业之间的关系——这正是建设项目的情况。为了避免混淆，在项目治理研究中，有必要对项目治理和项目管理做出明确的区隔。这需要不仅在概念上和哲学意义上说明项目和其他组织形态的区别（Morris，2013）；而且要对两种类型的项目（组织内项目与组织间项目）做出明确的界定。

本文借用科斯克拉和豪厄尔（Koskela and Howell，2002）的观点，认为项目治理的理论基础可以分为项目理论和治理理论两部分。本文还认为，对建设项目治理的深入理解应该建立在以下三个区别的基础之上：项目与市场、企业的区别，组织内项目与组织间项目的区别，治理与管理的区别。因此，本文的剩余部分安排如下：下一节识别项目有别于市场和企业的特征，区分项目的两种基本类型——企业间（Ⅰ型）项目和企业内（Ⅱ型）项目，并对项目的性质做出详细考察。然后对建设项目的特性做出具体分析。第三节讨论治理的内涵，对管理与治理做出比较清晰的区别，并且从复杂性和灵活性的角度分析治理的多层次性质。第四节研究建设项目治理的概念，并且从博弈论的角度分析三个治理范畴（垂直治理、水平治理、针对项目经理的治理）。结论部分总结研究结果，并提出今后的研究方向。

2 项目的性质

威廉姆森（Williamson，1991）指出，经济组织有三种基本形态：市场、科层组织（hierarchy）和混合型组织（hybrid）。项目，特别是建设项目，以不完全的长期合同为特征，属于混合型组织的范畴（Turner and Keegan，2001；Sha，2011）。就其与母组织的关系而言，建设项目属于组织间项目的范畴（Archibald，1992；Turner and Keegan，2001）。为了准确把握建设项目的性质，需要首先了解项目的基本性质，然后将组织间项目和组织内项目区分开来。

2.1 项目与市场、企业的区别

讨论项目的性质，最好从探讨“项目为什么存在”这个话题开始。在这方面，经典作者关于企业存在的理由的一些观点可以提供概念性的洞察力。奈特（1921）的观点可以概括为：（1）风险与不确定性是两个不同的概念。前者是可度量的（或是通过先验的推定，或是出于对以往经验的统计），后者是不可度量的。（2）有效的利润理论的基础是“真正的”不确定性，而不是风险。（3）归类合并和专业化是处理不确定性的两种基本方法；前者通过组合减少不确定性，后者选择某些人来承担不确定性。

威廉姆森（Williamson，1991）认为，交易有三个维度：资产专用性、不确定性和交易频率。它们使交易成本增加并且共同导致市场的失灵；其中最后一个维度在经验文献中所受的关注程度远不及前面两个（Geyskens *et al.*，2006）。威廉姆森（Williamson，1991）对纵向一体化的观点可以概括为：（1）资产专用性导致根本性转变（fundamental transformation）——市场中原本独立的有关各方变成相互依存的利益相关者。（2）专用性资产的投资人将受其他人“敲竹杠”（hold-up，索取高价）的威胁。（3）治理成本是资产专用性的函数：较高的资产专用性要求较高水平的纵向一体化。

如图1所示，奈特的推理逻辑是：不确定性引起对归类合并和专业化的需求；这一需求又导致企业以及企业家角色的产生。威廉姆森的推理逻辑是：资产专用性导致“敲竹杠”问题的出现，继而引发纵向一体化，包括企业和项目。将这两个推理逻辑结合起来考虑，我们可以把不确定性作为企业和项目存在的一个理由，作为它们有别于市场的一个特性。

接下来要做的事情就是把项目和企业区分开来。项目的出现可以归因于“企业生产—市场交易”这种常规模式的失灵。在常规模式下，企业在市场这只“看不见的手”的指挥下开展生产和经营；顾客在市场中购买现成的产品和服务。企业和顾客各得其

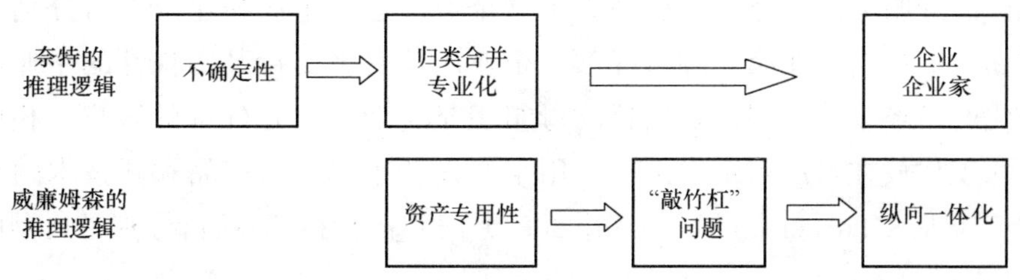

图 1　关于企业存在理由（纵向一体化）的两种推理逻辑

所；市场扮演着“万能的”中间人角色。然而，当顾客无法在市场中买到中意的产品或服务时，就要雇佣某些人或某些组织为其提供特定的产品或服务，从而产生一种新的生产模式——定制。从组织的角度来看，客户雇用一个企业或一组企业为其提供特定的产品或服务的这种方式，既不是市场，也不是企业（科层组织），而是市场和企业的混合体——这正是建筑项目的情况。有些时候，为了应对复杂多变的商业环境带来的挑战，企业会针对潜在的客户发起一些项目来开发新产品或新技术——这正是软件开发项目的情况。在上述两种情况中，无论是建设项目，还是软件开发项目，大多数的过程既不是常规性的，也不是重复性的。这就有别于企业中相对稳定并且是重复进行的常规性生产。因此，一次性或者是非重复性可以看作是项目有别于企业的特殊性质。

项目的非重复性与它的临时性密切相关。一般来说，市场是没有穷尽的。企业中的生产是连续的、稳定的和重复进行的，因而是常规性的。而项目中的生产过程在时间上是有限的，因而是临时性的。正是因为这个原因，不同的学派都把临时性作为项目的基本特征：临时性的努力或过程（PMI，2013）；临时性的生产系统（Koskela and Ballard，2006）；临时性的多边组织（Turner and Müller，2003；Turner，2006；Winch，2006）。需要说明的是，这里的临时性是相对于项目的母组织来说的，因此是一个相对的概念。

综上所述，正是由于客户独特而新颖的需求，以及复杂多变的商业环境，才使得“企业加市场”的常规模式失灵，进而导致新的经济组织形式——项目的出现。项目之所以有别于市场和企业，就在于它同时具备以下三个特征：不确定性、临时性和非重复性。

2.2　组织间项目与组织内项目的区别

根据与其母组织之间的关系，项目可以划分为两种类型（Archibald，1992；Turner and Keegan，2001）。Ⅰ型项目处于市场之中，因而属于企业间组织。Ⅱ型项目处于企业的科层组织之中，因而属于企业内组织。在第一种情况下，客户是项目的母组织。客户把项目的工作置于市场之中，企业作为“法人雇员”被客户雇佣，来开展项目的工作（Turner，2004）。相应地，那些把项目作为主要业务甚至是唯一业务，向客户提供定制的产品或服务的企业应该被划为Ⅰ型企业。建筑企业和建设项目分别是典型的Ⅰ型企业和Ⅰ型项目。在第二种情况下，企业用项目来支持其常规性的主业，以便赶上迅速变化的市场步伐。因此，项目的母组织是企业而不是外部的客户。相应地，那些把项目的工作放在科层组织中进行，用来开发新市场、新产品和新技术的企业应该被划为Ⅱ型企业（Turner and Keegan，2001）。IT企业和IT项目分别是典型的Ⅱ型企业和Ⅱ型项目。

不同类型的组织和任务需要不同的管控方法。在“纯”项目管理的领域，核心问题是成本、工期和质量。在这个领域，经典的项目管理（PM）方法对于Ⅰ型项目和Ⅱ型项目都是适用的。然而，在项目治理领域，似乎需要对这两种项目采用不同的方法。当前占支配地位的标准和指南（Office of Government Commerce，2007；APM，2011；PMI，2013；DIN，2013）主要关注科层组织内部的“项目—母组织”关系，它们对Ⅱ型项目是适用的。设想在一个软件开发公司里有若干个项目同时进行。公司（母组织）可以比较容易地使不同项目的目标与公司的短期利益、长远利益保持一致。在这里，项目是执行公司战略的手段和工具（Ahola *et al.*，2014）。然而，如果涉及市场交易和组织间关系的话，PM方法的局限性就会显现出来，就需要新的治理方法。以建设项目为例，为了向客户提交定制产品，项目联合体要求法律上独立的企业将其资源、能力和知识临时组合在一起。既然客户和所有的参与方拥有不同的战略目标和长远利益，项目的目标必须在有关各方协商、谈判和相互妥协的基础上才能确定下来。在这种情况下所能做的事情是使项目有关各方为实现共同目标而在一起工作，这个目标在本质上是短期的（Winch，2010；Ahola *et al.*，2014）。

总之，当我们把研究视角从“纯”项目管理扩展到项目治理时，必须对Ⅰ型项目和Ⅱ型项目做出区隔。把母组织的利益作为判断基准的观念适用于Ⅱ型项目；而Ⅰ型项目需要一种新的观念，一种同时考虑客户的利益以及项目有关各方利益的观念，它肯定要比Ⅱ型项目复杂得多。

2.3 建设项目的特性分析

建设项目可以看作是一系列正式合同与非正式合同的集合。建设项目有关各方之间的关系是典型的“承包方—发包方”关系，这种关系不同于Ⅱ型项目中的“项目—母组织”关系，后者更像是一个企业中的“雇员—雇主”关系。由于明确规定一系列特定权利的成本很高，建设项目合同肯定是不完全的；这为剩余控制权（Grossman and Hart，1986）和剩余索取权（Fama and Jensen，1983）留下大的空间。

建设项目的一个显著特征是在一般产品市场环境中难以发现的很强的不确定性（Winch，1989）。建筑业面所临的不确定性的来源有：（1）由小批量生产造成的任务不确定性，（2）由于对气象和地质条件等方面的不可预见性造成的自然不确定性，（3）由项目团队临时性特征造成的组织不确定性，（4）由于预算和竞标过程中的误差造成的合同不确定性（Winch，1989）。如此强的不确定性对专业化提出很高的要求。建筑业众多的专业注册资格体系可以看作是为应对不确定性而做出的制度安排。专用知识，特别是隐性知识，是专业注册资格体系的核心，属于人力资产专用性的范畴。根据前面提到的威廉姆森的推理逻辑，由于资产专用性程度高，建设项目理应采用科层治理结构。然而在现实中，建设项目采用的是混合型结构，超出了威廉姆森的预期。为了解释这个悖论，沙凯逊（Sha，2011）放松了威廉姆森的一些假设，把不确定性、应对不确定性的专用知识以及信息成本纳入分析框架。研究表明，在一定条件下，建设项目治理结构的选择方式可能偏离经典理论的预设路径。如果不确定性超过一定程度，它对生产成本的影响可能会大于"敲竹杠"问题对交易成本造成的影响。不确定性对生产成本的压力可能会抑制客户在事后讨价还价中"敲竹杠"的积极性。因此，生产成本和交易成本之间的权衡结果可能导致混合型结构，而不是科层结构（Sha，2011）。

总之，作为典型的Ⅰ型项目，建设项目可以视为在不确定性很强，因而专业化程度很高的条件下，生产成本和交易成本之间权衡的结果。它可以被简明地定义为"从事一次性定制任务的临时性的多边组织"。

3　治理的内涵

治理范式关乎新的观念和方法，是一门艺术，一门用来管控多个当事人、机构和系统的复杂艺术（Jessop，2003）。治理范式的兴起缘于组织或国家在科层协调中遇到的困难（Miller and Lessard，2000）；这些困难又缘于以快速变化的相互依存方式为特征的日益复杂的商业环境（Jessop，1998），以及日益频繁的跨越各种预设边界的互动（Scharpf，1994）。虽然治理一词有许多不同的含义，它的基本含义是"为有序规则和集体行动创造条件"（Stoker，1998）。

根据新制度经济学，社会、政治、法律和经济制度可以划分为四个范畴或层次：（1）社会基础或文化基础，也就是嵌入性（embeddedness）；（2）基本制度环境；（3）治理制度；（4）短期的资源配置（Williamson，2000）。第三个层次的目的是获得正确的治理结构，其主要任务是"精心营造秩序，进而减少冲突，实现共同的利益"（Williamson，2000），使管理活动在给定的治理结构中正常有效地进行（Biesenthal and Wilden，2014；Too and Weaver，2014）。与日常的管理活动相比，治理是相对稳定的制度，其变化频率一般用"年"或者是"十年"来衡量（Williamson，2000）。

除了上面所说的在目的、职能和变化频率方面的不同之外，管理与治理的根本区别在于它们价值取向和思维模式。下面的"二元体"体现了它们之间的不同：权威 *vs.* 共识（Ahern *et al.*，2014）；面向控制的方法 *vs.* 面向参与的方法（Toivonen and Toivonen，2014）；自上而下的集体性 *vs.* 自下而上的交互性（Ahern *et al.*，2014）；

科层协调 *vs.* 对等协调（Jessop，2003）；较高的“权力距离”文化 *vs.* 较低的“权力距离”文化（Hofstede，1980）。权力距离可以用来反映组织中权力较小的成员对不平等权力的接受和期待的程度。在权力距离较大的社会中，人们接受科层组织，每个人都有一个属于自己的位置，而不需要任何的理由。在权力距离较小的社会中，人们寻求权力的平等。这些“二元体”有助于理解管理与治理这两种范式的联系与区别。

在管理的语境中，人被分为管理者与被管理者两种类型。管理中的科层协调以“管理者懂得最多”这样一种价值观为基础。这种价值观的根源可以追溯到弗雷德里克·泰勒（Taylor，1911）。泰勒对工人的看法可能是有偏见的和侮辱性的。他曾把不太聪明的工人叫做“傻瓜”，并把他们比作牲畜：“对于把搬运铁块作为正常职业的工人的第一个要求是，他是如此愚笨和冷漠，以至于在心理构成上更像是公牛而不是别的东西。”（Taylor，1911）因此，在管理的语境中，受到更多关注的是计划、组织、命令、协调和控制（Donnelly Jr.，*et al.*，1987）。这种基于控制的性质在 PDCA（plan—do—check—act）循环中得到生动的体现；其中的持续改进过程恰如控制理论中的负反馈回路。

而在治理的语境中，受到更多关注的是自治、分权、结构扁平化、相互信任，以及通过组织结构的“非完整性”（underspecification）而实现的自组织（Müller *et al.*，2014）。所有的当事人，无论是个人、团体还是组织，都可以视为自组织的对等结构（self-organizing heterarchy）中的利益相关者。对等结构是一种元素网络，其中每一个元素都拥有同等的地位和权威。从复杂问题解决（complex problem solving，CPS）的角度来看，治理的观念和方法是一种分散的协调机制，这种机制是以“相互利益的共同意志”为基础，通过波兰尼（Polanyi，1967）所说的“相互控制”而实现的。“共同意志”是指有关各方通过自下而上的对话与协商而形成的共识。在“相互控制”的结构中，当事人的相互控制以下面两个原则为基础：（1）通过相互权威实现的自我约束，（2）通过相互调节实现的自我协调（Polanyi，1969；Ahern *et al.*，2014）。

治理是关于复杂性的一门艺术，它在不同层次上通过不同形式的灵活性得以实现。一般说来，层次越高，复杂性越强，要求的灵活性也就越大。较低层次所要求的是有关方法和过程选择方面的灵活性；而较高层次所要求的是在人们的观念以及工作态度方面的灵活性。在项目领域，治理通过以下灵活性来实现：（1）项目层面上，治理方式的特点和权限方面的灵活性，（2）组织层面上，灵活的组织结构和思想观念，（3）项目环境层面上，治理性（governmentality）安排方面的灵活性（Müller *et al.*，2014）。

区别对待（discriminating）是处理不同层次复杂性问题的基本原则。交易成本经济学认为，产品或服务的供应必须与其治理方式放在一起考虑。中心任务是以区别对待的方式，把不同性质的交易与具有不同成本和能力的治理结构（市场、科层和混合型组织）结合起来，进而实现有效的匹配关系（Williamson，2000）。这就意味着，对于经济组织和经济活动而言，没有一种万能的治理方法；相反，只能以一种随机应变的方式进行管控。

总之，管理和治理就像一枚硬币的两面。它们的目的都是为了追求组织的效率和效益，但是各自采取不同的方式。管理主要考虑日常工作的执行，在战术层面上通过科层协调来控制业务。而治理主要考虑组织的战略目标（Biesenthal and Wilden，2014），它追求人们的集体利益，使他们自愿服从情景框架，该框架影响当事人的行为，但是未必决定个体的具体行动（Clegg *et al.*，2002；Müller *et al.*，2014）。治理需要更加灵活的观念和方法。

4　对建设项目治理的再认识

以上分析表明，企业和项目是两种不同类型的经济组织；项目可以分为Ⅰ型项目和Ⅱ型项目；管理和治理是两种不同的管控组织的方法。如图 2 所示，对于一个建筑公司来说，它有四项基本任务：企业管理、公司治理、项目管理和项目治理。一般说来，项目比企业复杂，这是因为前者是后者与市场的混合体；Ⅰ型项目比Ⅱ型项目复杂，这是因为前者属于企业间组织，而后者是企业内组织；治理比管理复杂，这是因为，前者是一种更高层次的结构（Biesenthal and Wilden，2014）。因此，可以料想到建设项目治理（Ⅰ型项目治理）是四项任务中最具挑战性的任务。

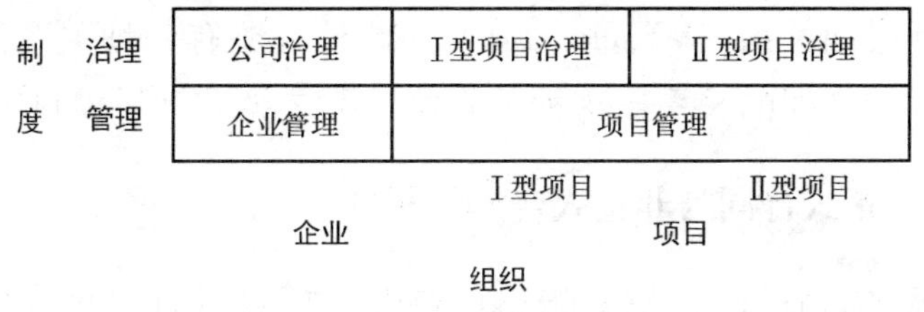

图 2　组织—制度四方图

4.1　对建设项目治理的概念化

项目治理最具代表性的定义是："通过项目发起人和项目团队实现的项目目标与母组织战略之间的协调一致"（PMI，2013）。这一定义隐含了一个假设：项目治理是基于项目的组织从外部单向施加到项目上的动作（Ahola *et al.*，2014）。然而，对建设项目而言，客户与有关企业之间的互动是双向进行的（Ahola *et al.*，2014）。此外，法律上独立的有关各方的战略目标和长远利益未必一致，有时甚至是相互冲突的。因此，建设项目治理需要另一种更加注重不同参与者利益诉求平衡的方法。

在有限理性、自利和机会主义行为的假设条件下，建设项目治理可以概括为一种努力，它使法律上独立的、具有不同战略目标和长远利益的项目参与各方能够为共同的利益而一起工作，取得共赢的结果。这意味着一个良好的制度环境，它能够激励个人、团体或组织做正确的事情，并且把事情做好。从本质上说，这是一个形成并影响参与人态度的框架，而不是直接决定组织成员的每一个行动。规范参与人行为的工作可以分为三个层次（Sha and Wu，2016）：

- 通过合理配置责、权、利，提高激励强度，这可能会使人们不愿违规；
- 通过严格的监督和约束，以及通过制衡机制来保证透明度、追责制和明确的角色定位（Müller，2009）提高违规的难度，这可能会使人们不能违规；
- 通过法律、经济、社会（主要通过同业群体）和心理上（通过认知悔悟）（Henisz *et al.*，2012）的严厉制裁提高违规的风险与成本，这可能会使人们不敢违规。

相关的治理机制包括：补偿机制（工程变更、索赔与反索赔），互助机制（工程保险）和保险机制（工程保险、抵押、留置和保证金）等。从理论上讲，以上三道防线可以有效地防止建设项目中的机会主义行为。然而，任何制度安排的设计与执行都是有成本的。因此，治理结构和治理机制的实际效果取决于成本与收益的平衡。尽管如此，它们指出了建设项目治理的可行途径。

4.2 三个治理范畴

在英国学者温奇（Winch，2001）提出的分析框架中，建设项目治理被划分为垂直治理和水平治理两个范畴。前者关注客户与项目的关系，也就是温奇所说的客户与一阶供应者（总承包商）之间的交易关系；而后者关注的重点是供应链，也就是一阶供应者之后的一系列合同关系（Winch，2010）。此外，还有一种关系需要治理，这就是施工企业与项目经理之间的关系，这种关系可以称之为“针对项目经理的治理”。

4.2.1 垂直治理：正式合同与非正式合同的视角

荷兰学者特纳（Turner，2004）指出，对建设项目垂直治理的研究可以从两个维度上展开：项目采购方式（project procurement route，PPR）和支付方式（合同类型）。PPR 决定了供应的作用和范围——传统方式（design—bid—build，DBB）、一体化方式（design—build，DB）、项目管理方式（construction management，CM），以及 PPP（public—private partnership）等等。支付方式（合同类型）决定了风险的分配和激励强度，涉及固定价格（fixed price）、成本加费用（cost plus）、实测（remeasurement）、目标成本（target cost）等多种合同形式。多数情况下，一种项目采购方式往往涉及多个委托代理关系。每个委托代理关系都需要一定的合同来规范。不同的项目采购方式与不同的合同类型组合在一起，就会产生不同的契约安排（Sha，2011）。

委托代理理论已被广泛地应用于一般的治理理论之中，它对于研究客户与项目之间的关系是有效的。设想一个由两个当事人组成的建设项目，这两个当事人分别是风险中性的客户和风险厌恶的代理人。代理人从客户那里得到的报酬是 $w=\alpha+\beta Y$，其中 α 是固定报酬，β 是激励系数（$0\leqslant\beta\leqslant1$），$Y$ 是可观察到的项目产出。客户的问题是：

选择 α 和 β，在满足代理人参与约束和激励相容约束的条件下，使自己的期望支付最大化。

建模的关键在于根据研究目的和问题的性质来确定产出函数 $Y(\cdot)$。例如，产出函数可以简单地表示为 $Y=e+x$，式中 e 是代理人的努力水平，x 是反映风险水平的随机变量。在分析建设合同中付出—收益的分享安排时，项目的产出被表示为两项成本之差：$Y=C-\overline{C}$，式中 $\overline{C}$ 是目标成本，C 是实际成本，它本身又是代理人努力水平的函数（Chang，2014）。为了分析不确定性和专用知识对治理结构选择的影响，项目的产出被表示为一个非线性函数 $Y=K^{\gamma}G^{1-\gamma}+x$，式中 K 和 G 分别是专用知识和一般性资料的数量，$\gamma(0<\gamma<1)$ 是用来反映“真正的”不确定性程度的信息缺口指数（Sha，2011）。

在实践中还存在关系型的项目交付安排，包括项目合伙（project partnering）、项目联盟（project alliancing）和一体化项目交付（integrated project delivery）等形式（Lahdenperä，2012）。在交易成本经济学领域，对关系型合同的研究考虑了重复博弈中声誉资本的作用。管家理论提出了不同于代理理论的描述人类行为的另一类方法（Biesenthal and Wilden，2014）。由三个“支柱”（规制、规范和认识）支撑的多学科分析框架提供了一种方法，可以把交易成本经济学、社会学和心理学等不同领域的不同观点结合在一起（Scott，2008；Henisz *et al.*，2012）。

4.2.2 水平治理：联盟博弈的视角

一般说来，与个人单干相比，合作能够带来较大的收益，从而达到“一加一大于二”的效果。合作本身要求两个条件：一个是通过合作而产生的超额收益（把蛋糕做大）；另一个是分配合作收益的公平性（以大家都接受的方式来分配蛋糕）。这些问题正是合作博弈理论关注的焦点。

联盟博弈理论是合作博弈理论的一个分支，它主要研究总联盟（grand coalition），也就是由所有参与人组成的联盟的稳定性。这里的基本假设是，总联盟是可以形成的。为了保持总联盟的稳定性，必须以某种公平的方式在参与人之间分配博弈的支付。在不同公平观的支持下，联盟博弈理论形成了几种解的概念，包括核（core）、夏普里值（Shapley value）、核仁（nucleolus）等（Saad *et al.*，2009）。

核以“交易收益”（gains from trade）的公平观为基础，它同时满足以下三个理性条件：（1）个体理性，即所有参与人得到的支付都不低于个人单干时的收益水平；（2）集体理性，即总联盟创造的收益恰好被分配完毕；（3）联盟理性，即不存在能够做出改进的联盟，也就是说，所有参与人都没有离开总联盟另组联盟的积极性。夏普里值在满足四个公理的前提下，对每个参与人赋予唯一的支付配置。实际上，它是参与人对总联盟的边际贡献的加权平均值，体现了“多劳多得”的公平观。核仁也给出一个唯一的支付配置，它使得某些参与人的不满意程度最小。这与罗尔斯的公平正义的差异原则是一致的："差异原则是使社会中最不利的成员获得最大利益"（Rawls，2001）。显然，在应用联盟博弈理论时，必须考虑人们对公平的看法。

4.2.3 针对项目经理的治理：共同代理的视角

项目经理的角色随着客户采购方式的不同而变化。在项目管理（PM）模式下，项目经理代表客户。而在设计—建造（DB）模式下，建筑公司通常指派自己的人员作为项目经理（Walker，2007；Fewings，2005）。实际上，他们常常被看作是与施工经理同样的职业（DOL，2015）。这里所要讨论的是建筑企业与项目经理之间的关系。

项目经理对施工管理的全过程负责，他们与不同的利益相关者打交道，处理在施工过程中随机发生的各项事务。因此，与制造业的车间主任和 IT 业的项目经理相比，他们拥有更大的自主权。这样可以保证效率和劳动生产率；另一方面，在利益不一致和信息不对称的条件下，容易产生逆向选择和道德风险的问题。

由于项目经理的决策同时对建筑企业和客户负责，因此，建筑企业在设计项目经理的选派与激励机制时，必须考虑客户的影响。项目经理、建筑企业和客户三者之间的关系可以描述为"一仆二主"的关系。这与共同代理博弈的情况是非常相符的。在共同代理博弈中，"一个特定的个体（代理人）所选择的行动不止影响一个人，而是影响若干人（委托人），委托人对各种可能行动的偏好通常是相互抵触的"（Bernheim and Whinston，1986）。有关共同代理的文献已经建立起可用来处理各种重要问题的分析框架（Carmona and Fajardo，2006；Attar *et al.*，2007）。因此，从共同代理的角度研究针对项目经理的治理问题，在技术上是可行的。

以上几个小节主要从博弈论的角度讨论了建设项目治理的三个范畴。博弈模型在许多方面可能过于简单，因而不可避免地具有局限性。然而，正如 Bowles（2004）所说的那样，"模型不解释所有的细节，但是它们可以告诉我们向何处去看。"不管这些模型是多么简单，它们确实可以为建设项目治理研究提供某些有用的线索。

5 结　论

项目已成为一种可以和市场、企业相提并论的，重要的经济组织形式。赫伯特·西蒙在研究不完全合同的交易时，曾经设想了一位"来自火星的神秘客人"，他乘坐飞船来到地球，

> 飞船上备有观察地面社会结构的望远镜。比方说，企业显示为绿色的实心区域……市场交易则表现为连接企业的红色线条……在发回火星的信息中，地球上的景象可能被描述为"由红色线条连接的大片绿色区域"（Simon，1991）。

今天，如果这架飞船再次光临地球，这位来客可能会看到更多的颜色：黄绿色

（绿色与少量红色的混合）或者是褐色（红色与少量绿色的混合），分别代表Ⅰ型项目和Ⅱ型项目。前者可以视为市场中类似于企业的组织，也就是 Eccles（1981）所说的准企业；后者则可以看作是科层组织中类似于市场的过程（Lindkvist，2004）。

Ⅰ型项目出现在十九世纪的英国建筑业，远远早于Ⅱ型项目。后者是二战之后在美国的航天工业中发展起来并实现正规化的（Winch，2000；Winch，2006）。然而，经典的项目管理（PM）方法主要是从Ⅱ型项目中派生出来的。正如温奇所说，“它原本不是用来处理企业之间的差异，而只是用来处理一个组织内部不同职能部门之间的差异”（Winch，1989）。对建设项目的深入理解取决于把关注点从科层组织内的“项目—母组织”关系扩展到自组织对等结构中的“承包方—发包方”关系。

与管理相比，治理处于较高的层次；它通过不同的灵活性而得以实现。这意味着较少的控制和较多的自主权。在建设项目的研究领域，治理结构和治理机制可以概括为基于对等协调的制度的总和，它为项目参与各方之间的制衡提供了基础。基本框架可以表示为两个维度：（1）治理范畴（垂直治理、水平治理、针对项目经理的治理）；（2）参与人的行为规制（使人们不想、不能和不敢违规）。理想的状态应该是：参与人通过相互妥协形成“共同意志”，大家在“共同意志”的支配下一起行动，各得其所。但是，由于建设项目面临的不确定性、有关各方的有限理性，以及治理范式所固有的复杂性，这种理想状态只是理论上可行的。由此可以得出结论：对于给定的建设项目，没有“最好”的，只有“最合适”的治理方法。

建设项目治理位于制度层次结构中的第三个层次，它在其上层（建筑交易体制，在英国简称为 contracting system）和下层（项目管理）之间发挥着承上启下的作用。建筑交易体制是基础性的制度环境，它影响着治理层的决策，同时又受到这些决策的影响（Winch，2010；Sha，2013）。另一方面，如果没有管理体系的有效支持，治理体系也无法运转（Too and Weaver，2014）。为了深入了解建筑交易体制、项目治理和项目管理之间的互动关系，需要在更广泛的框架内开展进一步研究。

在多项目的研究领域，项目群和项目组合的集体治理所面临的挑战与单一项目治理有很大不同（Aritua *et al.*，2009；Müller and Lecoeuvre，2014），这使得Ⅰ型项目和Ⅱ型项目的差别愈加明显。以项目群治理为例，对于Ⅱ型项目而言，项目群中的所有项目可以按照鱼刺图的形式进行治理，其中母组织扮演“鱼头”的角色（Turner and Keegan，2001）。然而，在建设项目领域，问题要复杂得多。设想有一个客户（比方说一个地方政府）发起一个项目，该项目由三个承包商来完成。人们可以发现，这个项目群中有四条“鱼”（客户和三个承包商），每一方都有自己的战略目标。另一方面，建筑企业往往参与若干个由不同客户发起的项目。如何从组织间的视角来分析不同的“鱼”之间类似于网络的复杂关系，并且找到合适的治理方法？这是一个有趣的，并且富有挑战性的问题，可能需要新的研究范式来解决。

Understanding construction project governance: an inter-organizational perspective

Abstract: In essence, construction projects belong to the category of inter-firm projects that can be viewed as firm-like organization in the market, differing from intra-firm projects that can be regarded as market-like processes within the hierarchy. The aim of this paper is to make a better understanding of construction project governance by expanding the focus from project—parent relationships within the hierarchy to contractor—contractee relationships in a self-organizing 'heterarchy'. The characteristics that distinguish the project from the market and the firm are identified. Two basic types of projects—type I and type II projects—are classified. The essence of governance is examined, making a clearer distinction between governance and management. Construction project governance is then conceptualized as an effort to make legally independent participants with divergent long-term interests and strategic goals work together towards the shared goals. Three governance categories (vertical, horizontal and project manager related governance) are classified and examined from a game theory perspective, providing insights into inter-relationships between diverse participants of construction projects. A key question that is addressed is how to create a favorable institutional environment in which people are willing to do the right things.

Key Words: Project governance, organization, institution, heterarchic coordination, building sector

DOI: http://dx.doi.org/10.7492/IJAEC.2016.012

1 INTRODUCTION

Projects are playing an increasingly important role in social and economic development, not only delivering products, services or infrastructure but also being used strategically to transform organizational practices and processes (Bjørkeng *et al.*, 2009). The increasing 'projectification' of society indicates that the business environment has become a more project-based economy (Lundin and Söderholm, 1998; Turner and Keegan, 2001). However, scholars and practitioners have long been suffering from project failures. A recent report (PM Solutions, 2011) states that 37% of projects fail. For other authors the number is even higher, e. g. , McManus and Wood-Harper (2014) report that in the information technology (IT) sector only one in eight projects can be considered truly successful. In the building sector project failures are often accompanied by serious accidents, side fatality, catastrophic collapses of buildings, facilities, and bridges, as well as political and/or business scandals (Bologna and Del Nord, 2000; Loosemore, 2000; Pietroforte and Miller, 2002; Sha, 2004).

In the face of frequent project failures, Cobb (1995) outlined his paradox asking: 'We know why projects fail; we know how to prevent their failure—so why do they still fail?' This is indeed a dilemma of project research. To a great extent, project failure is more a failure of project theory than a failure of the project itself. A growing number of scholars and practitioners are recognizing that the future of project management is dependent on its theory and that it is time to develop a wider and more powerful theoretical foundation to substitute the obsolete one (Koskela and Howell, 2002). As a result, research perspectives have been expanded from 'project management' as a toolbox approach to the 'management of projects' as a strategic approach (Morris, 1997), and from pure technical rationality, or projects as 'rational objects', to socio—technical rationality, or projects as 'rational actors' (Ahern *et al.* , 2014). Statistics indicate that the number of journal papers on project governance increased sharply in 2005 and has remained at a high level since then (Biesenthal and Wilden, 2014), indicating that governance has become a significant topic in the realm of projects.

Project governance is too multifaceted and complex to be analyzed through any single theoretical lens (Ahola *et al.* , 2014). The research on project governance has drawn substantially from economics, organization theory, political science, sociology and psychology, and particularly, from corporate governance theories. Literature analyses indicate that principal—agency theory, stakeholder theory and transaction cost economics are three basic theories that not only underpin general governance theories but also are adapted to the project governance context to a greater extent than other theories (Biesenthal and Wilden, 2014; Ahola *et al.* 2014).

From different points of view, project governance is defined in various ways; as a central tool for controlling the risk exposure of individual projects (Turner and Keegan, 2001), as a set of principles, structures, and processes for undertaking the management of projects (Crawford and Cooke-Davies, 2009), as a set of relationships between the project's management, its sponsor (or executive board), its owner and other stakeholders (Turner, 2009), as an overarching business function to provide a framework for organizational processes, decision-making models and project management tools, which support the successful delivery of projects, programs and portfolios in project-based organizations (PMI, 2013), and as an essential strategy to assist project teams understand, and respond to various stakeholder groups as an enabler of collaboration and reflection (Biesenthal and Wilden, 2014) amongst others. It is worthy to note that in spite of diverse definitions, two basic views of project governance can be identified: project governance as external to any specific project or as internal to a specific project (Ahola *et al.*, 2014). The former focuses on intra-organizational relationships, while the latter concentrates on inter-organizational relationships.

Research has been conducted at multiple levels through different approaches. In the vertical dimension, project governance is classified as project governance (the governance of individual projects) and governance of projects (the collective governance of a program or portfolio of projects). The former is mainly concerned with ensuring that 'projects are undertaken in the right way to deliver the right products, and to ensure the products will deliver the desired benefits' (Turner *et al.*, 2010). The latter takes a broader view than the individual project (Williams *et al.*, 2010), and comprises the values system, responsibilities, processes, and policies that allow projects to achieve organizational objectives (Müller, 2009). In addition, the project management office (PMO) is taken as the middle level that links parent organization (corporate governance) to the governance of a particular project (Biesenthal and Wilden, 2014); and governmentality is taken as the overall governance culture in the organization (Müller *et al.*, 2014).

In the horizontal dimension, various research orientations are often presented in the form of dyads, e.g., hard aspects *vs.* soft aspects (Walker *et al.*, 2008); control *vs.* involvement (Toivonen and Toivonen, 2014); *ex-ante* regulative governance mechanisms *vs.* *ex-post* normative and cognitive governance processes (Henisz *et al.*, 2012); internal process *vs.* external process, and flexibility *vs.* control (these two dyads together form a competing values framework) (Aubry *et al.*, 2014); stakeholder orientation *vs.* shareholder orientation, and behavior control *vs.* outcome control (these two dyads act as the two axes of the model of organizational enablers for governance of projects) (Müller and Lecoeuvre, 2014). Furthermore, the knowledge-based approach focuses on distributed coordination mechanism (Ahern *et al.*, 2014). The systems engineering based approach emphasizes the transformation from 'project governance' to 'system governance' (Locatelli *et al.*, 2014).

In spite of significant advances, the project governance research is still a fledgling field that has the potential to make a major scholarly and practical contribution (Pitsis *et al.*, 2014). Literature analyses illustrate that there are considerable differences in both themes and concepts between non-project management and project management journals. The former specifically deals with the concept of governance, whereas the latter is more concerned with the aspect of project management (Biesenthal and Wilden, 2014), retaining many elements of localism (Pitsis *et al.*, 2014). Currently dominant standards and guides relating to multi-project management and project governance (Office of Government Commerce, 2007; APM, 2011; PMI, 2013; DIN, 2013) are underpinned by a theoretical framework that regards project governance as a subset of corporate governance, or enterprise/strategic project management (Too and Weaver, 2014). Under such a framework, 'governance' is only a concept within 'management' (Biesenthal and Wilden, 2014), with quite many sources claiming that the project governance discourse has been built on representing the project management discourse itself (Ahola *et al.*, 2014). This theoretical framework may be effective for addressing intra-organizational relationships within a project-based organization. However, as the ensuing analysis will demonstrate, it is not well suited for dealing with inter-organizational relationships between legally independent firms participating in a specific project, as is the case with construction projects alone. In order to avoid the confusion around project governance research, it is essential to make a clearer distinction between project governance and project management. To do so will require not only specifying how projects are distinct from other forms of organizing conceptually and philosophically (Morris, 2013), but also telling the two types of projects, intra-firm and inter-firm projects, apart from each other clearly.

Borrowing from Koskela and Howell (2002), this paper argues that the underlying theoretical foundation of project governance can be divided into a theory of project and a theory of governance, and that a better understanding of construction project governance could be made by distinguishing the project from the firm and the market, distinguishing inter-firm from intra-firm projects, and distinguishing governance from management. Accordingly, the rest of this paper is structured as follows: The next section scrutinizes the nature of the project by identifying the characteristics that distinguish the project from the firm and the market, and classifies the two basic types of projects—interfirm (type Ⅰ) and intra-firm (type Ⅱ) projects. Later it analyzes the idiosyncrasy of construction projects. In the third section, the essence of governance is examined, making a clearer distinction between management and governance, and the multi-level nature of governance is analyzed through a lens of complexity and flexibility. In the fourth section, the concept of construction project governance is reviewed, and three governance categories, vertical, horizontal and project manager related governance, are examined from a game theory perspective. The conclusions section provides a summary of the research findings and identifies directions for further research.

2 THE NATURE OF THE PROJECT

According to Williamson (1991), there are three generic forms of economic organizations—market, hierarchy and hybrid. Characterized by long-term incomplete contracts, projects and construction projects, in particular, belong to the hybrid category (Turner and Keegan, 2001; Sha, 2011). In the matter of the relationships with their parent organizations, construction projects belong to the category of the inter-firm project (Archibald, 1992; Turner and Keegan, 2001). In order to grasp the nature of construction projects, it is necessary to first understand the basic properties of the project, and then differentiate inter-firm projects from intra-firm projects.

2.1 Distinguishing the project from the market and the firm

A good question to begin a discussion of the nature of the project is: 'Why does it exist?' In this regard, classical authors' opinions about the *raison d'être* of a firm can provide conceptual insight. Knight (1921)'s opinions can be summarized as follows: (1) Risk and uncertainty are two different concepts—the former is measurable (either through calculation a priori or from statistics of past experience) whereas the latter cannot be measured. (2) It is 'true' uncertainty, rather than risk, that forms the basis of a valid theory of profit. (3) Consolidation and specialization are the two fundamental methods of dealing with uncertainty—the former is based upon reduction by grouping; while the latter upon selection of individuals to 'bear' it.

According to Williamson (1991), there are three dimensions of transactions which raise transaction costs and combine to create market failure. They are asset specificity, uncertainty, and transaction frequency, the last one paying far less attention to the empirical literature than the first two (Geyskens *et al.*, 2006). Williamson (1991)'s opinions about vertical integration can be summarized as follows: (1) Asset specificity brings about a fundamental transformation, where originally independent parties in the market are transformed into interdependent stakeholders. (2) Those who have invested capital in asset specificity will be menaced by the hold-up of others, which weakens the power of asset specificity investors in *ex-post* haggling and, ultimately, increases the transaction cost. (3) Governance cost is a function of asset specificity, thus a higher degree of asset specificity requires a higher level of vertical integration.

As illustrated in Figure 1, Knight infers that uncertainty creates demand for consolidation and specialization, which in turn brings about the firm as well as the role of entrepreneur. Williamson, however, suggests that asset specificity causes the hold-up problem, which in turn entails vertical integration, including the firm and the project. By combining these two similar positions together, one can identify uncertainty as a *raison d'être* of both the firm and the project, or as a characteristic to distinguish them from the market.

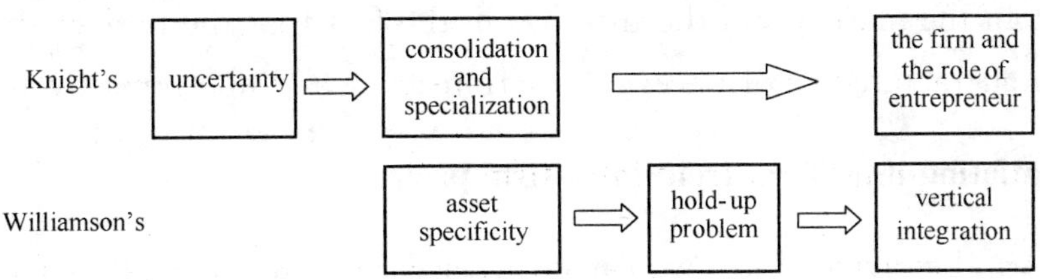

Figure 1 Two loci of inference about the *raison d'être* of the firm (vertical integration)

What should be done next is to tell the project apart from the firm. The emergence of the project can be attributed to the failure of the normal mode of routine production in firms plus transaction in the market. Under normal circumstances, firms carry out their business under the guidance of the market's invisible hand; while customers buy ready-made goods or services from the market—both firms and customers gain what they want, with the market acting as an 'omnipotent' intermediary. However, when a customer cannot find desirable goods or services in the market, he or she has to hire someone to provide bespoke products or services, bringing about a new mode of production—customization. From the viewpoint of the organization, the way in which a client hires a firm or a group of firms to provide bespoke products or services is neither the market nor the firm (hierarchy), but a hybrid of them. This is just the way construction projects are. Sometimes, in order to meet the challenges arising from a volatile business environment, firms may initiate projects to develop new products or technologies for potential clients, as is the case for software development projects. In both cases, most processes are neither routine nor repetitive. This is in contrast to the firm where the routine production is relatively stable and repetitive. Hence, one-off or non-repetitive features can be identified as a distinctive characteristic to tell the project from the firm.

The non-repetitive feature of the project is closely related to its transiency. Generally speaking, the market is endless. The production process in firms is continuous, stable and repetitive, and thus is routine in nature, whereas in a project the production process is limited in time, and thus is transient in nature. It is for this reason that transiency is coincidentally accepted by various schools as a distinctive characteristic of the project: 'temporary endeavor or process' (PMI, 2013), 'temporary production system' (Koskela and Ballard, 2006) and 'temporary multi-organization' (Turner and Müller, 2003; Turner, 2006; Winch, 2006). Note that so-called transiency here is with respect to the parent organization of the project, and thus is a relative concept.

In summary, it is the clients' unique and novel requirements as well as volatile business environments that make the normal mode of 'market plus firm' no longer appropriate, entailing a new form of economic organization—the project. What distinguishes the project from the market and the firm lies in the fact that the project simultaneously possesses the characteristics of uncertainty, transiency and non-repetitiveness.

2.2 Differentiating inter-firm from intra-firm projects

Projects can be divided into two categories according to the relationships with their parent organizations (Archibald, 1992; Turner and Keegan, 2001). Type Ⅰ projects are undertaken in the market, and are inter-organizational in nature; whereas type Ⅱ projects are undertaken within the hierarchy, and belong to intra-firm organizations. In the first case, clients play the role of parent organization of projects. They place their project work in the market and hire firms as 'legal person employees' to carry out the work (Turner, 2004). Correspondingly, firms that undertake projects as their main or even exclusive business, supplying bespoke products or services to clients should be classified as type I firms. Construction companies and construction projects are typical type I firms and type I projects respectively. In the second case, it is the firm that has projects supporting its mainline business, which is routine in nature, to keep pace with rapid market changes. So the parent organizations of projects are firms rather than external clients. Correspondingly, firms that retain project work within the hierarchy should be classified as type II firms, where projects are undertaken in the support function to create new markets, products or technologies (Turner and Keegan, 2001). IT companies and IT projects are typical type II firms and type II projects respectively.

Different types of organizations and different tasks require different methods to steer. In the domain of 'pure' project management where the focus is cost, time and quality, the canonical Project Management approach is suitable for both type I and type II projects. However, in the domain of project governance, it seems that different approaches are needed for each type. Currently, dominant standards and guides (Office of Government Commerce, 2007; APM, 2011; PMI, 2013; DIN, 2013) which put the focus on project—parent relationships within the hierarchy are suitable for type II projects. Imagine a software development company within which several projects are carried out simultaneously. It is easier for the company (the parent) to align the goals of various projects with its short- and long-term goals, and thus ensure that projects serve as vehicles that execute its strategies (Ahola *et al.*, 2014). However, if market transactions and inter-organizational relationships are involved, limitations of this approach become evident, which calls for a new governance approach. Take a construction project for instance. The project coalition requires several legally independent firms to temporarily pool together their resources, capabilities, and knowledge to deliver bespoke products. Since the client and all involved parties have divergent long-term interests and strategic goals, the project's goal must be determined on the basis of negotiations between and concessions from relative parties. In this case, what can be done is to align involved parties to work together towards shared goals that are short-term in nature (Winch, 2010; Ahola *et al.*, 2014).

In summary, when research perspective is expanded from 'pure' project management to project governance, it is essential to make an explicit distinction between type I and type II projects. The opinion that takes the parent organization's interests as the benchmark is suitable for type II projects. Whereas type I projects need a new strategy that takes the interests of both the client and all involved parties into account simultaneously, which is bound to be a much more complex issue than in type II projects.

2.3 Analyzing the idiosyncrasy of construction projects

A construction project can be viewed as a nexus of formal and informal contracts. Relationships between various participants in construction projects are typical contractor—contractee relationships, differing from project—parent relationships in type II projects which are more like employee—employer relationships within a firm. Because of the high cost of specifying a long list of the particular rights, contracts on construction projects are necessarily incomplete, leaving big room for residual rights of control (Grossman and Hart, 1986) and residual claims (Fama and Jensen, 1983).

Construction projects distinguish themselves by a high degree of uncertainty that can hardly be found at the aggregate level of the product market environment (Winch, 1989). Some of the sources of uncertainty facing the industry include: (1) task uncertainty due to the small units of production, (2) natural uncertainty due to the unpredictability about weather and geological conditions, and so on, (3) organizational uncertainty due to the temporary character of the project team, and (4) contracting uncertainty due to errors in estimating and competitive tendering (Winch, 1989) . Such a high level of uncertainty creates the strong demand for specialization. The broader and well-developed chartered professional certification system in the building sector can be regarded as an institutional arrangement designed for addressing uncertainty. Specialized knowledge, especially tacit knowledge, is at the core of the chartered professional certification system and belongs to the category of human asset specificity. According to Williamson, as mentioned above, it is reasonable for the construction project to adopt a hierarchy structure because of its high degree of asset specificity. In practice, however, construction projects adopt a hybrid structure, which exceeds Williamson's expectations. To explain the paradox, uncertainty, specialized knowledge to deal with uncertainty and information cost are included into the analysis framework by relaxing some assumptions made by Williamson (Sha, 2011). The analysis indicates that under some conditions, the approach of selecting the governance structure of construction projects might deviate from the path anticipated by canonical theories. If uncertainty exceeds a certain degree, its influence on the production cost may be greater than that of the hold-up problem on the transaction cost. The pressure of uncertainty on the production cost may restrain the client's enthusiasm for a hold-up in *ex-post* haggling, which will reduce construction firms' tendency towards vertical integration. In consequence, the tradeoff between production and transaction cost may bring about a hybrid, rather than a hierarchy structure (Sha, 2011).

In summary, as a typical type I project, the construction project can be regarded as a consequence of the tradeoff between production cost and transaction cost under the circumstance where great uncertainty creates strong demand for specialization, and could be concisely defined as a temporary multi-organization to undertake a one-off customization-based endeavor.

3 THE ESSENCE OF GOVERNANCE

As the complex art of steering multiple agencies, institutions and systems, the governance paradigm is about a new mindset and methods (Jessop, 1997). The rise of governance stems from difficulties of hierarchical coordination by organizations or the state (Miller and Lessard, 2000), which, in turn, is a consequence of increasingly complex business environments characterized by rapidly changing patterns of reciprocal interdependence (Jessop, 1998) and increasingly frequent interactions across all types of pre-established boundaries (Scharpf, 1994). In spite of diverse and contrary usages, governance is, in essence, 'concerned with creating the conditions for ordered rule and collective action' (Stoker, 1998).

According to new institutional economics, social, political, legal and economic institutions may be divided into four categories or levels: (1) social or cultural foundations, or embeddedness, (2) basic institutional environment, (3) institutions of governance, and (4) short-term resource allocation (Williamson, 2000). At the third level where the purpose is to get the governance structures right, the main task is to define structures and processes, and 'craft order, thereby to mitigate conflict and realize mutual gains' (Williamson, 2000), while requiring assurance that management is operating effectively and properly within the defined structures (Biesenthal and Wilden, 2014; Too and Weaver, 2014). As compared to day-to-day management, governance is a relatively stable institution with a change time-frame of one to ten years (Williamson, 2000).

Besides the above-mentioned differences in terms of purpose, function and change time-frame, the fundamental distinction between management and governance lies in their values orientation and way of thinking, which can be depicted by the following dyads: authority *vs.* consensus (Ahern *et al.*, 2014), control-oriented *vs.* involvement-oriented approach (Toivonen and Toivonen, 2014), collective top—down *vs.* mutual bottom—up characterization (Ahern *et al.*, 2014), hierarchical *vs.* heterarchic coordination (Jessop, 1997), and higher 'power distance' *vs.* lower 'power distance' culture (Hofstede, 1980). The term 'power distance' refers to the extent to which the less powerful members in organizations accept and expect power to be distributed unequally. Individuals in a society that exhibit a high degree of power distance accept hierarchies in which everyone has a place without the need for justification. Societies with low power distance seek to have equal distribution of power. These dyads are helpful to understand the connection and distinction between the two paradigms.

In the context of management, people are classified into two categories: those who manage others and those who are managed by others. The hierarchical coordination of management is based on the values of 'managers know best' which can be traced back to Taylor (1911). Taylor's view of workers may be considered prejudiced or insulting. He called less intelligent workers 'stupid', and compared them to draft animals: 'Now one of the very first requirements for a man who is fit to handle pig iron as a regular occupation is that he shall be so stupid and so phlegmatic that he more nearly resembles in his mental make-up the ox than any other type' (Taylor, 1911). Consequently, in the context of management, more attention is paid to planning, organizing, commanding, coordinating and controlling (Donnelly Jr. *et al.*, 1987). The control-based feature of management is vividly presented in the plan—do—check—act (PDCA) cycle in which the continuous improvement process is just like negative feedback loops in control theory.

In the context of governance, however, more attention is paid to autonomy, decentralization, flatness of structure, mutual trust, and self-organization achieved by 'underspecification' of structure (Müller *et al.*, 2014). All involved parties, whether individually, in groups, or in organizations, could be regarded as stakeholders in a self-organizing 'heterarchy', or a network of elements in which each element shares the same 'horizontal' position of power and authority. Using the lens of complex problem solving, governance approach can be viewed as a distributed coordination mechanism that is underpinned by a 'common will' of mutual interest and operates through what Polanyi (1966) calls 'mutual control'. A 'common will' as a consensus among all involved parties is achieved through bottom-up dialogues and negotiations. In a 'mutual control' structure, agents exercise control over each other, based on the twin principles of self-discipline through mutual authority and self-coordination through mutual adjustment (Polanyi, 1969; Ahern *et al.*, 2014).

Governance as an art of complexity is enabled through different forms of flexibility at different levels. Generally speaking, the higher the level, the greater the complexity, and the greater the degree of flexibility that would be required. It is argued that lower levels require flexibility in the choice of methods and processes, while higher levels of governance require flexibility in people's mindset and attitude towards work. In the realm of projects, governance is executed by: (1) flexibility in the idiosyncrasy of governance approaches and authority at the project level, (2) flexible organization structures and mindsets of people at the organizational level, and (3) management's flexibility in deployment of governmentality in project settings (Müller *et al.*, 2014).

Discriminating alignment is a fundamental principle to deal with complexity at different levels. Transaction cost economics asserts that the supply of a good or service and its governance must be examined simultaneously. The central exercise is to align transactions which differ in their attributes with governance structures (market, hierarchy and hybrid) which differ in costs and competencies in a discriminating way so that an economizing match is achieved (Williamson, 2000). This implies that there is no omnipotent approach to governing economic organizations and activities; instead, they must be steered in a contingent manner.

In summary, management and governance are just like two sides of the same coin. Both of them serve the same purpose of pursuing organizational effectiveness and efficiency, but they do this in different ways. Management is mainly concerned with the execution of daily work and operational control through hierarchical coordination at tactical level; whereas governance is mainly about strategic objectives (Biesenthal and Wilden, 2014), which aspires to the collective interests of people and the consent which leads them to voluntarily obey contextual frameworks that shape, but not necessarily determine, the actions of individuals (Clegg *et al.*, 2002; Müller *et al.*, 2014), demanding more flexible mindsets and methods.

4 RETHINKING CONSTRUCTION PROJECT GOVERNANCE

Above analyses indicate that the firm and the project are two different types of economic organizations, that projects can be classified into type I and type II, and that management and governance are two different approaches to steering diverse organizations. As illustrated in Figure 2, there are four basic tasks for a construction corporation: enterprise management, corporate governance, project management and project governance. Generally speaking, the project is more complex than the firm since the former is a hybrid of the latter and the market; type I projects are more complex than type II projects since the former belongs to inter-firm organization, while the latter is intra-organizational in nature; and governance is more complex than management since the former represents a higher level structure (Biesenthal and Wilden, 2014). Therefore, it can be expected that construction project governance (as type I project governance) is the most challenging one among the four tasks.

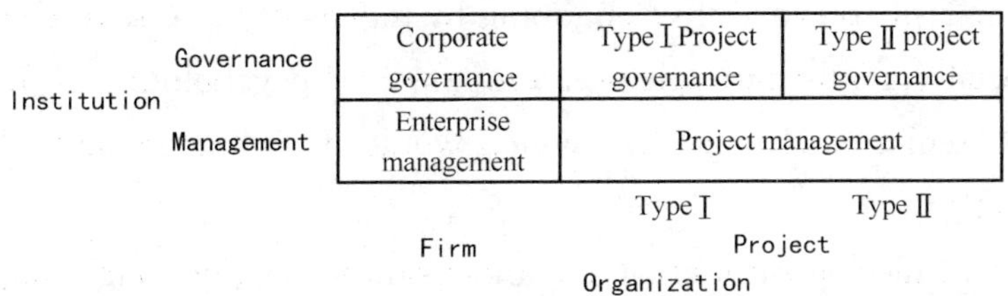

Figure 2 An organization/institution grid

4.1 A conceptualization of construction project governance

Project governance is typically defined as 'the alignment of project objectives with the strategy of the larger organization by the project sponsor and project team' (PMI, 2013). This definition implies an assumption that project governance is an activity that is externally, and unidirectionally, imposed by the project-based organization on the focal project (Ahola *et al.*, 2014). In the context of construction projects, however, the client and involved firms interact with each other in a bidirectional way (Ahola *et al.*, 2014). Furthermore, the strategic goals and long-term interests of legally independent participants are not necessarily consistent and can even be conflicting. Therefore, construction projects governance requires an alternative approach that pays more attention to balancing the interests and claims of different participants.

Under the assumption of bounded rationality, self-interest, and opportunistic behavior, construction project governance can be conceptualized as an effort to make legally independent participants with divergent long-term interests and strategic goals work together towards a shared goal, achieving positive results for all parties. This implies a favorable institutional environment that gives people, whether individually, in groups, or in organizations, the motivation to do the right things in the right way. In essence, it is a framework to shape and influence the attitude of participants, rather than directly determining every action of organizational actors. The job of regulating participants' behavior can be divided into three categories (Sha and Wu, 2016):

- To increase incentives by means of more reasonable allocation of responsibilities, rights, and interests, which would make participants unwilling to behave opportunistically.
- To increase the difficulty of wrongdoing by means of stricter supervision and restrictions, as well as a check and balance mechanism that enables transparency, accountability and defined roles (Müller, 2009), which would make participants unable to behave opportunistically.
- To increase the risk and cost of wrongdoing by means of more severe sanctions, legal, economic, social (mainly through peer groups) and psychological (through cognitive dissonance) (Henisz *et al.*, 2012), which would make participants dare not behave opportunistically.

Some relevant mechanisms involve compensation (engineering change, claim, and counterclaim), mutual aid (engineering insurance) and security (engineering guarantee, mortgage, lien and deposit). Theoretically speaking, these three lines of defense can effectively prevent opportunistic behaviors from occurring in construction projects. However, any institutional arrangement cannot be designed and executed without a cost. So the real effects of governance structures and mechanisms are dependent on the balance of their costs and benefits. Nevertheless, they do indicate practical approaches to governing construction projects.

4.2 Three governance categories

In the framework defined by Winch (2001), the governance structure of construction projects is divided into vertical governance and horizontal governance. The former focuses on the relationship between the client and the project, or as Winch noted, the transactions between the client and its first-tier suppliers; whereas the latter pays most attention to the supply chain, or a series of contracts developed behind the first-tier suppliers (Winch, 2010). In addition, there is another kind of relationship to be steered—the relationship between construction firms and project managers, which could be classified as the category of 'project manager related governance'.

4.2.1 *Vertical governance: formal vs. informal contract perspective*

The vertical governance of a construction project can be examined in two dimensions, as Turner (2004) suggested: project procurement route (PPR) and payment terms. The PPR determines the roles and scope of supply—traditional (design—bid—build, DBB), integrative (design—build, DB), construction management (CM), public—private partnership (PPP) and so on—while payment terms determine the allocation of risk and the incentive intensity, including fixed price, cost plus, re-measurement, target cost contracts and so on. In most cases, one kind of PPR may involve several principal—agent relationships. Each relationship should be regulated by a certain contract. Combining different types of PPR and payment terms yields various contractual arrangements (Sha, 2011).

Principal—agency theory has been widely applied in general governance theories and is useful for examining the relationship between the client and the project. Consider a construction project composed of two parties: a risk neutral client and a risk averse agent. The payment that the agent gains from the client is $w = \alpha + \beta Y$, where α is constant payment, β is incentive coefficient ($0 \leqslant \beta \leqslant 1$), and Y is observable output of the project. The client's problem is to select α and β so as to maximize its expected payoff under the condition that both participation constraint and incentive compatibility constraint of the agent are satisfied.

The key to modeling lies in selecting the outcome function $Y(\cdot)$ in accordance with the research purpose and the features of the problem to be solved. For example, the outcome may be simply represented as $Y = e + x$ where variable e is the agent's effort, and random variable x is a measure of risk. When analyzing a standard pain—gain sharing arrangement in construction contracts, the outcome is represented as the difference between fixed target cost $\overline{C}$ and outturn cost C: $Y = C - \overline{C}$, where C, in turn, is a function of agent's effort (Chang, 2014). With the aim of examining the influence of uncertainty and specialized knowledge on selecting the governance structure, the outcome is represented as a non-linear function $Y = K^{\gamma}G^{1-\gamma} + x$, where K and G are the amount of specialized knowledge and general producer goods respectively, γ $(0<\gamma<1)$ is the index of information gap to reflect the degree of 'true' uncertainty (Sha, 2011).

In practice, there are relational project delivery arrangements, including project partnering, project alliancing and integrated project delivery (Lahdenperä, 2012). In the domain of transaction cost economics (TCE), the research on relational contracting incorporates the role of reputational capital in repeated games. Stewardship theory provides an alternative description of human behavior compared to agency theory (Biesenthal and Wilden, 2014). An interdisciplinary governance framework that is supported by 'three institutional pillars' (regulative, normative and cognitive) provides a powerful way to unify the disparate and fragmented insights from TCE, sociology and psychology into a more unified theory that can allow us to better understand and manage relational project governance (Scott 2008; Henisz *et al.*, 2012).

4.2.2 *Horizontal governance: a coalitional game perspective*

Generally speaking, cooperation can generate more benefits as compared to single-handed practices, getting the result of '1+1>2'. Cooperation practices, in turn, require two preconditions. One is that the excess benefits from cooperation (making the cake bigger); the other is that the fairness in distributing the cooperation gains (cutting the cake in a way acceptable to all parties). These issues are exactly what the cooperative game theory focuses on.

As a sub-area of the cooperative game theory, coalitional game theory is mainly concerned with the stability of the grand coalition, or the coalition of all players. The fundamental assumption here is that the grand coalition will form. In order to guarantee the stability of the grand coalition, it is essential to allocate the payoff among the players in a fair way. Several solution concepts have been developed based on different notions of fairness, including core, Shapley value, and nucleolus (Saad *et al.*, 2009).

Based on the notion of 'gains from trade', the core simultaneously satisfies (1) individual rationality (no player receives less than what he could get on his own), (2) group rationality (the payoff vector exactly splits the total value) and (3) coalitional rationality (there is no coalition that can improve upon it), so no group of players has an incentive to leave the grand coalition to form another coalition. The Shapley value assigns a unique payoff allocation among the players, while satisfying four axioms. It is, in essence, a weighted average marginal contribution of the player to the grand coalition, representing the notion of 'more pay for more work'. The nucleolus provides a unique payoff allocation that minimizes the dissatisfaction of some players. It is well compatible with Rawls' difference principle of justice as fairness, which states that inequalities are to be to the greatest benefit of the least-advantaged members of society (Rawls, 2001). Obviously, when applying coalitional game theory, the local population's perception of fairness must be taken into consideration.

4.2.3 *Project manager related governance: a common agency perspective*

The roles of construction project managers can vary depending on the procurement route chosen by the client. In the case of executive project management or PM mode, they act on behalf of the client. On the other hand, design—and—building companies usually designate their own persons as project managers (Walker, 2007; Fewings, 2005). In practice, they are often treated as the same occupation as construction managers (DOL, 2015). What is to be discussed here is the relationship between construction firms and their project managers.

Construction project managers are responsible for all phases of the construction management process, interacting with a variety of stakeholders, and handling any issues that arise during construction in a contingent manner. That is why they have more autonomy as compared to workshop managers in the manufacturing industry and project managers in the IT sector. Having more autonomy can ensure efficiency and productivity, while, in the presence of conflicting interests and asymmetric information, it can bring about the problems of adverse selection and moral hazard.

When designing mechanisms for designating and stimulating project managers, construction firms must take the client's influence into account because a project manager making decisions may be responsible both to the construction firm and to the client. The relationships between the three parties can be described as 'one servant of two masters', which is well compatible with the scenario of common agency game where the action chosen by a particular individual (the agent) affects not just one, but several other parties (the principals) whose preferences for the various possible actions typically conflict (Bernheim and Whinston, 1986). The common agency literature has developed an analytical framework to tackle a variety of important problems (Carmona and Fajardo, 2006; Attar *et al.*, 2007). So it is technologically feasible to examine project manager related governance from a common agency perspective.

In the above sub-sections, three governance categories have been discussed mainly from a game theory perspective. Without a doubt, the game models may be unrealistically simple in many aspects, and inevitably have limitations. However, as Bowles (2004) argued, 'models do not explain all the details, but they tell us where to look'. Regardless of their simplicity, these models are capable of providing some clues for studying construction project governance.

5 CONCLUSION

The project has become a major form of economic organization, to the point of being on par with markets and firms. When examining the exchanges with incomplete contracts, Herbert Simon imagined a 'mythical visitor from Mars' approaching Earth in a spaceship

> equipped with a telescope that reveals social structures. The firms reveal themselves, say, as solid green areas.... Market transactions show as red lines connecting the firms forming a network in the spaces between them.... A message sent back home, describing the scene would speak of 'large green areas interconnected by red lines.' (Simon, 1991)

Today, if the spaceship approached Earth once again, the visitor might see more colors: yellow green (a mixture of green and a little red) and brown (a mixture of red and a little green), indicating type I projects that can be viewed as firm-like organization in the market, or quasi-firms as Eccles (1981) called, and type II projects that can be regarded as market-like processes within the firm (Lindkvist, 2004) respectively.

Type I projects emerged in the UK building sector during the 19th century, much earlier than type II projects that were developed and formalized in the US aerospace sector in the post-war period (Winch, 2000; Winch, 2006). However, the canonical Project Management approach was mainly derived from type II projects. As Winch suggested, it was 'not originally designed to handle differences between firms, only differences between functional departments within single organizations' (Winch, 1989). A better understanding of construction project governance depends on expanding the focus from project—parent relationships within the hierarchy to contractor—contractee relationships in a self-organizing 'heterarchy'.

Being at a higher level than management, governance is enabled through different forms of flexibility. This implies less control and more autonomy. In the realm of construction projects, governance structure and governance mechanism can be summarized as the sum of heterarchic coordination-based institutions to lay a foundation for the check and balance between diverse participants of the project. The basic framework can be illustrated in two dimensions: governance category (vertical, horizontal and project manager related governance) and approach to regulating participants' behavior (making people unwilling to, unable to, and dare not behave opportunistically). The ideal state should be one where all parties act together under a common will that is achieved *via* compromise between them, with each party finding the right niche for itself. However, it is just theoretically realizable due to uncertainty facing construction projects, bounded rationality of diverse participants, and flexibility inherent in the governance paradigm. Therefore, it can be concluded that there is no best approach, but rather a most suitable one to governing a given construction project.

In the multi-level structure of institutions, construction project governance serves as a connecting link between the upstream (construction business system, or 'contracting system' for short in the UK) and the downstream (project management). As a kind of basic institutional environment, the construction business system shapes, and is shaped by decisions made at the governance level, which in turn have a great influence on the process level as well as the performance of construction projects (Winch, 2010, p. 13; Sha, 2013). On the other hand, governance system cannot operate without effective support of the management system (Too and Weaver, 2014). Further studies should be conducted in a broader framework to grasp the interactions between construction business system, project governance and project management.

In multi-project environment, the collective governance of a program or portfolio of projects presents challenges that are fundamentally different from single project governance (Aritua *et al.*, 2009; Müller and Lecoeuvre, 2014), making the difference between type I and type II projects more evident. Take the governance of a program of projects for example. In type II project settings, all projects within a program may be steered as a fish-tail, with the parent organization acting as the fish head (Turner and Keegan, 2001). In the realm of construction projects, however, the problem is much more complex. Consider a client, say a local government that initiates three projects undertaken by different contractors, one can find four 'fishes' (the client plus three contractors) within the program, each having its own strategic goals. On the other hand, construction firms often participate in several projects sponsored by different clients. How to analyze the complex network-like relationships between various 'fishes' from inter-organizational perspective; and find appropriate approaches to steering them? This is an interesting but challenging subject, which might bring about a new research paradigm.

REFERENCES

Ahern, T., Leavy, B. and Byrne, P. J. (2014) Complex project management as complex problem solving: A distributed knowledge management perspective, *International Journal of Project Management*, **32** (8), 1371—1381.

Ahola, T., Ruuska, I., Artto, K. and Kujala, J. (2014) What is project governance and what are its origins? *International Journal of Project Management*, **32**(8), 1321—1332.

APM (2011) *Directing Change: A Guide to Governance of Project Management*, Association for Project Management, UK.

Archibald, R. D. (1992) *Managing High-Technology Programs and Projects* (2nd edition), Wiley, New York.

Aritua, B., Smith, N. J. and Bower, D. (2009) Construction client multi-projects—A complex adaptive systems perspective, *International Journal of Project Management*, **27**(1), 72—79.

Attar, A., Piaser, G. and Porteiro, N. (2007) A note on Common Agency models of moral hazard, *Economics Letters*, **95**(2), 278—284.

Aubry, M., Richer, M.-C. and Lavoie-Tremblay, M. (2014) Governance performance in complex environment: The case of a major transformation in a university hospital, *International Journal of Project Management*, **32**(8), 1333—1345.

Bernheim, B. D. and Whinston, M. D. (1986) Common agency, *Econometrica*, **54**(4), 923—942.

Biesenthal, C. and Wilden, R. (2014) Multi-level project governance: Trends and opportunities, *International Journal of Project Management*, **32**(8), 1291—1308.

Bjørkeng, K., Clegg, S. R. and Pitsis, T. S. (2009) Becoming (a) practice, *Management Learning*, **40** (2), 145—159.

Bologna, R. and Nord, R. Del (2000) Effects of the law reforming public works contracts on the Italian building progress, *Building Research and Information*, **28**(2), 109—18.

Bowles, S. (2004) *Microeconomics: Behavior, Institutions and Evolution*, Princeton University Press, Princeton.

Carmona, G. and Fajardo, J. (2006) On the definition of equilibrium in common agency games with adverse selection, available at http://www.researchgate.net/publication/228555375, (accessed 16 October 2015).

Chang, C. Y. (2014) Principal-agent model of risk allocation in construction contracts and its critique, *Journal of Construction Engineering and Management*, **140**(1), 04013032—1—9.

Clegg, S. R., Pitsis, T. S., Rura-Polley, T. and Marosszeky, M. (2002) Governmentality matters: designing an alliance culture of inter-organizational collaboration for managing projects, *Organization Studies*, **23**(3) 317—337.

Cobb, M. (1995) *Unfinished voyages*, Presentation at CHAOS University, Sponsored by The Standish Group, Chatham, MA.

Crawford, L. and Cooke-Davies, T. (2009) Project governance: the role and capabilities of the executive sponsor, *Project Perspectives*, vol. XXXI, 66—74.

DIN (2013) *Multi Project Management - Management of Project Portfolios, Programs and Projects—*

Part 1: *Fundamentals*, Deutsches Institut für Normung, Berlin.

DOL (2015) *Occupational Outlook Handbook*, United States Department of Labor, Washington, D. C., USA.

Donnelly Jr., J. H., Gibson, J. L. and Ivancevich, J. M. (1987) *Fundamentals of Management* (6th Edition), Business Publications Inc., Homewood, Illinois.

Eccles, R. G. (1981) The quasifirm in the construction industry, *Journal of Economic Behavior and Organization*, **2**(4), 335—357.

Fama, E. F. and Jensen, M. C. (1983) Agency problems and residual claims, Journal of Law and Economics, **26**(2), 327—349.

Fewings, P. (2005) *Construction project Management: An Integrated Approach*, Taylor and Francis, Abdingdon, Oxon, UK.

Geyskens, I., Steenkamp, J. B. E. M. and Kumar, N. (2006) Make, buy, or ally: a transaction cost theory meta-analysis, *Academy of Management Journal*, **49**(3), 519—543.

Grossman, S. J. and Hart, O. D. (1986) The costs and benefits of ownership: a theory of vertical and lateral integration, *The Journal of Political Economy*, **94** (4), 691—719.

Henisz, W. J, Levitt, R. E. and Scott, W. R. (2012) Toward a unified theory of project governance: economic, sociological and psychological supports for relational contracting, *Engineering Project Organization Journal*, **2**(1-2), 37—55.

Hofstede, G. (1980) *Culture's consequences: International differences in work-related values*, Sage Publications, Beverly Hills, CA.

Jessop, B. (1998) The rise of governance and the risks of failure: the case of economic development, *International Social Science Journal*, **50**(155), 29—45.

Jessop, B. (2003) The governance of complexity and the complexity of governance: preliminary remarks on some problems and limits of economic guidance, published by the Department of Sociology, Lancaster University, Lancaster LA1 4YN, available at http://www.comp.lancs.ac.uk/sociology/papers/Jessop-Governance-of- Complexit y.pdf, (accessed 20 June 2015).

Knight, F. H. (1921) *Risk, Uncertainty and Profit*, Houghton Mifflin Company, Boston.

Koskela, L. and Ballard, G. (2006) Should project management be based on theories of economics or production?, *Building Research and Information*, **34**(2), 154—163.

Koskela, L. and Howell, G. (2002) The underlying theory of project management is obsolete, In Slevin, D., Cleland, D. and Pinto, J. (Eds.), *Proceedings of PMI Research Conference* (293-302), Project Management Institute, Seattle.

Lahdenperä, P. (2012) Making sense of the multi-party contractual arrangements of project partnering, project alliancing and integrated project delivery, *Construction Management and Economics*, **30**(1), 57—79.

Lindkvist, L. (2004) Governing project-based firms: promoting market-like processes within hierarchies, *Journal of Management and Governance*, **8**(1), 3—25.

Locatelli, G., Mancini, M. and Romano, E. (2014) Systems Engineering to improve the governance in complex project environments, *International Journal of Project Management*, **32**(8), 1395—1410.

Loosemore, M. (2000) *Crisis Management in Construction Projects*, ASCE Press, Virginia.

Lundin, R. A. and Söderholm, A. (1998) Conceptualizing a projectified society, In Lundin, Rolf A. and Midler, C. (Eds.), *Projects as Arenas for Renewal and Learning Processes*, Kluwer Academic, Boston, 13—23.

McManus, J. and Wood-Harper, T. (2014) *A study in project failure*, BCS, The Chartered Institute for IT, available at http://www.bcs.org/content/ ConWebDoc/19584 (accessed 19 July 2014).

Miller, R. and Lessard, D. R. (2000) *The Strategic Management of Large Engineering Projects: Shaping Institutions, Risk and Governance*, MIT Press, Cambridge, MA.

Morris, P. W. G. (1997) *The management of projects*, Thomas Telford, London.

Morris, P. W. G. (2013) *Reconstructing project management*, John Wiley & Sons, Oxford.

Müller, R. (2009) *Project governance*, Gower Publishing, Aldershot, UK.

Müller, R. and Lecoeuvre, L. (2014) Operationalizing governance categories of projects, *International Journal of Project Management*, **32**(8), 1346—1357.

Müller, R., Pemsel, S. and Shao, J. (2014) Organizational enablers for governance and governmentality of projects: A literature review, *International Journal of Project Management*, **32**(8), 1309—1320.

Office of Government Commerce (2007) *Management of Portfolios*, The Stationery Office, London.

Piteroforte, R. and Miller, J. B. (2002) Procurement methods for US infrastructure: historical perspective and recent trends, *Building Research and Information*, **30**(6), 425—434.

Pitsis, T. S., Sankaran, S., Gudergan, S. and Clegg, S. R. (2014) Governing projects under complexity: theory and practice in project management, *International Journal of Project Management*, **32**(8), 1285—1290.

PMI (2013) *A Guide to the Project Management Body of Knowledge*, 5th ed., Project Management Institute, Inc., Newtown Square, PA, USA.

Polanyi, M. (1967) *The Tacit Dimension*, Doubleday, Garden City, NY.

Polanyi, M. (1969) *Knowing and Being: Essays by Michael Polanyi*, In Grene, M. (Eds), University of Chicago Press, Chicago, IL.

PM Solutions (2011) *Strategies for Project Recovery*.

Rawls, J. B. (2001) *Justice as Fairness: A Restatement*, E. Kelly (ed.), Harvard University Press, Cambridge, MA.

Saad, W., Han, Z., Debbah, M., Hjørungnes, A. and Basar, T. (2009) Coalitional game theory for communication networks, *IEEE Signal Processing Magazine*, **26**(5), 77—97.

Scharpf, F. W. (1994) Games real actors could play: positive and negative coordination in embedded negotiations, *Journal of Theoretical Politics*, **6**(1), 27—53.

Scott, R. W. (2008) *Institutions and Organizations: Ideas and Interests*, 3rd ed. Sage Publications, Thousand Oaks, CA.

Sha, K. X. (2004) Construction business system in China: an institutional transformation perspective, *Building Research and Information*, **32**(6), 529—537.

Sha, K. X. (2011) Vertical governance of construction projects: an information cost perspective, *Construction Management and Economics*, **29**(11), 1137—1147.

Sha, K. X. and Wu, S. Y. (2016) Multilevel governance for building energy conservation in rural China, *Building Research and Information*, **44**(5—6), 619—629.

Simon, H. (1991) Organizations and markets, *Journal of Economic Perspectives*, **5**(2), 25—44.

Stoker, G. (1998) Governance as theory: five propositions, *International Social Science Journal*, **50** (155), 17—28.

Taylor, F. W. (1911) *The Principles of Scientific Management*, Harper & Brothers, New York, NY.

Toivonen, A. and Toivonen, P. U. (2014) The transformative effect of top management governance choices on project team identity and relationship with the organization——An agency and stewardship approach, *International Journal of Project Management*, **32**(8), 1358—1370.

Too, E. G. and Weaver, P. (2014) The management of project management: A conceptual framework for project governance, *International Journal of Project Management*, **32**(8), 1382—1394.

Turner, J. R. (2004) Farsighted project contract management: incomplete in its entirety, *Construction Management and Economics*, **22**(1), 75—83.

Turner, J. R. (2006) Towards a theory of project management: the nature of the functions of project management, *International Journal of Project Management*, **24**(4), 277—279.

Turner, J. R. (2009) *The Handbook of Project-based Management*, McGraw-Hill, London.

Turner, R. J., Huemann, M., Anbari, F. T. and Bredillet, C. N. (2010) *Perspectives on Projects*, Routledge, Abingdon, Oxon.

Turner, J. R. and Keegan, A. (2001) Mechanisms of governance in the project-based organization: roles of the broker and steward, *European Management Journal*, **19**(3), 254—267.

Turner, J. R. and Müller R. (2003) On the nature of the project as a temporary organization, *International Journal of Project Management*, **21**(1), 1—8.

Walker, A. (2007) *Project Management in Construction* (5th edition), Blackwell, Oxford.

Walker, D. H. T., Segon, M. and Rowlinson, S. (2008) Business ethics and corporate citizenship, In: Walker, D. H. T. and Rowlinson, S. (Eds.), *Procurement Systems——A Cross Industry Project Management Perspective*, Taylor and Francis, Abdingdon, Oxon, UK.

Williams, T., Klakegg, O. J., Magnussen, O. M. and Glasspool, H. (2010) An investigation of governance frameworks for public projects in Norway and the UK. *International Journal of Project Management*, **28**(1), 40—50.

Williamson, O. E. (1991) Comparative economic organization: the analysis of discrete structural alternatives, *Administrative Science Quarterly*, **36**(2), 269—296.

Williamson, O. E. (2000) The new institutional economics: taking stock, looking ahead, *Journal of Economic Literature*, **38**(3), 595—613.

Winch, G. M. (1989) The construction firm and the construction project: A transaction coat approach, *Construction Management and Economics*, **7**(3), 331—345.

Winch, G. M. (2000) Institutional reform in British construction: partnering and private finance, *Building Research and Information*, **28**(2), 141—55.

Winch, G. M. (2001) Governing the project process: a conceptual framework, *Construction Management and Economics*, **19**(7), 799—808.

Winch, G. M. (2006) Towards a theory of construction as production by projects, *Building Research and Information*, **34**(2), 164—174.

Winch, G. M. (2010)*Managing Construction Projects: Information Processing Approach* (2nd edition), Wiley-Blackwell, Oxford.

绪　言

这本书是《建设项目治理》（沙凯逊，2013）一书（以下简称《治理》）的姊妹篇。如果说，《治理》一书致力于形式化建模和数学推导，旨在追求理论解析的“深入”；那么，本书的目的是走出象牙塔，在娓娓道来的文字中实现“浅出”。本书希望通过浅显易懂的方式介绍建设项目治理和建筑交易体制演化的相关问题，不至于令人望而却步。

建筑业是典型的基于项目（project-based）的行业。建设项目是建筑业的微观基础——它既是建筑业的基本生产单元，又是建筑市场上各种利益主体的交汇点。基础不牢，地动山摇。研究和解决建筑业的问题很多时候需要从建设项目入手。

当前，我国建筑业所承担的任务是举世无双的，它所面临的问题和挑战也是世间少见的。这些问题为建设项目理论提供了独特的研究素材和创新空间。改革开放以来，特别是进入21世纪新的历史时期，我国建筑业在规模和质量等方面均取得长足进展，然而，利润水平低下的问题一直没有得到解决。2014年建筑业总产值达到17.67万亿元，占国内生产总值（GDP）的27.8%，与1985年相比增加了260多倍；劳动生产率也比1985年增加了3.8倍。然而，建筑企业产值利润率只有3.9%，与1985年相比不仅没有提高，反而有所下降❶（国家统计局，1986；国家统计局，2015）。医治我国建筑业“大而不强”的顽疾，首先要找到病因，要在理论和实践的结合上解释以下问题：

- 为什么建筑企业利润率的改善远远落后于劳动生产率的提高，甚至出现劳动生产率上升而利润率下降的现象？
- 为什么在我国会出现建筑企业资质等级越高，规模越大，利润率反而越低的现象？
- 如何理顺建筑企业和建设项目之间的关系，走出“一放就乱，一抓就死”的怪圈？
- 为什么在发达国家取得成功的制度和方法，被移植到我国却不能取得同样的成效，甚至走向反面？
- 为什么帕累托无效❷的建筑交易体制会长期存在？

---

❶ 与1986年的《中国统计年鉴》相比，2014年的统计口径和方法有所变化。把全民所有制和城镇集体所有制建筑施工企业的相关数据类型综合在一起，可以算出1985年建筑业的劳动生产率是7398元/人，建筑企业的产值利润率是4.5%。

❷ 这是意大利经济学家维弗雷多·帕累托（Vilfredo Pareto，1848—1923）提出的概念。要解释帕累托无效，需要从**帕累托改进**（Pareto improvement）谈起。假设可供分配的资源和参与分配的人数不变，如果从一种分配状态到另一种状态的变化过程中，在没有使任何人状况变坏的前提下，使得至少一个人的状况变得更好，这就是帕累托改进。如果一个状态不可能发生帕累托改进，该状态就是**帕累托最优**（Pareto optimality）；反之则是**帕累托无效**（Pareto inefficiency）（普雷斯曼，2000，p. 165）。

如此等等，不一而足。这些问题已经超出了传统管理理论的范畴，需要采用新的思维方式和新的视角，在新的制度层面上研究解决。

在制度分析的层次结构中，管理（management）、治理（governance）和体制（system）是三个不同的范畴（Williamson，2000）。体制是项目运行的外部环境；项目治理为项目管理提供了运行基础和责权利体系框架，因而在很大程度上决定了项目管理的模式特征，并最终决定项目的绩效水平。把研究视角从管理的层面扩展到治理和体制的层面，这是建设项目理论创新的内在要求，也是建筑业制度创新的必要条件。

自20世纪80年代中后期以来，“治理”成为国际社会科学文献中最为流行的术语之一。在经济全球化的背景下，治理问题成为诸多学科领域的研究重点（俞可平，2002）。中共十八届三中全会把全面深化改革的总目标确定为“完善和发展中国特色社会主义制度，推进国家治理体系和治理能力现代化”（文件起草组，2013）。这一重大突破不仅在宏观层面上开启了国家治理和社会治理的新局面，而且在微观层面上对公司治理和项目治理的研究和实践提供了强大的动力，并将产生深远的影响。

推进国家治理体系和治理能力现代化，首先要树立起“治理思维”（李维安，2013）。如图0.1所示，从统治到管理，再到治理，反映了思维方式的历史变迁。两千多年前，《孟子·滕文公上》中就有“或劳心，或劳力。劳心者治人，劳力者治于人”的论断。劳力者和劳心者之间的关系，是统治与被统治的关系。在统治思维的框架中，统治者具有绝对的权威；统治者与被统治者之间存在很大的“位势差”或**“权力距离”**（Hofstede，1980）[1]——那种把地方官员称为“父母官”的做法，正是这种“位势差”的真实写照。一百多年前，泰勒[2]创建了科学管理理论，将管理职能从生产职能中独立出来。这固然是一次飞跃，然而在对工人的认识上仍有相当大的局限性。泰勒认为，工人只能严格按照管理者的指示去做，只能服从命令和接受工资。他对生铁搬运工的要求是：“他应该是如此愚钝，以至于在心理构成（mental make-up）方面更接近于公牛而不是其他的类型。”（Taylor，1911，p. 59）经过一个多世纪的发展，现代管理的理论和实践都发生了深刻的变化；尽管如此，在管理思维的框架中，管理者与被管理者之间还是存在着一定的“位势差”。七十多年前出现的“经理革命”[3] 开启了现代治理的新时代（周新军，2007）。治理思维重视当事人之间的策略性活动，承认“上有政策、下有对策”的事实，要求政策制定者在制定政策时尽量考虑可能出现的对策，通

---

[1] 权力距离（power distance）是用来表示人们对组织中权力分配不平等情况的接受程度。它的大小可以用权力距离指数PDI（power distance index ）来表示。在PDI较高的组织中，人们通常能够接受权力分配不平等的现实；而在PDI较低的组织中，人们对权力分配的不平等现象会表现出较强的反抗精神。

[2] 弗雷德里克·温斯洛·泰勒（Frederick Winslow Taylor，1856—1915）是美国古典管理学家，科学管理的创始人；他被管理界誉为科学管理之父。

[3] 随着股份制公司的发展、股权的分散以及企业所有权和经营权的分离，企业的主导力量逐步由股东转向经理阶层，这一现象被称为经理革命。1932年，伯利和米恩斯在《现代公司和私有财产》一书中系统论述了经理革命的思想，认为所有权和经营权的分离使得经理阶层事实上取得了对企业的控制权。波恩汉姆在1941年出版的《经理革命：世界上正在发生的事情》一书中正式提出了经理革命的概念。

过适当的制度安排，激励人们有积极性去做正确的事情，并且把事情做好（do right things right）。在治理思维的框架中，博弈双方之间的“位势差”要小得多，有时甚至可以忽略不计。

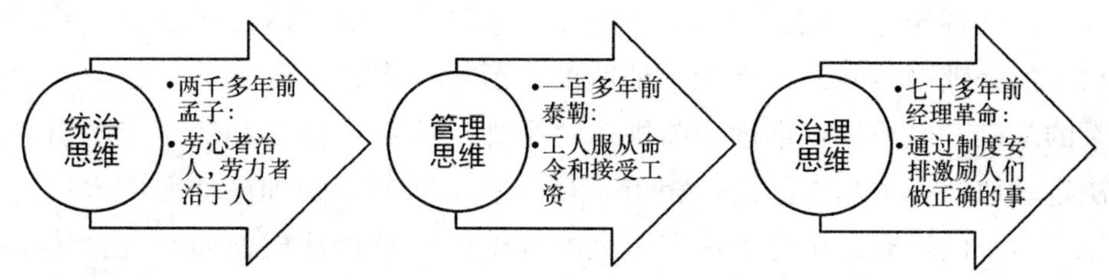

图 0.1　从统治思维到治理思维：权力距离逐步缩小的过程

“分析经济形式，既不能用显微镜，也不能用化学试剂。两者都必须用抽象力来代替。”（马克思，1975，p. 8）在经济管理领域，各种理论的成功之处都源于它们各自做出的抽象和假设，而这些抽象和假设不可避免地会产生一定的局限性。在管理学的“理论丛林”中，存在着管理过程学派、决策理论学派和行为科学学派等诸多研究范式和学派。这些学派从不同的定义和假设出发，对管理问题做出不同解释，各具优势与局限（Koontz，1980）。在每一个学派中，又有不同的分支。例如，在行为科学学派中，麦格雷戈[1]提出的 X 理论和 Y 理论对人性做出了截然不同的假设；前者是传统管理模式（“胡萝卜加大棒”）的基础，后者为参与式、团队式等新型管理模式提供了依据。我们很难说这两种理论孰优孰劣，因为它们各有自己的适用范围。

经济管理理论的基本假设涉及两个方面。一是对人的假设：

- 在决策时，人的理性程度如何？是完全凭感情用事，完全理性的，还是有限理性的[2]？
- 在与他人相处时，人的行为方式如何？是自利的，利他的，互惠的，还是采取机会主义的行为方式[3]？
- 在风险面前，人的态度如何？是风险规避的，风险偏好的，还是风险中性的？

二是对市场条件的假设：

---

[1] 麦格雷戈（Douglas M. McGregor，1906—1964）是美国著名的行为科学家，人性假设理论创始人，管理理论的奠基人之一。

[2] 在西方的许多民族语言中，“理性”和“合理性”均源于拉丁语词根 ratio，它的意思是计算。人的理性取决于接收、存贮和处理信息的能力，因此可以用决策者的认知能力与问题的复杂程度的比值来衡量。当这个比值等于 1 时，属于**完全理性**（perfect rationality）的情况；当该比值小于 1 时，属于**有限理性**（bounded rationality）的情况。所谓**程序理性**（procedural rationality），是指决策者的认知能力远远低于问题的复杂程度，该比值接近于 0 时的情况；在这种情况下，当事人只能按照**经验法则**（rule of thumb）行事（亨德里克斯，2007，p. 17）。

[3] 自利行为假设从性善论的立场出发：人人追求自我利益的最大化，其动机是强烈的，并且是光明正大的，没有损人之心，因而不说谎，不欺骗，并信守诺言。机会主义行为假设则坚持性恶论的立场：经济社会中的人不但自利，而且只要能够利己，就不惜损人。机会主义的当事人会借助于不正当的手段谋取利益，其动机强烈而复杂：当事人会随机应变，投机取巧，会有目的、有策略地利用信息，按个人目标对信息加以筛选和扭曲，如说谎、欺骗等，并且会违背对未来的承诺（贺卫，王浣尘，2000）。

- 市场中的竞争状况如何？是充分竞争，还是不充分竞争？
- 市场中的信息条件如何？是完全信息，还是不完全信息？
- 交易双方对信息的了解有无差异？信息是对称的，还是不对称的？

在经济管理理论中，假设（assumption）不同于假说（hypothesis）。前者相当于欧氏几何中的公理（axiom），是无须证明的；后者则有待于证实或证伪。假设是整个理论体系的基础，也是逻辑推理的前提。一个理论体系的性质和适用范围由它的基本假设所决定。放松一个基本假设，相当于打开一扇通向新的理论体系的大门，同时意味着对原有体系的扬弃。历史上许多重大的理论创新都是从放松原有理论体系中的基本假设开始的。例如，对欧氏几何第五公理的质疑和否定，导致数学界公认的“19世纪最富有启发性和最值得注意的成就”——非欧几何的诞生与发展。在经济管理领域，西蒙[1]继承并发展了巴纳德[2]的思想，用“有限理性”假设取代古典经济学的“完全理性”假设，用“满意”标准取代“最优”标准，进而创建了有限理性决策理论（西蒙，2007）。实践证明，“有限理性”假设的提出，在经济管理理论发展史上具有划时代的意义。

在建设项目研究领域，目前有基于系统科学的范式、基于新制度经济学的范式和基于生产理论的范式等不同流派。如表0.1所示，这些研究范式建立在不同的假设条件之上，具有不同的目的和内容，所采用的技术路线和分析工具也各不相同。其中占据主导地位的是以美国项目管理协会（PMI）的项目管理知识体系（PMBoK）为代表的基于系统科学的范式（PMI，2013）。作为我国建设项目研究的集大成者，《建设工程项目管理规范》（GB/T 50326—2006，GB/T 50326—2014）与国际标准ISO10006一脉相承；它们同属于基于系统科学的范式。

建设项目领域的三种研究范式 **表0.1**

	基于系统科学的范式	基于新制度经济学的范式	基于生产理论的范式
对项目的定义	临时性的努力或过程	临时性的多边组织	临时性的生产系统
主要目标	工期、成本、质量 客户满意	减少不确定性 降低交易成本	实现转化、消除浪费、 增加价值
主要职能	计划、执行与控制	代理人的选择与激励	生产系统的设计、运行与改进
核心问题	工作分解结构	不确定性	无效流
基本分析单元	项目活动	交易	业务流程
主要分析工具	系统科学 运筹学	交易成本理论、委托代理 理论、不完全合同理论	转化理论、流理论、 价值理论

（资料来源：沙凯逊等，2009）

---

[1] 赫伯特·A. 西蒙（Herbert Alexander Simon，1916—2001）是美国经济组织决策管理大师。由于在决策理论研究方面的突出贡献，他在1978年获得诺贝尔经济学奖。

[2] 切斯特·巴纳德（Chester I. Barnard，1886—1961）是美国管理学家，系统组织理论的创始人。他被誉为现代管理理论的奠基人。

基于系统科学的研究范式实际上隐含了以下假设：项目范围和方法的不确定性足够小，项目活动之间的关系简单并且前后衔接，项目活动之间的边界是刚性的，根据标准进行的控制可以保证活动的结果（Koskela and Howell，2002）。此外，基于系统科学的范式和基于生产理论的范式还有一个不可忽视的假设：治理结构是外生给定的，这使它们在很大程度上失去了在项目治理范畴的话语权。

基于新制度经济学的范式把建设项目看作是以合同作为章程的**临时性多边组织**（temporary multi-organization）（Winch，1989），把交易作为基本分析单元，以交易成本理论、委托代理理论和不完全合同理论为主要分析工具。该范式认为，项目实质上是一种组织创新，是交易各方之间的一种相互依存的资产与能力的合作关系；不确定性（信息短缺）是项目组织的核心问题；降低交易成本是项目组织的主要目标。临时性多边组织这一命题的提出，不仅为新制度经济学和其他前沿理论的应用开启了门户，也为建设项目治理研究提供了合适的视角。

本书延续了《治理》一书的传统，坚持项目本位的立场，采用新制度经济学的视角，将项目治理和建筑交易体制内生化。所谓项目本位的立场，就是从由客户（Client）、设计方（Conception）、施工方（Construction）和控制方（Control）组成的4C结构的整体出发（Winch，2002，p. 19；沙凯逊，2010），而不是从建筑企业的立场出发——注意，建筑企业只是4C结构中的一个节点。所谓新制度经济学的视角，就是把项目看作是介乎于市场和企业之间的混合型（hybrid）组织，把建设项目看作是从事一次性定制任务的临时性的多边组织；把治理看作是制度层次结构中的关键环节，把项目治理看作是为一种努力，它使法律上独立的、具有不同战略目标和长远利益的项目参与各方能够为共同的利益而一起工作，取得共赢的结果；把建筑交易体制看作是建筑市场中各种参与人之间长期的、未经协调的、带有偶然性的行动后果。

本书的结构体系和主要内容如图0.2所示。前面五讲主要介绍基本概念和方法，并在此基础上建立起建设项目的整体分析框架。后面五讲以基于博弈论的制度分析为主线，按照“垂直治理—水平治理—针对项目经理的治理—关系治理与行业自律—建筑交易体制动态演进”的逻辑展开。第1讲简要介绍市场理论、企业理论的发展脉络与基本观点。第2讲从新制度经济学的角度讨论项目的性质，旨在确立适合于治理研究的“项目观”。第3讲简要介绍制度的基本概念和分析层次、制度分析的基本特征，以及博弈论的基本概念和方法。第4讲讨论治理的内涵，旨在使治理摆脱管理

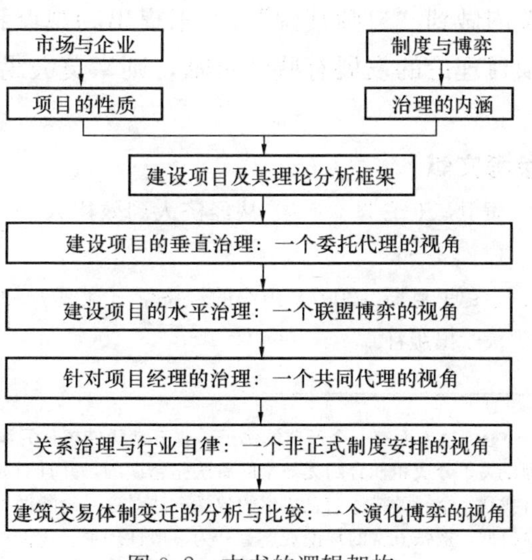

图0.2　本书的逻辑架构

的“阴影”，取得相对独立的地位。在以上工作的基础上，第5讲建立起关于建设项目的理论框架体系。第6讲以委托代理理论的解释逻辑为主，研究建设项目的垂直治理问题。第7讲从联盟博弈的视角研究建设项目的水平治理问题。第8讲以共同代理的解释逻辑为主，研究针对项目经理的治理问题，并涉及规范建设单位行为的问题。第9讲以关系治理的解释逻辑为主，研究建设项目治理中的非正式制度安排，涉及关系治理、建筑专业体制和行业自律。第10讲从演化博弈的视角研究建筑交易体制的变迁问题。

本书和《治理》一书可以互为参考。从方法论的角度来看，《治理》一书的特点是基于博弈模型的形式化分析。经济模型的优势主要在于其精炼、准确的品格以及对经济学洞察力的泛化能力，也就是从特殊上升为一般的能力❶。然而，学习和掌握经济模型需要足够的数学基础。因此，《治理》一书注定是面向“小众”的。本书尽量使用非技术性的语言，以便让更多感兴趣的人，无论是否具备相应的数学知识，都能读得下去。对博弈模型感兴趣的读者，可以参照《治理》一书中的相关内容，或许能够取得较好的效果。

本书在写作上力求做到简单明了、通俗易懂，但是在参考文献引用的规范性方面没有降低标准，依然保持着对他人劳动的尊重和对知识产权的敬畏之心。本书对参考文献的引用和标注均按照哈佛体系（Harvard System）——即“作者—日期体系”（author—date system）——的规定进行：在引用参考文献时，将出版物的年份列在作者姓名之后；在正文中被引用的参考文献，均根据汉语在前、英语在后的原则，按照作者的汉语拼音或英文字母的先后次序在各章的最后列出。

建设项目理论的发展有赖于多种学术流派的交叉与融合。不同的学术流派和研究范式之间应该是相辅相成的互补关系，而不是非此即彼的替代关系。本书以新制度经济学的理论和方法为主要分析工具，在一定假设的基础上构建分析框架，力求在此框架内做到“自圆其说”。本书提出的观点和论断只是一得之见和一家之言，若能对建设项目理论的发展有些许贡献，则幸莫大焉。

参考文献

1. 贺卫，王浣尘（2000）从经济人到效用人——经济学中人性假设的飞跃，山西财经大学学报，**22**（3），1—6.
2. 亨德里克斯（2007）组织的经济学与管理学，中译本，胡雅梅，张学渊，曹利群译，北京：中国人民大学出版社.

❶ 这方面有一个经典的例子。张五常凭借超凡的洞察力，在1969年出版的《佃农理论》一书中首先指出，传统理论关于分成租佃合约无效率的看法是错误的，并且对分成地租中的信息成本问题提出了开创性的论断。但是，他没有找到一个好的描述信息成本的数学方法对这一论断做出进一步的提升。1974年，斯蒂格利茨通过建立严格的道德风险模型，把张五常的理论观点上升为一般性理论。凭借对信息经济学的贡献，斯蒂格利茨获得2001年诺贝尔经济学奖（张五常，2000）。

3. 国家统计局（1986）中国统计年鉴，北京：中国统计出版社.

4. 国家统计局（2015）中国数据，http：//data. stats. gov. cn/easyquery. htm? cn=C01.

5. 李维安（2013）推进全面深化改革的关键：树立现代治理理念，光明日报，2013 年 11 月 29 日 11 版.

6. 马克思（1975）资本论（第一卷上），中译本，中共中央马克思恩格斯列宁斯大林著作编译局译，北京：人民出版社.

7. 普雷斯曼（2000）思想者的足迹：五十位重要的西方经济学家，中译本，陈海燕，李倩，陈亮译，南京：江苏人民出版社.

8. 沙凯逊（2010）建设项目理论重构初探：一个新制度经济学的视角，项目管理技术，**8**（3），13—16.

9. 沙凯逊（2013）建设项目治理，北京：中国建筑工业出版社.

10. 沙凯逊，宋涛，亓霞，华冬冬（2009）建设项目理论研究范式探析，项目管理技术，**7**（5），13—18.

11. 文件起草组（2013）中共中央关于全面深化改革若干重大问题的决定，北京：人民出版社.

12. 西蒙（2007）管理行为（原书第 4 版），中译本，詹正茂译，北京：机械工业出版社.

13. 俞可平（2002）全球治理引论，马克思主义与现实，（1），20—32.

14. 张五常（2000）经济解释，北京：商务印书馆.

15. 周新军（2007）企业管理与公司治理：边界确定及实践意义，中南财经政法大学学报，（5），107—112.

16. Hofstede，G.（1980）*Culture's Consequences：International Differences in Work-related Values*，Sage Publications，Beverly Hills，CA.

17. Koontz，H.（1980）The Management Theory of Jungle Revisited，*Academy of Management Review*，**5**（2），175—187.

18. Koskela，L. and Howell，G.（2002）The underlying theory of project management is obsolete，Slevin，D.，Cleland，D. and Pinto，J.，*Proceedings of PMI Research Conference*，Seattle：Project Management Institute，293—302.

19. PMI（2013）*A Guide to the Project Management Body of Knowledge*（5th edition），Project Management Institute，Inc.，Newtown Square，PA，USA.

20. Taylor，F. W.（1911）*The Principles of Scientific Management*，Harper & Brothers，New York，NY.

21. Williamson，O. E.（2000）The new institutional economics：taking stock，looking ahead，*American Economic Review*，**38**（3），595—613.

22. Winch，G. M.（1989）The construction firm and the construction project：a transaction coat approach，*Construction Management and Economics*，**7**（3），331—345.

23. Winch，G. M.（2002）*Managing Construction Projects：An Information Processing Approach*，Blackwell Science，Oxford.

第 1 讲　市 场 与 企 业

- □ 市场的本质在于通过价格机制实现的自发性适应，企业的本质则是通过命令实现的协作性适应。项目同时具备市场和企业的性质，是一种混合型的组织或制度安排。
- □ 新古典经济学的一般均衡理论揭示了一个深刻的道理：充分竞争和价格机制有利于资源的有效配置。但是，该理论赖以存在的基本假设也为市场失灵以及后瓦尔拉范式的兴起埋下了伏笔。
- □ 新古典企业理论把企业看作是生产函数，由此产生企业“黑箱”问题。新制度经济学把交易成本的概念引入经济分析之中，为打开企业“黑箱”提供了理论基础。
- □ 现代企业理论从个人交易行为的角度理解企业。把企业看作是个人之间产权交易的一种合作组织，是一系列契约关系的结合体。

研究项目治理，首先要搞清楚项目的性质。根据新制度经济学的观点，项目属于介乎于市场和企业之间的混合型（hybrid）组织。因此，研究项目的性质，离不开市场和企业，也离不开市场理论和企业理论的支持。基于以上考虑，本书在研究项目的性质之前，首先介绍有关市场与企业的问题；并且把“市场与企业”和“项目的性质”分别作为第 1 讲和第 2 讲的标题。实际上，这两讲可以看作是一个单元。第 1 讲简要介绍市场理论、企业理论的发展脉络与基本观点，以及我国市场经济体系和国有企业改革的发展历程。第 2 讲则在第 1 讲的基础上，着重讨论项目的性质以及与项目理论有关的问题。

1.1　市场与市场经济理论

市场是社会分工和交换的产物，因而属于历史的范畴（马克思，1975，p. 718）。市场大体上可分为“硬件”和“软件”两个范畴。一个被广泛接受的定义是：市场是商品和劳务交换的场所，这实际上是市场空间的概念，属于“硬件”的范畴。下面的一些定义或概念则可以划归为“软件”的范畴：马克思把市场抽象为商品所有者的全部相互关系的总和。这一抽象不仅反映了市场所反映的物与物的关系，而且揭示了在物的掩盖之下的人与人的关系。新古典经济学综合派的代表人物萨缪尔森[1]认为，市场是一种通过把买者和卖者汇集在一起交换物品的机制。交易成本理论的创始人科斯[2]认为，市场和企业一样，都是经济组织的表现形式。而在社会学家韦伯[3]看来，市场是理性合作的共存和结果，市场因人们的社会行为而存在（吴萌，高玉林，2001）。

市场的复杂性只有被纳入经济生活及社会生活的整体中去才能被理解，而经济生活与社会生活是逐年变化的；这种复杂性本身不断在进化和演变，因而随时会改变其意义或影响（布罗代尔，1993，p. 226）。

主流经济学的市场理论经历了以下几个发展阶段：古典市场经济理论（亚当·斯密的“看不见的手”）、新古典综合派（“完美”的价格机制）、宏观调控理论（凯恩斯革命）、新自由主义（绝对市场化）和新制度经济学（交易成本理论）。在现代经济学的语汇中，完全竞争范式、一般均衡范式、新古典范式和瓦尔拉范式是同义语；而交易成本理论属于后瓦尔拉范式。

1.1.1 亚当·斯密与“看不见的手”

说起市场与市场经济理论，人们自然会想起亚当·斯密[4]，以及他所提出的“看不见的手”（the invisible hand）的著名论断：

> 由于每个个人都努力把他的资本尽可能用来支持国内产业，都努力管理国内产业，使其生产物的价值能达到最高程度，他就必须竭力使社会的年收入尽量增大起来。确实，他通常既不打算促进公共的利益，也不知道他自己是在什么程度上促进那种利益。……他所盘算的也只是他自己的利益。在这场合，像在其他许多场合一样，他受着一只看不见的手的指导，去尽力达到一个并非他本意想要达到的目的。也并不因为事非出于本意，就对社会有害。他追求自己的利益，往往使他能比在真正出于本意的情况下更有效地促进社会的利益。（斯密，1997b，p. 27）

斯密认为，经济活动的基础是分工；个人利益是人们从事经济活动的根本动力：

> 我们所需要的食物和饮料，不是出自屠户、酿酒家或面包师的恩惠，而是出于他们自利的打算。（斯密，1997a，p. 14）

---

[1] 保罗·萨缪尔森（Paul A. Samuelson，1915—2009）是第一位获得诺贝尔经济学奖（1970）的美国经济学家。他的经典著作《经济学》被翻译成四十多种语言，是全世界最畅销的经济学教科书。

[2] 罗纳德·哈里·科斯（Ronald Harry Coase，1910—2013）是美籍英裔经济学家，新制度经济学的主要创始人。他在1991年因“揭示了‘交易价值’在经济组织结构的产权和功能中的重要性”而获得诺贝尔经济学奖。

[3] 马克斯·韦伯（Max Weber，1846—1920）是德国政治经济学家和社会学家；他被公认为现代社会学和公共行政学最重要的创始人之一。

[4] 亚当·斯密（Adam Smith，1723—1790）是英国古典政治经济学的主要创立者。普雷斯曼（2000）认为，亚当·斯密、马克思和凯恩斯是历史上最重要的三位经济学家。

长期以来，亚当·斯密被符号化为“自由放任主义经济思想之父”。实际上，这在很大程度上是一种误读。斯密的自由竞争学说，原本是针对18世纪欧洲的重商主义和殖民主义所带来的特权及其负面影响而提出的，但自20世纪以后，却逐渐被“简化”为鼓吹“自私自利”和“看不见的手”等教条。近十多年学术界有关斯密思想的研究，对“倡导自私自利”和“放任自流”的斯密形象，提出了有力的质疑，重新发掘出一个被遗忘了的、强调公正和关注工人福祉的亚当·斯密（许宝强，2007）。1976年是亚当·斯密思想开始全面复兴的关键一年。为了纪念《国富论》发表二百周年，包括几乎全部诺贝尔经济学奖得主在内的数百名经济学家在英国格拉斯哥大学聚会。在此前后的几年时间里，牛津大学和格拉斯哥大学出版了最为齐全的斯密文集。学术界凭借对相关文献的深入解读，惊奇地发现，斯密并不是人们想象的那样，是一味鼓吹“看不见的手”的经济学家。斯密在晚年耗时四年对《道德情操论》的第六版修订，也能充分体现出他本人从早年的自由放任主义到具有某种建构倾向的德性主义的转变（罗卫东，2010）。

1.1.2 福利经济学基本定理与瓦尔拉范式

自亚当·斯密以来，经济学家们的所有努力都在试图构建通过价格机制协调经济体制运行的那只看不见的手的理论体系（科斯，2003）。其中最具代表性的是瓦尔拉[1]和阿罗[2]、德布鲁[3]。前者因创建一般均衡分析的理论体系而著称；后者证明了一般均衡的存在性。正因为如此，一般均衡也常称为瓦尔拉均衡；阿罗—德布鲁体系也成了一般均衡理论的代名词。

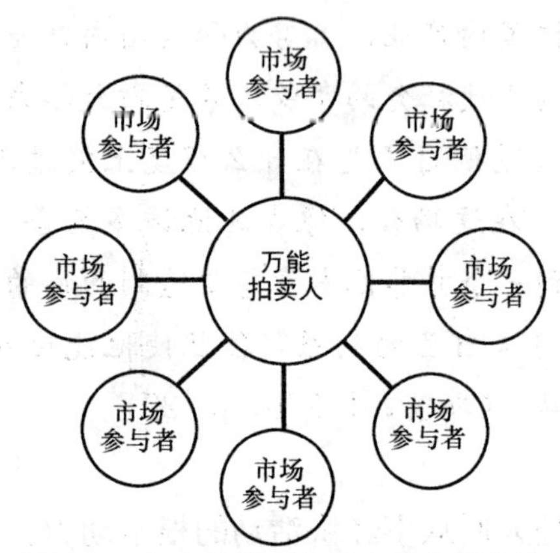

图1.1 瓦尔拉拍卖人的信息沟通结构
（资料来源：亨德里克斯，2007，p. 52）

所谓**一般均衡**（general equilibrium），是指市场上所有商品的供给和需求相等，也就是**市场出清**（market clearing）的状态。瓦尔拉的模型将经济体抽象为一系列相互关联的数学方程。瓦尔拉坚信，只要方程组中方程的个数等于未知数的个数，就可以证明一般均衡的存在。瓦尔拉提出的虚拟拍卖人——**瓦尔拉拍卖人**（Walrasian auctioneer）——相当于亚当·斯密的“看不见的手”。如图1.1所示，这

---

[1] 里昂·瓦尔拉（Léon Walras，1834—1910）是法国经济学家。普雷斯曼（2000）认为，瓦尔拉是经济学史上六位左右最重要的人物之一。这里的瓦尔拉是根据《英汉专名词典》中的Walras词条译出的。Walras是法国人，法语单词最后一个字母s是不发音的，故不宜翻译为瓦尔拉斯。

[2] 肯尼斯·约瑟夫·阿罗（Kenneth Joseph Arrow，1921—）是美国经济学家。他在1972年因“深入研究了经济均衡理论和福利理论”而获得诺贝尔经济学奖。

[3] 杰拉德·德布鲁（Gerard Debreu，1927—2004）是美籍法裔经济学家。他在1983年由于“概括了帕累托最优理论，创立了相关商品的经济与社会均衡的存在定理”而获得诺贝尔经济学奖。

个全知全能的拍卖人处于信息中心的位置，他从所有人那里收集信息，然后根据这些信息计算市场出清的价格，最后将这些价格信息报告给有关各方（亨德里克斯，2007，p. 52）。然而，冯·诺依曼[1]发现，瓦尔拉的解法并不能排除负价格的出现，而负价格在现实中不存在，因而是没有意义的（普雷斯曼，2000，p. 110）。1954年，阿罗和德布鲁在十分严格的假设条件下，分别独立证明了福利经济学第一基本定理：完全竞争市场经济的一般均衡都是帕累托最优的。

福利经济学第一基本定理揭示了一个深刻的道理：充分竞争和价格机制有利于资源的有效配置。下面的例子生动地阐明了这个道理：

> 譬如你想添置一盏台灯，它需要与房间内的插座相连，还要与地毯的颜色相匹配。但是，台灯制造商既不生产插座和制造台灯的电子零件，也不拥有发电厂、超市和零售店。许多事情都有可能出错，但是却没有。因为许许多多的厂商为了自身的利益生产了相互兼容的商品，并提供优质的服务：商店里面保证有你中意的台灯，并且便于你驱车前往购买；开发商建造房屋时，安装的插座与台灯的插头是匹配的；电力供应商提供的电压符合灯泡的要求；即使你日后搬家，新家里的插座也与你旧家电相匹配，电压也和老房子一样；灯泡坏了，你也没有必要跑很远的路去买新的灯泡……。一切都是如此方便；而所有这些便利都是在市场这只“看不见的手”的指挥下，无数人努力的结果（亨德里克斯，2007，p. 47）。

需要指出的是，阿罗—德布鲁体系不仅抽象掉了市场运行的制度环境和法律结构，而且把“经济人”的道德价值排除在经济分析的范围之外：“市场结果是公平的，但是当然，只有当它们来自公平的初始分配时才是如此……因此，在完美竞争的条件下，道德在市场没有用武之地。”（Gauthier，1986，p. 93）

1.1.3　市场失灵与后瓦尔拉范式

一般均衡理论构造了一个不存在交易成本的理想社会：价格机制可以保证个人利益和社会利益的和谐；存在一组可以使市场出清的均衡价格；每个生产者和消费者只要遵循这些均衡价格就可以保证其自身和社会的福利同时达到最大化。在市场经济的“古典阶段”，“乌托邦资本主义”（Bowles，2004，p. 208）的情况似乎确实如此：经济的运行基本上是靠市场和价格发挥作用；政府只是充当“守夜人”的角色。这种一元调节机制曾经使工业革命时期的社会生产力得到飞速发展。正如马克思和恩格斯（1964）在《共产党宣言》中所说：“资产阶级在它的不到一百年的阶级统治中所创造的生产力，比过去一切世代创造的全部生产力还要多，还要大”。然而，历史证明市场

---

[1] 约翰·冯·诺依曼（John von Neumann，1903—1957）是美籍匈牙利裔数学家和信息科学家。他在现代计算机、博弈论和核武器等诸多领域均有杰出建树，被誉为计算机之父和博弈论之父。

不是万能的。随着市场经济的发展，由于外部性、不确定性、市场垄断和公共产品等原因，**市场失灵**（market failure）的问题逐渐暴露出来。资源浪费、两极分化、劳资矛盾尖锐、社会动荡不安等缺陷“破坏了看不见的手的理论所假定的完全竞争的田园诗般的画面”（萨缪尔逊，诺德豪斯，1996）。由于信息总是不充分的，市场总是不完全的，因此市场总是不具备受约束的帕累托效率的。正如斯蒂格利茨[1]所说，亚当·斯密的看不见的手之所以是“看不见”的，是因为它就像皇帝的新衣一样，原本就不存在（崔之元，1999）。

在很大程度上，上面所说的种种问题和缺陷与其说是市场失灵，不如说是经济人假设和市场完全性假设失效的结果。如前所述，福利经济学基本定理是在十分严格的假设条件下得以证明的。这些假设条件包括：

- 人是自利的和完全理性的，
- 交易者的数量趋于无穷并且是非合谋的，
- 进入成本和退出成本可以忽略不计，
- 市场出清价格由处于信息中心的瓦尔拉拍卖人决定，
- 市场各方之间没有直接的信息沟通和明示协议，他们都是价**格接受者**（price taker）。

如果这些假设条件不能完全满足，福利经济学基本定理自然不能成立，整个瓦尔拉范式也就失去了基础。正因为如此，美籍日裔学者福山指出：新古典主义经济学有百分之八十是正确的，而剩下的百分之二十只能给出拙劣的解释（赵汀阳，2003）。新古典主义经济学的局限性给后人的研究留下了可观的余地和空间。以科斯和威廉姆森为代表的新制度经济学家创立和发展了交易成本理论、委托代理理论和不完全契约理论，使得产权和交易成本经济学很快就明确无误地成了一种范式（张五常，2000，p. 11），并且终将可以与边际主义在新古典经济学中所占据的位置相媲美（张五常，2000，p. 425）。

瓦尔拉范式与后瓦尔拉范式的比较 　　**表 1.1**

研究范式	均衡分析类型	交往性质		理性假设	行为假设
瓦尔拉范式	局部均衡分析	完全竞争市场中的匿名交往		完全理性	自利行为
	一般均衡分析				
后瓦尔拉范式	策略均衡分析	策略性交往	个体对他人的最优反应	有限理性	机会主义行为
	演化均衡分析		种群体对自身的最优反应	程序理性	

资料来源：沙凯逊（2010）

科斯在他的分析框架中一方面排除了“瓦尔拉拍卖人”，从而开启了经济学史上后

[1] 约瑟夫·斯蒂格利茨（Joseph E. Stiglitz，1943—）是美国经济学家，2001年诺贝尔经济学奖得主。他在1997至2000年间，曾担任世界银行高级副行长兼首席经济学家的职务。

瓦尔拉范式的大门；另一方面引入了外部性、私人交易和谈判机制，从而为纳什均衡分析开拓了空间。如表 1.1 所示，瓦尔拉范式和后瓦尔拉范式之间，以及不同类型的均衡分析之间的差别都源于它们的基本假设。瓦尔拉均衡，也就是一般均衡，是非策略性交往的均衡：在完全自由竞争的市场中，无数完全理性的市场参与者通过瓦尔拉拍卖人进行匿名交易，最终的均衡结果是帕累托最优的。纳什均衡则是策略性交往的均衡：数量有限的有限理性交易者之间的交易不是匿名的，而是根据他人的策略做出自己的最优反应，最终的均衡结果不一定是帕累托最优的。在演化博弈中，我们假设种群体由程序理性的个体组成。演化稳定策略也可以看作是一种纳什均衡，不过是种群体对自身的最优反应（沙凯逊，2010）。

1.1.4　我国市场经济体制的发展进程

市场经济既不是自给自足的自然经济，也不是指令性的计划经济。市场经济的特点主要表现在以下几个方面：自主决策、合同、竞争、平等和开放。市场机制主要包括供求机制、价格机制、竞争机制和风险机制；通过价格的波动、市场主体对利益的追求、市场供求的变化来调节经济运行。不同的专业市场具有其特有的市场机制，例如金融市场上的利率机制，外汇市场上的汇率机制和劳动力市场上的工资机制等。法治和诚信是市场经济的基础。

市场制度的核心是它的自由价格制度。所谓“市场在资源配置中的基础性作用”，就是指由自由竞争形成的，能够反映供求状况的价格决定资源的流向（吴敬琏，马国川，2013，p. 6）。我国经济体制改革的实践充分证明，价格具有高效的信息传导功能，市场配置资源是最有效率的经济形式。作为改革开放的亲历者，作者本人对市场机制的非凡力量有着切身的感受。

背景资料：计划经济与市场经济体制的鲜明对比

1983 年春节过后的大年初六，作者从县城到省城济南办事，当时济南和县城之间的交通十分不便，一天只有两趟长途客车。由于无法当日返回，只好找了一家招待所住下。因错过了招待所晚饭的开饭时间，便试图到附近找点吃的东西。不料整条街上的饭店和商店都因春节期间缩短营业时间而提前关门。作者不得已在昏暗的路灯下沿街搜索，冒着严寒走了将近十里路，最后才在火车站的小卖部买到一包饼干，得以充饥。这件事让作者着实领教了效率低下与商品短缺之苦。

三十多年过去，情况发生了根本性的变化。今年春节过后，作者打算外出旅游，足不出户就在网上订好了车票和旅馆。入住旅馆后，随即与当地的旅行社取得联系，把行程安排妥当。在饮食方面更是令人满意，当地的特色小吃物美价廉，令人目不暇接。回想起三十一年前在济南沿街觅食的经历，真是恍如隔世。仔细一想，以上所说的种种便利，不是出自铁路部门、旅店老板或饭店老板的恩惠，实在是拜改革开放之赐——如果市场这只“看不见的手”没有从计划体制的桎梏中解放出来，恐怕现在我们还处于短缺经济的梦魇之中。

如图 1.2 所示，我国的社会主义市场经济是在改革开放实践中逐步形成和发展起来的。如何处理政府（计划）与市场的关系，是贯穿三十多年经济体制改革进程的核心问题。从最初讳言“市场”一词，到最终提出“使市场在资源配置中起决定性作用”，决策部门、学界和媒体经历了多年的思考、争论和激辩，经济政策也几经探索和反复[❶]。1992 年，中共十四大确立了我国经济体制改革的目标是建立社会主义市场经济体制，提出要使市场在国家宏观调控下对资源配置发挥基础性作用。这是一个重大的理论突破。此后的二十多年间，对政府和市场关系，人们一直在寻找新的科学定位。2013 年，中共十八届三中全会明确指出，经济体制改革是全面深化改革的重点，核心问题是处理好政府和市场的关系，使市场在资源配置中起决定性作用和更好发挥政府作用（文件起草组，2013）。这次会议拉开了我国新一轮改革的大幕。

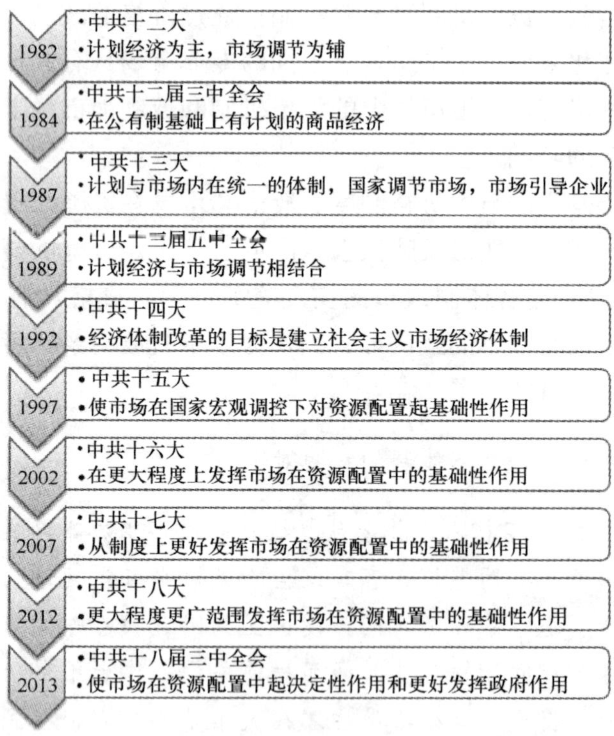

图 1.2　我国的经济体制改革：从计划到市场

我国从 20 世纪 70 年代末开始走上了市场取向的改革之路，经过三十多年的曲折

❶ 《重启改革议程——中国经济改革二十讲》（吴敬琏，马国川，2013）一书以详实的第一手资料生动讲述了从“摸着石头过河”到提出到确立“市场在资源配置中的基础性作用”的艰难曲折的探索过程。本书的作者吴敬琏是卷入论战最多的经济学家之一，他对市场经济的坚定捍卫为他赢得了“吴市场”的称号。

发展，取得了空前巨大的成就。但是，改革并没有获得完全成功，还有许多“大关”没有过（吴敬琏，马国川，2013，p. 241）。随着改革进入“深水区”，许多深层次的问题和矛盾都显露出来，环境污染严重、贫富差距拉大、腐败现象愈演愈烈。这些问题和矛盾，恰恰证明改革没有完全到位。当前我国市场经济运作中的最大问题是，政府在引入市场的同时，它本身不但没有退出，反而是愈加强势地参与其中，成为最强大的、最主要的和无处不在的市场主体。政府不仅指挥市场、驾驭市场，还直接参与市场的竞争和运作。在后面的分析中可以看出，建筑市场中的种种乱象，在很大程度上都可以归咎于地方政府，特别是政府客户的不当行为。尽管存在这样那样的问题，对市场化改革的方向应该有清醒的认识和坚定的信心。

还应该指出，市场在资源配置中起决定性作用，并不是起全部作用。“使市场在资源配置中起决定性作用”和“更好发挥政府作用”，两者之间是辩证统一的关系。确定好市场发挥作用的边界，同时也就确定了政府发挥作用的边界。明确政府更好发挥作用的边界，使政府既不“缺位”，也不“越位”，有所为有所不为，有进有退，才能使市场在资源配置中更好发挥决定性的作用。建立“有效市场”和“有为政府”，并处理好这两者之间的关系，是我国经济健康发展和成功转型的制度前提。前者应该准确反映各种要素的相对稀缺性；后者应使制度环境和基础设施能够随着资本的积累、比较优势的变化和产业的升级进行相应完善（林毅夫，2016）。

1.1.5　建筑市场的内涵

建筑业有广义和狭义之分。按照传统的统计分类，建筑业主要针对建筑产品的生产（即施工）活动而言，因而是狭义的建筑业；广义的建筑业则涵盖了建筑产品的生产以及与建筑生产有关的所有的服务内容，包括规划、勘察、设计、建筑材料与成品及半成品的生产、施工及安装，建成环境的运营、维护及管理，以及相关的咨询和中介服务等等，这反映了建筑业真实的经济活动空间（Seaden and Manseau，2001）。准确把握建筑市场的含义，需要从广义建筑业的概念出发。

作为国民经济统计体系的内容之一，狭义建筑业概念的存在是必要的，也是合理的。但是，建筑业活动范围和发展空间不受狭义建筑业概念的限制。国民经济核算体系和行业分类中的“建筑业”是按照产品的同质性原则进行界定的，这样做的目的在于进行统计分析，而不是为了行业管理。统计分析与行业管理是性质不同的两回事，不能混为一谈。工业发达国家在国民经济核算和统计时均采用了狭义建筑业的概念，而在行业管理中均采用了广义建筑业的概念。历史的经验证明，在考虑行业定位和行业发展时采用狭义建筑业的概念，会给建筑业的发展带来致命的束缚。构筑我国建筑业持续、健康发展的平台，必须从广义建筑业的概念出发，跨越第二产业和第三产业的界限，综合考虑建筑产品、建筑市场和建筑交易制度等多方面的因素（沙凯逊，2003）。

从广义建筑业的立场出发，建筑市场应该看作是参与建筑工程活动的各方主体之间的交易场所和交易制度。交易场所包括有形建筑市场和无形建筑市场；交易制度包括相关的法律、法规、规章以及行业规范和惯例；其中的“各方主体”，是指建设项目的建设单位和参与工程建设活动的企业或单位以及相关从业人员，涉及勘察、设计、施工、建筑材料与成品及半成品的生产与供应、项目的运营、维护与管理、相关咨询和中介服务等活动。

1.2 企业与企业理论

适应性（adaptation），也就是组织对干扰或失调的恢复能力，是经济组织的核心问题。经济学大师哈耶克[1]（Hayek，1945）和现代管理理论之父巴纳德（Barnard，1938）都坚持这一观点；不过前者强调的是组织对市场变化的适应，后者强调的是组织内部的适应。如果说，市场的本质在于通过价格机制实现的自发性（autonomy）适应；那么，企业的本质则是通过命令（fiat）实现的协作性（cooperation）适应（Williamson，1991）。从组织形式的角度来看，企业可分为个人独资企业、合伙企业和公司企业（包括有限责任公司和股份有限公司）。

企业已经有几百年的历史了。这种经济组织形式在经济社会发展中扮演着重要角色。为了说明企业和市场之间的关系，西蒙曾经设想了一位来自火星的“神秘客人”从空中俯瞰地球社会结构的场景。在这位火星人的眼中，企业是绿色的区域，市场交易表现为红色的线条：

> 无论我们的客人来到美国、苏联、都市中国还是欧共体，其下方空间的大部分都是绿色的区域，因为几乎所有居民都是企业的雇员，因而位于企业的边界之内。组织是这幅图景的主要特征。在发回火星的信息中，地球上的景象可能会被描述为“由红色线条连接的大片绿色区域”，而不是“连接绿点的红色网络”（Simon，1991，p. 27）。

企业理论的研究对象是市场经济中的企业。在所有者与经营者合为一体的古典企业中，基本问题是企业存在的理由和企业边界等问题；而在所有者与经营者相分离的现代企业中，基本问题还包括公司治理的问题。企业理论的发展过程大体上可以划分为新古典企业理论和现代企业理论两个阶段。

---

[1] 弗里德里希·奥古斯特·冯·哈耶克（Friedrich August von Hayek，1899—1992）是英籍奥地利裔经济学家，新自由主义的代表人物。1974年，哈耶克和他在理论上的对手默达尔一同获得了诺贝尔经济学奖，以表彰他们“在货币政策和商业周期上的开创性研究，以及他们对于经济、社会和制度互动影响的敏锐分析”。

1.2.1　新古典企业理论与企业“黑箱”

在新古典经济学的厂商理论中，企业被视为在市场经济中完全有效运转的、为获取利润而从事商品生产活动的经济单位。它可以是个体生产者，也可以是规模庞大的公司。该理论赋予企业以“经济人”的含义，这意味着厂商在经济活动中具有完全理性，并掌握完全信息。企业对投入和产出水平的选择都是为了使利润最大化。这种理论在市场完全竞争的假设条件下，在一般意义上强调技术的作用，在特定意义上强调规模收益作为企业规模的重要决定因素，对于理解产业（或企业）的整体行动，以及企业间的互动结果等问题，都是十分有用的。

然而，新古典经济学具有明显的局限性，主要是因为它没有把企业看作是一种组织，而是当作一种以利润最大化为目标的生产函数（production function）。如图1.3所示，企业被当作一个“黑箱”，输入的是资本K和劳动力L，输出的是产出Y。企业内部所发生的事情，以及相关的协调和激励等问题，都被掩盖在“黑箱”之中。正如哈特（1998）所说，这种研究范式“完全忽略了企业内部的激励问题。企业被看作是一个完全有效的‘黑箱’，在它的内部，任何事情都十分顺利地运行着，每个人都在做着指派给他的工作。”然而，“对任何企业，哪怕只瞥上一眼，就能知道这是不现实的。”由于基本假设造成的先天不足，新古典企业理论无法解释企业的基本问题。正是在对新古典企业理论的质疑中，现代企业理论应运而生。企业理论研究一些貌似简单、实则深刻的问题——例如，既然亚当·斯密的看不见的手可以通过市场机制配置资源，为什么不能使用契约关系处理所有的经济活动，而要求企业存在？企业与市场的边界在哪里？企业内部的雇佣关系、所有权结构、融资结构，是怎样决定的？这些问题的解答与许多闪耀着思想光芒的名字联系在一起——科斯的交易成本理论被用来解释企业的存在；阿尔钦重视监督成本的概念；威廉姆森分析了资产专用性在企业中的作用；再向前则可以追溯到奈特，其著名的“不确定性”概念也被联系到企业理论中。

图1.3　作为生产函数的企业是一个“黑箱”

（资料来源：亨德里克斯，2007，p. 48）

1.2.2　科斯革命与现代企业理论

历史上的许多重大理论突破都是从提出“真问题”开始的。牛顿提出的“苹果落地”的问题就是一个很好的例子。在当时的普通人看来，提出这个问题的人是不是疯了——苹果不落向地面，难道会向天上飞去不成？然而，正是在这个貌似“弱智”的问题的启发下，牛顿发现了万有引力定律，并最终构建起经典力学体系。由此可见，这种具有划时代意义的“真问题”只有伟大的头脑才提得出来。

现在，人们研究企业的性质和企业理论，不得不从科斯谈起。因为正是他提出的“企业为什么存在”的问题打开了新古典经济理论中的企业“黑箱”：

> 既然人们通常认为协调要通过价格机制来实现，那么，为什么这样的组织是必需的呢？在企业之外，价格运动指挥生产，这是通过市场上一系列买卖交易来协调的。……在企业之内，这些市场交易被取消，指挥生产的企业家—协调者取代了复杂的市场结构和买卖交易。显然，存在着协调生产的其他方法。尽管有这样的假设，即假如生产由价格运动来调节，生产就能在没有任何组织的情况下进行，我们还是要问：组织为什么存在？（Coase，1937，p. 388）

在伦敦经济学院就读期间，二十岁出头的科斯通过了商学士考试并获得一笔旅行奖学金。依靠这笔奖学金，科斯在美国度过了1931—1932学年，并且把大部分时间用来访问工厂和企业的主管。回到英国后，科斯在1934年完成了《企业的性质》的初稿。三年后，这篇文章几乎未经修改就得以发表。在这篇文章中，科斯首次提出交易存在成本的问题：

> 建立企业有利可图的主要理由似乎是，利用价格机制是有成本的。通过价格机制“组织”生产的最明显的成本是发现相关价格的费用。（Coase，1937，p. 388）

在1960年发表的《社会成本问题》一文中，科斯首次明确使用了交易成本的概念，并且对交易成本的内容做出进一步的界定。

针对企业的性质和边界问题，科斯提出了极富洞见的思想。关于企业存在的理由，科斯认为，企业的显著特征就是对价格机制的替代。企业的存在是为了节约市场交易成本，即用成本较低的企业内部协调代替成本较高的市场交易。当市场的交易成本高于企业内部的协调成本时，企业便产生了。关于企业的边界，科斯认为，交易成本与管理成本的对比，确定了企业的边界——当企业内部的协调成本低于市场的交易成本时，企业的规模可以扩大；反之，则应该缩小。当企业内部的协调成本等于市场的交易成本时，企业就达到了最佳规模。

《企业的性质》的发表揭开了“科斯革命”的序幕。然而，这篇文章并没有取得立竿见影的效果。直到20世纪70年代，交易成本学说才成为现代经济学异军突起的一派，并引发了大量的学科交叉和学术创新，逐步发展成当代经济学的一个新的分支——新制度经济学。正如科斯所说的那样：

> 一般人们认为，新制经济学的诞生是以我那篇《企业的性质》论文的发表为准，这篇文章明确地把交易成本的概念引入经济分析之中。不聚小溪无以成江海，理论的积累发展尤为如此。在此，我不仅仅只想到了经济学家，如奥利弗·威廉姆森、哈罗德·德姆塞茨和张五常等人对新制度经济学的贡献，尽管他们的工作都很重要，但我要特别提及的是在其他学科领域，如法学、人类学、社会学、政治

学以及社会生物学等学科同仁们的工作对新制度经济学的重大贡献。（科斯，2003，p. 10）

在新制度经济学的形成和发展过程中，威廉姆森[1]发挥了至关重要的作用。他因此被誉为重新发现"科斯定理"[2]的人。实际上，"新制度经济学"这个词汇是由威廉姆森最早提出的。

20世纪70年代经济学发生的另一重大进展是微观经济学基础理论的革命性突破。以博弈理论为基础的信息经济学、激励理论、契约理论和委托代理理论等新的理论和方法为企业理论的发展注入了新的活力（钱颖一，1989）。由此，企业理论得到迅速发展，成为主流经济学中最富有成果的领域之一。

现代企业理论从个人交易行为的角度研究企业。它把企业看作是个人之间产权交易的一种合作组织，是一系列契约关系的结合体。企业行为则是所有企业成员博弈的结果。像任何新兴学科一样，现代企业理论至今还未形成一套公认的系统结构，但至少包括以下四个方面的研究范畴：（1）企业的性质和边界。涉及企业的定义、企业与市场的界限、企业所有权的含义等问题。（2）企业内部的科层制度。涉及企业内部的组织结构设计、企业对员工的激励等问题。（3）企业的资本结构。涉及企业股权与债券的比例、企业破产的经济含义与机制等问题（4）企业所有权与控制权的分离。涉及对经理的激励和约束、对所有者的权益保护、不同类型的所有者的利益协调等问题（钱颖一，1989）。其中第三和第四个问题属于公司治理的范畴。

从20世纪70年代开始，企业理论主要沿着两个方向发展。一是交易成本理论，二是委托代理理论。前者着眼于企业与市场的关系；后者则侧重于分析企业内部组织结构及企业成员之间的委托代理关系。这两种理论的共同点是强调企业的契约性，因此被称为"企业的契约理论"。

20世纪80年代后期，交易成本理论的一个重要突破是不完全合同理论。该理论认为，产权安排的重要性在于合同的不完全性（张维迎，2006）。该理论由格罗斯曼（Grossman）、哈特[3]（Hart）和莫尔（Moore）等人共同创立，因而又被称为GHM理论。GHM理论放松了传统的"合同完全性"假设，相当于在合同上打开了一个

---

[1] 奥利弗·威廉姆森（Oliver Williamson，1932—）是美国经济学家。他在2009年因"在公共经济管理理论，特别是企业边界理论的研究"而获得诺贝尔经济学奖。

[2] 据说，在经济学文献中频频出现的"科斯定理"一词是由1982年诺贝尔经济学奖得主，美国经济学家施蒂格勒（George Joseph Stigler，1911—1991）发明的，科斯自己并没有这样说。如果科斯必须拥有一个定理，那么，可以将它概括成以下三种说法。第一，产权的界定是市场交易的必要前提。第二，如果产权被明晰地界定，且所有的交易成本为零，那么资源的利用效率与谁拥有产权无关。（这是最流行的有关科斯定理的一种说法，而且它成了某些争论的主题。）第三，如果权利能被清晰地界定且交易成本为零，那么，帕累托条件（或经济效率）将能够实现（张五常，2000，p. 11）。

[3] 哈佛大学的奥利弗·哈特（Oliver Hart，1948—）和麻省理工学院的本特·霍姆斯特罗姆（Bengt Holmström，1949—）因"对契约理论的贡献"获得2016年诺贝尔经济学奖。后者是完全合同理论和委托代理理论的代表。

"缺口"。正是通过这个"缺口"，GHM 理论把产权制度引入合同理论，并使之成为"剩余控制权"安排的重要依据。现在，不完全合同理论已成为企业理论研究领域的重要分析工具。

现代企业理论，特别是有关公司治理的理论和方法，对于建设项目治理研究具有重要的参考价值。由于受篇幅的限制，这里只是对相关理论的发展脉络做一简单梳理。后面的讨论会结合建设项目治理的具体问题，对相关理论做出较为详细的评介。

1.2.3 我国的国有企业改革

在计划经济体制下，国家像是一座统一的"大工厂"，而企业只是这座"大工厂"中的一个"生产车间"，因而不是经济学意义上的"企业"。自 20 世纪 80 年代以来，国有企业改革一直是中国经济改革的重要课题。

市场和企业是两种不同的制度安排、组织形式或运行机制。从计划经济向市场体制过渡，实际上是用市场和企业这两种制度、两种组织或两种机制，去代替中央集权指令计划这一种制度、一种组织或一种机制，进而实现对经济活动的协调、激励以及对资源的有效配置。

国有企业改革的目的，不仅是为了塑造与市场经济相适应的微观基础，而且是为了建立在生产和交易活动中具有比较优势的现代企业制度。也就是说，不仅要使企业成为能对市场信号做出恰当反应的利益实体，而且要使企业成为与市场机制相匹配的经济组织。为了实现上述目标，一是要正确划分政府和企业的界限，做到政企分离；二是要正确划分市场与企业的界限，确定企业的产权边界和产权结构（费方域，2006，p. 2）。

如图 1.4 所示，经过三十多年的改革，我国国有企业的管理体制与经营机制发生了深刻变化，国有企业总体上已经同市场经济相融合（文件起草组，2013）。但是，国有企业走向市场化、国际化的任务仍相当繁重。这里主要有三个方面的障碍。一是企业内部因素。相当一部分国有大型企业公司制股份制改革步伐缓慢，国有企业的公司治理还不完善，企业经营机制还不能完全适应市场经济要求，市场化选人用人和激励约束机制还未真正形成。二是历史包袱。国有企业还有大量的历史遗留问题尚未解决，企业办社会的现象仍普遍存在。三是外部环境。外部配套改革还不到位，对全面深化国有企业改革形成不利影响。当前和今后一个时期，深化国有企业改革，要重点抓住两个关键环节。一是加快国有企业股权多元化改革，积极发展混合所有制经济。二是深化国有企业管理体制改革，健全完善现代企业制度（黄淑和，2014）。

1.3 结　论

这一讲的内容可以沿着三条线索来解读。第一条是市场理论的发展脉络：从亚当

初期的放权让利阶段

- 1978年，中共十一届三中全会确立以扩大企业自主权为主要内容的国有企业改革方针，在企业内部建立各种形式的经济责任制；在企业领导体制上实行厂长（经理）负责制；重点调整国家与企业的责权利关系。
- 1983年，国有企业开始试行“利改税”的改革方案。

以承包经营责任制为主要内容的国企改革

- 1984年，中共十二大指出，经济体制改革的中心环节是搞活国营大中型企业。出现了承包经营责任制、租赁制、资产经营责任制、税利分流以及股份制试点。
- 1984年12月，上海飞乐音响公开发行股票，揭开了股份制改革的序幕。
- 1986年8月，沈阳市防爆器械厂宣布破产，成为新中国第一家破产企业。

国企改革沿市场化方向深入推进

- 1993年中共十四届三中全会指出，建立现代企业制度是我国国有企业改革的方向；现代企业制度的基本特征是“产权清晰、权责明确、政企分开、管理科学”。
- 1993年12月，《公司法》颁布出台，加快了国有企业规范的公司制改革特别是境内外重组上市的步伐，推动国有资本进入市场。

国企战略性改组加快步伐

- 1997年中共十五大指出，调整和完善所有制结构；公有制实现形式可以而且应当多元化；要着眼于搞好整个国有经济，抓好大的，放活小的；对国有企业实施战略性改组，实行鼓励兼并、规范破产、下岗分流、减员增效和再就业工程，形成企业优胜劣汰的竞争机制。

国有资产管理体制改革新阶段

- 2003年，中共十六届三中全会指出，要大力发展国有资本、集体资本和非公有资本等参股的混合所有制经济，实现投资主体多元化，使股份制成为公有制的主要实现形式；竖持政府公共管理职能和国有资产出资人职能分开；建立归属清晰、权责明确、保护严格、流转顺畅的现代产权制度，是构建现代企业制度的重要基础。

国企总体上实现与市场经济的融合

- 2013年，中共十八届三中全会指出，国有企业总体上已经同市场经济相融合，必须适应市场化、国际化新形势，以规范经营决策、资产保值增值、公平参与竞争、提高企业效率、增强企业活力、承担社会责任为重点，进一步深化国有企业改革。

图 1.4　国有企业的改革历程

·斯密的“看不见的手”、瓦尔拉的虚拟拍卖人、阿罗和德布鲁所证明的一般均衡理论，到后瓦尔拉范式。第二条是企业理论的发展脉络：从新古典厂商理论的企业“黑箱”、打开企业“黑箱”的“科斯革命”，到现代企业理论。第三条是三十多年来我国以市场为导向的改革的发展脉络：在市场层面上，从最初讳言“市场”一词、1992 年提出“建立社会主义市场经济体制”的目标，到最终提出“使市场在资源配置中起决定性作用和更好发挥政府作用”；在企业层面上，从初期的放权让利、企业承包经营责任制、调整和完善所有制结构，到总体上同市场经济相融合。每条线索上都有具有几个里程碑意义的人物和事件。抓住了这些人物和事件，就是抓住了问题的实质。

从发展的先后顺序来看，市场早于企业、企业早于项目。与此相对应，在理论层面上，市场理论领先于企业理论，企业理论领先于项目理论。因此有理由相信，项目理论可以而且应该从市场理论和企业理论中汲取有益的成分。如果通过这一讲的介绍，能够对市场理论和企业理论有一个比较全面和充分的认识，下一讲对项目性质的探索就有了较好的基础。

参考文献

1. 布罗代尔（1993）十五至十八世纪的物质文明、经济和资本主义（第2卷），中译本，施康强，顾良译，上海：三联书店.
2. 崔之元（1999）“看不见的手”范式的悖论，北京：经济科学出版社.
3. 费方域（2006）企业的产权分析，上海：上海三联出版社.
4. 哈特（1998）企业、合同与财务结构，中译本，费方域译，上海：上海人民出版社.
5. 亨德里克斯（2007）组织的经济学与管理学，中译本，胡雅梅，张学渊，曹利群译，北京：中国人民大学出版社.
6. 黄淑和（2014）国有企业改革在深化，求是理论网，http：//www. qstheory. cn/zxdk/2014/201403/ 201401/ t20140127 _ 316812. htm.
7. 科斯（2003）新制度经济学，梅纳尔主编，制度、契约与组织：从新制度经济学角度的透视，中译本，刘刚，冯健，杨其静，胡琴译，北京：经济科学出版社，10—14.
8. 林毅夫（2016）照搬西方主流经济理论是行不通的，求是，（20），http://www. qstheory. cn/dukan/qs/ 2016-10 /15/c_1119708317. htm.
9. 罗卫东（2010）亚当·斯密的启蒙困境，读书，（12），25—31.
10. 马克思（1975）资本论（第三卷），中译本，中共中央马克思恩格斯列宁斯大林著作编译局译，北京：人民出版社.
11. 马克思，恩格斯（1964）共产党宣言，中译本，中共中央马克思恩格斯列宁斯大林著作编译局译，北京：人民出版社.
12. 普雷斯曼（2000）思想者的足迹：五十位重要的西方经济学家，中译本，陈海燕，李倩，陈亮译，南京：江苏人民出版社.
13. 钱颖一（1989）企业理论，汤敏，茅于轼主编，现代经济学前沿专题（第一集），上海：商务印书馆.
14. 萨缪尔逊，诺德豪斯（1996）经济学（第12版）中译本，萧琛等译，北京：北京经济学院出版社.
15. 沙凯逊（2003）诠释建筑业，建筑经济，（9），3—6.
16. 沙凯逊（2010）建设项目治理：从外生到内生，项目管理技术，**8**（10），13—17.
17. 斯密（1997a）国民财富的性质和原因的研究（上卷），中译本，郭大力，王亚南译，北京：商务印书馆.
18. 斯密（1997b）国民财富的性质和原因的研究（下卷），中译本，郭大力，王亚南译，北京：商务印书馆.
19. 吴敬琏，马国川（2013）重启改革议程——中国经济改革二十讲，北京：生活·读书·新知三联书店.
20. 吴萌，高玉林（2001）市场概念研究，江汉论坛，（10），5—9.
21. 文件起草组（2013）中共中央关于全面深化改革若干重大问题的决定，北京：人民出版社.
22. 许宝强（2007）自由竞争的真义，读书，（4），12—16.

23. 张维迎（2006）序二，费方域，企业的产权分析，上海：上海三联出版社，13—17.
24. 张五常（2000）经济解释，北京：商务印书馆.
25. 赵汀阳（2003）博弈问题的哲学分析，读书，(2)，77—86.
26. Barnard，C. I.（1938）*The Functions of the Executive*，Harvard University Press，Cambridge.
27. Bowles，S.（2004）*Microeconomics：Behavior，Institutions and Evolution*，Princeton University Press，Princeton.
28. Coase，R. H.（1937）The Nature of the Firm，*Economica*，**4**（16），386—405.
29. Gauthier，D.（1986）*Morals by Agreement*，Clarendon Press，Oxford.
30. Hayek，F. A.（1945）The use of knowledge in society，*American Economic Review*，**35**（4），519—530.
31. Seaden，G. and Manseau，A.（2001）Public policy and construction innovation，*Building Research and Information*，**29**（3），182—196.
32. Simon，H.（1991）Organizations and markets，*Journal of Economic Perspectives*，**5**（2），25—44.
33. Williamson，O. E.（1991）Comparative economic organization：the analysis of discrete structural alternatives，*Administrative Science Quarterly*，**36**（2），269—296.

第2讲　项目的性质

□ 临时性、不确定性和非重复性是项目的三个显著特征。这三个特征均源自定制这一基本属性，而客户独特、新颖的需求是产生定制的原因。

□ Ⅰ型项目和Ⅱ型项目是项目的两种基本类型。前者处于企业之外，属于企业间组织；后者处于企业之内，属于企业内组织。建设项目是典型的Ⅰ型项目。

□ 如果把交易成本比作摩擦力，那么，新古典理论可以看作是一种"无摩擦理论"，现代理论则是一种"摩擦理论"。在项目管理领域占据主导地位的系统学派基本上不考虑交易成本，由此导致项目"灰箱"的问题。系统学派把项目看作是过程、努力或开放系统，没有完全走出新古典阶段。

□ 对于建设项目治理来说，派生于Ⅱ型项目的主流项目理论具有先天的局限性。

□ 建设项目治理研究需要坚持基于新制度经济学的"项目观"。

上一讲介绍了市场理论和企业理论的发展脉络和基本观点。这一讲从新制度经济学的角度讨论项目的性质，旨在确立适合于治理研究的"项目观"。与市场和企业一样，项目也是人类社会发展到一定程度才出现的生产方式和组织形态(Winch，2006)。如图2.1所示，在项目及其相关理论的发展过程中，有三个值得关注的时间节点：(1)19世纪30年代，在第一次工业革命浪潮的推动下，现代建设项目和建筑交易体制开始在英国出现（Winch，2000)。(2) 20世纪40年代，由于军事工业的蓬勃发展，项目管理的理论和方法在美国初步形成。(3) 20世纪70年代，随着石油危机的爆发和信息技术（IT）的进步，以"福特制"为代表的大批量生产模式的局限性越来越明显，致使基于项目的组织（project-based organization）大量涌现，进而催生了基于项目的经济（project-based economy）(Turner and Keegan，2001)；与此同时，经济学和企业理

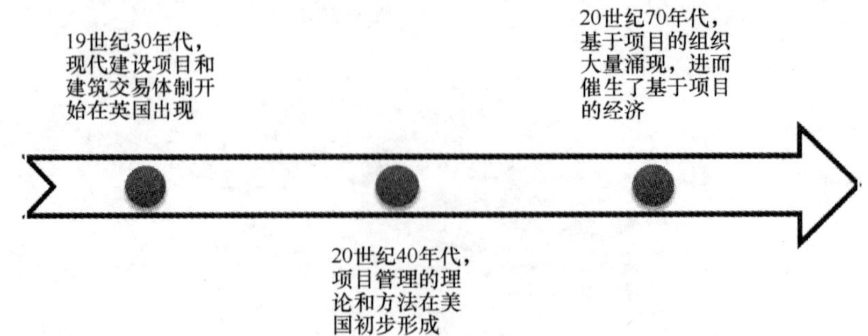

图2.1　项目及其相关理论的发展进程

论的革命性进展为项目管理知识体系注入新的活力；从此现代项目管理进入了新的发展阶段。

2.1　项目的基本特征

项目在不同的语境中被赋予不同的含义，因而是一个多面性（multi-faceted）的术语。尽管存在许多不同的观点和学派，人们对于项目的一些基本特征的看法还是一致的。例如，引言部分提到了建设项目研究领域的三种主要流派——基于系统科学的范式、基于新制度经济学的范式和基于生产理论的范式——它们对项目的定义分别是“临时性的努力或过程”、“临时性的多边组织”和“临时性的生产系统”。从中可以看出，尽管对项目本质的认识差别很大，这三种学派对项目的“临时性”特征都是认可的。

一般来说，企业中的生产是连续稳定、重复进行的日常性（routine）过程；项目则具有明确的起止时间，而且是一次性的。这里所说的临时性是一个相对的概念。以一所学校的图书馆建设项目为例，也许该项目的生命周期会超过某些小企业——它可能会持续几年的时间，而在这几年中，社会上一些小企业已经完成从注册成立到宣告破产的全过程；但是，相当于作为项目发起者的学校来说，它是临时性的过程或组织——图书馆建成之后，项目随之结束（这里暂且不考虑项目的全生命周期），而学校对图书馆的使用才刚刚开始。这个项目之所以是临时的和一次性的，是因为它是根据学校的特殊要求而量身定制的。

项目为客户提供量身定制的产品或服务。定制是项目的基本特征。之所以需要定制，是因为企业中连续稳定、重复进行的日常性生产方式无法满足客户提出的某些独特和新颖的需求。一般情况下，企业面向整个市场开展生产和营销活动，客户从市场购买现成的商品和服务，企业与客户各得其所，不存在定制的问题。如果客户在市场上买不到自己所需要的商品或服务，就需要向企业定制。还是以上面提到的图书馆为例，馆内的图书和其他设备（如计算机、书架、桌椅等）可以从市场中采购，图书馆的主体建筑则要通过项目在现场建造。建筑企业是典型的基于项目的组织。这类企业提供的产品或服务，基本上是根据客户的需要而特别定制的。

总之，项目同时具备临时性、不可重复性和不确定性这三个特性；这是项目区别于市场和企业的根本性标志。临时性给项目带来时间上的紧迫性压力；客户的独特性和新颖性要求则带来不确定性的压力。独特性和新颖性也意味着不可重复性——在每一个项目之前和之后，都很难出现完全相同的项目。因此，项目面临的不确定性要超过企业。项目也因此被视为管理不确定性的机构（Turner and Müller，2003）。

2.2　项目的两种基本类型

在正式讨论项目的分类问题之前，先举一个例子以增加感性认识。设想一家 IT

企业同时进行若干个研发项目——阳光政务云整体解决方案、面向中小企业的虚拟化解决方案、海量存储研发项目、高端容错计算机研制项目等等。这些项目都是由公司总部直接发起，属于企业内部的组织。这些研发项目虽然会涉及一些外包（outsourcing）或者众包（crowdsourcing）业务，但是在本质上还是属于"科层组织中类似于市场的过程"（Sha，2016）。为了兴建新的产业大楼，该企业又专门发起一个建设项目。和以上研发项目不同，这个建设项目涉及诸多的外部组织——设计事务所、工程总承包、分包商、监理公司等，该企业和外部组织之间的关系是市场中的交易关系，因此，这个建设项目本质上属于"市场中类似于企业的组织"（Sha，2016）。

从上面的例子可见，现实中确实存在两种不同类型的项目。它们之间的根本区别在于项目与其**发起者**（sponsor）[1] 或**母组织**（parent organization）之间的关系——第一种是组织之间（inter-organization）的关系，第二种则是组织内部（intra-organization）的关系。从后面的分析可以看出，项目治理的核心问题在于处理好有关各方的责权利关系；而组织内部和组织之间的关系是两种不同性质的关系。因此，研究项目治理，首先要对项目的这两种基本类型做出明确的界定。

如表 2.1 所示，Ⅰ型项目属于**企业间组织**（inter-firm organization）：项目处于企业之外、市场之中；项目的发起者是外部实体——客户；项目和客户之间是组织之间

项目和基于项目的企业：两种不同的组织关系　　表 2.1

	Ⅰ型	Ⅱ型
客户、企业和项目之间的关系示意图	企业　客户　项目　市　场	客户　企业　项目　市　场
项目发起者	客户	企业
项目的位置	项目在企业之外 客户将项目置于市场之中	项目在企业之内 客户在科层内部管理项目
项目的性质	企业间组织	企业内组织
典型项目	建设项目	企业的产品研发项目、软件开发项目等
典型企业	建筑企业	军工企业、信息技术（IT）企业等

[1] 在项目管理的文献资料中，经常会出现 sponsor，client 和 owner 这几个含义相近的词汇。在多数情况下，它们都代表同一个角色。有些时候，则要对它们做出区别。根据 Project Management Questions（2015）的解释，sponsor 是项目的出资者，可翻译成"项目发起者"或"项目出资方"。client 和 owner 都是项目的使用者和受益者。client 可翻译成"客户"；owner 可翻译成"业主"。

的关系；作为项目的承揽者，企业是客户雇佣的法人组织。Ⅱ型项目则属于**企业内组织**（**intra-firm organization**）：项目处于企业的科层组织之中；项目的发起者是企业；项目和企业之间是组织内部的关系。与上述两类项目相对应，基于项目的企业也可以分为两种类型。Ⅰ型企业（如建筑企业）把一次性项目（**one-off project**）作为自己的主要的、甚至是唯一的业务。这类企业的客户将项目置于市场之中。Ⅱ型企业（如军工企业、**IT** 企业等）通过项目这种组织形式来支持其日常性主业，旨在研发新产品，开拓新市场。这类企业的客户在科层内部管理项目（**Turner and Keegan，2001**）。

2.3　项目理论的发展脉络

在讨论项目的概念时，德国著名社会学家曼海姆（2000）的观点很有启发性："我们应当首先意识到这样一个事实：同一术语或同一概念，在大多数情况下，由不同境势中的人来使用时，所表示的往往是完全不同的东西。"荷兰学者 Turner（2006b）把项目管理的研究归纳为以下八个学派：(1)最优化或者系统学派，(2)过程学派，(3)组织学派，(4) 成功学派，(5) 决策学派，(6) 权变学派，(7) 治理学派，(8) 营销学派。这些学派都是项目理论力图与时俱进的表现。需要指出的是，某一学派的存在并不意味着其他学派就是错误的，只是表明独特视角下的研究重点而已。因此，这些学派之间的关系是相辅相成的互补关系，而不是非此即彼的对立关系。在八个学派中，组织学派和治理学派是紧密相连的。由于篇幅所限，下面只对系统学派、组织学派和基于生产理论的范式做一简要介绍。

2.3.1　占据主导地位的系统学派与项目"灰箱"

虽然以建设项目为代表的Ⅰ型项目出现的时间要比Ⅱ型项目早一个多世纪，主流项目管理的理论和方法却是派生于后者而不是前者。一般认为，20 世纪 40 年代，美国为研制原子弹而实施的"曼哈顿计划"[❶] 是现代项目管理的起点。项目管理（PM）最初是围绕工期、质量和成本三大目标，以系统科学和运筹学为主要工具，制定项目实施的最优方案。20 世纪 50 年代后期，洛克希德公司在北极星导弹计划中研发了**计划评审技术**（PERT，Program Evaluation and Review Technique）；杜邦公司在化工项目中采用了**关键路径法**（CPM，Critical Path Method）。随后，又出现了其他工具和方法，如**产品分解结构**（PBS，Product Breakdown Structure）、**工作分解结构**（WBS，Work Breakdown Structure）、**组织分解结构**（OBS，Organization Breakdown Structure）和**挣值分析法**（EVA，Earned Value Analysis）等等；由此形成了最优化学派或

---

❶ "曼哈顿计划"由英文 Manhattan Project 翻译而来。从项目管理发展历史的角度来看，这里的"计划"一词翻译成"项目"恐怕更为合适。

者系统学派。在项目管理的诸多学派中，系统学派一直占据主导地位。《系统分析与项目管理》一书（Cleland and King，1968）是项目管理领域最具影响力的著作之一。美国项目管理协会（PMI，Project Management Institute）制定的《项目管理知识体系》（PMBoK，Project Management Body of Knowledge）的内容主要源自该学派。PMBoK已成为美国项目管理的国家标准之一，也是当今项目管理知识与实践领域事实上的国际标准。

系统学派延续了新古典企业理论的传统，把项目当作生产函数来看待（Turner and Müller，2003）。该学派对项目给出了各种定义，例如"复杂工作"（complex effort）、"独特努力"（unique endeavor）、"人为努力"（human endeavor）、"临时性努力"（temporary endeavor）和"事情"（something）等等，但是都没有涉及"组织"的概念：

- 为了在规定时间和预算范围内实现特定目标而进行的复杂工作（Cleland and King，1968）。
- 为了做前所未有的事情而付出的一次性的独特努力（Smith，1985）。
- 产生变化的人为努力，具有时间和范围的限制，拥有混合的长远目标和具体目标，涉及各种资源，并且是独特的（Andersen *et al.*，1987）。
- 具有起点和终点的事情（Barnes，1989）。
- 为了生产独特产品或提供独特服务而做出的临时性努力（PMI，2000）。

从国际标准《质量管理——项目管理质量指南》（ISO 10006：1997）对项目的定义也可以看出系统学派在项目管理知识体系中的地位和影响：

> 由一组有起止日期、相互协调的受控活动组成的独特过程，过程的实施要达到规定的目标，要满足时间、费用、资源等约束条件限制[1]（刘福恒，2003）。

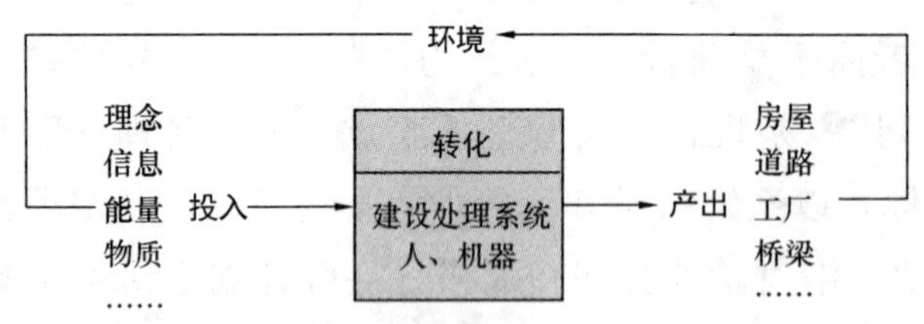

图 2.2　作为开放系统的建设项目是一个"灰箱"
（资料来源：Walker，2007，p. 38）

第 1 讲已经指出，新古典企业理论把企业看作是生产函数，由此产生企业"灰箱"问题。与此相类似，在系统学派看来，项目是一个开放的投入—产出系统（Walker，2007）。图 2.2 给出了一个建设项目的系统示意图[2]。关键路径法、挣值分析法等工具可以较好地解释项目计划对风险的响应机制，分析项目与项目之间，

[1] 该定义的英文原文是：Unique process consisting of a set of coordinated and controlled activities with start and finish dates, undertaken to achieve an objective conforming to specific requirements, including constraints of time, cost and resources.

[2] 在原图中（Walker，2007，p. 38），中间的方框没有涂成灰色。

以及项目与企业之间的交互作用。尽管如此，由于没有涉及项目的组织结构这一关键问题，系统学派的理论和方法在资源配置、利益相关者之间的关系以及项目的边界等问题面前显得能力不足（Turner and Müller，2003）。因此可以认为，在系统学派的分析框架内，项目在很大程度上是一个“灰箱”。

荷兰学者特纳（Turner，2006a）指出，缺乏完整的理论是阻碍项目管理被认可为管理学科的一个因素。被系统观念所支配的项目管理理论更多地被看作是工程学科的分支，而不是管理学科。在《项目管理的基础理论已经过时》（The underlying theory of project management is obsolete）一文中，精益项目管理的代表人物科斯克拉和豪厄尔（Koskela and Howell，2002）指出，需要放宽 PMBoK 所隐含的假设条件，研究并回答诸如项目存在的理由、项目边界的确定、建设项目契约多样性等一系列问题。

2.3.2　新兴的组织学派和治理学派

从 20 世纪 70 年代开始，科斯革命的影响日益彰显。在经济学领域，交易成本理论得到快速发展；博弈论和信息经济学等新的理论和方法出现重大突破；新制度经济学发展成为一个重要的经济学分支。与此相呼应，企业理论也从新古典阶段进入现代发展阶段，企业“黑箱”被逐步打开。在这种背景下，对项目的研究视角也从生产成本扩展到交易成本，从项目的实施过程扩展到项目的组织模式和激励机制，从组织内的科层关系扩展到组织间的契约关系。于是项目被赋予更多的含义：临时性组织（Cherns and Bryant，1984；Cleland and Kerzner，1985；Winch，1989）、信息处理系统（Winch，2006）、实现变革的机构、资源利用机构、不确定性管理机构等等（Turner and Müller，2003）。

组织学派与系统学派之间的本质区别在于对项目的认识。系统学派认为，项目的本质是“过程”或“努力”；而组织学派认为，“努力”只是项目组织为了实现自身目标的手段。组织学派一个有代表性的定义是：

> 项目是一个临时性组织，为了实现有益的变革目标，它被赋予资源，从事一项独特、新颖和暂时的努力来管理内在不确定性和整合的需求[❶]（Turner and Müller，2003）。

根据这个定义，项目的本质是组织，该组织的目标是实现有益的变革；为了实现这一目标，需要通过独特、新颖和暂时的努力；工作的重点在于管理不确定性和整合资源。

把项目定义为临时性组织，使得项目管理稳固地成为组织理论和管理理论的一部

❶ 该定义的英文原文是：A project is a temporary organization to which resources are assigned to undertake a unique，novel and transient endeavor managing the inherent uncertainty and need for integration in order to deliver beneficial objectives of change.

分（Turner，2006a），并且进一步引发对项目治理和委托代理关系的思考。治理学派关注的重点是：（1）与项目相关的交易成本，（2）客户与承包商之间的委托代理关系，（3）项目治理的机制、角色和责任，（4）项目利益相关者之间的冲突和谈判（Turner，2006b）。如果说，传统的组织理论主要考虑组织内部的关系，治理学派则更多地关注组织之间的关系。后者对于建设项目来说，是十分有用的。需要指出的是，组织学派和治理学派都可以划归为基于新制度经济学的研究范式。

2.3.3 基于生产理论的研究范式

基于生产理论的范式自认为是对系统学派的改进，同时对基于新制度经济学的范式持批评态度（Koskela and Ballard，2006）。该范式把项目看作是一种临时性的生产系统，把业务流程作为基本分析单元，以转化理论、流理论和价值理论作为主要分析工具；它以最大限度减少浪费为主要目标，把项目管理等同于生产管理。

精益项目管理的倡导者认为，生产理论应该是项目理论创新的主要动力，而精益生产❶的思想和方法是最合适的切入点（Koskela and Ballard，2006）。表 2.2 列出了精益项目与传统项目之间的差别。可以看出，精益项目管理并不是简单地把制造业精益生产技术移植到建筑业，而是试图用精益思想对建设项目进行全方位、全过程的改造，使项目管理在目标、组织、决策过程和实施过程等方面产生很大的改变。

精益思想给项目管理带来的变化　　表 2.2

	传统项目管理	精益项目管理
关注焦点	企业之间的交易与合同	企业内部的生产系统
目　　标	“投入—产出”转化	“投入—产出”转化、减少无效流、价值
决策过程	不同的专业人士按先后顺序分别进行决策	下游的组织和人员可参与上游的决策
设计过程	先完成产品设计，然后开始工艺设计	产品设计和工艺设计同时进行
设计内容	未考虑建筑产品生命周期的所有阶段	考虑建筑产品生命周期的所有阶段
行动方式	尽可能快地开展工作	在可靠的最后一刻开展工作
供应方式	不同的组织通过市场发生联系并进行交易	通过系统的努力来减少供应链中的交付时间
学　　习	学习是零星的和分散的	学习过程与项目、企业以及供应链管理融合在一起
利益关系	利益相关者的利益不一致	利益相关者的利益相一致
缓冲区	为局部优化而设置	为吸收系统变异而设置

（资料来源：沙凯逊等，2009）

❶ 精益生产（Lean Production，简称 LP）又称精良生产，是一种以最大限度减少生产所占用的资源和降低管理和运营成本为主要目标的生产方式；其中的“精”表示精准和精美，“益”表示利益和效益。这一概念是美国麻省理工学院的学者在一项名为“国际汽车计划”的研究项目中提出的。他们在做了大量的调查和对比后认为，日本丰田公司的即时制造（JIT，just in time）方式以零缺陷、零库存为目标，可以有效地消除浪费和故障，因而是适用于现代制造企业的一种生产组织管理方式。精益生产方式的优越性不仅体现在生产制造系统，同样也体现在产品开发、协作配套、营销网络以及经营管理等诸多方面。

2.3.4　项目群与项目组合

近年来，随着市场环境的变化和工程技术的发展，越来越多的项目以多项目（multi-project），也就是项目群（project program）和项目组合（project portfolio）的形式存在。项目管理的理论和实践也从单一项目管理发展成为项目群管理和项目组合管理。美国项目管理协会（PMI）专门编制了《项目群管理标准》（PMI，2006a）和《项目组合管理标准》（PMI，2006b）。PMI对项目群和项目组合的定义分别是：

> 项目群是通过协同管理以取得单独管理时无法获取的利润和控制的相互联系的一组项目❶。（PMI，2006a）
>
> 项目组合是为了便于有效管理以实现战略经营目标，由项目和（或者）项目群以及其他工作组成的集合体❷。（PMI，2006b）

从上面的定义可以看出，项目群和项目组合的结构成分不同。项目群由若干项目组成；项目组合不仅可以包括项目，还可以包括项目群。除此之外，项目群和项目组合还有两个不同之处。一是不同的关注焦点。项目群是目标导向的，项目组合则侧重于资源的有效利用。二是不同的稳定性。与项目群相比，项目组合具有更强的稳定性。

图2.3给出了一个项目群的鱼刺图。客户项目群是“鱼头”，项目群中的各个项目是“鱼刺”。所有的“鱼刺”随“鱼头”而动。项目群为一组项目提供战略方向；这些项目为实现这一战略目标而共同努力。当最后一个项目的任务完成时，整个项目群也随之结束。

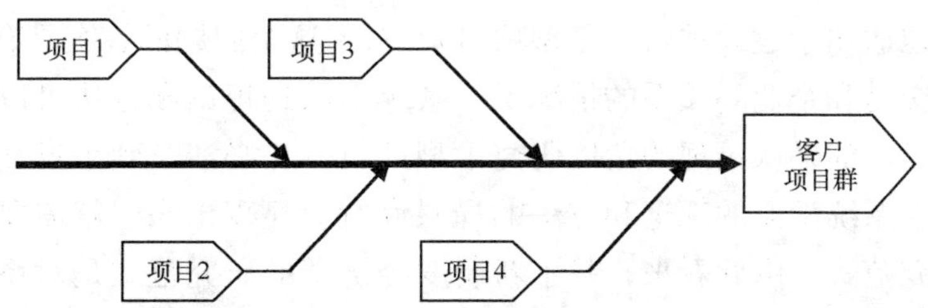

图2.3　项目群示意图（资料来源：Turner and Keegan，2001，p. 257）

如图2.4所示，项目组合可以看作是共享同一个**资源池**（resource pool）的一组项目。某一个项目或一个项目群可以根据需要加入这个项目组合，也可以在完成自己的任务之后退出，而项目组合可以长期存在下去（Turner and Müller，2003）。正所谓“铁打的组合，流水的项目”。

---

❶ 该定义的英文原文是：A Program is a group of related projects managed in a coordinated manner to obtain benefits and control not available from managing them individually.

❷ 该定义的英文原文是：A portfolio is a collection of projects and/or programs and other work grouped together to facilitate effective management of that work to meet strategic business objectives.

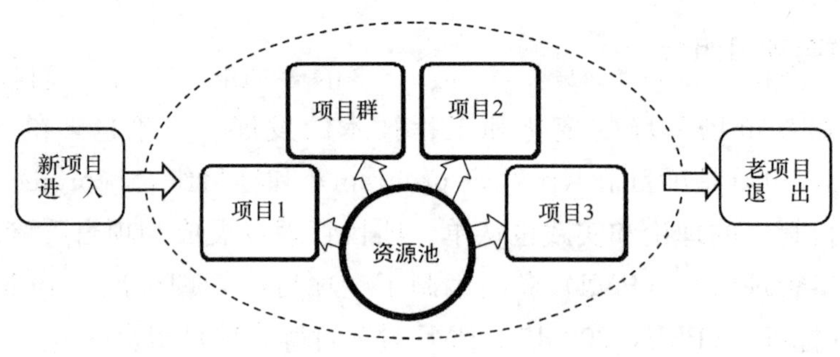

图 2.4 项目组合示意图

如果说，单一项目所关注的只是项目自身的目标和价值；多项目则涉及到战术和战略两个层面的问题。在基于项目的组织中，多项目处于战略和战术之间的中枢位置。多项目管理不是多个单一项目管理的简单加总，而是意味着从“硬范式”向“软范式”的范式转换（Arituaet *al.*，2009）。

2.4 主流项目管理理论的适用性问题

当前在项目管理领域占据主导地位的是系统学派。在运用主流项目管理的理论和方法时，需要考虑它们的适用性问题。系统学派的理论和方法最初起源于Ⅱ型项目，是为了处理单一组织内部不同职能部门之间的关系而设计的，并没有涉及到组织之间的关系（Winch，1989）。然而，Ⅰ型项目的成员之间，以及项目成员和客户之间的关系属于市场交易的范畴。于是就有了下面的适用性问题：产生于Ⅱ型项目的理论和方法能否无条件地适用于建设项目（Ⅰ型项目）？对于这个问题的答案是有条件适用——在不涉及市场交易和企业间关系的情况下，系统学派的理论和方法可以较好地适用于Ⅰ型项目；然而，如果从治理的角度研究Ⅰ型项目，势必涉及到市场交易和企业之间的关系，这时，系统学派的理论和方法的局限性就会显现出来，就需要采用基于新制度经济学的研究范式。由此看来，基于新制度经济学的研究范式是对系统学派的理论和方法的有益补充。

在运用多项目管理的相关理论和方法时，尤其需要注意区分两种不同的项目类型。近日，作者在审阅国家自然基金申请书的过程中，发现有的申请者把项目群定义为“同属于一个建筑企业承揽的、影响企业成长的众多项目的集合”。这种概念上的“移花接木”是没有道理的。设想一个建筑企业从 n 个（n>1）不同的客户那里承揽了建设项目，这些客户的战略目标各不相同，并且该企业与这些客户的战略目标也不相同。接下来的问题是：这个“项目集合”是真正意义上的项目群吗？答案是否定的。这是因为对于一个真正的项目群来说，发起者的战略目标是它的唯一目标，项目群中的各个小项目都围绕这一目标开展工作（一个鱼头，n 条鱼刺）；而上述“项目集合”中就存在 n+1 个不同的战略目标（n+1 条鱼）。

与单一项目相同，项目群也是为它们的发起者的战略目标服务的。因此，在运用项目群的相关理论和方法时，需要从项目发起者的立场出发。借鉴项目群管理的理论和方法来分析建筑企业与它所承揽的众多项目之间的关系是可以的，但是首先必须搞清楚项目群本身的概念，以及建筑项目（Ⅰ型项目）和Ⅱ型项目的区别。Ⅱ型项目（航天项目、软件开发项目等）处于企业之中，项目的发起者是企业。在这种情况下，项目群的目标服从于企业的战略目标；问题相对简单（一个鱼头，n 条鱼刺）。而建设项目（Ⅰ型项目）处于市场之中，客户是项目的发起者，建筑企业是项目的承揽者。在这种情况下，项目群的目标由客户的战略目标所决定，未必和建筑企业的战略目标保持一致（n+1 条鱼）。

上述错误的性质在于混淆了项目发起者（客户）和项目承揽者（建筑企业）的角色。错误的根源很可能是因为忽略了以下事实：(1) 项目群的概念，以及项目群管理的理论和方法均产生于Ⅱ型项目。(2) 建设项目（Ⅰ型项目）的发起者是客户，而不是建筑企业。(3) 建筑企业、客户和建设项目三者之间的关系要比Ⅱ型项目的情况复杂得多。

2.5　结　　论

任何有组织的人类活动——从陶罐制作到人类登月——都会产生两种最基本的而且是方向相反的要求：一是劳动的分工，二是任务的协调（Mintzberg，1979，p. 64）。市场、企业和项目都是社会分工的产物。由此看来，市场理论、企业理论和项目理论都是关于劳动分工与任务协调的理论。

项目属于介乎于市场和企业之间的混合型组织，因此同时具备市场和企业的性质。就适应性而言，项目既有通过价格机制实现的自发性适应，也有通过命令实现的协作性适应。Ⅰ型项目可以看作是市场中的**“准企业”**（quasi-firm）（Eccles，1981）；Ⅱ型项目则可以看作是企业中的“类市场”过程（market-like process）（Lindkvist，2004）。因此，对项目的研究离不开市场和企业。项目理论可以而且应该从市场理论和企业理论中汲取有益的成分。第 1 讲用了大量篇幅介绍市场理论和企业理论，原因就在于此。

市场、企业和项目本身在不断发展变化，人们对它们的认识也在不断深化。如图 2.5 所示，市场理论经历了古典阶段和新古典阶段，现已进入由后瓦尔拉范式主导的发展阶段；企业理论也从新古典阶段发展到现代阶段；但是，项目管理知识体系目前仍由系统科学的观念所支配，没有完全走出新古典阶段。

是否考虑交易成本是区分新古典理论和现代/后现代理论的一个重要标志。新古典理论（一般均衡理论、企业“黑箱”）的局限性在于它们赖以存在的基本假设。在完全理性、完全信息等假设的基础上，新古典理论构造了一个不存在交易成本的理想社

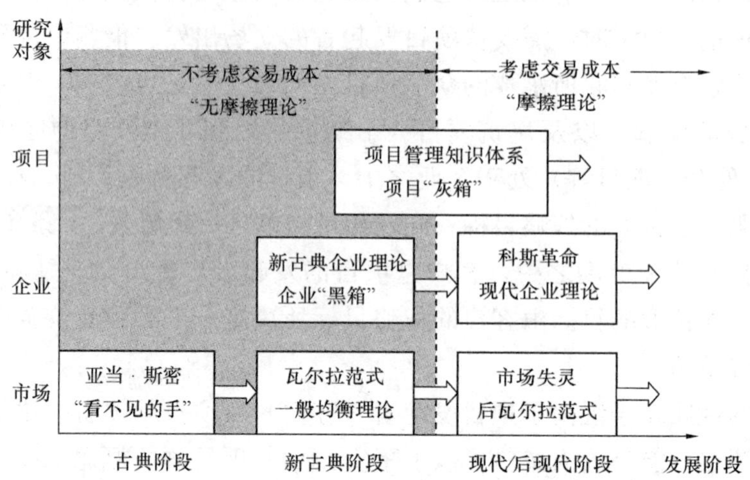

图 2.5 市场理论、企业理论和项目理论的不同发展阶段

会。然而，交易成本为零的世界，有如物理学中没有摩擦力的世界，是不现实的。有鉴于此，威廉姆森把交易成本形象地比作摩擦力（Williamson，1981）。新制度经济学中的交易成本理论、委托代理理论和不完全契约理论，正是与现实经济社会运行情况比较接近的"摩擦理论"。

由于在项目管理领域表现出较强的优势，基于系统科学的范式一直占据主导地位；然而，该范式也有不可忽视的局限性：一是"项目观"的问题。该范式把项目看作是过程、努力或开放系统，不考虑交易成本，由此导致项目"灰箱"的问题。二是对Ⅰ型项目的适用性问题。现有的项目管理知识体系主要是在Ⅱ型项目基础上发展起来的，基本上没有考虑组织之间的关系；而Ⅰ型项目涉及到市场交易和组织间关系，情况要复杂得多；这时系统学派的适用性就成了问题。

基于新制度经济学的范式把项目视为临时性的多边组织，把交易成本作为重要的分析对象，有助于打开认识项目"灰箱"的大门，有助于复杂关系的分析。因此，在建设项目治理领域需要坚持基于新制度经济学的"项目观"；范式转换则是建设项目治理研究的前提。

参考文献

1. 刘福恒（2003）项目管理质量应用指南，北京：中国标准出版社.
2. 曼海姆（2000）意识形态与乌托邦，中译本，黎鸣、李书崇译，北京：商务印书馆.
3. 沙凯逊，宋涛，亓霞，华冬冬（2009）建设项目理论研究范式探析，项目管理技术，**7**（5），13—18.
4. Andersen，E. S.，Grude，K. V.，Haug，T. and Turner，J. R.（1987）*Goal directed project management*，Kogan Page/Coopers & Lybrand，London.
5. Aritua，B.，Smith，N. J. and Bower，D.（2009）Construction client multi-projects-a complex adaptive

systems perspective, *International Journal of Project Management*, **27** (1), 72—79.

6. Barnes, NM. (1989) Have projects, will manage, BBC2, London.
7. Cherns, A. B. and Bryant, D. T. (1984) Studying the client' s role in construction management, *Construction Management and Economics*, **2** (2), 177—184.
8. Cleland, D. I. and Kerzner, H. (1985) *A project management dictionary of terms*, Van Nostrand Reinhold, New York.
9. Cleland, D. I. and King, W. R. (1968) *Systems Analysis and Project Management*, McGraw-Hill, New York.
10. Eccles, R. G. (1981) The quasi-firm in the construction industry, *Economic Behavior and Organization*, **2** (4), 335—357.
11. Koskela, L. and Ballard, G. (2006) Should project management be based on theories of economics or production? , *Building Research and Information*, **34** (2), 154—163.
12. Koskela, L. and Howell, G. (2002) The underlying theory of project management is obsolete, Slevin, D. , Cleland, D. and Pinto, J. , *Proceedings of PMI Research Conference*, Project Management Institute, Seattle, 293—302.
13. Lindkvist, L. (2004) Governing project-based firms: promoting market-like processes within hierarchies, *Journal of Management and Governance*, **8** (1), 3—25.
14. Mintzberg, H. (1979) *The Structure of Organizations*, Prentice-Hall, Englewood Cliffs, NJ.
15. PMI (2000) *A guide to the project management body of knowledge* (4th edition), Project Management Institute, Newtown Square, PA.
16. PMI (2006a) *The Standard for Program Management*, Project Management Institute, Pennsylvania.
17. PMI (2006b) *The Standard for Portfolio Management*, Project Management Institute, Pennsylvania.
18. Project Management Questions (2015) available at: http: //www. projectmanagementquestions. com/4544/, (accessed 2 December 2015).
19. Sha (2016) Understanding construction project governance: an inter-organizational perspective, *International Journal of Architecture, Engineering and Construction*, **5** (2), 117—127.
20. Smith, B. (1985) Project concepts, In: *Effective project administration*, Institution of Mechanical Engineers, London.
21. Turner, J. R. (2006a) Towards a theory of project management: the nature of the functions of project management, *International Journal of Project Management*, **24** (4), 277—279.
22. Turner, J. R (2006b) 项目管理的八个学派，师冬平译，项目管理技术，**4** (10), 69—72.
23. Turner, J. R. and Keegan, A. (2001) Mechanisms of governance in the project-based organization: roles of the broker and steward, *European Management Journal*, **19** (3), 254—267.
24. Turner, J. R. and Müller R. (2003) On the nature of the project as a temporary organization, *International Journal of Project Management*, **21** (1), 1—8.
25. Walker, A. (2007) *Project Management in Construction* (5th edition), Blackwell, Oxford.
26. Williamson, O. E. (1981) The economics of organization: the transaction cost approach, *American Journal of Sociology*, **87** (3): 548—575.
27. Winch, G. M. (1989) The construction firm and the construction project: a transaction coat approach,

Construction Management and Economics, **7** (3), 331-345.

28. Winch, G. M. (2000) Institutional reform in British construction: partnering and private finance, *Building Research and Information*, **28** (2), 141—55.

29. Winch, G. M. (2006) Towards a theory of construction as production by projects, *Building Research and Information*, **34** (2), 164—174.

第3讲　制度与博弈

- □ 制度分析的方法把制度作为内生变量，既考虑经济因素，又考虑非经济因素的影响；因而是比较接近现实经济活动的分析方法。
- □ 以科斯和威廉姆森为代表的新（new）制度经济学和以加尔布雷思为代表的"新"（neo-）制度经济学具有不同的制度观、方法论和价值判断。前者适用于制度的均衡分析，后者适用于制度的演化分析。
- □ 制度可分为内嵌性制度、基本制度环境、治理制度和短期的资源配置制度等不同层次。它们具有不同的研究目的，需要用不同的时间尺度来衡量其变化频率，并且采用不同的研究方法。
- □ 博弈论是制度分析的重要工具。博弈论的主要贡献在于它的一些具有哲学深度的思想发现。其中最重要的可能是囚徒困境博弈所揭示的道理：由于个人理性与集体理性的矛盾，纳什均衡不一定导致帕累托有效。

研究项目治理，既要搞清楚项目的性质，也要正确理解和把握治理的内涵。根据新制度经济学的观点，治理属于制度的范畴。在制度分析的层次结构中，治理处于承上启下的关键位置。一方面，治理结构和治理机制是在一定的社会文化氛围和基本制度环境下形成的，另一方面，治理又会对日常管理产生基础性的作用与影响。因此，对项目治理的理解和认识需要从制度和制度分析入手。基于以上考虑，本书在讨论治理的内涵问题之前，首先介绍有关制度与制度分析的问题；并且把"制度与博弈"和"治理的内涵"分别作为第 3 讲和第 4 讲的标题。实际上，这两讲可以看作是一个单元。第 3 讲简要介绍制度的基本概念和分析层次、制度分析的基本特征。第 4 讲则在第 3 讲的基础上，重点讨论治理的概念与内涵，以及公司治理的相关问题。由于博弈论是制度分析的重要工具，有关博弈论的内容也放在这里一并介绍。从全书的整体结构来看，本书采用新制度经济学的视角，按照"垂直治理—水平治理—针对项目经理的治理—关系治理—交易体制动态演进"的逻辑展开；因此，这一讲的内容不仅为第 4 讲的讨论创造了条件，也为后面的一系列分析打下了基础。

3.1　制度的基本概念与分析层次

传统经济学以经济人假设为前提，在制度不变的前提下研究经济问题。制度经济学则把制度作为分析对象，采用新的假设和观点，建立了较为接近现实经济活动的制度分析方法，从而引发了经济学的一次革命。

3.1.1 两种不同的制度观

制度（institution）是一个涵盖面广、内容丰富的范畴。哈耶克倾向于把制度视为一种秩序（order），科斯则把制度看作一种建制结构（structural arrangement 或 configuration），而在诺斯[1]看来，制度是一种博弈规则（韦森，2003；黄新华，于正伟，2010）。任何定义都是整个理论的一个浓缩，正如黑格尔所说，“概念的展开就是全部理论”（汪丁丁，2004）。这些不同的定义，反映出不同学派在立场、观点和方法论上的差异。

比较制度分析学派的代表人物青木昌彦提出了两种截然不同的制度观，一是“作为博弈规则的制度”，二是“作为博弈内生结果的制度”（Aoki，2001）。由此产生的问题是：制度与博弈孰先孰后？这个类似于“鸡生蛋—蛋生鸡”的问题，实际上源于制度经济学的两个学派。为了解释这个问题，需要对制度经济学的发展脉络做一个简单的梳理。

制度经济学是在批判传统经济学的基础上发展起来的。如图 3.1 所示，从方法论上讲，制度经济学可以追溯到 19 世纪 40 年代的德国历史学派。该学派反对英国古典学派所采用的抽象演绎的自然主义方法，主张运用具体实证的历史主义方法从整体上考察社会的变迁。19 世纪末、20 世纪初在美国形成的制度经济学延续了德国历史学派的传统。制度经济学的代表人物凡勃伦认为，经济学是演化的科学；社会分析应当从体现人类关系的制度开始，而不是从任意的心理学法则开始（谢尔曼，2005）。

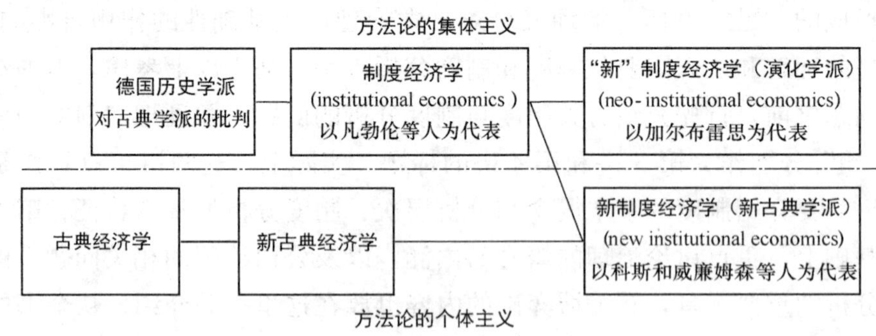

图 3.1 制度经济学的发展脉络

以凡勃伦为代表的（老）制度经济学在演进过程中形成了左、右两个分支（谢尔曼，2005）。一个是以加尔布雷思为代表的“新”制度经济学（演化学派）（neo-insti-

[1] 道格拉斯·诺斯（Douglass C. North，1920—2015）是美国经济学家。他在 1993 年因“建立了产权理论、国家理论和意识形态理论等制度变迁理论”而获得诺贝尔经济学奖。

tutional economics)，另一个是以科斯和威廉姆森等人为代表的新制度经济学（新古典学派）(new institutional economics)[1]。第一个分支承袭了凡伯伦和康芒斯的传统。该学派以生物进化中的“自然选择”为基础，重点分析制度与经济的互动以及整体经济的演化；坚持方法论的集体主义（methodological collectivism)，反对通过个体来解释社会整体的本质和发展动力。第二个分支则把自身的理论视为对新古典经济学的发展。该学派运用新古典经济学的逻辑和方法分析制度的构成和运行，以及这些制度在经济体系运行中的地位和作用。它坚持方法论的个体主义（methodological individualism)，以交易成本为基础，以静态（或比较静态）均衡分析为重点，其自身又形成了交易成本理论、产权理论、契约理论和制度变迁理论等分支。“交易成本”的概念是新制度经济学的核心。正如诺斯所强调的那样，因为有了“交易成本”的概念，制度经济学才称得上是“新”的（王红，2015)。

这两个分支不仅在方法论上有很大的区别，而且在价值判断上也是泾渭分明。以科斯和威廉姆森等人为代表的学派主张私有化和市场化，因而被冠以“右翼制度经济学”的称号。以加尔布雷思为代表的演化论观点与新古典主义的主张——永恒的心理学法则、均衡趋势和资本主义别无替代等——完全相反。该学派坚持认为，资本主义制度并非像新古典学派鼓吹的那样是永恒的和不可替代的，它的命运将像此前的原始社会、奴隶制度和封建制度一样走向灭亡（谢尔曼，2005)。

在制度起源的问题上，新制度经济学（新古典学派）持构建论的立场；“新”制度经济学（演化学派）则认为，制度是由长期的演化选择形成的。从构建论的立场出发，制度被视为“博弈的规则”；从演化论的立场出发，制度则是“博弈的内生结果”。构建论本身又可分为基于自由主义的构建论（制度是个体为了自身利益最大化、通过理性算计有意识建构形成的）和基于权威主义的构建论（制度可以依靠权威机构或社会精英设计、颁布和组织实施)。自由主义的构建论和权威主义的构建论之间存在明显的对立，几乎不可调和；而演化论和新古典的建构论却并非完全对立或绝对不可交流。

为了揭示制度演进的内在逻辑及其影响因素，青木昌彦（Aoki，2010）提出了“双重二元性”（dual-dualities）的命题。如图 3.2 所示，第一重是认知（主观）与行为（客观）之间的二元性，第二重是当事人（个体）与社会（群体）之间二元性。青木昌彦认为，制度演进是一个非线性的循环往复过程：当事人行动→社会博弈状态→

[1] 在英文中，neo-institutional economics 和 new institutional economics 是很容易区别的。而国内不少文献把它们都翻译成“新制度经济学”，这容易造成误解。英文中的 new 和 neo-都有“新”的意思，但是，neo-所说的“新”更多地具有“复制、模仿先前事物”的意思。在西方哲学中，大凡有“复兴”、“复古”和“返回”倾向的思潮或流派，例如“新柏拉图主义”、“新托马斯主义”和“新康德主义”等，它们的英文名称都戴着 neo一这顶仿古的“新”帽子（李小科，2006)。在我国的新制度经济学研究领域，为了区分以加尔布雷思为代表的学派和以科斯、威廉姆森等人为代表的学派，有人将前者称为“后制度经济学”，将后者称为“新制度经济学”；有人根据其理论关联，将前者称为“新制度经济学”，而将后者称为“新古典制度经济学”（张林，2001)；还有人把它们分别称之为“演化学派”和“新古典学派”（黄少安，2007)。为了做到既忠实于原文，又不引起误解，本书将 neo-institutional economics 译为“‘新’制度经济学（演化学派)”，而将 new institutional economics 译为“新制度经济学（新古典学派)”。

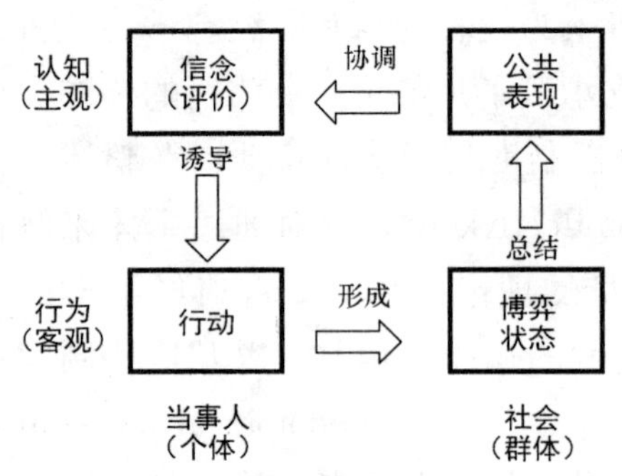

图 3.2 制度演进中的“双重二元性”
(资料来源：Aoki，2010)

社会公共表现→当事人信念→新的当事人行动→……。正如毛泽东（1966，p. 285）所说，“实践、认识、再实践、再认识，这种形式，循环往复以至无穷，而实践和认识之每一循环的内容，都比较地进到了高一级的程度”。

制度能否构建？是构建还是演化而成？回答以上问题，可能要考虑制度的不同层面，以及制度的生命周期——短期的和具体的制度往往可以构建，而长期的基本的制度却难以构建。演化可能是更为本质的现象，而建构是演化到达到某一阶段的产物。可以说，任何建构都是局部和短期的均衡，是长期演化过程中的某一个驻点（黄少安，2007）。讨论至此，上述“制度与博弈孰先孰后”的问题似乎有了一个折中的答案。

综上所述，以科斯和威廉姆森等人为代表的新制度经济学（新古典学派）和以加尔布雷思为代表的“新”制度经济学（演化学派）具有不同的制度观、方法论和价值判断，适用于不同性质的制度分析。在方法论上，前者继承了新古典经济学的传统，适用于制度的均衡分析；后者与德国历史学派一脉相承，适用于制度的演化分析。表 3.1 对这两个学派的不同点做出了归纳。基于以上考虑，本书在项目治理的均衡分析中，采用新制度经济学（新古典学派）的观点，把制度看作是博弈的规则；而在建筑交易体制的演化分析中，采用“新”制度经济学（演化学派）的观点，把制度视为长期动态重复博弈的结果。

制度学派的两个分支 **表 3.1**

	新制度经济学（新古典学派）	“新”制度经济学（演化学派）
制度观	制度是博弈的规则	制度是长期动态重复博弈的结果
方法论	方法论的个体主义	方法论的集体主义
制度的起源	构建论	演化论
时间尺度	短期的制度	长期的制度
制度分析	均衡分析	演化分析

3.1.2 制度分析的四个层次

威廉姆森指出，制度是分层次的。如图 3.3 所示，在四个层次中，第一层是内嵌于各种习俗、传统和社会文化中的非正式制度；第二层是诸如宪政、法律和产权等的基本制度环境；第三层是针对各种具体交易形成的治理制度；第四层是在上述三个层次支持下的资源配置制度。它们具有不同的研究目的，需要用不同的时间尺度来衡量其变化频率，并且采用不同的研究方法。制度的层次越高，其持续时间越长，影响范围越大（Williamson，2000）。图中的锥形结构，象征着不同层次制度之间的依存关系：首先，管理是在一定的治理结构条件下进行的；其次，治理结构是在一定的基本制度环境下形成的；最后，各种习俗、传统和社会文化等非正式制度对其他三个层次产生深远的影响。制度在不同层面上表现出不同的时间特性。管理层面上的变化是随时发生的，治理结构的生命周期需要用年或十年来衡量，衡量体制的演化需要用十年甚至百年的时间尺度，而在文化层面，制度具有“超稳定”的时间特征。

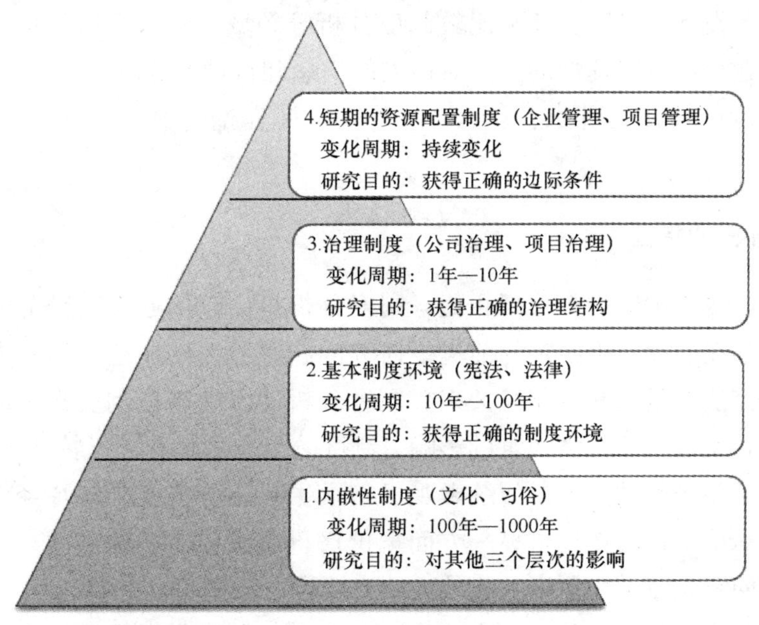

图 3.3　制度分析的四个层次

对于某一个经济组织（企业、项目）来说，内嵌性制度（文化、习俗）、基本制度环境（宪法、法律）、治理制度（公司治理、项目治理）和短期的资源配置制度（企业管理、项目管理）这四个层次分别发挥着“气场”、“规则库”、“关系场”和“工具箱”的作用。其中，“气场”的影响最为广泛和深远——文化是渗透在骨子里，融化在血液中的东西，是一种人们在决策时会不假思索地采取的“缺省策略”（default strategy）（Aoki，2010）。文化是决定一个民族、一个国家是否是一个伟大的民族、伟大的国家的最根本、最内在的“软实力”。几千年来，中华文明虽饱受磨难而绵延不绝，这在很大程度上要归因于文化的力量。在世界各国、各民族中间漂泊流荡、备受摧残和蹂躏而没有被消灭与同化的以色列也可以证明这一点。应该指出的是，现代经济学和管理学的理论和方法基本上是在西方的社会文化背景下发展起来的，在应用这些理论和方法解决我国的问题时，一定要考虑到中西方之间的文化差异，切忌生搬硬套。

3.2 制度分析与博弈论简介

制度分析方法的产生是经济学方法论上的一次革命。制度分析旨在揭示制度自身的发展规律，理解和把握制度、行为和结果之间的联系，以及制度与社会经济发展的相互影响作用。制度分析既包括制度均衡分析，又包括制度演化分析；涵盖外部性经济的治理、机制设计、制度变迁和比较制度分析等领域。从认识论的角度来看，制度分析的核心问题是：有限理性的个人对他人的信念和行动能理解多少？是如何理解的？在这方面，制度的作用是什么？（Aoki，2010）博弈论是制度分析中主要的方法和工具。

3.2.1 制度分析的特征

与新古典经济学中的均衡分析相比，制度分析是比较接近现实经济活动的分析方法。传统经济学在制度外生给定的前提下研究问题，习惯于在经济体系内部考察经济现象，只关注经济变量之间的相互关系。制度分析的方法则把制度作为内生变量，既考虑经济因素，又考虑非经济因素的影响。制度分析方法具有以下特征。

一是对制度差异的敏感性。传统微观经济学主要用价格差异解释经济行为；制度经济学一方面承认价格的作用，另一方面把价格机制看作是一种制度，对价格差异解释不了的那些问题，就采用制度分析的方法来解释（汪丁丁，2004）。

二是强调历史和**路径依赖**（path dependence）[1]。制度变迁理论认为，一些微小的历史事件可能导致某些制度产生。制度变迁一旦走上某条路径——无论这条路径是“好的”还是“坏的”——都会在以后的发展中得到自我强化，从而形成制度变迁轨迹的路径依赖。这与物理学中的惯性相类似。“技术变迁与制度变迁是社会与经济演进的基本核心，这两者都呈现出路径依赖性的特征。”（诺斯，1994，p. 138）“路径依赖性意味着历史是重要的。如果不回顾制度的渐进演化，我们就不可能理解当今的选择（并在经济绩效的模型中确定它们）。”（诺斯，1994，p. 134）

三是对信息的重视。信息是制度分析的核心要素。有限理性假设、委托代理和不完全合同等概念和理论都与信息密不可分。因此，有人在本体论层面上将制度与信息视为“同一枚硬币的正反两面”，认为“制度的基本功能就是信息功能”，“制度作为编码体系而存在。”（许文彬，2010）

四是重视制度的时间尺度（timing）。研究尺度不仅是单位之间的换算问题，而且

[1] 路径依赖的概念最早产生于20世纪50年代生物进化的研究领域。1975年，美国经济史学家David在《技术选择、创新和经济增长》一书中，利用路径依赖的思想分析技术变迁问题，首次把这一概念引入经济学的研究范畴。十年后，有关路径依赖的研究涵盖了从单个组织到社会制度体系的多个层次，成为经济学发展最快的领域之一（刘汉民，2010）。

会对研究结果产生重大影响。测量海岸线要用千米而不能用纳米做单位；测量物质微观结构的情况则正好相反。与此相类似，在制度分析中，制度的时间尺度问题也十分重要。不同性质的制度需要采用不同的分析方法——演化分析适合于全局性的长期制度，均衡分析则适合于局部性的短期制度。

背景资料：

1967 年，数学家曼德布洛特在《科学》杂志上发表一篇短文，提出了一个“看似不成问题”的问题：“英国的海岸线有多长?”他证实，用一毫米长的尺子和十千米长的尺子测量海岸线的长度，前者的数值要比后者大得多。而当尺子的长度小到能够计量每粒沙子的尺寸时，海岸线的长度可能是无限长。换言之，海岸线的长度不是定值，而是随着尺子长短的变化而变化。这使人们认识到，几千年来，人类对自然科学中最基本的度量的理解，竟然存在如此深刻的局限性（殷雅俊，2010）。

五是注重人的观念和意识形态。诺思在他的分析框架里引入了心智结构（mental construct）的概念。心智结构中包括个体的生活史、观念史和意识形态等因素。心智结构不仅影响个体的日常决策，而且影响群体的制度选择。一个人受何种观念的教育和熏陶，对他的行为当然有影响，而制度只不过是与人的行为模式相配的一套规范。有什么样的人，就有什么样的制度（汪丁丁，2004）。

3.2.2　博弈论简介

制度经济学和博弈论在研究对象和研究方法上有许多天然的联系。博弈论是制度分析的重要工具。新制度经济学（新古典学派）中的委托代理、不完全合同等理论模型都是在非合作博弈理论的基础上建立起来的，而演化博弈论则为演化经济学提供了重要的技术支持。当前，博弈论在制度分析中的应用主要集中在制度的资源配置效率、机制设计、制度自我实施的微观动机、制度的生成与演化等研究领域（黄凯南，2010）。由于本书不打算采用形式化建模的方式来分析问题，因此这里只用很小的篇幅介绍博弈论的一些最基本的概念和原理。

博弈不同于人们在市场中的一般性匿名交往，它是一种**策略性交往**（strategic interaction）。在市场中，价格发挥**充分统计量**[1]（sufficient statistics）的作用，个人的决策无须考虑和他人的相互影响关系；而在策略性交往中，个人的行动后果依赖于他

---

[1] 统计量一般都有压缩数据的功能，只是程度不同而已。然而，数据的过分压缩会造成信息损失。有人曾举过这样一个案例：在一个咖啡店里坐着十几个身无分文的流浪汉，凑巧世界首富比尔·盖茨也来喝咖啡。此时有纳税官进来统计，他的统计结果是“咖啡馆内的人均财富达亿万美元”。这个案例说明，用“人均数”的统计和表述，不利于表明收入差距的真实情况。贫富差距越大，这个“平均数”就会越偏离实际。统计学把“不损失信息”的统计量称为充分统计量。比如，均值和方差是正态分布的充分统计量，这是因为，只要知道均值和方差，无须其他信息，就可以确定总体的条件分布（成平等，1985）。

人的行动；并且所有的当事人都会意识到这种相互依赖的关系（Bowles，2004，p. 31）。如果说，一般均衡理论研究的是当事人之间通过瓦尔拉拍卖人实现的间接互动，那么，博弈论研究的则是当事人之间的直接互动。

博弈论旨在探讨参与人（player）如何合理选择策略（strategy），使自己的支付（payoff）最大化，最终求得均衡解。博弈论发展到现在，已经形成合作博弈论、非合作博弈论和演化博弈论等不同流派。表 3.2 列出了博弈论的基本类型和相应的解的概念。

按照参与人策略性交往的制度结构，也就是能否达成一个有约束力的合作协议（binding cooperative agreement），博弈可分为**合作博弈**（cooperative game）与**非合作博弈**（non-cooperative game）。非合作博弈论的重点是个体理性和个人最优决策，其结果可能是有效率的，也可能是无效率的；合作博弈则强调集体理性、效率和公平（张维迎，1996，p. 5）。在博弈论发展的初始阶段，合作博弈受到了比非合作博弈更多的重视。20 世纪 70 年代，随着信息经济学的发展，非合作博弈论在经济学研究领域的作用才日益突显出来。

博弈论的基本类型与解的概念　　表 3.2

<table>
<tr><td rowspan="8">博弈论</td><td rowspan="4">非合作博弈论</td><td>完全信息静态博弈
（纳什均衡）</td></tr>
<tr><td>完全信息动态博弈
（子博弈精炼纳什均衡）</td></tr>
<tr><td>不完全信息静态博弈
（贝叶斯纳什均衡）</td></tr>
<tr><td>不完全信息动态博弈
（精炼贝叶斯纳什均衡）</td></tr>
<tr><td rowspan="2">合作博弈论</td><td>常规联盟博弈
（核、夏普里值、核仁）</td></tr>
<tr><td>联盟形成博弈</td></tr>
<tr><td rowspan="2">演化博弈论</td><td>演化稳定策略</td></tr>
<tr><td>复制者动态</td></tr>
</table>

在非合作博弈中，信息结构（行动的时间顺序以及可获取的信息量）是最重要的因素。根据参与人采取行动的先后顺序，可以把博弈分成**静态博弈**（static game）和**动态博弈**（dynamic game）。静态博弈是指参与人同时选择行动，或者是参与人虽不是同时行动，但后行动者并不知道先行动者采取了什么行动。动态博弈是指参与人的行动有先后顺序，并且后行动者能够观察到先行动者的选择。“剪刀—石头—布”之类的游戏属于静态博弈；而象棋和围棋等棋类游戏则属于动态博弈。根据参与人对其他参与人的特征、策略及支付函数等信息的了解程度，博弈可划分为**完全信息博弈**（complete information game）和**不完全信息博弈**（incomplete information game）。完全信息博弈，是指每个参与人对所有其他参与人的特征、策略和支付函数等信息有完全准确的了解；否则，就是不完全信息博弈。

3.2.2.1　非合作博弈：以囚徒困境博弈为例

非合作博弈论以理性假设为基础。和前面提到的“完全理性”、“有限理性”和“程序理性”中的“理性”有所不同，这里的理性可以概括为两点，一是纳什准则，二是**共同知识**（common knowledge）。所谓纳什准则，就是个人的选择不能有损于自己的利益。也就是说，“要把你自己的策略建立在假定对手会按其最佳利益而行动的基础之上”（Sen，1987）。所谓共同知识，就是指“所有参与人知道，所有参与人知道所有参与人知道，所有参与人知道所有参与人知道所有参与人知道……”这样一个事实。在博弈论中，一般假定参与人的行动空间和行动顺序是所有参与人的共同知识（张维迎，1996，p. 48）。对规则的共同认知，是社会博弈的显著特性（Aoki，2010）。

博弈的标准表达式由三个要素构成：（1）**参与人**（player），即博弈中的决策主体，其目标是通过合理选择一定的策略使自己的支付最大化。（2）**策略**（strategy），即参与人针对博弈中所遇到的每一种情况（也就是给定其他参与人可能采取的各种行动）所采取的行动。应该指出的是，策略和行动是两个不同的概念，策略是行动的规则（对他人行动做出的反应），而不是行动本身，尽管在静态博弈中，两者是相同的。举例来说，“人不犯我，我不犯人；人若犯我，我必犯人”是一种策略，而“犯”和“不犯”则是两种行动（张维迎，1996，p. 51）。（3）**支付**（payoff），即参与人在一定的策略组合下得到或预期得到的收益，它可以是正值，也可以是负值。

纳什均衡（Nash equilibrium）是完全信息静态博弈解的一般概念，同时也适用于所有非合作博弈。在求解博弈问题时，首先要确定每个参与人的**最优反应**（best response）。所谓最优反应，是指针对所有其他人给定的策略，参与人所选择的对自己最有利（能够产生最大支付）的策略[1]。如果某个**策略组合**（strategy profile）中所有的策略都是最优反应，这时每个参与人都没有理由改变自己的策略，因而实现某种均衡，这种均衡便是纳什均衡。换句话说，纳什均衡是由所有参与人的最优策略组成的，是一个没有内生变动源的结果（Bowles，2004，p. 52）。在一个博弈中，可能存在多个纳什均衡，这就是所谓的策略互补的情况。纳什均衡带来的启示是：不满足纳什均衡要求的协议是没有意义的，因为至少有一个参与人会违背这个协议。下面给出的囚徒困境的例子将表明，纳什均衡不一定有效率。

当参与人的支付用连续的效用函数表示时，最优反应就不能用单个的策略来表

---

[1] 在博弈中可能存在比最优反应更强的策略，这就是**占优策略**（dominant strategy）。所谓占优策略，是指那些不管别人采取什么策略，参与人都会选择的策略（因为这样做会产生最大的支付）。正所谓“你有千条妙计，我有一定之规”。在囚徒困境博弈中，“坦白”是占优策略——不管对方采取何种策略，当事人都会选择“坦白”。

示，而是表现为**最优反应函数**（best response function）。给定所有其他人的行动，最大化个人的效用，可以得到个人的最优反应函数。在最优反应函数曲线的交点处，每个参与人都没有理由改变自己策略，于是就达到纳什均衡（Bowles，2004，p. 34）

非合作博弈中的经典案例是囚徒困境（prisoner's dilemma）博弈。它已成为当代社会最伟大的寓言之一。这个故事讲的是，两个嫌犯被警察抓住，分别在不同的房间里接受审讯。警察知道两人有罪，但缺乏足够的证据；于是提出以下条件供两人选择：(1) 如果两个人都保持沉默，不揭发对方，则由于证据不够确凿，每人获刑一年；(2) 若一人揭发，而另一人沉默，则揭发者因为立功而立即获释，沉默者因证据确凿并且态度不好而获刑十年；(3) 若互相揭发，则因证据确凿，二人都获刑八年。每个囚徒都面临两种选择：坦白或抵赖。两人的选择合在一起构成一个策略组合。表 3.3 给出了该博弈的支付矩阵。其中每个单元格中的第一个数字是囚徒甲的支付，第二个数字是囚徒乙的支付。例如，策略组合（坦白，坦白）的支付是（−8，−8）——甲、乙两人的支付均为−8，二人都获刑八年。策略组合（坦白，抵赖）的支付是（0，−10）——甲的支付是 0，立即获释；乙的支付是−10，获刑十年。矩阵中用下划线标注的数字是最优反应的支付。如果一个单元格中的两个数字都用下划线标注，这个策略组合就是纳什均衡。

囚徒困境博弈的支付矩阵 **表 3.3**

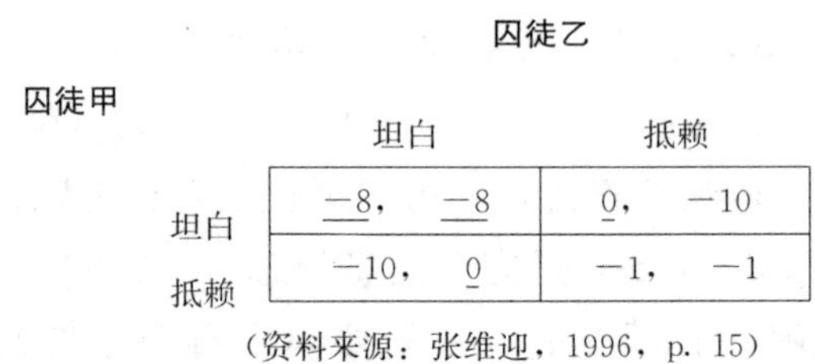

囚徒甲 \ 囚徒乙	坦白	抵赖
坦白	−8，−8	0，−10
抵赖	−10，0	−1，−1

（资料来源：张维迎，1996，p. 15）

囚徒甲会根据以下推理做出自己的选择：(1) 如果囚徒乙坦白、自己也坦白的话，自己将获刑八年；如果自己抵赖，将获刑十年。两害相比取其轻，因此，在囚徒乙坦白的情况下，自己应该选择坦白。(2) 如果囚徒乙抵赖，自己坦白的话，自己将获释；如果自己也抵赖，将获刑一年。显然，在囚徒乙抵赖的情况下，自己应该选择坦白。(3) 由前面两条可以得出结论：不管囚徒乙做何选择，自己都应该选择坦白。与囚徒甲相同，囚徒乙也会根据类似的推理做出自己的选择。最终的结果是，两个嫌犯都选择坦白，各被判刑八年。策略组合（坦白，坦白）是纳什均衡。

然而，从囚徒的整体立场出发，策略组合（坦白，坦白）不是帕累托最优的，策略组合（抵赖，抵赖）才是最好的结果。因为两人都坦白的结果是各坐牢八年；而如果两人都选择抵赖，结果是各坐牢一年；显然两人各坐牢一年的结果要比各坐牢八年的结果好得多。在现实生活中，这种由个人理性导致集体非理性的例子比比皆是。由此可以得出囚徒困境博弈的经济学意义：由于个人理性与集体理性的矛盾，纳什均衡不一定导致帕累托有效。囚徒困境博弈的结果向“个人效用最大化行为必然导致社会福利最优”这一新古典经济学的基本命题提出了挑战。

囚徒困境的结果是人们所不愿看到的。为了走出囚徒困境，需要通过引进一些改进机制，对支付进行必要的调整。例如，可以引进分隔机制，将种群体中的随机配对转化为非随机配对。再比如，引进重复博弈机制和善意的针锋相对（nice tit for tat）策略[1]，也可以把囚徒困境博弈转化为合作—背叛信心博弈（Bowles，2004，p. 242）。通过类似的转换，可以把帕累托无效纳什均衡转换为帕累托有效纳什均衡。关键在于对具体问题进行具体分析，引进适当的变量，形成合适的效用函数和支付矩阵。这就要求对研究对象以及相应的分析工具进行深入的学习和理解。由此可见，所谓制度变迁，就是游戏规则的改变，以及随之而来的利益格局的改变。

3.2.2.2 合作博弈：以“三妻分产”博弈为例

从表面上看，非合作博弈理论所研究的是关于非合作的规律，实际上，它的更深的目标是寻求合作之路（赵汀阳，2003）。一般说来，与不合作相比，当事人之间的合作会产生较大的收益，即所谓“一加一大于二”的效果，这部分额外的收益是合作带来的剩余，也就是**组织租金**（organizational rent）。从合作的角度来研究组织租金的形成与分配，有三种可供选择的技术路径。一是建立联盟博弈（coalitional games）模型，二是建立谈判博弈（bargaining games）模型，三是建立无限次重复博弈（infinitely repeated games）模型。这里的合作博弈主要是指联盟博弈。

从是否考虑合作成本的角度出发，联盟博弈可分为**常规联盟博弈**（canonical coalitional game）和**联盟形成博弈**（coalition formation game）。前者只考虑合作带来的收益，不考虑合作时可能发生的成本。从效用是否可以转移的角度考虑，联盟博弈又可划分为**可转移效用的联盟博弈**（coalitional game with transferable utility，TU）和**不可转移效用的联盟博弈**（coalitional game with non-transferable utility，NTU）。这里着重介绍 TU 联盟博弈的相关内容。

TU 联盟博弈涉及多种解的概念（solution concept），其中最主要的是以下三种：**核**（core）、**夏普里值**（Shapley value）与**核仁**（nucleolus）。对核、夏普里值与核仁的求解，都是围绕着对组织租金分配的公平性展开的。然而，对“公平”的理解是一个见仁见智的问题。如表 3.4 所示，这三种解的概念源自不同的公平观，因而在存在性、唯一性和空间分布上具有不同的特性。它们都可以用来解释 TU 联盟博弈的稳定性，各有长处和局限性，而且相互联系。第 7 讲 7.2 节将会比较详细地介绍这几种解的概念。

合作博弈中的经典案例是“三妻分产”博弈。这个故事出自公元前 500 年至公元

---

[1] 善意的针锋相对是这样一种策略：在第一回合采取合作，在后面所有的回合中模仿对方上一回合的行动。

500 年间编撰的犹太教典籍《塔木德》（译自希伯来语 Talmud，意思是“伟大的研究”）。该书的《妇女部·婚书卷》中记载了一场财产纠纷及其解决方案。一个富翁在婚书中向他的三个妻子许诺，他死后将给第一个妻子 100 个单位的遗产，给第二个妻子 200 个单位的遗产，给第三个妻子 300 个单位的遗产（遗产的单位用金币计）。但是，人们在富翁死后清算遗产的时候发现，他的财产不够 600 块金币，只有 100 枚、200 枚或者 300 枚金币。这时的问题是：这三个妻子各应分得多少金币？拉比（犹太人中的一个特别的阶层，意指老师和智者）提出的分配方案如表 3.5 所示。

TU 联盟博弈的三种解的概念 **表 3.4**

	核（core）	夏普里值（Shapley value）	核仁（nucleolus）
基本思想	基于交易收益（gains from trade）的公平观：无论从个体、联盟还是集体（大联盟）的角度来看，分配方案都应该是有效率的	基于多劳多得的公平观：分配方案应该使参与人的支付水平与他的期望边际贡献相当	基于罗尔斯的平均主义的公平观：分配方案能够使满意度最小的联盟的满意度实现最大化（最大最小原则）
存在性	必要条件：超可加性 充分条件：凸博弈 充要条件：Bondareva Shapley 定理（平衡博弈）	存在	存在
唯一性	不确定	唯一	唯一

“三妻分产”的解决方案 **表 3.5**

遗产数量	第一个妻子所得	第二个妻子所得	第三个妻子所得
100	100 / 3	100 / 3	100 / 3
200	50	75	75
300	50	100	150

按照常人的逻辑，这个方案存在严重的问题——按照婚约，这三个妻子应得遗产的比例为 1∶2∶3，而在拉比的裁决中，只有在遗产为 300 枚金币的情况下这一比例才成立。很多人早就看出了这个问题，至于为什么会发生这种问题，这些分配方法的背后是否存在着一个贯穿始终的分配原则，却无人能给出一个合理的解释。于是这个问题便成为一个千古之谜。1985 年，奥曼[1]和马斯库勒从现代博弈论的角度证明了古代犹太人的裁决完全符合现代博弈论的原理（Aumann and Maschler，1985）。古代犹太人提出的遗产分割方案正是三人联盟博弈的核仁解。从联盟博弈的角度来看，该方案体现了罗尔斯的平均主义的公平观，也就是所谓的“最大最小原则”——在判断社

[1] 罗伯特·约翰·奥曼（Robert John Aumann，1930—），美国和以色列（双重国籍）经济学家。他在 2005 年因“通过博弈论分析促进了对冲突与合作的理解”获得诺贝尔经济学奖。

会福利最大化时，把最穷的人的福利是否最大化作为衡量标准（高东茁，2010）。

3.2.2.3　演化博弈：以鹰鸽博弈为例

前面介绍的非合作博弈与合作博弈适用于制度的均衡分析；演化博弈则适用于制度的演化分析。演化博弈分析的焦点不是**个体**（individual），而是**种群体**（population）的行为规则（Bowles，2004，p. 60）。对个体的过分关注，以及对当事人智力水平的过高估计，影响了经典博弈论的解释能力和分析能力。实际上，采取总体的研究视角是十分必要的。在很大程度上可以说，对个体的研究正是为了对总体的理解和把握。此外，现实社会中的各类当事人也没有经典博弈论所假设的那么高的智力水平；这也是值得注意的事实。

演化稳定策略（ESS，evolutionarily stable strategy）和**复制者动态**（replicator dynamic）是演化博弈论的两种主要分析工具。前者可以为演化稳定性提供"静态"的概念性分析（McKenzie，2009）；后者可以用来解释个体的适应性（fitness），也就是后代的成活率的变动情况。在演化博弈的分析中，**演化稳定状态**（evolutionarily stable state）是十分重要的概念——如果一个种群体在经受扰动的情况下，只要这种扰动不是太大，其结构能够恢复原状，那么，该种群体就处于演化稳定状态。

从本质上说，ESS 是对纳什均衡的一种扩展或改进。如前所述，纳什均衡是一种策略组合——如囚徒困境博弈中的（坦白，坦白）——其中所有参与人的策略都是对该组合中其他策略的最优反应。纳什均衡体现了方法论的个体主义。而 ESS 是一种**策略**而不是**策略组合**。ESS 是对其本身的最优反应——如果种群体成员都采取这一策略，该种群体就能够抵制那些采取其他策略的个体的入侵，因而保持相对稳定——这是一种方法论的集体主义。

"物竞天择、适者生存"，严复用这八个字高度概括了达尔文进化论的内涵。生物进化论利用适应性（fitness）的概念来描述种群体中个体的生存能力：如果某一个体的适应性优于其他个体，那么它就具有较强的繁育后代的能力。复制者动态的概念与此相类似：种群体中高于平均支付水平的策略将被其他个体采纳，从而提高它们在种群体中的比例（Bowles，2004，p. 70）。第 10 讲 10.1.2 节将会比较详细地介绍复制者动态的相关内容。

演化博弈中的经典案例是鹰鸽博弈。假设在一个无限大的种群体中存在两种策略：以老鹰为代表强势策略与以鸽子为代表的温和策略。可以证明，当老鹰之间争斗失败的成本大于所要分配的价值，鹰鸽博弈具有唯一的混合策略[1]均衡——整个种群

---

[1] 混合策略是相当于纯策略而言的。在每一个给定的信息条件下，如果参与人在其策略空间中选取唯一确定的策略，这种策略则称为纯策略，简称策略；如果参与人采取的不是唯一的策略，而是以某种概率随机选择不同的行动，这种策略称为混合策略。在博弈的标准表达式中，混合策略可以定义为纯策略空间中的概率分布（张维迎，1996，p. 100）

体由老鹰和鸽子混合组成。尽管当种群体完全由鸽子组成时，它的平均支付将达到最大值，但是最终的结果是，种群体由老鹰和鸽子混合组成，老鹰所占比例稳定在一定的水平（Bowles，2004，pp. 79—81）。这种均衡是一种负反馈机制所造成的——当老鹰的数量超过这一比例时，老鹰会因为内耗过高而减少；反之，当老鹰的数量小于这一比例时，老鹰的数量会因为对鸽子的剥夺而增加。因此，这种均衡是稳定的：在受到外界扰动的情况下，只要扰动足够小，种群体的比例结构在扰动消除后都能恢复到原来的均衡状态。鹰鸽混合的 ESS 是对市场失灵的一个生物学类比——市场不能达到全部由鸽子所代表的温和派组成的和谐状态，总会存在一部分弱肉强食者，并且会造成效率的下降。这就是鹰鸽博弈的经济学意义。第 10 讲 10.1.3 节将会比较详细地介绍鹰鸽博弈的相关内容。

3.3 结　　论

这一讲的内容可以沿着两条线索来解读：一条是以加尔布雷思为代表的“新”制度经济学（演化学派），另一条是以科斯和威廉姆森为代表的新制度经济学（新古典学派）。在对待制度的态度上，这两个学派都继承了以凡勃伦等人为代表的（老）制度经济学的传统，把制度作为内生变量，重视对社会、历史、法律和伦理等非经济因素的影响。但是在方法论上，前者与凡勃伦等人所倡导的方法论的集体主义是一脉相承的，后者则坚持新古典经济学所推崇的方法论的个体主义。由此产生了两种不同的制度观。

新制度经济学（新古典学派）认为，制度是博弈的规则；均衡是共同体成员自由选择的结果，它使得每个成员在理性地思考自己的利益时，总是没有积极性打破这一均衡（赵汀阳，2003）。在这种语境下，个体具有完全的能动性，能够理性地算计，依靠个体追求制度创新潜在利益的动力，将制度从一个均衡转向另一个均衡（黄少安，2007）。从方法论的角度出发，该学派可以看作是“均衡”学派；它以静态（或比较静态）均衡分析为特征，以经典博弈论为主要分析工具。

“新”制度经济学（演化学派）认为，制度是长期动态重复博弈的结果。个体在制度演化过程中是无意识的，没有能动性；制度变迁是由某种凌驾于个体意识之上的力量驱动的（黄少安，2007）。该学派以动态演化分析为特征，以演化博弈论为主要分析工具。

制度是重要的。俗话说得好，没有规矩，不成方圆。哈耶克曾经说过，一种坏的制度会使好人做坏事，而一种好的制度会使坏人也做好事。制度并不是要改变人利己的本性，而是要利用人这种无法改变的利己心去引导他做有利于社会的事。在某种程度上可以说，制度比人性和政府更重要（梁小民，2002）。所谓制度自觉，是指生活在一定制度环境中的人，要明白制度的来历、制度的形成过程、它的特色和发展趋势。培养制度自觉的意识，有助于增强个体和组织在制度转型中的自主能力。

背景资料：

犹太人通过法规解决刑讯逼供的难题是一个正面的例子。古今中外，刑讯逼供造成无数的冤假错案，成为社会的顽疾。在解决这个难题时，犹太人表现出了高度的智慧。犹太经典《塔木德》规定，事主若做出对自己不利的证词，则证词无效。既然招供不被采信，刑讯逼供自然就不会发生了（何柏生，2009）。

下面是制度改变行为，取得立竿见影效果的一个典型案例。向老人发放免费公交卡，一向被视为城市敬老的重要举措。不过，随着城市化进程的加快以及老龄化社会的到来，城市公交显得日渐逼仄和拥挤，“让座”冲突也时有发生。此前不少人呼吁老年人“错峰出行”，把高峰时段的公共交通资源让给年轻人。但是，这种基于道德的倡议并没有取得多大实际效果。2016 年，上海市政府从制度创新入手，把“暗补”改为“明补”，促使老年人理性出行。从 5 月 1 日起，政府通过老年综合津贴的方式，把交通补贴直接打入“敬老卡”。每个老年人按年龄档次的不同可获得从 75 元到 600 元不等的补贴。据估计，这项制度涉及 260 万老年人，预计年财政投入超过 45 亿元。随后，从 6 月 26 日起停止“敬老卡”免费乘车制度。记者实地观察发现，公交车站及地铁上的老年乘客明显减少。交通拥堵现象有所缓解。有的线路老年乘客比以往下降了八成以上（胡印斌，2016）。

然而，制度不是万能的。在讨论制度问题的时候，我们面对的是能动主体复杂的社会行为。而在在制度决定论者看来，似乎只要有了“正确”的制度，一切问题都不在话下；不少人往往把复杂问题简单化，甚至把人简化为“巴甫洛夫的狗”：似乎铃声一响，狗就会分泌唾液，人就会吃东西（尹伊文，2008）。这种观点忽视了人的自觉意识和主观能动性，属于机械论和结构决定论的思维方式。因此，在充分认识制度重要性的同时，还要警惕制度决定论陷阱；少一点工具理性，多一点人文关怀。

背景资料：

20 世纪 60 年代后期，美国通过立法要求生产汽车必须配备安全带，旨在提高汽车行驶的安全性，但是实施效果却很不理想。配备安全带固然可以减少驾驶员的危险性，但同时也降低了他们谨慎开车的程度。统计数字表明，实施这项法律后，每次车祸中死亡的司机和乘客减少了，而发生车祸的次数、因车祸死亡的行人和未系安全带的乘客数量却大大增加（梁小民，2003）。

博弈论的贡献不仅在于它产生了一系列能够预测人类行为的分析模式，而且在于它的一些具有哲学深度的思想发现。博弈论正在并将进一步对传统经济学做出深刻的改造。萨缪尔森在他的经典教科书中曾引用过这样的话：“你可以使鹦鹉成为训练有素的经济学家，它必须要学的只是两个词：供给和需求”。现在，这两个词或许可换成“博弈”和“均衡”(董保民等，2008，p. 2)。

当然，博弈论也有它的局限性。尽管经典博弈论宣称它所研究的是多人的策略互动问题，而实际上却是一个人的心智博弈。在封闭的模型中，由于所有参与人都拥有有关博弈形式的全部知识，实际上共享一个心智模型，博弈结果能够在事前借助理性的演绎得到。即便是所谓的动态博弈或重复博弈，其策略均衡解也能在事前求出。因此，在经典博弈中，永远不会存在“意外”的事件。除此之外，演化博弈论在技术层面上还面临着两个问题。首先是“时间问题”。在研究生物进化时可以只考虑种群体的长期博弈，而对于人则不得不考虑个体对自己有限生命的自觉意识和利益衡量。集体的博弈时间虽长，人的生命却是有限的。人生苦短，这大概会更多地鼓励自私。其次是“人数问题”。二元是关于“多”的最简单的表达方式，因此，在对人际问题进行简化处理时，人们最容易想到的模式是二人博弈。但是，二人博弈无法表达许多重要的人际关系，如结盟、选举和“搭便车”问题（free rider problem）等。因此，逻辑上足够正确表达人际关系的最简单模式应该是三人关系。三人博弈模式增加了行为的许多可能性，而这些新的可能性所带来的几乎都是产生损人利己现象的条件。因此，即使假定人性是善的，那么世界却不得不被假定为“恶”的。在一个“恶”的世界里如何使善良的共同体最后胜出，问题恐怕不像演化博弈论在电脑中的实验那么简单（赵汀阳，2003)。人类社会是如此复杂，现实生活中的约束条件是如此之多，以至于我们不得不放弃“最优解”，转而求其次；不得不在一定情况下放弃定量分析，转而求助于定性分析的方法。

参考文献

1. 成平，陈希儒，陈桂景，吴传义（1985）参数估计，上海：上海科技出版社，35—52.
2. 董保民，王运通，郭桂霞（2008）合作博弈论，北京：中国市场出版社.
3. 高东苗（2010）最大最小化原则：功利主义和公平的社会契约，北京科技大学学报（社会科学版），(3) 162—168.
4. 何柏生（2009）意见一致，判决无效，读书，(12)，59—61.
5. 黄凯南（2010）主观博弈与制度内生演化，经济研究，(4)，134—146.
6. 黄少安（2007）关于制度经济学的几个基本理论问题，学术月刊，(1)，81—85.
7. 黄新华，于正伟（2010）新制度主义的制度分析范式：一个归纳性述评，财经问题研究，(3)，17—25.
8. 胡印斌（2016）上海为何有底气取消老人免费乘车，中国青年报，2016-06-28，02 版.
9. 李小科（2006）澄清被混用的新自由主义——兼谈对 New Liberalism 和 Neo-Liberalism 的翻译，复旦学报（社会科学版），(1)，60—66.
10. 梁小民（2002）制度比人性和政府更重要，万象，**4** (5)，32—34.
11. 梁小民（2003）安全带不安全与制度设计，人民日报，2003 年 3 月 27 日第 7 版.
12. 刘汉民（2010）路径依赖理论及其应用研究：一个文献综述，浙江工商大学学报，(2)，58—72.
13. 毛泽东（1966）实践论，毛泽东选集（第一卷），北京：人民出版社.

14. 诺斯（1994）制度、制度变迁与经济绩效，中译本，刘守英译，上海：上海三联书店.
15. 沙凯逊（2013）建设项目治理，北京：中国建筑工业出版社.
16. 王红（2015）张军对话诺斯：什么才是最有效的经济制度，http://www. d1money. com/user/space?oid=20549,2015 年 12 月 4 日.
17. 汪丁丁（2004）制度分析的特征及方法论基础，社会科学战线，(6)，51—61.
18. 韦森（2003）哈耶克式自发制度生成论的博弈论诠释，中国社会科学，(6)，97—99.
19. 谢尔曼（2005）演化的政治经济学——在获得凡勃伦-康芒斯奖时的讲话，朱培译，国外理论动态，(12)，16—21.
20. 许文彬（2010）制度的信息意义考察：理论与模型，经济研究，(12)，97—108.
21. 尹伊文（2008）"制度决定论"的神话，读书，(7)，25—33.
22. 殷雅俊（2010）超级分形雪花与埃舍尔的画作，水木清华，(7)，47—49.
23. 张林（2001）两种新制度经济学：语义区分与理论渊源，经济学家，(5)，56—60.
24. 张维迎（1996）博弈论与信息经济学，上海：上海三联出版社.
25. 赵汀阳（2003）博弈问题的哲学分析，读书，(2)，77—86.
26. Aoki, M. (2001) *Towards a Comparative Institutional Analysis*, MIT Press, Cambridge.
27. Aoki, M. (2010) Between game theory and institutional studies: the dual-dualities of the institutional process, available at SSRN: http: //ssrn. com/abstract=1624003, (accessed 2 December 2014).
28. Aumann, R. J. and Maschler, M. (1985) Game-theoretic analysis of a bankruptcy problem from the Talmud, *Journal of Economic Theory*, **36** (2), 195—213.
29. Bowles, S. (2004) *Microeconomics: Behavior, Institutions and Evolution*, Princeton University Press, Princeton.
30. McKenzie, A. J. (2009) Evolutionary game theory, *The Stanford Encyclopedia of Philosophy* (*Fall* 2009 *Edition*), Zalta, E. N. (ed.), URL=http://plato. tanford. edu/archives/fall2009/entries/game-evolutionary/.
31. Saad, W., Han, Z., Debbah, M., Hjørungnes, A. and Basar, T. (2009) Coalitional game theory for communication networks, *IEEE Signal Processing Magazine*, **26** (5), 77—97.
32. Sen, A. K. (1987) Rational Behavior, in Eatwell, J., Milgate, M. and Newman, P. (eds.), *The New Palgrave: a Dictionary of Economics*, Macmillan, London, (4), pp. 68—76.
33. Taylor, P. D. and Jonker, L. B. (1978). Evolutionarily stable strategies and game dynamics, *Mathematical Biosciences*, **40** (1—2), 145—156.
34. Williamson, O. E. (2000) The new institutional economics: taking stock, looking ahead, *American Economic Review*, **38** (3), 595—613.

第4讲 治理的内涵

- □ 对治理的研究沿着两个不同的维度进行。在新制度经济学家看来，治理是一种制度安排；为了降低交易成本，治理结构必须和交易性质相匹配。而在政治学家看来，治理是一种基于协调的过程；这种协调是对等的，旨在保证社会秩序和集体行动。
- □ 为了正确理解和把握治理的内涵，需要回答三个问题，即治理的基本属性（What）、治理产生的原因（Why）、治理方式与治理机制（How）。如果针对这三个问题选出三个关键词来描述治理的性质，它们应该是：相对稳定的制度、复杂性和多中心的对等协调。这三个关键词有助于理解治理和管理之间的区别。
- □ 上善若水。在老子看来，水之“上善”在于包容与不争。这与现代治理理念是高度契合的：以其不争，故天下莫能与之争，此乃效法水德也。
- □ 治理中的对等协调分为事前和事后两个环节：事前通过平等协商形成共识或规则，事后按照所商定的规则行事。因此，治理在很大程度上是一种“法治”（rule of law）。
- □ 公司治理的出现缘于现代企业所有权的分散，以及所有权与控制权的分离。公司治理的核心在于通过责权利的合理配置，使具有不同目标函数的所有者和经营者“不同心而同力”。

长期以来，对项目的研究主要集中在项目管理的范畴；“重管理、轻治理”的倾向是如此强烈，以至于项目治理被笼罩在项目管理的“阴影”之中（沙凯逊，2010）。这一讲讨论治理的内涵，旨在使治理摆脱管理的“阴影”，取得相对独立的地位。

治理这个词早已存在；然而，治理范式的兴起却没有多长的时间。英文中的治理（governance）源于古希腊文中的“掌舵”（steer）一词，意思是控制、引导和操纵。在传统意义上，governance和government几乎没有什么区别，都表示国家/政府权力的统治、管辖、支配和控制。图4.1给出了governance与government两个词从互为同义词到相去甚远的演进过程。20世纪40年代，随着股份制公司的发展、股权的分散以及企业所有权与经营权的分离，企业的主导力量逐步由股东转向经理阶层，出现了所谓的“经理革命”，由此产生**公司治理**（corporate governance）的理论与实践；治理一词也被赋予新的含义。20世纪80年代，社会科学研究领域存在的过分简单的非此即彼的二分法❶，使得许多学科无法描述和解释真实世界所发生的复杂现象，从而引发了社会科学的“范式危机”。在此背景下，治理理论在政治学和社会学领域得以蓬勃发展；治理一词成为在许多语境中大行其道的“时髦术语”（Jessop，1998）。冷战结束后，国际社会经历了从两极到多极的结构性转变。在全球治理的语境里，国际社会是一个没有政府的社会——没有一个位于所有行为主体之上的最高权威对各行为主体进行规制；于是便有了所谓的“没有政府的治理”（governance without government）（罗西瑙，2001）。

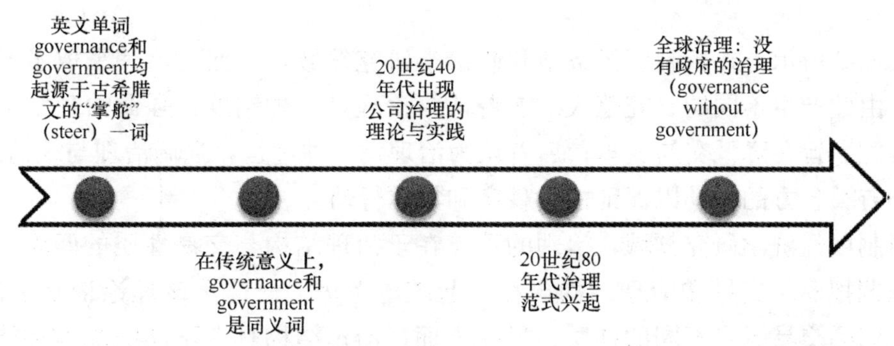

图 4.1　从统治到治理：词义的源流与演进

4.1　治理的类型

治理是一个用途十分宽泛的词汇。在经济管理领域，公司治理成为理论和实际工作者所关注的热点问题。在环保领域，生态治理和雾霾治理被提到重要的议事日程。在国家层面上，我国把“完善和发展中国特色社会主义制度，推进国家治理体系和治理能力现代化”作为全面深化改革的总目标（文件起草组，2013）。在世界范围内，气候变化和禽流感等问题常常和全球治理联系在一起。世界银行和国际货币基金组织则把“善治”（good governance）作为发放贷款的条件。表 4.1 列出了不同分类标准下的治理类型。

治理的不同类型　　表 4.1

分类标准	治理类型
按治理层次划分	社区治理、公司治理、项目治理、公共治理、国家治理、全球治理
按治理领域划分	环境治理、网络治理、社会治安综合治理
按治理模式划分	规制性（regulatory）治理、参与式（participatory）治理、多级（multi-level）治理、协作式（collaborative）治理、元治理（meta-governance）

为什么治理一词有如此广泛的用途？治理到底是什么意思？对这些问题的回答可

❶　这种二分法包括：经济学中的市场对科层、政策研究中的市场对计划、政治学中的私人对公众、国际关系中的无政府状态对主权国家等（Jessop，1998）。

能是多种多样的。然而在一般意义上，治理可以理解为各种类型的社会协调和管理模式（Bevir，2013）。治理涉及行为界定、权力让渡与绩效核验等决策过程。治理过程可以通过政府（自上而下的科层结构）、市场（价格机制和竞争机制）和社会网络（公私合伙制或社区合作机制）来实施，涉及家庭、部族、正式组织、非正式组织和不同的地域范围（国家和地区）；治理的手段包括法律、规范、权力和语言等（Bevir，2013）。

4.2 治理研究的两种范式

如表 4.2 所示，在新制度经济学和政治学研究领域，人们对治理采取了不同的研究视角，由此产生不同的研究范式。前者认为治理是一种制度，强调治理结构与交易性质的匹配，旨在降低交易成本；后者认为治理是一种过程，强调治理与统治的区别，旨在协调有关各方的行动以保证社会秩序和集体行动。

在新制度经济学研究领域，治理的重点在于治理结构与交易性质的匹配。交易成本理论强调把商品交易和治理结构放在一起统筹考虑——这是该理论最基本的原则。一方面，商品交易具有不同的性质；另一方面，治理结构具有不同的成本和能力；为了降低交易成本，必须以一种区别对待（discriminating）的方式，使治理结构与交易性质相匹配（Williamson，1988；Williamson，1991）。在经济组织的比较分析中，威廉姆森以交易作为基本分析单位[1]，以合同法、适应性和治理手段作为基本维度[2]，分析不同治理结构（市场、科层与混合结构）与交易性质（资产专用性、不确定性与交易频率）的匹配关系，以及它们在不同制度环境下的成本与效率，较好地解释了经济组织的治理逻辑（Williamson，1991）。在这里，市场、科层与混合结构都作为可供选择的治理结构而存在，因而都属于治理的范畴。

新制度经济学和政治学：两种不同的治理研究范式 **表 4.2**

新制度经济学	
• 治理是一种制度 • 强调治理结构与交易性质的匹配 • 旨在降低交易成本	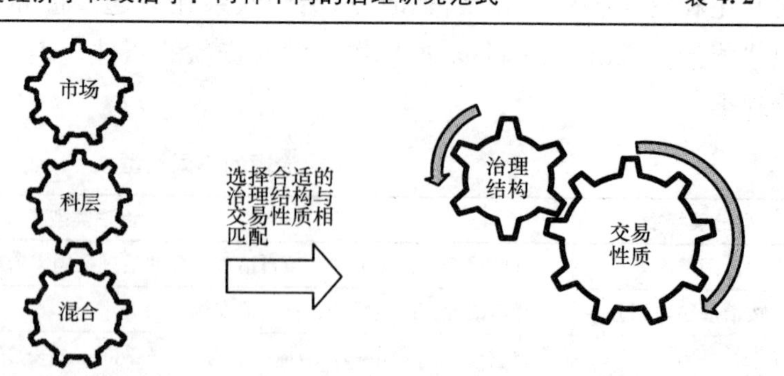

[1] 康芒斯（2009）在《制度经济学》中指出："将法律、经济和伦理道德联系在一起的最基本的活动单位必须包括冲突、相互关系和秩序这三个原则。这个单位就是交易。"由于交易总是在一定合同关系下进行的，因此，基本的分析方法应该是合同的方法。

[2] 合同法（contract law）实际上是争端解决机制，是经济组织的法律基础；适应性（adaptation）是组织对干扰或失调的恢复能力；治理手段（instrument）包括激励和控制两个方面。

续表

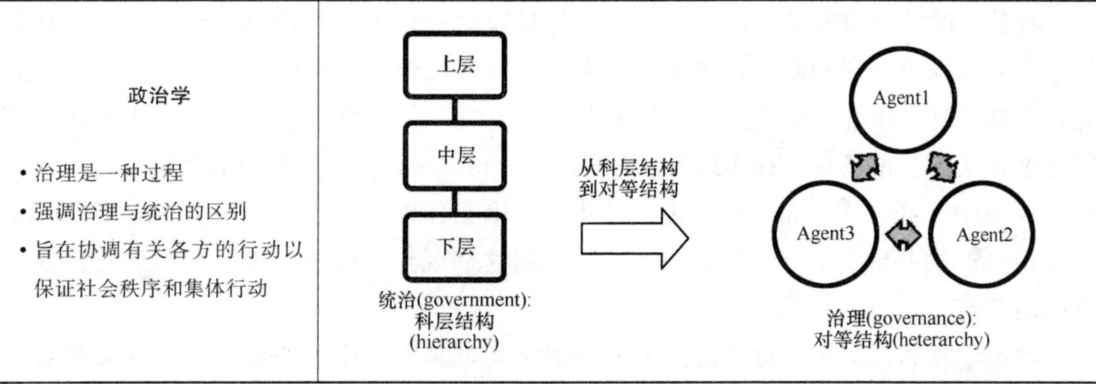

在政治学研究领域，治理的重点在于相互依存的个人或组织之间的协调（Jessop，2003）。对治理的理解大致上可分为广义和狭义两种看法。从广义上看，治理可以是对相互依存活动的任何协调模式，其中主要的三种模式是市场、科层和**自组织的对等结构**（self-organizing heterarchy）[1]。而从狭义上看，治理仅限于自组织的对等结构。为了和广义的治理相区别，这类治理又叫作“对等治理”（hierarchical governance）（Jessop，1998）。

在一些政治学家和社会学家看来，治理从一开始就要和传统的政府统治的概念区别开来（戈丹，1989）。在狭义的治理领域，治理（governance）与统治（government）的本质区别在于，前者是**对等协调**（heterarchical coordination）后者是**科层协调**（hierarchical coordination）。在**科层结构**（hierarchy）中，组织的“头脑”位于最顶层，其他部分只是执行单元；而在**对等结构**（heterarchy）中，位于各个层次上的每一个单元都像包含整体信息的“神经元”，都有思考和决策的功能；因此可认为，“整个组织都是头脑”（Hedlund，1986）。从这个角度看，科层协调与对等协调的区别在

[1] Heterarchy 一词由两部分组成：前缀词 heter 的意思是“其他的”、“不同的”；后缀词 archy 具有“统治”和“支配”的意思。牛津词典对该词的解释是“他人的统治”（the rule of an alien）（Hedlund，1986）。中文文献对该词有不同的译法，但都不够准确。例如，在人工智能领域，这个词被译为“变态分层结构”。在社会科学领域，它被译为“异层级”（王凤彬，2009）。这里的“变态”和“异”与前缀词 heter 相对应，而“分层结构”和“层级”则与后缀词 archy 的原意有较大差异——archy 的原意是“统治”和“支配”，并没有“层”的含义。显然，这两种翻译都受“科层”（hierarchy）一词的影响。为了准确理解 heterarchy 的含义，有必要把它和 hierarchy 做一个比较。hierarchy 和 heterarchy 这两词的不同之处在于它们的前缀词。前缀词 hier 来源于希腊语 hieros，意思是“神圣的”或“上帝的”。在圣经中，hierarchy 是由九个等级组成的天使体系。这个体系被搬到人间，便形成了等级森严的教会制度。社会学家韦伯用这个词来表示理性化的等级体系或官僚制（bureaucracy）。在汉语中，官僚制往往和官僚主义联系在一起，而在韦伯那里，这个词并没有特别明显的贬义，因此，hierarchy 一词通常都被译为中性的科层制，用来表示各种系统中存在的等级关系。前缀词 heter 来源于希腊语 hétéros，意思是“两者中的另一方”（the other of two）或“不同的”。因此，heterarchy 的含义是“双方互相支配”。例如，在人工智能领域的“变态分层结构”中，智能体（agent）之间的关系是对等的，不存在控制与被控制的关系。既然不存在等级层次，硬翻译成“分层结构”就没有道理了。在有关治理的英文文献中，有的作者直接将 heterarchy 解释为“非科层”（non-hierarchy）。基于以上考虑，本书把 heterarchy 翻译为“对等结构”，把 hierarchy 翻译为“科层结构”。

于，前者是单中心的，后者是多中心的❶。

在狭义的治理研究领域，治理被看作是科层与市场失效的产物。政治学家和社会学家之所以提出治理的概念，之所以主张用治理替代统治，是因为他们在社会资源的配置中既看到了市场的失效，又看到了国家的失效（俞可平，2000）。英国著名政治学家杰索普认为，市场具有程序理性（procedural rationality），政府具有实质理性（substantive rationality）❷，而对等治理则是建立在第三种理性——反身理性（reflexive rationality）❸ 的基础之上（Jessop，1998）。根据这一观点，科层、市场和治理分别属于不同的范畴。

政治学家和社会学家对治理做出了许多定义，其中全球治理委员会的定义很有代表性：

> 治理是各种公共的或私人的个体和机构管理其共同事务的诸多方式的总和。它是使相互冲突的或不同的利益得以调和并且采取联合行动的持续过程。这既包括有权迫使人们服从的正式制度和规则，也包括各种人们同意或以为符合其利益的非正式的制度安排。(Commission on Global Governance，1995，p. 4)

这个定义概括了治理的四个特征：第一，治理不是一整套规则，也不是一种活动，而是一种过程。第二，治理过程的基础不是控制，而是协调。第三，治理既涉及公共部门，也包括私人部门。第四，治理不是一种固定的制度，而是持续的互动。

4.3 有关治理的三个基本问题

为了正确理解和把握治理的内涵，需要回答以下三个基本问题：（1）治理的基本属性，也就是治理是什么的问题（What）。（2）治理问题产生的原因，也就是治理为什么存在的问题（Why）。需要指出的是，治理问题产生的原因与治理的目的是密切相关的。（3）治理方式和治理机制，也就是如何治理的问题（How）。如前所述，对治理的研究是沿着两个不同的维度进行的。一个是以威廉姆森为代表的新制度经济学的研究范式，另一个是以杰索普为代表的政治学的研究范式（狭义的治理）。下面分别从这两个维度考察有关治理的三个基本问题，并对这两种范式进行比较和整合。

---

❶ 市场是一种分散化的决策机制。但是，在一般均衡理论的分析框架内，市场中的协调也可以看作是单中心的协调机制。如第1讲中的图1.1所示，在市场结构中，无所不能的瓦尔拉拍卖人位于信息中心的位置，市场各方之间没有直接的信息沟通和明示协议，他们都是价格的接受者。

❷ 对程序理性的解释，详见绪言部分的脚注6。实质理性（substantive rationality）也称价值理性（value rationality），是以主体为中心的理性。它从某些特定的价值理念（如公平、正义、忠诚、荣誉等）的角度来判断行为的合理性。

❸ 简而言之，反身性就是相互决定性。反身性承认人们思维和实际状况之间的双向互动。这种理性取得成功的关键在于不断地承诺对话以产生和交换更多的信息（Jessop，1998）。

在治理的基本属性（What）问题上，两种范式的认识有较大差别，但同时存在整合的余地。在新制度经济学家看来，治理是一种制度安排。在制度分析的层次结构中，治理处于第三个层次；其他三个层次分别是内嵌性制度、基本制度环境和短期的资源配置制度。这些层次之间的一个重要差别在于制度的时间尺度。例如，短期的资源配置制度是持续变化的，而在治理的层次上，制度是相对稳定的，其变化周期是 1 年—10 年。在政治学家看来，治理是一种基于协调的过程，与它相对应的是科层（统治）与市场。如前所述，全球治理委员会给出的定义一方面强调治理“是持续的过程”，另一方面也给制度留下了空间：“既包括有权迫使人们服从的正式制度和规则，也包括各种人们同意或以为符合其利益的非正式的制度安排。”综合考虑这两种范式对治理基本属性的认识，本书把治理视为“相对稳定的制度安排”。这是因为，（1）如前所述，全球治理委员会给出的定义中并没有完全将制度排除在外。（2）根据辩证唯物主义的运动观，一切事物的存在和发展都是绝对运动和相对静止的统一。在承认运动绝对性的同时，也应该承认存在着某种相对静止的状态。因此，“相对稳定”的说法比“持续的互动”的说法更为恰当。

在治理产生的原因（Why）问题上，两种范式的看法基本一致，都把复杂性看作是治理问题产生的根源。说到底，治理是劳动分工的产物。随着社会进步和经济发展，劳动分工越来越细，人们之间的交互式依存程度越来越高，关系越来越复杂，保证社会秩序和集体行动的难度越来越大，交易成本也随之提高。在传统方法失效的情况下，治理范式便应运而生。正因为如此，治理被视为“关于复杂性的艺术”（Jessop，2003）。例如，公司治理出现的原因是企业所有权和经营权的分离所带来的管理上的复杂性。再比如，对于雾霾问题之所以要采取治理的方式来解决，是因为雾霾的产生和消除都是如此复杂，以至于单靠政府、市场或企业都难以奏效。在治理的目的方面，两种范式的侧重点有所不同；新制度经济学家强调交易成本的降低；而政治学家强调保证社会秩序和集体行动（Stoker，1998，p. 155）。实际上，降低交易成本和保证社会秩序以及集体行动两者并不矛盾；两者是高度一致的。综合考虑这两种范式对治理问题产生的原因以及对治理目的认识，本书把治理产生的原因归结为复杂性，而把治理的目的理解为低成本、高效率地保证组织的秩序和集体行动。

在治理方式与治理机制（How）问题上，两种范式的看法有较大差异。新制度经济学家强调治理结构与交易性质的合理匹配。威廉姆森认为，市场、科层与混合结构都是可供选择的治理结构。政治学家则强调对等协调。例如，杰索普认为，治理是科层与市场失效的产物；市场、科层和治理具有不同的理性基础和协调逻辑，分属不同的范畴。

对以上两种不同的观点进行整合，需要解决以下两个问题。第一个问题是：市场、科层与混合结构是否属于治理的范畴？对于这个问题，新制度经济学家的回答显然是肯定的。在政治学领域，对治理的理解存在广义和狭义两种看法。一方面，杰索普等人对科层、市场和治理做出了比较明确的切割；另一方面，把三者放在一起讨论的也大有人在。实际上，治理和科层、市场的关系不是绝对的排斥和对立，而是相辅相成、互为补充的。例如，在社会治理中，政府和市场都应该而且可以发挥积极的作用。在雾霾治理中没有政府的参与也是不可想象的。基于以上考虑，本书认为，市场、科层与混合结构都属于治理的范畴。于是就产生第二个问题：在认定科层结构属于治理范畴的前提下，能否接受对等协调的概念？从逻辑上讲，“科层属于治理范畴”和“治理是对等协调”这两个命题似乎无法同时成立。这是因为，科层结构与对等结构是相互对立的两个概念。然而，从实际出发，似乎应该同时接受这两个命题。这是因为，第一，对等协调中的平等关系不是绝对的，有时也需要一定的权威。政治学家和社会学家一方面强调治理的对等属性，另一方面也承认，治理作为一种政治管理过程，也像政府统治一样需要权威和权力（俞可平，2000）。此外，科层中的等级关系也不是绝对的，在许多情况下，上下级之间也需要一定的协商。第二，交易本身意味有关当事人之间的对等关系。威廉姆森所说的“治理结构与交易方式的匹配”，是指交易双方签订合同之前需要考虑的问题。以一项资产专用性较高的合同为例，考虑到交易的性质，双方选择科层结构与之相匹配，以降低交易成本。注意，在签订合同时，交易双方是平等的。一旦签订了合同，当科层结构成为事实，当事人之间的关系才会发生变化。由此可见，当事人之间存在“事前”（*ex ante*）的对等关系和“事后”（*ex post*）的科层关系，两者并不矛盾。马克思对这种从“事前”到“事后”的变化做出了生动的描述：

> 劳动力的买和卖是在流通领域或商品交换领域的界限以内进行的，这个领域确实是天赋人权的真正乐园。那里占统治地位的只是自由、平等、所有权和边沁。自由！因为商品例如劳动力的买者和卖者，只取决于自己的自由意志。……平等！因为他们彼此只是作为商品占有者发生关系，用等价物交换等价物。所有权！因为他们都只支配自己的东西。边沁！因为双方都只顾自己。……一离开这个简单流通领域或商品交换领域，……就会看到，我们的剧中人的面貌已经起了某些变化。原来的货币所有者成了资本家，昂首前行；劳动力所有者成了他的工人，尾随于后。一个笑容满面，雄心勃勃；一个战战兢兢，畏缩不前，像在市场上出卖了自己的皮一样，只有一个前途——让人家来鞣（马克思，1975，pp. 199—200）。

基于以上分析，本书认为，治理的特点主要体现在多中心的对等协调。这种协调分为事前和事后两个环节：事前通过平等协商形成共识或规则，事后按照所商定的规则行事。

表 4.3 列出了对两种范式进行比较、分析与整合的结果。本书对治理的理解是：与管理相比，治理是一种相对稳定的制度安排；治理问题产生的根源在于交互式依存

关系带来的复杂性；市场、科层与混合结构都属于治理的范畴；治理的特点主要体现在多中心的对等协调，旨在低成本、高效率地保证组织的秩序和集体行动。

有关治理的三个基本问题：两种范式的比较、分析与整合　　**表 4.3**

	新制度经济学范式	政治学范式（狭义的治理）	对两种范式的整合
治理的基本属性 （How）	与管理相比，治理是一种相对稳定的制度安排	治理是一种基于协调的、持续互动的过程	治理是一种相对稳定的制度安排
治理产生的原因 （Why）	复杂性导致交易成本升高	治理是科层与市场失效的产物；交互式依存关系带来的复杂性导致保证社会秩序和集体行动的难度增大	治理产生的根源在于交互式依存关系带来的复杂性；旨在低成本、高效率地保证组织的秩序和集体行动
治理方式与治理机制 （How）	选择合适的治理结构（市场、科层、混合结构）与交易性质（资产专用性、不确定性、交易频率）相匹配	多中心的对等协调	治理的特点主要体现在多中心的对等协调；事前通过平等协商形成共识或规则，事后按照所商定的规则行事

综上所述，为了正确理解和把握治理的内涵，需要回答三个问题，即治理的基本属性（What）、治理产生的原因（Why）、治理方式与治理机制（How）。如果针对这三个问题选出三个关键词来描述治理的性质，它们应该是：相对稳定的制度、复杂性和多中心的对等协调。

这三个关键词有助于理解治理和管理之间的区别。首先，在威廉姆森提出的四层次分析框架中，管理属于短期的资源配置制度，而治理的变化周期是 1 年—10 年。由此可见，与管理相比，治理是相对稳定的制度安排。其次，管理和治理都是社会分工的产物；分工越细，问题的复杂程度越高。泰勒的科学管理出现在一百多年之前，引发现代治理的“经理革命”则发生在七十多年前。显然，与管理相比，治理是更高层次上的分工的产物，面对的问题更加复杂。最后，治理以对等协调为基本特征，强调当事人之间的平等关系；因此，治理在很大程度上是一种“法治”（rule of law）[1]。而在管理学科的语境中，总是存在“管理者”和“被管理者”。新管理主义提出“使管理者管理”（make managers manage）和“让管理者来管理”（let managers manage）的主张，使得管理者的主体地位愈加突出（Kettl，1997）；因此，管理在很大程度上是一种“人治”（rule of the individual）。在现代社会，人民群众不是社会管理的消极受体，而是社会管理的主体和实施者。这就是治理与管理的本质区别。

[1] 法治（rule of law）的本质是：法律高于一切，法律面前人人平等，人人都要依法办事。而对于法制（rule by law）来说，法律只是一种工具；由于主体不明确，法制往往会变成人治（rule of the individual）。

背景材料：全球治理的中国智慧

2015 年 8 月 4 日，时任联合国秘书长的潘基文把自己的“上善若水”书法横幅作为生日礼物赠给美国总统奥巴马，巧妙地传递了潘基文本人对全球治理中“善治”(good governance) 的思考和期盼（易平，2015)。

“上善若水”出自《老子》第八章。在老子看来，水之善在于包容与不争。这与现代治理理念是高度契合的：以其不争，故天下莫能与之争，此乃效法水德也。在全球化加速发展、各国利益日益融合的今天，国际社会就是一个大家庭，需要我们以中国古代哲学家老子在《道德经》中所阐述的那样，在对外交往中倡导利益交融、休戚与共的命运共同体理念，当前特别要发扬“上善若水”和“同舟共济”的精神，协调宏观经济政策，共同破解难题（何亚非，2014)。

治理需要通过不同层次的灵活性来实现。根据治理关系的复杂程度，治理本身可以分为三个层次。与治理有关的三种嵌入性社会组织包括：人际关系的社会性嵌入 (social embeddedness)、组织间关系的机构性嵌入（institutional embeddedness）和体系间关系的社会功能性嵌入（‘societal’ embeddedness）[1]（Jessop，2003)。在这三个层次中，第一个层次最为简单，例如，社区治理涉及的对象主要是人际关系；第三个层次最为复杂，例如，全球治理涉及的对象主要是国际关系。层次越高，复杂性越强，所要求的灵活性也就越大。

项目治理与公司治理的性质相近，但是，前者要比后者复杂。这是因为，项目（特别是Ⅰ型项目）治理涉及的对象主要是组织间的关系，属于前面所说的第二个层次；而公司治理涉及的对象介乎于一、二层次之间——在公司的利益相关者中，有的可能是法人，有的可能是自然人。因此，与公司治理相比，项目治理要求更大的灵活性。尽管如此，这并不妨碍前者把后者的研究成果作为其重要的思想渊源。

4.4 公司治理理论简介

经过几十年的发展，公司治理的理论与实践已经相当成熟，并且积累了大量的研究成果和实际经验。在公司治理研究成果的基础上开展项目治理研究，这是一条事半功倍的技术路径。因此，有必要对公司治理理论的研究现状及发展趋势做一简要的梳理。

---

[1] 嵌入（embeddedness）一词的原义是指一个系统有机地结合到另外一个系统之中，即某一事物内生于其他事物的现象。这个概念最早是由匈牙利哲学家波兰尼（2007）在 1944 年出版的《大转型：我们时代的经济与政治起源》一书中提出，用来强调社会关系对经济过程的重要性。经过多年的发展，嵌入性理论现已成为新经济社会学的重要研究领域。

4.4.1　公司治理的概念

公司治理也是一个多角度多层次的概念。从公司治理问题产生与发展的角度来看，可以从狭义和广义两方面去理解这个概念。狭义的公司治理，是指所有者（主要是股东）对经营者的一种监督与制衡机制。即通过一种制度安排来合理地配置所有者与经营者之间的权利与责任关系。公司治理的目标是保证股东利益的最大化，防止经营者对所有者利益的背离。其核心问题是由股东大会、董事会、监事会和管理层所构成的公司治理结构。广义的公司治理不限于股东对经营者的制衡，而是涉及广泛的利益相关者，包括股东、债权人、供应商、雇员、政府和社区等与公司有利益关系的个人或组织。从广义的角度来看，公司治理是通过一套正式的或非正式的、内部的或外部的制度或机制来协调公司与所有利益相关者之间的关系，以保证公司决策的科学化，维护与公司有关的各方面的利益。（李维安，2001，pp. 31—32）。

背景材料：

近二十年来，治理理论得到长足的发展，但是，关于公司治理的概念至今还没有统一的标准。据有关资料统计，国内外有关公司治理的定义就有 22 种之多（周新军，2007)，这反映出该领域多元化的发展态势。

美国经济学家奥利弗·哈特（1996）将代理问题与合同的不完全性作为公司治理存在的条件和理论基础。他认为，只要以下两个条件存在，公司治理问题就必然在一个组织中产生。第一个条件是代理问题，确切地说是组织成员（可能是所有者、工人或消费者）之间存在利益冲突；第二个条件是，交易费用是如此之大，以至于使代理问题不可能通过合同来解决。

美国学者玛格丽特·布莱尔（1999）从狭义和广义两方面给公司治理结构做出定义。狭义地讲，公司治理结构是指有关公司董事会的功能、结构和股东权利等方面的制度安排；广义地讲，公司治理结构是指公司剩余控制权和剩余索取权分配的一整套法律、文化和制度安排，它决定着公司目标，谁在什么状态下实施控制，如何进行控制，风险与收益如何在不同成员之间分配等问题。

吴敬琏（1994）认为，所谓公司治理结构，是指由所有者、董事会和高级执行人员即高级经理三者组成的一种组织结构。在这种结构中，上述三者之间形成一定的制衡关系。

费方域（1996）认为，公司治理的概念应该是一个知识体系。知识的最小表述单位是判断，所以，它可以用一系列互为补充的判断来加以说明：(1) 公司治理的本质是一种合同关系；(2) 公司治理的功能是配置权、责、利；(3) 公司治理的起因在产权分离；(4) 公司治理有多种形式。

张维迎（1999，p. 106）认为，公司治理结构就是这样一种解决股份公司内部各种代理问题的机制。它规定着企业内部不同要素所有者的关系，特别是通过显性和隐性的合同对剩余索取权和控制权进行分配，从而影响企业家和资本家的关系。

李维安（2001）认为，公司治理是一个由主体和客体、边界和范围、机制和动能、结构和形式等诸多因素构成的体系。公司治理主体是以股东为核心的诸多利益相关者，公司治理的客体由治理边界加以限定。公司治理机制包括激励机制、约束机制及决策机制，这些机制发挥作用的前提是存在合理的公司治理结构。公司治理结构包括内部治理与外部治理两个方面，内部治理是基于正式的制度安排，外部治理则建立于非正式的制度安排的基础之上。

在实践中，将治理和管理混为一谈的现象普遍存在。一项针对跨国公司在华投资企业的调查表明，受访的绝大多数外籍首席执行官和中方主管都把治理问题当成了管理问题（周新军，2007）。这种状况既不利于管理水平的提高，又有碍于公司治理制度的实施，致使不少公司的治理结构徒有其名。因此，有必要简要介绍公司治理和企业管理之间的联系与区别。

最早对公司治理和企业管理做出区分的是英国学者特里克教授。他认为，企业管理的重点是公司的运营，而公司治理的重点则是确保这种运营处于正确的轨道之上。他还明确指出，战略管理是公司治理与企业管理的联结点（Tricker，1984）。美国学者肯尼斯·代顿认为，治理与管理是同一枚硬币的正反两面，它们相互依存，又互有区别。现代企业总是同时存在着管理和治理的问题。公司治理是指董事会用来监管企业高管的过程、结构和关系，而企业管理则是企业高管确定企业目标以及为实现目标所做的事情（Dayton，1984）。刘伟（1994）认为，公司治理结构并非一般的企业管理，而是指规范所有者和资产受托者，以及受托者与代理者之间的权、责、利的制度安排。或者更具体地说，它是指一组联结并规范所有者（股东）、支配者（董事会）、管理者（经理）、使用者（工人）相互权力和利益关系的制度安排。费方域（1996）从三个方面对治理和管理做出了区别：治理的中心是外部的，管理的中心是内部的；治理是一个开放系统，管理是一个封闭系统；治理是战略导向的，管理是任务导向的。一言以蔽之，治理关心的是“公司向何处去”，而管理关心的是“使公司怎样到达那儿”。从上面的分析可以看出，在公司治理与企业管理的关系问题上，尽管表述的方式各有不同，多数学者认为在制度安排的层级中，公司治理是高于企业管理的。

4.4.2 公司治理理论的主要内容和发展趋势

正如第1讲所指出的那样，公司治理是企业理论的重要组成部分。1932年，伯利和米恩斯在《现代公司与私有财产》一书中首次提出Berle—Means命题，也就是现代公司所有权分散以及所有权与控制权分离的问题❶（伯利，米恩斯，2005）。从那时开始，众多学者从不同角度对公司治理理论开展研究，形成了两权分离理论（伯利、米恩斯和钱德勒）、利益相关者理论（杜德、布莱尔）和超产权理论（法马、马丁、帕克）等不同研究范式。与此同时，公司治理的实践也在广度和深度两方面不断发展。由于受篇幅的限制，这里只简要介绍公司治理理论的主要框架。

公司治理理论主要关注两个问题。一是分散投资者的集体行动问题，二是不同的权益所有者之间利益冲突的调解问题。由于企业所有者（主要是股东）与管理者（经理层）的效用函数不一致，以及两者之间的信息不对称，前者需要通过公司治理对后者进行监督和控制。公司治理的核心问题是：如何确定哪些人应该参与公司治理？如何解决监管公司管理层的集体行动问题？如何规制公司收购和大投资者的行为？董事会应该如何构成？如何定义管理者的诚信责任❷？针对管理层的权力滥用，合适的法律行动是什么？所有这些问题都没有唯一的简单答案（Becht *et al.*，2005）。

在公司治理研究领域，对**内部治理**（internal governance）和**外部治理**（external governance）的划分得到普遍的认同。内部治理是针对公司内部参与者之间的权力制衡问题而做出的制度安排，涉及所有权结构、董事会及其下属委员会、内部控制、风险管理、透明性与财务报告等内容（Ahmed，2008）。外部治理主要是指公司外部的利益相关者所采用的各种控制措施，涉及代理表决权争夺❸、债务契约❹、公司绩效信息的公开与评估、政府规制、经理人市场、媒体压力、收购、兼并或直接购入股票等（Manne，1965；Becht *et al.*，2005）。无论是内部治理还是外部治理，都涉及各种有形的组织和无形的机制，正式和非正的制度安排。

在**治理结构**（governance structure）和**治理机制**（governance mechanism）的关系问题上，也存在不同看法。大部分人认为，治理结构是为了实现公司内部相互制衡而设置的组织机构或制度安排；股东大会、董事会和监事会等机构是治理结构的主要表现形式。治理机制包括激励机制、约束机制和决策机制。与治理结构相比，治理机制在内容上更广、在层次上更深（李维安，2001）。一些经济学家则把公司治理的本质理解为产权的安排。他们认为，完备的公司治理应该同时包括治理结构（产权安排）和治理机制两个层次。产权安排处于公司治理的基础地位，各种治理机制的设计与实施是实现公司治理目标的保障。前者向投资者提供投资的激励，后者向经理层提供经营

❶ 实际上，这一问题最早由亚当·斯密提出。他在1776年出版的《国富论》（即《国民财富的性质和原因的研究》）中指出，“作为其他人所有的资金的经营者，不要期望他会像自己所有的资金一样获得精心照顾。”（斯密，1997）

❷ 在英美的公司法中，诚信责任（fiduciary duties）主要是指公司董事和经理对股东及公司负有忠实和勤勉的义务。美国一些州的判例主张，公司股东之间也负有类似的义务。

❸ 代理表决权争夺（proxy voting contests）是指由不同股东组成的利益集团通过争夺股东的委托投票权，以获得股东大会的控制权，进而达到控制董事会和改变公司战略的行为。

❹ 债务契约（debt covenants）是指企业经理人员代表股东与债权人签订的、用于明确债权人和债务人双方权利和义务的一种法律文书，包括各种贷款契约、债券发行契约等。它的主要作用是限制经理人员的行为以保护债权人合法权益。

的激励（郑志刚，2004）。

在公司治理中经常采用的方法和措施有：（1）选举代表股东利益的董事会；CEO（Chief Executive Officer，总经理，首席执行官）为董事会负责；（2）恶意收购[1]或代理表决权争夺；（3）大宗股票持有者（银行、持股企业、养老基金等）持续的主动监控；（4）通过高管薪酬契约使管理层与投资者利益保持一致；（5）明确界定CEO的诚信责任，并辅之以集体诉讼（Becht *et al.*，2005）。

治理模式的比较研究是公司治理理论的一个重要方面。现代公司的治理模式主要有两种：一种是以英美为代表的“单层董事会”模式，另一种是以德国为代表的“双层董事会”模式。在英美模式中，董事会对股东大会负责，董事会下设若干委员会。该模式建立在证券市场主导的金融体制的基础之上；它的一个重要特点是借助证券市场的力量对经理层进行监督和激励。投资者通过抛售股票（即所谓的“用脚投票”），或者通过随时可能出现的恶意收购，使得公司经营管理者需要随时保持警惕。因此，英美模式又叫作“外部监控模式”。德国模式仿效政治上三权分立的做法，设置股东大会、执行董事会和监督董事会，分别作为公司的决策机构、执行机构和监督机构。执行董事会由执行董事组成，行使执行职能。监督董事会由非执行董事组成，行使监督职能。执行董事会的人选与政策目标由监督董事会决定。由此可见，监督职能高于执行职能（高程德，2000，p. 107）。德国模式建立在银行主导的金融体制的基础之上；它的一个重要特点是由银行和大股东直接监控公司。以银行为主的金融机构不但提供融资，而且控制公司的监事会，凭借内部信息优势发挥实际的控制作用。因此，德国模式又叫作“内部监控模式”。

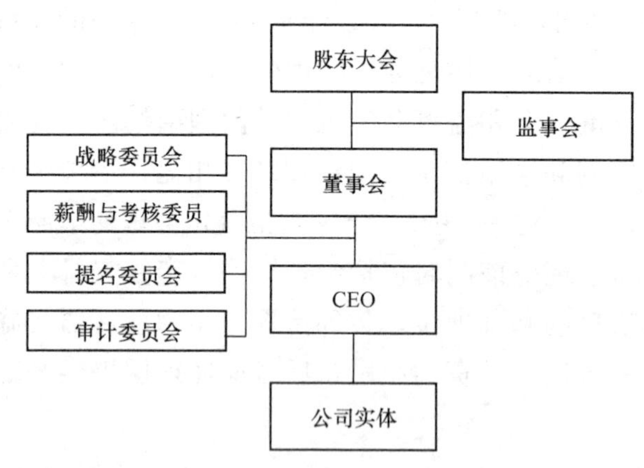

图 4.2　一个典型的公司治理结构

我国的公司法在法律形式和用语方面大体上使用德国的表达方式，而实际运作则与英美式“单层董事会”的制度相接近。也就是说，代表高层执行人员的执行董事（美国称为内部董事）和代表所有者及其他利害相关者的非执行董事（美国称外部董事）都在董事会中（吴敬琏，2001）。图4.2给出了一个典型的公司治理结构。股东大会拥有最终控制权，董事会（下设若干委员会）拥有实际控制权，监事会拥有监督权，经理层拥有经营权，这四种权力相互制约，共同形成公司的内部

[1] 恶意收购（hostile takeovers）又称敌意收购，是与善意收购相对的一种收购方式。它是指收购公司在未经目标公司董事会允许，不管对方是否同意的情况下所进行的收购活动。

治理。

近三十年来，公司治理理论沿着从单个公司到企业集团、从传统企业到网络组织的发展脉络，逐步形成了股权至上逻辑下的单边治理、利益相关者合作逻辑下的共同治理以及协同竞争逻辑下的网络治理等不同研究范式（李维安，王世权，2007）。公司治理的理论与实践已经从发达国家扩展到转型经济和新兴市场经济国家。研究内容从治理结构与治理机制扩展到治理模式与治理原则。公司治理质量与治理环境受到更多的关注。公司治理评价成为新的研究重点（李维安，2006）。

在我国，公司治理的理论研究和实践活动相互促进，相得益彰，取得了长足的进步。20 世纪 90 年代初，国内一部分经济学家就指出，现代企业制度的核心是公司治理结构。在 1999 年召开的中共中央十五届四中全会上，“法人治理结构”被正式写入有关国有企业改革的决定中。新公司法（2005 年 10 月）和新证券法（2005 年 10 月）的出台，以及国务院批转证监会“关于提高上市公司质量的意见”（2005 年 11 月）的发布，标志着国有企业改革进入了以公司治理为主要内容的新阶段。这方面具有代表性的研究成果和政策法规文件包括：《中国公司治理原则》（2000 年 11 月）、《独立董事制度指导意见》（2001 年 8 月）、《中国上市公司治理准则》（2002 年 1 月）、《关于上市公司股权分置改革的指导意见》（2005 年 8 月）、中国公司治理评价系统（2003 年 4 月）和中国公司治理指数（简称南开治理指数，$CCGI^{NK}$）（2004 年 2 月）等（李维安，2006）。在 2013 年 11 月中共中央十八届三中全会上通过的《关于全面深化改革若干重大问题的决定》重申了“健全协调运转、有效制衡的公司法人治理结构”的任务，并把它作为坚持和完善我国基本经济制度的重要内容。可以预期，我国在公司治理领域的实践将为公司治理理论增添新的内容，做出特殊的贡献。

4.5　结　　论

这一讲的内容可以沿着三条线索来解读。一是以威廉姆森为代表的新制度经济学的研究范式，二是以杰索普为代表的政治学的研究范式（狭义的治理），三是公司治理的相关理论与实践。本书对治理内涵的理解得益于对两个研究范式的比较、分析与整合。例如，在治理的基本属性（What）问题上，关键词“相对稳定的制度”出自新制度经济学的研究范式；而在治理方式与治理机制（How）问题上，关键词“对等协调”出自政治学的研究范式。公司治理的理论成果也为正确理解治理的内涵提供了很好的基础。只有博采众长，兼收并蓄，才能在较高层次上将不同范式的特色与精华融合起来，并且有所创新。

治理的目的是使具有不同目标函数的利益相关者“不同心而同力”（吴敬琏，2001）。有效的治理应该在以下四个方面发挥作用：（1）简化有关复杂性的模型和实践，（2）开发动态的社会知识，（3）建立协调行动的方法，（4）形成共同的世界观和元治理系统（Jessop，2003）。

在制度的层次结构中，治理处于承上启下的关键位置，因而是十分重要的。但是，治理也有其自身的局限性。一方面，治理受社会文化和基本制度环境的制约。例如，在公司治理领域，以英美为代表的“外部监控”模式和以德国为代表的“内部监控”模式之间的差异，实际上是这些国家在历史、政治、经济、法律和文化等方面诸多差异的反映。另一方面，治理也不能代替管理，并且受管理活动的影响。“重管理、轻治理”的做法固然不对，“重治理、轻管理”的做法也不足取。这是因为，管理活动是实现组织目标的“最后一公里”，离开有效的管理，设计再好的治理结构和治理机制也无济于事。因此，研究治理问题，需要和其他层次的制度联系起来，做到上下贯通和相互衔接。

参考文献

1. 伯利，米恩斯（2005）现代公司与私有财产，甘华鸣，罗锐韧，蔡如海译，北京：商务印书馆.
2. 波兰尼（2007）大转型：我们时代的经济与政治起源，中译本，冯钢，刘阳译，杭州：浙江人民出版社.
3. 布莱尔（1999）所有权和控制：重新思考二十一世纪的公司治理，中译本，张荣刚译，北京：中国社会科学出版社.
4. 费方域（1996）什么是公司治理？上海经济研究，(5) 36—39.
5. 高程德（2000）公司组织与管理，北京：北京大学出版社.
6. 戈丹（1999）现代的治理，昨天和今天：借重法国政府政策得以明确的几点认识，陈思译，国际社会科学，(中文版)，(2)，49—58.
7. 哈特（1996）公司治理：理论与启示，中译本，朱俊，汪冰，顾恒中译，经济学动态，(6) 60—63.
8. 何亚非（2014）全球治理的中国智慧和中国思想，中国新闻周刊，(43) 46—47.
9. 康芒斯（2009）制度经济学（上），中译本，于树生译，北京：华夏出版社.
10. 李维安（2001）公司治理，天津：南开大学出版社.
11. 李维安（2006）中国公司治理：从“违规”到合规，南开管理评论，(1)，3.
12. 李维安，王世权（2007）利益相关者治理理论研究脉络及其进展探析，外国经济与管理，**29** (4)，10—17.
13. 刘伟（1994）公司法人产权与治理结构，改革，(4)，50—60.
14. 罗西瑙（2001）没有政府的治理，中译本，张胜军，刘小林等译，南昌：江西人民出版社.
15. 马克思（1975）资本论，第一卷（上），中译本，中共中央马克思、恩格斯、列宁、斯大林著作编译局译，北京：人民出版社出版.
16. 沙凯逊（2010）建设项目理论重构初探：一个新制度经济学的视角，项目管理技术，**8** (3)，13—16.
17. 斯密（1997）国民财富的性质和原因的研究（上卷），中译本，郭大力，王亚南译，北京：商务印书馆.
18. 王凤彬（2009）科层组织中的异层级化趋向——基于宝钢集团公司管理体制的案例研究，管理世界，(2)，101—122.
19. 文件起草组（2013）中共中央关于全面深化改革若干重大问题的决定，北京：人民出版社.
20. 吴敬琏（1994）现代公司与企业改革，天津：天津人民出版社.
21. 吴敬琏（2001）我国公司治理结构存在的问题和改善的途径，载改革：我们正在过大关，139—150，北京：三联书店.

22. 易平（2015）奥巴马过生日 潘基文赠汉字书法“上善若水”，http：//news. 163. com/15/0807/14/ B0E0P7R00001121M. html，2015-8-7.
23. 俞可平（2000）治理与善治，北京：社会科学文献出版社.
24. 张维迎（1999）企业理论与中国企业改革，北京：北京大学出版社.
25. 郑志刚（2004）公司治理的内涵：治理结构和治理机制的分层，第四届中国制度经济学年会议论文，available at http：//www. unirule. org. cn/xiazai/2007082404. pdf，(accessed 12 October 2014）.
26. 周新军（2007）企业管理与公司治理：边界确定及实践意义，中南财经政法大学学报，（5），107—112.
27. Ahmed，N.（2008）*Internal and External Aspects of Corporate Governance*，Routledge Press，Abingdon，Oxon.
28. Becht，M.，Bolton，P. and Röell，A.（2005）*Corporate Governance and Control*，available at http：//ssrn. com/abstract_id= 343461，(accessed 2 December 2014).
29. Bevir，M.（2013）*Governance：A very short introduction*，Oxford University Press，Oxford，UK.
30. Commission on Global Governance（1995）*Our Global Neighbourhood：The Report of The Commission on Global Governance*，Oxford University Press，Oxford，UK.
31. Dayton，K. N.（1984）Corporative governance：the other side of the coin，*Harvard Business Review*，**62**（1），34—37.
32. Hedlund，G.（1986）The hypermodern MNC—A heterarchy? *Human Resource Management*，**25**（1），9—35.
33. Jessop，B.（1998）The rise of governance and the risks of failure：the case of economic development，*International Social Science Journal*，**50**（155），29—45.
34. Jessop，B.（2003）The Governance of complexity and the complexity of governance：preliminary remarks on some problems and limits of economic guidance，published by the Department of Sociology，Lancaster University，Lancaster LA1 4YN，available at http：//www. comp. lancs. ac. uk/sociology/papers/Jessop— Governance—of—Complexity. pdf，(accessed 2 October 2014).
35. Kettl，D. F.（1997）The global revolution in public management：driving themes，missing link，*Journal of Policy Analysis and Management*，**16**（3），446—462.
36. Manne，H. G.（1965）Mergers and the market for corporate control，*The Journal of Political Economy*，**73**（2），110—120.
37. Stoker，G.（1998）Governance as theory：five propositions，*International Social Science Journal*，**50**（155），17—28.
38. Tricker，R. I.（1984）*Corporate Governance：Practices，Procedures and Powers in British Companies and Their Boards of Directors*，The Corporate Policy Group，Gover Publishing Company Limited，Oxford，UK.
39. Williamson，O. E.（1988）Corporate finance and corporate governance，*The Journal of Finance*，**43**（3），567—591.
40. Williamson，O. E.（1991）Comparative economic organization：the analysis of discrete structural alternatives，*Administrative Science Quarterly*，**36**（2），269—296.

第 5 讲　建设项目及其理论分析框架

- □ 建设项目的存在是市场和科层组织失灵的结果；而两者失灵的主要原因又在于不确定性，以及由此产生的专业化需求和组织间协调的需求。
- □ 建设项目是由若干个法人单位组成的临时性的联合体。它的基本结构可以概括为由客户（Client）、设计方（Conception）、施工方（Construction）和控制方（Control）组成的 4C 模式。
- □ 把研究视角从管理的层面扩展到治理和体制的层面，这不仅是项目管理理论创新的内在要求，也是我国建筑业制度创新的必要条件。
- □ 从制度分析的角度出发，可以得出一种比较全面的“项目观”：建设项目不仅是一种过程，而且是一种组织；不仅是一种生产力，而且是一种生产关系；项目区别于企业的本质属性不仅在于它的一次性，而且在于它的适应性。
- □ 研究建筑业的绩效问题，既要面对企业和项目并存的事实，又涉及到管理、治理和体制三个不同的制度范畴。在这方面，面向双重对象的三层次分析框架具有较强的解释能力。
- □ 建设项目治理内生化意味着在立场、观点和方法论等方面的一系列根本性变化：研究立场由企业本位转为项目本位，研究重点从生产力转向生产关系，研究方法从瓦尔拉范式变为后瓦尔拉范式。
- □ 不同研究范式之间应该是相辅相成的互补关系而不是非此即彼的替代关系。在对不同流派进行多元整合的基础上，可以得到由两个基本研究范畴（项目管理和项目治理）和一个相关领域（建筑交易体制）组成的理论研究体系。

前面四讲介绍了项目的一般性质和治理的基本内涵。其中第 1 讲和第 2 讲从经济组织的角度分析了项目与市场、企业之间的不同；第 3 讲和第 4 讲则从制度的角度分析了治理与管理的区别和联系。从现在开始，本书进入建设项目这一主题。这一讲旨在建立一个关于建设项目的理论研究框架体系。后面的五讲将在这一框架内，按照“垂直治理—水平治理—针对项目经理的治理—关系治理与行业自律—交易体制动态演进”的逻辑展开。

作为一个完整的体系，建设项目理论需要回答以下问题。第一是项目的性质问题（为什么项目不能由企业或市场所取代），第二是项目的边界与规模问题（是将两个项目合并为一个、拆分为四个、还是保持两个不变），第三是如何实现项目绩效目标的问题——这是建设项目理论研究的根本所在，应该成为理论框架的主线。上述问题在许多方面超出了传统管理理论的范畴，需要在制度层面上研究解决。

这一讲首先介绍建设项目的起源。然后从建筑业的特殊性出发，进一步探讨建设项目存在的理由，以及建设项目与建筑专业体制的内在联系。接下来介绍建设项目的基本结构、建设项目的构造性分析框架和文化环境，以及建筑企业和建设项目的关系。然后对三种不同的研究范式——基于系统科学的、基于新制度经济学的和基于生产理论的研究范式——进行比较分析。最后讨论了建设项目治理内生化的问题，并针对建设项目研究领域存在的问题，提出理论重构的主要原则和新的框架体系。

5.1　建设项目的起源

项目是人类社会发展到一定程度才出现的组织形态，因而属于历史的范畴（Winch，2006）。现代意义上的建设项目最早出现在英国；它的出现与总承包模式、建筑专业体制（professional system in construction）的兴起密不可分。19 世纪初，在第一次工业革命浪潮的推动下，总承包（general contracting）第一次在英国的房屋建筑领域取代了传统的分工种承包（separate trades contracting）；建筑专业体制也从无到有地发展起来。到 19 世纪 60 年代，建设项目和 DBB（Design—Bid—Build，设计—招标—建造）模式成为英国建筑业最主要的组织形态和生产交易方式（Winch，2000）。

背景材料：现代建设项目的形成与发展（资料来源：Winch，2000，pp. 141—143）

英国建筑业最重要的特性之一是总承包出现得非常早——这种方式 19 世纪上半叶就在英国出现了，而欧洲大陆在二战之后才采用这种方式。房屋建造中的分工种承包最早产生于文艺复兴时期意大利的佛罗伦萨，它在 17 世纪初传到英国。随着 1666 年伦敦大火之后的城市重建以及乡村住房的重建，这种方式得到广泛应用。在工业革命，特别是英法战争的压力之下，分工种承包体制开始瓦解。为了向为抵抗法国而动员起来的大量士兵提供住宿，在 1793 年成立了营房建设办公室。最初，营房建设办公室还是依靠分工种承包的方式，但是由于任务紧迫，促使向总承包方式的转变，即由一个承包商在一个合同中对全部工作承担财务责任。这种方式要求建筑师在招投标之前就要完成设计，要求建立工料测量体系，要求技工脱离与建筑师的直接联系。

在土木工程领域，发展的轨迹有所不同，但是得到了与房屋建造领域同样的结果。这个世界上第一个工业化国家的运河和铁路等基础设施建设由私人创办为基础。创办者有时是土地所有者和其他利益方，但是在铁路工程中，创办者自己有时又是工程师。最初，实际工程被分解为若干部分，由当地承包商在工程师的监督下进行，但是到了 19 世纪 30 年代，承担更多责任的总承包商的角色出现了。在 25 世纪最后 25 年里，对土木工程项目合同的竞标成为普遍的方式。咨询工程师变得更为重要。

这种新兴体制的一个重要特征是总承包商，他承担别人构思的工作并受制于独立的第三方。作为第一次，客户能够有效地转移建设过程固有风险的项目参与者出现了。总承包商的崛起也刺激了一些“圈外”人士，促使他们在不同专业的基础上组织起来。在此期间，专业人士成立了许多机构——1818 年的土木工程师学会（ICE），1834 年的英国皇家建筑师学会（RIBA）和 1868 年的皇家特许测量师学会（RICS）等。

承包商与专业人士之间的动态关系是 19 世纪中叶英国总的发展趋势的一部分，也就是从企业家理念占支配地位、由斯密的“看不见的手”管控的社会向专业人士的理念占支配地位的社会的开端发展。在这个社会中，专业人士在公众利益方面对自由市场起到规制作用。

到 19 世纪 60 年代，这种专业体制成为一种规范。除非工程量是由经过认证的工料测量师提供的，任何正规的建筑企业都不会投标，而工程量的计算要求建筑师提供完整的施工图和详细说明。建筑师、工程师和工料测量师已经建立了他们自己的专业组织——这种组织形式被建筑业其他团体所钦羡和效仿，并在 1980 年皇家特许建造学会（CIOB）成立时达到巅峰状态。

从以上背景资料可以看出，建设项目是第一次工业革命的产物。当生产力发展到一定阶段，原有的生产关系不能适应建筑业发展的需要，必然引起新的社会分工和生产关系的变革，由新的生产关系（总承包、建筑专业体制、工程招投标）取代旧的生产关系（分工种承包）。正是在这种情况下，建设项目应运而生，成为现代建筑业的微观基础。

5.2 建设项目存在的理由

在本书的代序“组织间关系视角下的建设项目治理”一文中，已经涉及“项目为什么存在”的问题，并且得出以下结论：

> 正是由于客户独特而新颖的需求，以及复杂多变的商业环境，才使得“企业加市场”的常规模式失灵，进而导致新的经济组织形式——项目的出现。项目之所以有别于市场和企业，就在于它同时具备以下三个特征：不确定性、临时性和非重复性。

在第 2 讲中，除了重申以上观点之外，又增加了定制的因素：

> 临时性、不确定性和非重复性是项目的三个显著特征。这三个特征均源自定制这一基本属性，而客户独特、新颖的需求是产生定制的原因。

这一节从建筑业的特殊性出发，进一步探讨建设项目存在的理由，以及建设项目与建筑专业体制的内在联系。

在《企业的性质》一文中，科斯提出了“企业为什么存在”的问题：“既然人们通常认为协调要通过价格机制来实现，那么，为什么这样的组织（企业，本书作者注）是必需的呢?”（Coase，1937，p. 388）对这个问题的探究引发了经济学的一场革命——“科斯革命”。对于建设项目来说，也存在类似的问题：为什么建筑产品的生产要通过项目的形式进行，而不是像汽车和电视机的生产那样，在企业中进行?

汽车和电视机的生产和交易是按照“企业生产—市场交易”的序贯（sequential）模式进行的：企业根据市场需求组织生产，并将产品投放到市场进行销售；客户根据自己的需要在市场选购中意的产品。生产和交易都在价格机制这只“看不见的手”的指挥下进行；企业和客户各得其所，但是相互之间并不发生直接的关系。而建设项目则采用“企业＋市场”的混合（hybrid）模式：客户和企业直接签订合同；由若干企业组成的项目联合体可以看作是市场中的“准企业”（Eccles，1981），其中既有市场的因素（合同关系），又有企业的成分（指令关系）。正如前面所说，项目的存在可以归因于“企业生产—市场交易”这种常规模式的失灵。接下来的问题是：是什么因素使得常规模式失灵？下面的分析将表明，不确定性是最主要的原因。

在许多情况下，不确定性和风险被看作是同义词，并且不加区别地交互使用。实际上，这两个词是有差别的。奈特最早指出不确定性和风险之间的区别——他把可度量的不确定性叫作风险，把不可度量的不确定性叫作“真正的”不确定性：

> 风险和不确定性这两个范畴之间的实际区别是，在前一种情况下，一组事件中的结果的分布是已知的（或是通过先验的推定，或是出于对以往经验的统计）；而对于不确定性来说，情况就不同了，究其原因，通常是因为所处理的问题极为独特，因而无法形成一组事件。（Knight，1921，p. 233）

从博弈论的角度看，不确定性是“自然”或虚拟参与人隐藏信息或隐藏行动的结果，并且这些结果是不可度量的，因而属于“未知的未知”（unknown unknowns）[1]。在远古时代，我们的先人面对不确定性，只能求助于占卜和神明。宗教的产生正是源于人们对未知或不可知的敬畏之心。在宗教信条中，不确定性是神的特质（李向平，2006）。在现代经济管理的语境中，不确定性的问题要通过有组织的经济活动来解决。奈特认为，归类合并和专业化是处理不确定性的两种基本方法；前者导致了企业的产生，后者将处理不确定性的职能集中在某些人和某些阶层的手中，由此产生了企业家；利润可以看作是对企业家承担不确定性的一种报偿。如果说，归类合并是对“事”的分类，那么，专业化则是对“当事人”的选择：

---

[1] 所谓“未知的未知”是指某些事情，它们不仅是未知的，而且人们不知道这些事情是他们所未知的。与此相对应，还有所谓的“已知的已知”（known knowns）、“已知的未知”（known unknowns）和“未知的已知”（unknown knowns）。

单个的面粉厂主或棉纺厂主可能只在市场交易一次，而投机商则是千百次地进入市场，因而他的判断错误肯定会表现出相应较强的相互抵消的趋势，因而使其工作有一个可预计的稳定回报。(Knight，1921，p. 256)

奈特的这一论断在建筑业中得到了充分印证。建筑业面临的不确定性当中，有许多是其他行业所没有的。例如，由市场需求波动和单件生产造成的任务不确定性，由气象、地质等因素造成的工程不确定性，由预算误差造成的合同不确定性等（Winch，1989）。在这种情况下，有关各方都缺少决策所需要的信息，信息短缺的问题成为主要矛盾。如此之多的不确定性对专业化提出了很强的需求。面向建筑业的专业注册资格多达十几个种类❶，远远超过其他行业，原因就在于此。

背景材料：

建筑物的大小和复杂程度的变化是没有穷尽的。与许多其他行业的产品相比，建筑物的生产在一种相对难以控制的环境下进行，因此，在建设项目中出现这样那样的问题是不足为奇的。例如，在其他行业，有多少管理者需要考虑秃鹫的繁育习性？这个问题似乎是可笑的。但是，承担美国怀俄明州蛇谷（Snake Canyon）高速公路施工任务的承包商就不得不停工六个月，这是因为这个地方是秃鹫的重要栖息地。这就意味着承包商必须在整个冬季施工，必须采用在零度以下施工的特殊技术（Loosemore，2000，p. 20）。

大量触目惊心的工程事故是建筑业不确定性的真实写照。且不说发展中国家，即便是在发达国家，此类事故也不能幸免。在1875年前的一段时间里，美国屡屡发生大坝、桥梁坍塌等恶性事故，平均每年有25座桥梁坍塌（沙凯逊等，2003）。20世纪以来，尽管科学技术有了巨大的进步，管理水平有了极大的提高，建筑领域的灾难性事故仍然不断发生（Loosemore，2000）：

- 1907年加拿大魁北克大桥在施工过程中发生结构性坍塌，造成82名建筑工人死亡；
- 1940年美国塔科马峡谷悬索桥坍塌；
- 1967年美国俄亥俄州银桥（Silver Bridge）坍塌，造成46名汽车乘客死亡；
- 1970年澳大利亚墨尔本西门大桥（West Gate Bridge）坍塌；
- 1981年美国堪萨斯市凯悦饭店的两条高架通道坍塌，造成113人死亡，186人严重受伤；

---

❶ 建筑业的专业注册师制度是通行的国际惯例。我国建筑业目前就设有注册建筑师、注册结构工程师、注册设备工程师、注册监理工程师、注册造价师、注册估价师、注册建造师等专业资格。

• 1995 年韩国购物中心倒塌，造成 501 人死亡，900 多人受伤。

这些事故似乎在不停地提醒人们：在一个充满不确定性的世界里，唯一可以确定的事情就是不确定性。不确定性对建筑业的影响以及建筑业与不确定性之间的较量永远不会停止。

以上分析表明，建筑业所面临的不确定性既多又强，由此导致独具特色的建筑专业体制。专业化意味着**资产专用性**（asset specification），资产专用性则使交易双方之间的关系发生所谓的“根本性转变”（fundamental transformation）——由相互独立转变为相互依存。此时，个人的效用函数不仅取决于本人的决策，而且依赖于他人的选择。

科斯在讨论企业规模时指出，在企业内部组织某些交易的成本似乎也有可能大于在公开市场上完成的交易的成本（Coase，1937）。将众多的专业组织整合到一家企业中（纵向一体化），固然可以降低市场上的交易成本，但是会导致企业内部协调成本的增加。因此，如果需要整合的关系太多，单靠一家企业的力量也是不行的，而是需要多家企业联合完成。

更为重要的一点是，由于不确定性和复杂性，建筑产品的最终形式和生产过程不可能在一开始就完全定义清楚，各个环节之间存在相互依存关系，客户与企业之间，以及多家企业之间需要保持沟通与协调。在这种情况下，项目联合体这种新的组织形式就产生了。由于项目联合体兼具市场和科层的特点，它能将不同的专业组织有效整合在一起。

为了进一步说明问题，不妨对农业和建筑业做一个简单比较。我们的问题是：既然这两个行业都面临着大量的不确定性，为什么项目这种组织形式在建筑业得到广泛应用，而在传统农业生产中却很少出现？为了回答这个问题，需要从这两个行业的生产性质入手。农业生产一方面在很大程度上是靠“天”吃饭的（“自然”隐藏信息或隐藏行动），另一方面又是年复一年重复进行的，许多方面的概率是可以知道的（可以度量），因而属于风险的范畴，这类问题可以通过风险决策和保险的方法来解决。建筑业的生产活动中存在大量新颖、独特的一次性任务，许多不确定性是“自然”造成的，并且是不可度量的，因此属于“真正的”不确定性。这种任务要求较高的专业化水平，需要多个组织合作完成，因此采用项目联合体的形式。

综上所述，建设项目的存在是市场和科层组织失灵的结果；而两者失灵的主要原因又在于不确定性以及由此产生的专业化需求和组织间协调的需求。正如英国学者温奇（Winch，2006）所说，不确定性是建设项目存在的重要理由。如果不确定性不大，建筑业就没有必要采用项目的方式进行生产。由于不确定性和昂贵的信息成本，客户不得不把决策权让渡给承包商和专业人士。为了调动承包商和专业人士正确决策的积极性，客户需要付出一定的代理成本。把大量处理不确定性的职能整合到一家总承包企业内，还是分散到若干个专业公司（设计师事务所、专业分包商、劳务分包商）中去，这取决于信息成本和代理成本之间的平衡，也取决于资源、能力与态度之间的匹配（沙凯逊等，2009b）。

5.3 建设项目及其制度分析层次

第2讲已经指出，根据项目与其发起者或母组织之间的关系，项目可以分为Ⅰ型和Ⅱ型两种类型。前者是企业间组织（inter-firm organization），后者是企业内组织（intra-firm organization）。建设项目属于典型的Ⅰ型项目。它是由若干个企业或单位组成的临时性的联合体（temporary coalition）。项目联合体涉及众多的利益相关者，如客户、承包商、供应商、设计单位和咨询单位等。它们都是独立的法人单位，拥有不同的战略目标、长远利益和自主决策的能力。项目联合体成员之间通过相互依存的合作关系，达到整合资源、节约成本、创造价值的目的。

5.3.1 建设项目的基本结构

温奇（Winch，2002）把现代建设项目的基本结构描述为由设计方（Conception）、施工方（Construction）和控制方（Control）组成的3C结构。这个结构中没有包括建设项目的母组织——客户（Client）；然而，对于项目治理模型来说，客户这个角色是不可或缺的。研究表明，项目法人缺失造成的市场参与者行为不规范是建筑业利润率低下的主要原因（沙凯逊，2009）。对客户行为的分析，应该成为我国建设项目治理研究的重点。基于以上考虑，沙凯逊和孙晓冰（2009）把3C结构扩展为图5.1所示的4C结构。在建设项目的众多结构形式中，4C结构具有典型意义，其他许多模式都可以由此演变和派生出来。

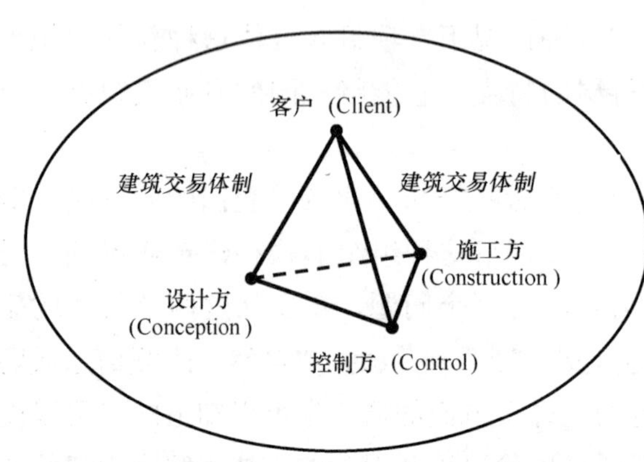

图5.1 建设项目的4C结构及其制度环境

（资料来源：沙凯逊，孙晓冰，2009）

作为项目的发起者，客户位于4C结构的顶端。在建设项目的诸多利益主体中，客户是矛盾的主要方面。建筑企业是典型的基于项目的经济组织。建筑企业和建设项目互为存在的前提；两者之间存在耦合[1]关系。建筑交易体制（construction business system）是建设项目和建筑企业运行的外部环境，也是项目管理和项目治理的制度基

[1] 耦合（coupling）原本是一个物理学的概念，这里被用来说明建筑企业和建设项目之间相互匹配、相互制约、共同发挥作用的效应。

础。研究建设项目，需要综合考虑项目的甲方、乙方和第三方之间，建筑企业和建设项目之间，以及体制、治理和管理三个层次之间的联系和相互影响关系。

5.3.2　建设项目的构造性分析框架

在威廉姆森的分析框架中，制度分为四个范畴或层次：(1) 社会基础或文化基础，(2) 基本制度环境，(3) 治理制度，(4) 短期的资源配置 (Williamson，2000)。如图 5.2 所示，在建设项目研究领域，温奇 (Winch，2010) 的构造性 (tectonic) 分析框架由体制、治理和过程三个层次组成 (过程层的内容与项目管理的范畴相对应)。图中的两组弧形箭头显示了不同层次之间的互动关系——右边的两个弧形箭头表示体制层对治理层、治理层对过程层的作用；左边的两个弧形箭头则表示过程层对治理层、治理层对体制层的反作用。

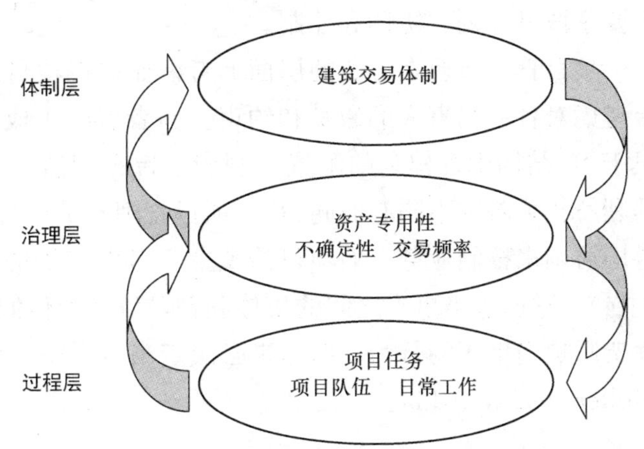

图 5.2　建设项目的构造性分析框架

(资料来源：Winch，2010，p. 11，Figure 1. 5)

建筑交易体制是建筑市场中不同利益主体之间进行博弈的一整套规则，它本身又是在博弈中产生的，是与工程质量低劣和腐败现象长期斗争的产物 (沙凯逊，邓晓红，2001)。建筑交易体制涉及国家法律体系、政府采购政策、建筑法规、劳动市场法规和地方法规。它的任务是提供正确的制度环境，协调各方关系，从而达到降低风险，增进合作，减少交易费用的目的。

根据交易成本理论，资产专用性、不确定性和交易频率是考虑经济组织治理结构的三个主要维度。有关项目治理的定义一般包括两重含义：(1) 项目治理为某些行为提供一种结构，这些行为包括：设定项目目标，确定实现项目目标的措施，确定监控项目绩效的措施；(2) 项目治理代表了包括业主和承包商在内的利益相关者的利益 (Clarke，2004；Turner，2006)。第一重含义讲的是项目治理的功能；第二重含义讲的是项目治理的目的。温奇 (Winch，2001) 把建设项目治理分为垂直治理和水平治理。国内有的学者把工程项目治理分为内部治理和外部治理。在他们看来，内部治理是体现投资主体与其他工程项目直接利益群体之间的内部决策过程和各利益相关者参与项目治理的方法和途径；外部治理是以工程项目其他利益相关者所构成的外部市场环境来约束工程项目直接利益主体。外部市场环境一般包括政府管理部门及其制定的法律法规、劳动力市场、技术市场、金融市场等 (王华，尹贻林，2004；严玲，赵黎明，2005)。由此可见，这里所说的外部治理在很大程度上相当于本书中建筑交易体制的范畴。

英国皇家特许建造学会（CIOB，2002）对项目管理的定义是：

为了在规定时间内按照核定成本和质量标准完成一个经济实用的项目，对项目从开始到结束的所有计划、协调和控制，旨在满足客户的需要[1]。

从中可以看出，建设项目管理的主要内容是工期、造价和质量（所谓的“铁三角”），主要手段是计划、协调和控制。

项目管理主要在方法的层面上考虑如何把项目做好；项目治理主要在动机的层面上考虑对各方当事人的激励和约束。前者着眼于成本、质量、工期三大目标；后者着眼于4C结构中责权利的配置与制衡，旨在营造一种制度环境，使具有不同目标函数的利益相关者“不同心而同力”。项目管理侧重于日常工作的执行，在战术层面上通过科层协调来控制业务；而项目治理主要考虑组织的战略目标（Biesenthal and Wilden，2014），它追求当事人之间的集体利益，以及使他们自愿服从治理体系框架的意愿，该框架影响当事人的行为，但是未必决定当事人每一个具体的行动（Clegg *et al.*，2002；Müller *et al.*，2014）。

5.3.3 建设项目的文化环境

建设项目和建筑交易体制都是在一定的社会历史文化背景下形成和发展起来的。因此，各国的建筑交易体制和建设项目管理模式无不打上文化的烙印。文化无形，却能以文“化”人。中西方文化之间存在很大不同。我国的传统文化重视家庭和宗族关系，长幼之间论资排辈，等级森严；而西方文化崇尚人格独立，长幼之间平等相处，较少计较老少界限。以姓名为例。中国人的姓在前、名在后，表现出集体主义精神和整体性的（holistic）思维方式；西方人的姓在后、名在前，凸显了人个人主义情节和分析性的（analytic）思维习惯。

背景材料：

《天涯晚笛》（苏炜，2013）一书说的是“民国时代最后一位才女”、合肥“张家四姐妹”中的小妹——张充和的故事。张充和兄弟姐妹十人，张家为这些孩子起名时，除了第三个字是表示辈分的“和”字之外，女孩名字的第二个字都带上了“两条腿”（元、允、兆、充），意味着女大不中留，注定要跟人家走；男孩名字的第二个字都有象征着家族的“宝盖头”（宗、寅、定、宇、寰、宁），表示男孩应当留在家里。显然，张家在给孩子的起名时把宗族情节发挥到了极致。

---

[1] 该定义的英文原文是：The overall planning，co-ordination and control of a project from inception to completion，aimed at meeting a client's requirements in order to produce a functionally and financially viable project that will be completed on time，within authorized cost and to the required quality standards.

从中国象棋和国际象棋的比较中，也能看出中西方文化的差异。在中国象棋中，“楚河汉界”划定了以将（帅）为中心的势力范围。将（帅）及其贴身护卫都有自己的活动范围，不能越雷池半步。这在很大程度上体现了定居民族生活空间的不变性，以及谨慎求稳、固守秩序的思想。而在国际象棋中，王到哪里，国家就到哪里；哪一方胜利，所有的地盘就都是它的属地。这折射出游牧民族随处而安，适应生活环境变化的特点，以及西方传统思想中勇于探险和挑战、鼓励个人奋斗的精神。

一般来讲，西方人具有较强的个人权利意识、契约意识和职业精神，遵循“法—理—情”的行事逻辑；而中国人注重族群关系、强调家国同构、礼法同构，具有按照“情—理—法”的逻辑办事的倾向（李东，2008）。根据行为科学中的动机与激励理论，人的行为是由动机引起的，而动机是由于人们本身内在的需要而产生的。不同的文化背景会导致不同的价值取向和需求。

背景材料：中美两国职工需求的跨文化比较研究（资料来源：喻春生等，1989. 141—143）

1988 年，中外学者针对职工在工作中需求的问题，在中国东部丝织、机械、制药、日用化工等行业的工厂，以及美国东南部地区的若干电力公司进行了问卷调查。结果见下表。

序列	美国样本（$N=454$）			中国样本（$N=301$）		
	项目	分值	%	项目	分值	%
1	能有作为，获得自我实现感	1205	17.7	工资和奖金较高	697	15.4
2	能做出成绩，获得成就感	667	9.8	能发挥我的才能	610	13.5
3	能发挥我的才能	636	9.3	有所作为，获得自我实现感	483	10.7
4	能从事有挑战性的工作	565	8.3	福利待遇较好	469	10.4
5	能做有意义的工作	509	7.5	能体现个人的价值	297	6.6
6	工资和奖金较高	494	7.3	工作有保障，职业稳定	249	5.5
7	能因为工作出色而受到表扬	411	6.0	能从工作中得到友情	208	4.6
8	工作有保障，职业稳定	401	5.9	有自信心	181	4.0
9	能晋级与提升	365	5.4	能做成绩，获得成就感	179	4.0
10	能体现个人价值	359	5.3	能做有意义的工作	173	4.0
11	有竞争感	225	3.3	有责任感	168	3.7
12	有责任感	221	3.2	能晋级与提升	157	3.5
13	能解决一些工作中的问题	162	2.4	地位较高	152	3.4
14	有自信心	153	2.2	能作重要的决策	93	2.1
15	感觉到是企业的成员，有归属感	110	1.6	能从事有挑战性的工作	92	2.0
16	能做重要的决策	109	1.6	有竞争感	92	2.0
17	福利待遇好	104	1.5	能解决一些工作中的问题	92	2.0
18	能得到别人的赏识和赞扬	48	0.7	感觉到是企业成员，归属感	92	2.0
19	能从工作中得到友情	38	0.6	能得到别人的赏识和赞扬	31	0.7
20	地位较高	28	0.4	能因为工作出色而受到赞扬	12	0.3

研究结果表明，在中美两国样本中有一些相当显著的差异。第一，在美国样本中，“工资和奖金较高”这一项不在最重要的5项需求之中，而在中国样本中，它却被是第一位的需求。第二，在美国样本中被列为第17位的“福利待遇较好”，在中国样本中却被列为第4位。第三，“能因为工作出色而受到赞扬”这一项，在美国样本中被列为第7位，而在中国样本中却被列为第20项中的最后一项。第四，“能从工人中得到友情”这一项，在中国样本中被列为第7位，而在美国样本中却被列为第19位。

我国的建筑交易体制和建设项目管理模式基本上是按照国际惯例，也就是工业发达国家的经验建立起来的。经过30多年的改革与发展，我国初步形成了以项目法人责任制、招标投标制、工程监理制和合同管理制为核心的工程建设管理体制框架。然而，建设市场的混乱局面表明，我们在制度设计上存在不少漏洞。建设项目法人缺位、招标投标流于形式、工程监理形同虚设、阴阳合同以假乱真的现象时有发生；与建设项目有关的贪污腐败行为屡禁不止；当初作为社会公正的重要符号而大力发展的中介组织，在不少地方和领域异化为腐败的温床，甚至蜕变为新的社会腐败主体。人们不禁要问，为什么这些国际通行的办法在我国建筑业的实施效果会大打折扣？古人说得好：“橘生淮南则为橘，生于淮北则为枳，叶徒相似，其实味不同。所以然者何？水土异也”。且不说基本制度的不同，单是文化上的差异就足以造成“水土不服”。学习和借鉴国外经验切忌食洋不化。所谓国际惯例，实际上主要是西方发达国家在长期的生产和交易过程中形成的一套游戏规则。我国的社会制度和文化背景与西方国家存在巨大差异，对此应该有充分的认识。

5.4 建设项目与建筑企业的关系

如前所述，基于项目的组织可以分为Ⅰ型和Ⅱ型两种类型。建筑企业把建设项目作为自己的主要业务，属于典型的Ⅰ型企业。作为项目的承揽者，建筑企业是客户雇佣的法人组织。如图5.3所示，围绕着建筑产品的生产和交易，建筑企业与建设项目之间形成网络关系。从企业的角度看，一家建筑企业可以组建多个项目部，同时参与不同的建设项目——请注意，正如第2讲所指出的那样，这些项目不能被理解为“项目群”。这些项目部各自进行独立核算，其内部是科层结构。建筑企业下属的各个项目部之间是共享/合伙式的相互依存关系（pooled interdependence）。同一家企业中不同项目部之间的协调就是图5.3中水平方向的“企业协调”。从项目的角度看，一个建设项目是由若干企业组成的联合体。项目联合体不是独立的经济

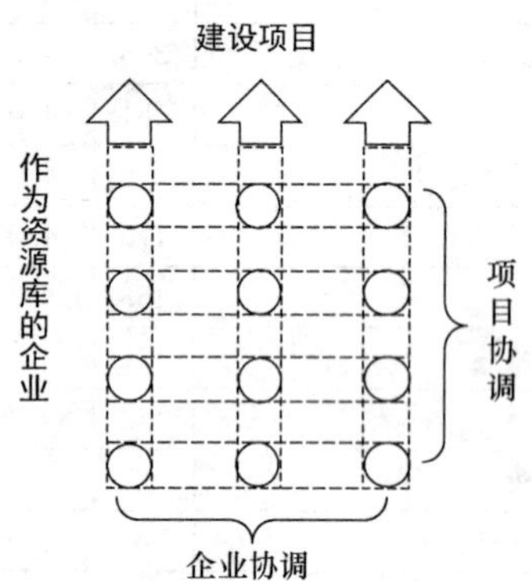

图5.3 建筑企业与建设项目之间的网络关系
（资料来源：Winch，2010，p. 9，Figure 1.4）

实体（Winch，1989）。联合体内部不同企业的短期目标和利益是相同的（共同努力把项目做好），而长期目标和利益未必相同；它们之间的关系基本上是市场交易关系，而不是科层关系。同一个项目联合体中不同企业之间的协调就是图 5.3 中垂直方向的"项目协调"。在管理和治理两个层面上，建筑企业和建设项目存在耦合关系。

建筑企业和建设项目之间的耦合是通过项目经理部实现的。建筑企业与项目经理之间的关系，在理论上属于上下级之间的科层关系，但在实际上并非这么简单。与一般企业中的车间主任相比，项目经理的责任和权力要大得多。由于建筑项目的分散性、流动性、复杂性和不确定性，企业不得不把相当大的决策权让渡给项目经理，与此同时，在权责分配、信息沟通、激励与控制等方面带来一系列新的问题。企业和项目之间能否实现良性互动，取决于决策权和剩余索取权的一致性。

5.5　面向双重对象的三层次分析框架

这个分析框架是在对我国建筑业"规模—利润率之谜"的探析过程中提出来的。利润水平低下是我国建筑业的老大难问题。针对这一顽症，业界人士不知开出了多少处方，至今却收效甚微。一方面，调整产业结构、改善市场行为的呼声日益高涨，另一方面却出现企业规模越大、利润率越低的反常现象（贾洪，赵宏彦，2008）。统计数据表明，2001 年以来的资质管理办法改变了我国建筑业的市场结构，但没有从根本上改善市场主体的行为和行业绩效。如表 5.1 所示，对总承包商而言，特级、一级企业的利润率不如二、三级或者三级以下的企业；对专业承包商而言，企业资质越低，利润率反而越高。于是就有了"规模—利润率之谜"：按照产业组织理论，企业规模扩张的动力应该是利润率的提高，而我国建筑企业的状况与产业组织理论相背离。

建筑企业利润率比较　　**表 5.1**

企业类型与等级		利润率（%）		
		2002 年	2004 年	2005 年
总承包企业	特级	1.56	2.22	2.62
	一级	1.24	1.68	1.68
	二级	2.03	2.58	2.78
	三级	2.14	3.03	3.26
	平均	1.71	2.25	2.38
专业分包企业	一级	2.89	2.9	3.04
	二级	3.19	3.86	4.11
	三级	4.00	5.11	5.50
	平均	3.38	3.93	4.15

（资料来源：贾洪，赵宏彦，2008）

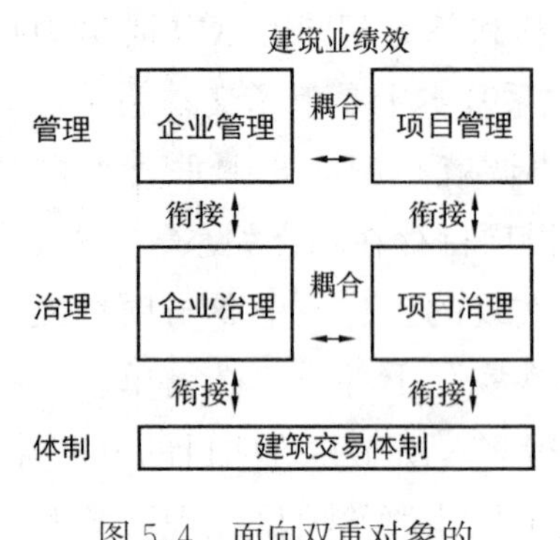

图 5.4 面向双重对象的三层次分析框架

（资料来源：沙凯逊，杨杰，2009）

研究建筑业的绩效问题，既要面对企业和项目并存的事实，又涉及管理、治理和体制三个不同的制度范畴。在这方面，图 5.4 给出的面向双重对象的三层次分析框架是一个有用的工具。该框架在横向上包含企业和项目两种组织形式，在纵向上分为管理、治理和体制三个层次，并且把横向耦合与纵向衔接关系纳入研究视野，从而大大拓宽了思路。从这个分析框架出发，可以得到一条绩效链。该链条以建筑交易体制为起点，以行业绩效为终点，在治理与管理两个中间环节上，存在着企业和项目两条平行的轴线。于是就有了一个基于绩效链的分析思路：行业绩效不佳，一定是在绩效链的某些环节上出了问题（沙凯逊，杨杰，2009）。

从企业与项目之间的耦合关系来看，当前存在的突出问题是，以包代管的现象普遍存在，部分项目经理权力过大，甚至出现项目经理部法人化、企业管理空心化的倾向。项目盈利而企业亏损的情况时有发生，建筑企业的利润中心地位有其名而无其实。此外，不少大型建筑企业盲目追求市场规模，出让资质、私招乱聘，结果是虚高的产值和恶化的利润水平。

从体制、治理和管理之间的衔接关系来看，体制、治理和管理三个层次之间存在脱节现象；特别是在项目治理领域，在理论和实践两方面都严重滞后。此外，建筑交易体制也不能充分适应于我国的国情。体制与社会文化背景之间的关系犹如“皮”与“毛”的关系。皮之不存，毛将焉附。一些经过精心设计并大力推行的管理方法和改革措施之所以不能取得预期效果，各种“潜规则”之所以大行其道，其源盖出于此。

总之，企业与项目之间关系不顺，体制、治理和管理之间的脱节，以及建筑交易体制对国情的不适应，是造成我国建筑业规模不经济的主要原因。这些缺陷导致建设项目法人缺失，进而形成压级压价、垫资施工和拖欠工程款的“三座大山”。这些正是“劣币驱逐良币”的原因所在——尽管大企业的企业管理、项目管理和公司治理的水平一般要比小企业高，但是在“三座大山”的压迫之下，利润水平反而不如小企业（沙凯逊，2009）。由此可见，要解决我国建筑业“大而不强”的问题，必须在项目治理和制度环境的改善方面下功夫。

5.6 多重视角下的建设项目研究范式

随着建设项目本身及其实施环境的变化以及相关理论的发展，研究视角正在从生产成本扩展到交易成本，从项目的实施过程扩展到项目的组织模式和激励机制，从企业内的科层关系扩展到企业间的合同关系。在这种背景下，建设项目被赋予更多的含义：生产系统、临时性的组织、信息处理系统、有益的变化等。在建设项目研究领域，目前主要有基于系统科学的范式、基于新制度经济学的范式和基于生产理论的范式三种流派。在绪言和第 2 讲中已经涉及这些流派，这里再做一些必要的补充。

5.6.1 基于系统科学的范式

基于系统科学的范式把建设项目看作是一种独特的一次性任务或过程，把项目活动作为基本分析单元，把系统科学和运筹学的原理和方法作为主要分析工具。该范式以美国项目管理协会（PMI）的项目管理知识体系（PMBoK）为代表。

在 PMBoK 的框架内，项目管理是知识、技能工具和技术在项目活动中的应用，它在技术层面上发挥组织内部不同职能之间的“统一总管”（unifying agent）的作用，旨在满足利益相关者对项目的需求（已经明确的要求）和期望（尚未明确的要求），并在以下几个方面，即项目的范围、时间、成本和质量之间、具有不同需求和期望的利益相关者之间以及需求和期望之间取得平衡（Duncan，1996；Turner，1993）。范围管理是项目成败的关键，范围定义则是通过工作分解结构（WBS，Work Breakdown Structure）实现的；因此，WBS 被认为是项目管理的中心环节（Morris，1994）。

PMBoK 实际上隐含了以下假设：项目范围和方法的不确定性不大，项目活动之间的关系简单并且前后衔接，项目活动之间的边界是刚性的，根据标准进行的控制可以保证活动的结果。这些假设在带来分析便利性的同时，也产生了较大的局限性（Koskela and Howell，2002）。

5.6.2 基于新制度经济学的范式

基于新制度经济学的范式把建设项目看作是以合同作为章程的临时性多边组织（Winch，1989），把交易作为基本分析单元，以交易成本理论、委托代理理论和不完全合同理论作为主要分析工具。该范式认为，项目实质上是一种组织创新，是交易各方之间的一种相互依存的资产与能力的合作关系；不确定性（信息短缺）是项目组织的核心问题，降低交易成本是项目组织的主要目标。

临时性多边组织这一命题的提出为新制度经济学和其他前沿理论的应用开启了门户。温奇（Winch，2001）提出的概念性框架将客户与一阶供应商（first-tier suppliers）之间的交易关系归入垂直交易治理；将水平交易治理归结为一阶供应商之后的供应链关系。荷兰学者特纳和基根（Turner and Keegan，2001）从交易成本的视角分析了四种不同治理结构下的项目治理机制、角色和责任。特纳（Turner，2004）对建设项目垂直治理的研究从两个维度上展开：项目采购方式（project procurement route，PPR）和支付方式（合同类型）；该研究修正了威廉姆森“工作成本与契约形式无关”的假设，并在此基础上研究建设项目合同形式的多样性以及不同合同的事前激励和事后治理机制。

各种类型的博弈模型在基于新制度经济学的范式中得到广泛的应用。在建设项目垂直治理的研究领域，沙凯逊（Sha，2011）将不确定性和信息成本纳入分析框架，用委托代理模型分析建设项目的采购方式和契约类型。研究结果表明，信息缺口和信息的相对成本系数是决定建设项目治理结构和报酬结构的重要因素。在研究对承包商的激励强度时，有人利用委托代理模型分析建设合同中风险分担的最优比例。研究表明，合同破裂的风险对承包商激励具有重要的影响作用（Chang，2014）。在水平治理的研究中，沙凯逊（2011）把项目联盟看作是合作博弈的均衡结果，把决策者处理信息的能力以及寻找合作伙伴的方式作为决定治理结构的重要影响因素。引入重置成本的概念，将参与人的谈判能力内生化，并在建设项目 3C 结构的基础上构建联盟博弈模型。应该看到，博弈模型都是建立在抽象的基础之上，因此不可避免地具有局限性，然而，它们却可以提供强大的洞察力，可以告诉我们研究的方向。

5.6.3 基于经济学还是基于生产：两种范式的对话

2006 年，基于生产理论的范式和基于新制度经济学的范式以学术期刊 *Building Research and Information* 为平台，展开了建设性的批评与反批评。首先是精益项目管理的代表人物科斯克拉和巴拉德（Koskela and Ballard，2006）对基于新制度经济学的范式提出质疑。他们的主要批评对象是温奇的代表作《管理建设项目：一种信息处理的方法》（Winch，2002），同时也涉及对交易成本理论和组织理论的批评。如表 5.2 所示，科斯克拉和巴拉德把温奇的观点称为基于经济学的项目管理，把自己的观点称为基于生产的项目管理，并且对这两种方法进行了对比。

基于经济学和基于生产的项目管理　　表 5.2

	基于经济学的项目管理	精益生产的项目管理
对项目性质的基本假设	通过交易而形成的一体化组织	生产系统
对项目的概念化	信息处理系统	转化、流、价值
内在目标	减少不确定性（也就是消除信息短缺）	生产房屋和设施、消除浪费、增加价值
管理性质	形成合同结构和组织结构	生产系统的设计、运行与改进

资料来源：Koskela and Ballard（2006）

在回应文章中，温奇（Winch，2006）把科斯克拉和巴拉德对他的批评归结为四点。一是重视交易而忽视生产；二是重视信息流而忽视物质流；三是把减少不确定性作为项目的核心问题；四是对组织所采用的构造性方法（tectonic approach）。关于前两个问题，温奇认为，交易成本理论所要解决的主要是“生产/购买”（make/buy）的决策问题，以及生产交易过程采用何种治理机制（市场/科层/混合）的问题，这些问题是任何建设项目都无法回避的，也是生产理论难以解决的。项目是由客户、设计方、承包商和供应商等“资源库”（resource base）组成的联合体。项目管理不同于资源库管理，前者的任务主要是协调“资源库”之间的交易关系，因此要重视信息流的作用；后者的任务主要是进行物质生产，因此要重视物质流的作用。关于不确定性，温奇指出，不确定性是项目存在的重要理由；如果不确定性不大，就没有必要采用项目管理的方式。不确定性会对组织及其生产系统产生重要影响。关于组织的构造性方法，温奇把信息处理和组织结构之间的关系比喻为河水与河床的关系：为了发挥河水发电的潜力，需要修建大坝；同样，为了改变信息流，就需要改变组织结构。

此外，温奇还对基于生产理论的范式所采用的 TFV（转化/流/价值）分析框架提出了四点批评。一是过分注重物质生产过程；二是分析中缺乏组织的概念；三是缺乏对风险和不确定性的分析；四是对价值的理解过于单一。关于价值，温奇认为，在建设项目中价值具有三方面的意义：对客户（买方）的贡献、对供应方（卖方）的贡献以及对社会的贡献。这三个方面有时会出现矛盾。例如，修建马路对政府和行人改善交通是有利的，但是可能会对周边的居民和自然环境带来不利影响。因此，只考虑第一种价值是片面的。

毫无疑问，不同范式之间的交流与对话是十分有益的。然而，上述对话双方似乎只是站在各自的立场上进行思辨，缺乏从总体上把握建设项目理论体系的高度。之所以出现这种情况，可能是因为争辩双方都忽略了以下事实：建设项目理论本身是分层次的；不同层次的问题需要采用不同的视角和方法，不能笼统地混为一谈。首先，科斯克拉和巴拉德的文章题目——项目管理应该以经济学理论还是以生产理论为基础？（Should project management be based on theories of economics or production?）——本身就是值得质疑的；这是因为，基于经济学的学派的研究对象主要是项目治理问题，并不属于项目管理的范畴。为了说明问题，这里打一个比方：写字和打仗是两回事；写字应该用笔，打仗应该用枪；这是人所共知的事实。因此，类似于“写字应该用枪还是用笔”这样的问题是没有意义的。在回应文章中，温奇指出，“批评者提出的经济学理论和生产理论的分野是没有意义的”（Winch，2006）。显然，温奇也没有将项目管理和项目治理严格区分开来，因而只说对了一半——这是因为，如果只是考虑项目管理这一范畴，生产理论或许就足够了，因而没有必要涉及经济学理论，然而，如果同时考虑项目管理和项目治理两个范畴，上述理论分野又是必不可少的。

5.7　建设项目理论重构

以上分析表明，建设项目理论不仅要回答管理层面的问题，而且要回答治理层面和体制层面的问题。从目前的情况看，对治理和体制的研究尚处于起步阶段，远远落后于项目管理领域的研究，在一定程度上存在图 5.5 给出的“冰山”现象；不仅不能满足实践的需求，而且落后于相关理论的发展。

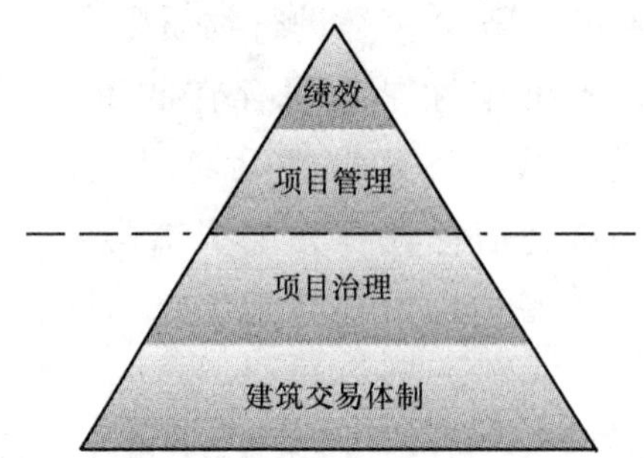

图 5.5 建设项目理论研究的“冰山”现象

（资料来源：沙凯逊等，2009a）

5.7.1 建设项目理论研究存在的主要问题

一是研究视角缺少高度。人们对事物的认识往往由看问题的立场和角度所决定；不同的视角导致不同的结论。东坡有诗云：“横看成岭侧成峰，远近高低各不同。不识庐山真面目，只缘身在此山中。”这首诗生动地说明了立场问题的重要性。在理论多元化的发展背景中，建设项目在不同的语境中被赋予不同的含义。然而，由于缺乏从总体上把握建设项目理论的高度，每个流派所关注的只是其中的某一侧面，难以真正看清建设项目的“庐山真面目”。

具体到某一流派，也有两种可供选择的立场：一是项目本位的立场，二是企业本位的立场。前者从建设项目 4C结构的整体出发；后者则是从建筑企业的立场出发，而建筑企业只是 4C 结构中的一个节点。如果把 4C 结构比作一座山，项目本位的立场就相当于站在山顶之上，而企业本位的立场则相当于站在山脚下的一点。当前在建设项目研究领域占据主导地位的是基于系统科学的研究范式。该范式基本上采取企业本位的立场。这种不从整体出发，而是从局部出发的做法难免会产生“见木不见林”的局限性。

二是研究范畴边界不清。早就有经典作者指出，经济学家应当尽可能地把握自己研究领域的边界与内涵。对此类问题的错误理解，可能导致对经济事实本身的错误认识，并最终损害经济科学的权威性和影响力（凯恩斯，2001)。然而在建设项目研究领域，管理和治理这两个不同的范畴至今仍然被混为一谈。这一点在前面提到的两种范式的学术交锋中表现得很明显。再比如，在项目管理领域颇具影响的学者特纳(Turner，2006）发表的文章，一方面对理论重构的重要性具有充分的认识，另一方面却把管理和治理混为一谈。文章题目是《项目管理理论探究：项目管理职能之性质》(Towards a theory of project management：The nature of the functions of project management)，而其中的许多内容却属于项目治理的范畴。在国内的相关文献中，不少作者把 EPC 、BOT、PPP[1] 连同代建制一起统统叫作建设项目的管理模式，有的作者把它们叫作建设工程交易模式，还有的作者把 BOT 和 PPP 等模式叫作建设项目的融资与合同管理模式（沙凯逊，孙晓冰，2009）。实际上，这些模式都属于项目治理的范畴。基本术语的不规范和不统一，说明了这样一个事实：对项目治理的研究尚未形成相对独立的体系，未取得与项目管理同等的地位。

三是项目治理理念缺失。为了实现建设项目的绩效目标，首先要解决的是“想不想做”的问题（如何使人们有积极性去做正确的决策），然后才是“能不能做”的问题（在人们有积极性去做正确决策的前提下，如何把事情做好）。前者着眼于利益相关者之间责权利的配置与制衡，属于治理的范畴。后者着眼于项目的成本、工期和质量，属于管理的范畴。此外，管理和治理都是在建筑交易体制提供的制度环境下进行的。如果没有良好的制度环境和正确的动机，再好的管理方法也无济于事。按理说，对治理的研究应该优先于对管理的研究。然而，实际情况却并非如此。重管理、轻治理的倾向导致了项目治理理念的缺失，在实践中产生了十分有害的后果（沙凯逊，2009）。

作为我国建设项目研究的集大成者，《建设工程项目管理规范》（GB/T 50326—2006，以下简称为《规范》）与国际标准 ISO10006一脉相承；它们同属于基于系统科学的研究范式。需要指出的是，基于系统科学的研究范式隐含了一个重要假设：治理结构是外生给定的。既然《规范》的宗旨是“规范建设工程项目管理行为”（编写委员会，2006），它对治理问题的舍象自然是题中应有之义。然而，正因为如此，《规范》在很大程度上失去了在项目治理范畴的话语权。

5.7.2 建设项目治理内生化

建设项目治理内生化既是建设项目理论创新的内在要求，也是建筑业制度创新的必要条件（沙凯逊，2008）。它要求采用新的思维方式和研究视角，借鉴主流治理理论的成果和经验，引入协调与激励、合作与竞争以及变迁与演化等因素，把相关制度变量纳入理论分析框架（沙凯逊，2010b）。

治理内生化必须以范式转换为前提，也就是从瓦尔拉范式转向后瓦尔拉范式。没有范式转换，治理不可能由外生转为内生。彻底的治理内生化必须从基本假设的改变开始：对当事人的行为假设由“自利行为”（从性善论的立场出发）转变为“机

---

[1] EPC 是英文 Engineering Procurement Construction 的缩写，即设计—采购—施工模式，也就是我们常说的总承包。BOT 是英文 Build—Operate—Transfer 的缩写，即建造—运营—移交模式。典型的 BOT 方式也叫做“公共工程特许权”，是政府同私营的项目公司签订合同，由项目公司融资和建设的基础设施项目。在协议期内，项目公司拥有设施、并且负责设施的运营和维护，通过收取使用费或服务费回收投资，并取得合理利润。协议期满后，设施的所有权无偿移交给政府。PPP 是英文 Public—Private Partnership 的缩写，即公私合伙模式。PPP 是指这样一种制度安排，即公共部门和私人实体通过共同行使权力，共同承担责任，共同投入资源，共同承担风险，共同分享利益的方式，以生产和提供公共的产品和公共的服务。

会主义行为”（从性恶论的立场出发）；对当事人的理性假设由“完全理性”（决策者的认知能力与问题的复杂程度的比值 $r=1$）转变为“有限理性”（$r<1$ 甚至“程序理性”（$r\to 0$））。与此相适应，建设项目的定义也应由“独特的一次性任务或过程”转变为“临时性的多边组织”。如果没有基本假设和定义的改变，治理内生化只能是徒有其名。

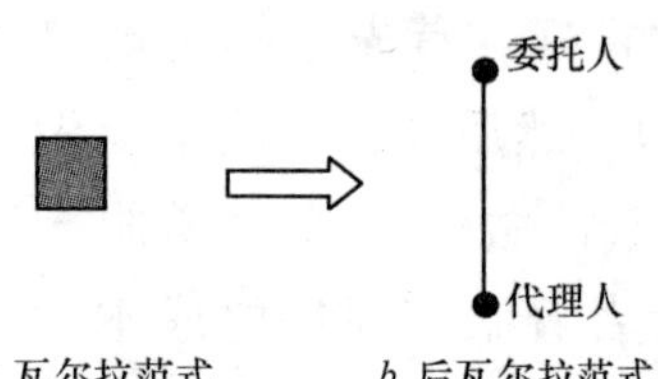

图 5.6 对企业的抽象：从一元结构到二元结构

（资料来源：沙凯逊，2010b）

在基本假设给定的条件下，理论体系的正确与否取决于对抽象力的把握。抽象不足和抽象过度都不可能得到理想的效果。抽象不足会使模型过于复杂，抽象过度则会把问题“抽空”。在一般均衡理论的阿罗—德布鲁体系中，企业被看作是生产函数。如图 5.6 所示，在瓦尔拉范式中，企业“黑箱”相当于牛顿力学中的质点。既然是“黑箱”，对企业内部责权利配置与制衡关系的分析就无从谈起，于是形成了治理的盲区。而在后瓦尔拉范式中，企业模型被抽象为委托人（企业所有者）与代理人（企业经营者）之间的策略性交往。模型由一元结构变为二元结构，问题发生了质的变化。原先无法讨论的治理问题，如利益相关者之间的协调与激励等，都可以纳入分析框架。一系列新的理论和方法——如交易成本理论、不完全合同理论、机制设计理论等——也因此得以产生和发展。

与企业相比，建设项目要复杂得多。如图 5.7*a* 所示，温奇（Winch，2002）把现代建设项目的基本结构抽象为由设计方、施工方和控制方组成的 3C 结构。沙凯逊和孙晓冰（2009）把 3C 结构扩展为 4C 结构（如图 5.7*b* 所示）。4C 模型在定性分析时表现出较大的优越性，然而，在建立博弈分析模型时却显得过于复杂：由 3C 变为 4C，虽然只增加了一个当事人，当事人之间的关系却从 3 个增加到 6 个，使分析的难度大大增加。如何使模型既能够分析客户和其他利益相关者的关系，又有较强的可操作性？图

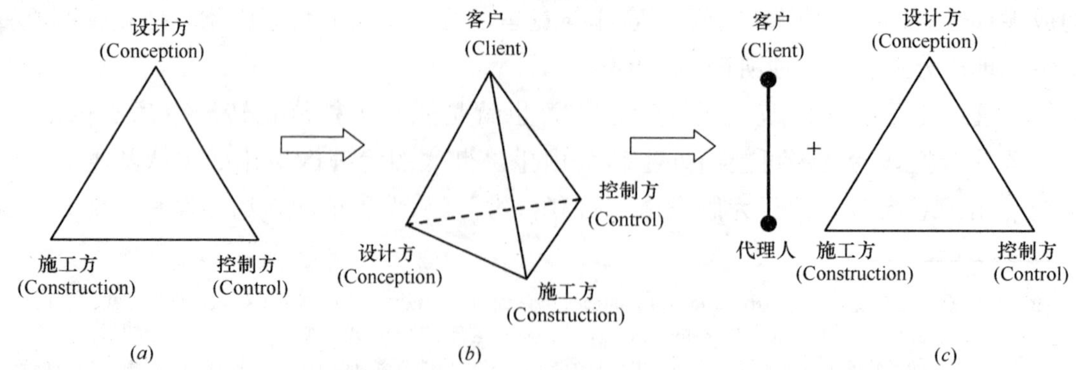

图 5.7 对建设项目的抽象：从 3C 到（1+3）C

（资料来源：沙凯逊，2010b）

（*a*）3C 模型；（*b*）4C 模型；（*c*）（1+3）C 模型

5.7*c* 给出的（1＋3）C 模型可能是一种比较合适的解决方案。根据温奇（Winch，2002）提出的原则，（1＋3）C 模型将建设项目治理分为垂直治理和水平治理两部分，从而把一个复杂的问题分解为两个相对简单的问题，大大提高了形式化分析的可操作性。

5.7.3　理论重构的基本原则与内容

当前，建设项目理论研究同时面临着机遇和挑战。一方面，相关学科和理论的发展成果不断为建设项目研究注入生机与活力；另一方面，在日益增加的不确定性和复杂性面前，原有理论的解释能力和判断能力受到质疑。因此，对建设项目理论进行梳理、整合与重构是十分必要的。虽然建设项目理论重构的涉及面很广，工作量很大，但是其基本原则和内容可以概括为以下几点，即调整立场，拓宽视野，厘清边界，多元整合（沙凯逊，2010a）。

所谓调整立场，就是要从企业本位转变为项目本位的立场。基于系统科学的范式基本上采取企业本位的立场，具有较大的局限性。例如，按照《规范》的逻辑，项目经理负责制是建设项目管理的基本制度，项目经理部是一次性的成本中心，企业是利润中心。《规范》要求建筑企业赋予项目经理充分的权力和职责，以保证项目的效率；然而，在建设项目 4C 结构关系失衡的条件下，放权的结果往往是利润中心失灵。在这方面，中建总公司在内部进行的“放权—收权”演变过程颇具代表性（苏京鳄，2009）。要走出“一放就乱、一收就死”的困境，必须调整立场和思路，从企业本位转变为项目本位。

所谓拓宽视野，就是要站在新的高度，全面审视建设项目的性质。根据威廉姆森提出的制度层次结构，可以较好地从总体上认识和把握建设项目的性质。如图 5.8 所示，项目管理与项目治理就好像一枚硬币的两面。前者把项目经理负责制作为基本制度，着眼于成本、质量、工期三大目标；后者把项目法人责任制作为基本制度，着眼于 4C 结构中责权利的配置与制衡。由此可以得出一种比较全面的“项目观”：建设项目不仅是一种过程，而且是一种组织；不仅是一种生产力[❶]，而且是一种生产关系；项目区别于企业的本质属性不仅在于它的一次性，而且在于它的适应性。

所谓厘清边界，就是要明确界定不同研究范畴的边界与内涵。任何研究范式都是在一定的抽象和假设的基础上建立和发展起来的，因此不是全能的，而是有一定的局限性和适用范围。就建设项目理论而言，基于系统科学的和基于生产理论的研究范式适用于项目管理，但不适于项目治理的研究。同样的道理，项目治理研究需要以基于新制度经济学的研究范式为主，而建筑交易体制研究需要采用基于演化经济学的研究范式，而不是其他的研究范式。不同研究范式之间应该是相辅相成的互补关系而不是

---

❶　张青林（2004）认为，建筑业改革的理论基石是项目生产力理论。

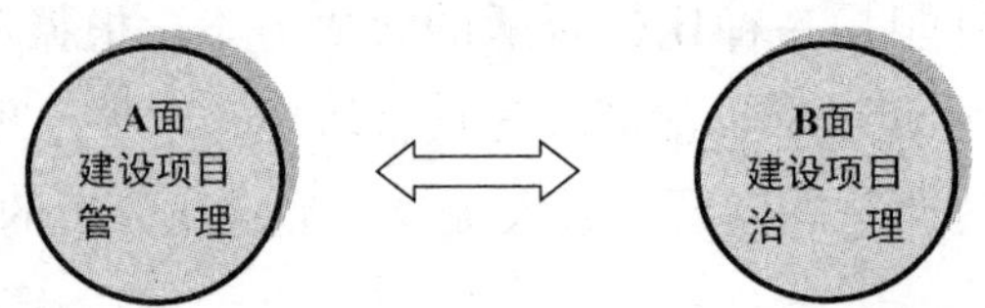

图 5.8　项目管理与项目治理：一枚硬币的两面

非此即彼的替代关系（沙凯逊等，2009a），认清这一点，是进行多元整合，构建新的分析框架的前提。

所谓多元整合，就是要在全面审视建设项目性质的基础上，集中不同流派的优势，形成新的分析框架。长期以来，在建设项目研究领域，基于系统科学的研究范式始终占据主导地位；从 PMBoK 和国际标准 ISO10006，到《中国项目管理知识体系》和《建设工程项目管理规范》，无不把项目作为一种过程来研究；而对建筑交易体制和项目治理的研究严重不足，甚至出现"张冠李戴"的现象，把原本属于项目治理的内容放到项目管理的范畴中讨论（Koskela and Ballard，2006；Winch，2006）。从科学发展史上看，许多科学的进步恰恰是因为一些看起来不同、甚至是对立的理论范式相互交叉与融合的结果。为了建立符合时代需求的建设项目理论体系，必须摒弃非此即彼的思维方式，代之以多元化的方法论，在多元竞争中使理论走向成熟。在对不同流派进行多元整合的基础上，可以得到一个新的理论研究体系（沙凯逊，2010c）。

如图 5.9 所示，对建设项目的理论研究包括两个基本研究范畴（项目管理和项目治理，用实线连接）和一个相关领域（建筑交易体制，用虚线连接）。项目管理的基本问题是，如何在给定的治理结构下实现资源的有效配置，进而实现成本、质量和工期等目标。项目治理的基本问题是，如何在给定的建筑交易体制下实现 4C 结构中的责权利的合理配置与制衡。垂直治理、水平治理和针对项目经理的治理属于正式制度安

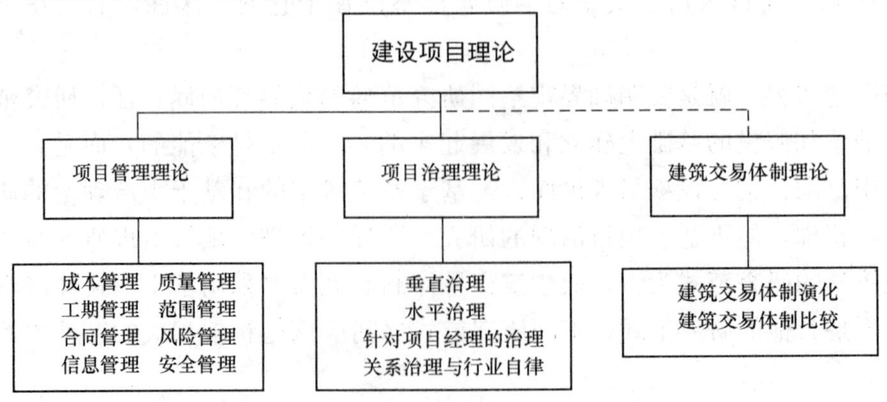

图 5.9　建设项目理论的研究体系

排的范畴；建设项目治理中的非正式制度安排涉及关系治理、建筑专业体制和行业自律等方面的内容。最后需要说明的是，建设项目属于微观的范畴，而建筑交易体制属于中观的范畴，之所以把建筑交易体制理论作为相关领域列出，是因为对建筑交易体制的研究经常涉及建设项目 4C 结构的问题，而且管理、治理和体制三个范畴之间的关系实在太密切，以至于无法完全分开的缘故。这个框架比较简单，却能够使项目治理摆脱项目管理的“阴影”，取得相对独立的地位。

5.8　结　　论

这一讲的内容可以沿着两条线索来解读。一是对建设项目的再认识，二是对建设项目理论研究的再思考。对建设项目的再认识导致了比较全面的“项目观”：建设项目不仅是一种过程，而且是一种组织；不仅是一种生产力，而且是一种生产关系；项目区别于企业的本质属性不仅在于它的一次性，而且在于它的适应性。对建设项目理论研究的再思考引发了研究范式的转换和一个新的理论研究框架。

以上两方面的工作都是围绕着提高建筑业绩效这一核心问题展开的。研究建筑业的绩效问题，既要面对企业和项目并存的事实，又涉及管理、治理和体制三个不同的范畴。在这方面，面向双重对象的三层次分析框架和基于绩效链的分析思路具有较好的解释能力。

由于认识水平和理论分析工具的限制等因素，长期以来，对建设项目的研究主要集中在项目管理的范畴。在理论与实践双重需求的驱动下，对建设项目的研究视角正在从管理的层面扩展到治理和体制的层面。系统研究建设项目的治理逻辑和建筑交易体制的演进规律，不仅可以丰富建设项目理论研究的内容，对建筑业的结构调整、业务流程再造、建设项目总承包、供应链管理等诸多课题，也有重要的现实意义。

从治理外生转变为治理内生，虽然只有一字之差，却意味着在立场、观点和方法论等方面的一系列根本性变化：研究立场由企业本位转为项目本位，研究重点从生产力转向生产关系，充分统计量从价格变量变为制度变量，分析结果从瓦尔拉均衡变为纳什均衡。

建设项目理论体系既包括科学层面和技术层面的问题，又涉及文化层面的问题。科学层面和技术层面的问题使得建设项目的管理与治理可以具有国际化的特性，而文化层面的问题则必须考虑我国的文化传统和特点。我国的建设项目理论研究，一方面要引进西方的理论和方法，同时要坚持本土化的正确方向。我国建筑业所承担的任务是世所罕见的，它所面临的问题也是世所罕见的。它们为建设项目理论提供了独特的研究素材和创新空间。从这个意义上讲，我国建筑业应该对建设项目理论的发展做出自己特有的贡献。

参考文献

1. 编写委员会（2006）建设工程项目管理规范实施手册（第二版），北京：建筑工业出版社.
2. 贾洪，赵宏彦（2008）基于绩效分析的建筑行业结构发展策略，建筑经济，(12)，5—9.
3. 凯恩斯（2001）政治经济学的范围与方法，中译本，党国英，刘惠译，北京：华夏出版社.
4. 李东（2008）我国企业管理的本土化问题，光明日报，2008-11-11.
5. 李向平（2006）私人信仰与社会结构的变迁——中国信仰的社会学解读，探索与争鸣，(9)，5—9.
6. 沙凯逊（2008）从管理到治理：建设项目理论演进探析，建筑经济，(6)，12—14.
7. 沙凯逊（2009）“规模—绩效之谜”再探，建筑经济，(8)，9—11.
8. 沙凯逊（2010a）建设项目理论重构初探：一个新制度经济学的视角，项目管理技术，**8**（3），13—16.
9. 沙凯逊（2010b）建设项目治理：从外生到内生，项目管理技术，**8**（10），13—17.
10. 沙凯逊（2010c）建设项目理论框架：立场、观点和方法论，建筑经济，(10) 95—97.
11. 沙凯逊（2011）基于联盟博弈的建设项目水平治理分析，项目管理技术，**9**（11），21—25.
12. 沙凯逊，邓晓红（2001）欧盟建筑交易体制比较研究：启发与思考，建筑经济，(3)，19—22.
13. 沙凯逊，宋涛，亓霞，华冬冬（2009a）建设项目理论研究范式探析，项目管理技术，**7**（5），13—18.
14. 沙凯逊，宋涛，亓霞，华冬冬（2009b）从不确定性看建设项目的治理逻辑，山东建筑大学学报，**11**（4），283—287.
15. 沙凯逊，宋涛，赵锦锴，殷涛（2003）从美日两国的历史经验看建设交易制度创新，建筑经济，(3)，10—12.
16. 沙凯逊，孙晓冰（2009）规范建设单位行为：一个项目治理的视角，项目管理技术，**7**（10）13—17.
17. 沙凯逊，杨杰（2009）“规模—绩效之谜”初探，建筑经济，(4)，5—7.
18. 苏京鳄（2009）中建总公司：法人层次管项目，90%盈利，建筑，(1)，10—21.
19. 苏炜（2013）天涯晚笛，桂林，广西师范大学出版社.
20. 王华，尹贻林（2004）基于委托—代理的工程项目治理结构及其优化，中国软科学，(11) 93—96.
21. 严玲，赵黎明（2005）论项目治理理论体系的构建，上海经济研究，(11)，104—110.
22. 喻春生，理查德 C. 休士曼，约翰 D. 哈特菲尔德（1989）职工需求与管理技巧模式及其跨文化比较，管理世界，(2)，154—163.
23. 张青林（2004）项目管理与建筑业，北京：中国计量出版社.
24. Biesenthal，C. and Wilden，R.（2014）Multi-level project governance：trends and opportunities，*International Journal of Project Management*，**32**（8），1291—1308.
25. Chang，C. Y.（2014）Principal—agent model of risk allocation in construction contracts and its critique，*Journal of Construction Engineering and Management*，**140**（1），04013032—1—9.
26. CIOB（2002）*Code of Practice for Project Management for Construction and Development*，3rd Edition，Blackwell Publishing，Oxford.
27. Clarke，T.（ed.）（2004）*Theories of Corporate Governance：the Philosophical Foundations of Corporate Governance*，Routledge，London.
28. Clegg，S. R.，Pitsis，T. S.，Rura—Polley，T. and Marosszeky，M.（2002）Governmentality mat-

ters: designing an alliance culture of inter-organizational collaboration for managing projects, *Organization Studies*, **23** (3) 317—337.

29. Coase, R. H. (1937) The nature of the firm, new series, *Economica*, **4** (16), 386—405.
30. Duncan, W. (1996) *A guide to the Project Management Body of Knowledge*, PMI Publications, Sylva NC.
31. Eccles, R. G. (1981) The quasi-firm in the construction industry, *Economic Behavior and Organization*, **2** (4), 335—357.
32. Knight, F. H. (1921) *Risk, Uncertainty and Profit*, Houghton Mifflin Company, Boston.
33. Koskela, L. and Ballard, G. (2006) Should project management be based on theories of economics or production?, *Building Research and Information*, **34** (2), 154—163.
34. Koskela, L. and Howell, G. (2002) The underlying theory of project management is obsolete, Slevin, D., Cleland, D. and Pinto, J., *Proceedings of PMI Research Conference*, Seattle: Project Management Institute, 293—302.
35. Loosemore, M. (2000) *Crisis Management in Construction Projects*, ASCE Press, Virginia.
36. Morris, P. (1994) *The Management of Projects*, Thomas Telford, London.
37. Müller, R., Pemsel, S. and Shao, J. (2014) Organizational enablers for governance and governmentality of projects: a literature review, *International Journal of Project Management*, **32** (8), 1309—1320.
38. Sha, K. X. (2011) Vertical governance of construction projects: an information cost perspective, *Construction Management and Economics*, **29** (11), 1137—1147.
39. Turner, J. R. (1993) *The Handbook of Project-based Management*, McGraw-Hill, London.
40. Turner, J. R. (2004) Farsighted project contract management: incomplete in its entirety, *Construction Management and Economics*, **22** (1), 75—83.
41. Turner, J. R. (2006) Towards a theory of project management: The nature of the functions of project management, *Project Management*, **24** (4), 277—279.
42. Turner, J. R. and Keegan, A. (2001) Mechanisms of governance in the project-based organization: roles of the broker and steward, *European Management Journal*, **19** (3), 254—267.
43. Williamson, O. E. (1991) Comparative economic organization: the analysis of discrete structural alternatives, *Administrative Science Quarterly*, **36** (2), 269—296.
44. Williamson, O. E. (2000) The new institutional economics: taking stock, looking ahead, *Journal of Economic Literature*, **38** (3), 595—613.
45. Winch, G. M. (1989) The construction firm and the construction project: a transaction coat approach, *Construction Management and Economics*, **7** (3), 331—345.
46. Winch, G. M. (2000) Institutional reform in British construction: partnering and private finance, *Building Research and Information*, **28** (2), 141—55.
47. Winch, G. M. (2001) Governing the project process: a conceptual framework, *Construction Management and Economics*, **19** (7), 799—808.
48. Winch, G. M. (2002) *Managing Construction Projects: An Information Processing Approach*, Blackwell Science, Oxford.

49. Winch, G. M. (2006) Towards a theory of construction as production by projects, *Building Research and Information*, **34** (2), 164—174.

50. Winch, G. M. (2010) *Managing Construction Projects: An Information Processing Approach*, 2nd Edition, Blackwell Science, Oxford.

第 6 讲　建设项目的垂直治理：一个委托代理的视角

- □ 委托人和代理人的利益不一致、信息不对称是造成委托代理问题的两个基本条件。解决由此所造成的逆向选择与道德风险问题，就是要解决如何让人说真话、如何让人不偷懒的问题。
- □ 风险与激励的合理匹配是委托代理理论的核心问题。委托人的问题是：在满足代理人参与约束和激励相容约束的前提下，设计一个合同，以最大化自己的期望效用。在期望效用模型中，最大化期望效用函数的问题可以转化为最大化确定性等价的问题。
- □ 建设项目的垂直治理空间由两个维度构成：一是项目采购方式，二是合同类型。垂直治理的主要任务就是根据当事人的风险态度和建设项目的实际条件，权衡利弊，选择合适的采购方式和合同类型。
- □ 当信息缺口达到一定程度，并且专用知识的比重超过一定程度时，建设项目采购方式的选择过程有可能不再沿着经典理论预设的方向发展，而是发生转折，也就是所谓的“二阶转变”。
- □ 在决定建设项目的采购方式时，不仅要考虑乙方“敲竹杠”给交易成本带来的压力，还要考虑不确定性给生产成本带来的压力。在决定建设项目的合同类型时，需要同时考虑不确定性，以及一般性资料和专用知识的成本。
- □ 在一定条件下，建设项目的当事人有可能不服从“委托人风险中性，代理人风险厌恶”也就是“中性—厌恶”的假设，而是表现为“偏好—厌恶”或“中性—偏好”的风险态度。这时就有必要放宽“中性—厌恶”的假设，在新的条件下求解委托代理模型。

第 5 讲建立了一个关于建设项目的理论框架体系。从这一讲开始，研究工作就按照该框架设定的逻辑展开。这一讲以交易成本和委托代理理论的解释逻辑为主，研究建设项目的垂直治理问题，也就是客户与一阶供应商（first-tier suppliers）之间的交易关系。首先简要介绍期望效用函数和委托代理理论的基本概念和方法，为下面的分析做准备。然后分析建设项目的垂直治理空间，该空间由采购方式与合同类型两个维度构成。接下来的研究沿着两个方向展开。一是将不确定性和信息成本纳入分析框架，构建委托代理模型，分析建设项目的采购方式和合同类型。二是从我国建设市场的实际出发，提出建设项目当事人风险态度多样性的命题，并在不同假设条件下求解委托代理模型，提出相应的激励策略。

需要指出的是，正如引言部分所讲的那样，本书的宗旨是不求“深入”，但求“浅出”，因此，这一讲省略了数学推导过程，只对相关模型及其基本结论做出简要说明。对数学推导过程感兴趣的读者，可以参照《建设项目治理》一书（沙凯逊，2013）中的相关内容。

6.1 委托代理理论简介

委托代理理论是新制度经济学的重要内容，也是这一讲的主要分析工具。信息经济学中的委托代理关系泛指任何一种涉及不对称信息的交易；其中拥有信息优势的一方称为**代理人**（agent），另一方称为**委托人**（principal）（张维迎，1996，p. 403）。概括地讲，委托代理理论所要解决的问题是，从委托人的立场出发设计一种合同，这个合同能够合理地分担风险和提供激励，使得代理人有积极性接受它，并且按照委托人的意愿去努力工作。

6.1.1 概述

委托代理理论的产生缘于现代企业中所有权与控制权的分离。如图 6.1 所示，在市场经济的古典阶段，企业的规模较小，技术水平较低，管理比较简单，生产经营的风险不大。在这种情况下，企业所有者一般又是企业的经营管理者，他们承担企业的全部风险和责任（无限责任）；企业内部不存在委托代理关系。随着企业规模的扩大和不确定性的提高，对管理者专业素质的要求越来越高，所有者难以胜任对企业的管理任务，不得不把经营权让渡给职业经理人。伯利和米恩斯在 1932 年出版的《现代公司与私有财产》一书中，分析了美国两百家大公司的情况，发现其中相当数量的公司是由高级管理人员控制的（伯利，米恩斯，2005）。20 世纪 40 年代，随着股份制公司的发展、股权的分散以及企业所有权与经营权的分离，企业的主导力量逐步由股东转向经理阶层，出现了所谓的“经理革命”。企业是否由支薪的职业经理管理成为现代企业与古典企业的分界线（钱德勒，1987）。

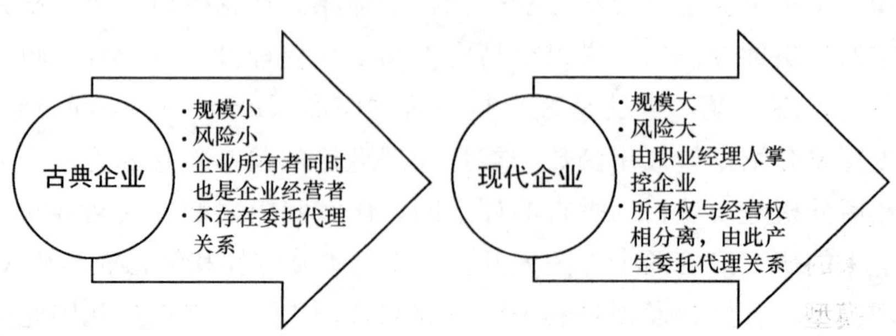

图 6.1 经理革命：所有权与经营权的分离

当股东将企业经营权让渡给职业经理人时，经济学意义上的委托代理关系便出现了。企业所有者（股东）是委托人，企业经营者（职业经理人）是代理人；两者具有不同的目标和利益。股东把公司视为一种投资手段，他们希望通过职业经理人的努力实现自身财富的最大化。职业经理人则利用自身的人力资本为股东创造价值，他们把公司视为获取报酬以及实现自我价值的资源。此外，职业经理人比股东更了解企业生产、收益和成本等方面的信息，因此具有信息优势。由于两者的利益不一致，信息不对称，职业经理人就有可能为了自身利益最大化而偏离股东利益最大化的方向，这时股东必须承受职业经理人机会主义行为所造成的代理成本。由此可见，委托人和代理人的利益不一致、信息不对称是造成委托代理问题的两个基本条件。

委托代理理论以非对称信息博弈论为基础。所谓**非对称信息**（asymmetric information），就是指某些参与人拥有而另一些参与人不拥有的信息。比如，商品房的内在质量如何，开发商最清楚，而购房者心中无数；这就是知识信息的不对称，又叫作隐藏知识（hidden knowledge）。又比如，承包商在施工中是否有偷工减料的行为，业主很难知道；这就是行动信息的不对称，又叫作隐藏行动（hidden action）。从时间的角度看，信息的非对称有可能发生在当事人签约之前，也可能发生在签约之后。这两种非对称分别称为事前（*ex ante*）非对称和事后（*ex post*）非对称。知识信息的不对称往往会导致合同前的机会主义，即**逆向选择**（adverse selection）。由于边际贡献难以衡量，在市场上只能以“平均贡献”来确定商品和劳务的价格，在这种平均原则下，就会发生“劣币驱逐良币”：高质量的商品和劳务有可能被低质量的商品和劳务赶出市场。行动信息的不对称则往往会诱发合同后的机会主义，即**道德风险**（moral hazard）。如表 6.1 所示，综合考虑非对称信息的类型和发生时间这两个因素，可以产生不同的委托代理模型。

背景材料：逆向选择和道德风险

这两个术语均起源于保险业。首先来看逆向选择。由于私人信息的存在，投保人在投健康保险时，有可能就他们的风险程度说谎；保险公司只能根据统计数据，按平均的发病率收取保险费。这对于身体健康的人来说是不合算的，于是一部分健康的人就会退出保险。这部分健康的人退出后，参加保险的人的发病概率就会提高。针对这种情况，保险公司就要提高保险收费。保险费越高，退出的人就越多，结果剩下来的人都是身体状况不好的人，这种选择就是逆向选择。其次来看道德风险。一旦人们办理了保险，往往就会自觉不自觉地降低对保险对象的关心程度，使保险公司承担较大的风险，这就是道德风险。

常用的委托代理模型 表 6.1

	隐藏知识（hidden knowledge）	隐藏行动（hidden action）
事前（*ex ante*）	逆向选择模型 信号传递模型 信息甄别模型	
事后（*ex post*）	隐藏知识的道德风险模型	隐藏行动的道德风险模型

（资料来源：张维迎，2006，p. 399）

需要指出的是，以上模型仅考虑了静态条件下单个委托人和单个代理人之间的委托代理关系，而且代理人仅从事单项工作。在现实生活中，委托人、代理人有可能不止一个；代理人被委托的工作不止一项；即使是一项，也有多个维度；而且有可能是多阶段动态博弈。这些比较复杂的情况需要比较复杂的委托代理模型来解决，如多阶段博弈动态模型、多任务模型、团队工作模型和共同代理（common agency）模型等。

通俗地讲，解决由非对称信息所造成的逆向选择与道德风险问题，就是要解决如何让人说真话、如何让人不偷懒的问题。衡量一个制度是否完善，就要看它在多大程度上能够让人们说真话、不偷懒。建设项目的客户面临着两个问题。一是对承包商的选择问题，即在对承包商的实际能力难以观察的情况下，通过什么样的机制能够保证最有能力的承包商来承担建设项目？二是对承包商的激励问题，即在对承包商的努力程度难以度量的情况下，如何使承包商努力工作，不偷工减料？第一个问题可通过工程招投标来解决。这一讲主要讨论后一个问题。

6.1.2 当事人的风险态度和效用曲线

当事人的风险态度是委托代理问题中的又一个重要因素。在现实生活中，不同的人对同一个问题往往采取不同的态度，表现出不同的风险态度（risk attitude）或风险偏好（risk preference）。**风险中性**（risk neutral）的决策者完全以损益值的大小作为方案选择的标准。**风险厌恶**（risk averse）的决策者不求超额的收益，但求损失较小。**风险偏好**（risk seeking）的决策者宁可冒险，也要追求较大的收益。不同的风险态度会导致不同的决策结果。一般来讲，过分保守会失去一些机会；而过度冒险会导致风险损失。

背景资料：企业家、冒险精神与风险管控

企业家是从事组织、管理并承担经营风险的人。没有甘冒风险和承担风险的魄力，就不可能成为企业家。在比尔·盖茨看来，成功的首要因素就是冒险。在任何事业中，把所有的冒险因素都排除掉的话，自然也就把所有成功的机会都消除掉了。也有人说过：只有被百分之九十九的人嘲笑过的梦想，才有资格谈及百分之一的成功。但是，冒险精神只是成功企业家的必要条件而非充分条件。企业家要想取得成功，不仅要敢

于冒险，还要有很强的风险分析和管控能力。

在风险决策理论中，决策者对收益和损失的感受和反应，称之为**效用**（utility）。效用是描述个人偏好的方法之一。应该强调指出，效用不同于实际收益，它只是人的主观心理感受。同样的商品或服务对于不同的人来说，它们带来的满足程度可能是不一样的。即便是同一个人，在不同条件下对同样的商品或服务的感受也可能截然不同。例如，菜品中的辣椒对于嗜好辣味的人来说是一种享受，而对不喜欢辣味的人来说可能是一种折磨。再如，对于同样一个面包，一个人在饥肠辘辘和酒足饭饱时的感觉是截然不同的。

背景材料：效用、边际效用和边际效用递减规律（资料来源：厉以宁，秦宛顺，1985）

在经济学中，效用是指商品或服务满足人的欲望或需要的能力。效用值没有量纲，通常情况下用 0 表示最小的效用值，用 1 表示最大的效用值。边际效用（marginal utility）是指消费者在一定时间内增加一个单位商品或服务所带来的新增效用。在其他条件不变的情况下，随着对某种物品消费量的增加，消费者从连续增加的每一单位物品中所得到的满足程度越来越小。例如，在著名的“吃面条”的小品中，尽管每碗面条都是一样的，陈佩斯在吃第一碗和吃第四碗面条时的满足程度显然是不一样的。这种普遍存在的现象在经济学中被总结为边际效用递减规律（The law of diminishing marginal utility）。

效用的概念最早由瑞士数学家丹尼尔·伯努利提出。关于不确定性决策的定量研究可以追溯到 17 世纪的数理统计理论。需要说明的是，这里的“不确定性”并不是奈特所说的“真正的”不确定性，而是奈特所说的“风险”。因此，这里所说的不确定性决策和风险决策没有实质性的区别。最初，人们把期望收益最大化作为不确定性条件下的理性决策原则。丹尼尔·伯努利在破解圣彼得堡悖论（St. Peterburg paradox）时发现，不确定性条件下的理性决策原则应该是**期望效用**（expected utility）最大化而不是期望收益最大化；也就是说，应该把“钱的函数的数学期望”作为决策函数，而不是把“钱的数学期望”作为决策函数（刘建洲，1993）。对圣彼得堡悖论的研究成果，构成了风险条件下现代决策理论的基石（Machina，1987 ）。

背景资料：圣彼得堡悖论与期望效用（资料来源：刘建洲，1993）

17 世纪的法国数学家帕斯卡和费玛是概率论的早期创立者。他们假设，一场公平赌博的吸引力是由它的期望值 $X=\sum_{i=1}^{n} p_i x_i$ 所决定的；式中 x_i 是第 i 个结果，p_i 是出现 x_i 的概率。公平赌博要求赌博各方的输赢数额和机会均等。以猜硬币赌博为例，如果猜对赢 2 元，猜错输 2 元，当硬币本身没有问题时，就是一场公平赌博。这场赌博的数学期望为零。如果在某场赌博中，某个局中人所赢的钱的期望值 E 大于零，那么此人应预先交出数量为 E 的钱，才能保证这场赌博的公平。

1728 年，瑞士数学家尼古拉·伯努利对以上假设提出挑战。问题源自一种叫作圣彼得堡游戏的赌博：将一枚均匀的硬币抛起，如果第一次猜对出现正面，可得 2 元；第一次没猜对，第二次猜对，可得 4 元……如果前 $n-1$ 次没猜对，第 n 次猜对，可得 2^n 元。伯努利的问题是，为使参赌者有资格参加这场赌博，他应该预先交出多少钱才能使这场赌博变得公平？按照帕斯卡和费玛的观点，参赌者应该预先交出等同于这场赌博的数学期望的钱来。既然硬币是均匀的，参赌者第一次猜中的概率是 1/2；第一次没猜对，第二次猜对的概率是 1/4；……前 $n-1$ 次没猜对，第 n 次猜对的概率为 $1/2^n$。这样，参赌者赢钱的数学期望就是无穷大：$1/2\times 2+1/4\times 4+\cdots+1/2^n\times 1/2^n+\cdots=\infty$，也就是说，无论交多少钱，这场赌博对参赌者都是有利的。然而，实际上没有多少人愿意花 25 元去参加一次这样的赌博。于是就产生了一个悖论：为什么一场理论上是公平的赌博，实际上只有傻瓜才会愿意出任意高价参加？这就是著名的圣彼得堡悖论。

1738 年，尼古拉·伯努利的堂弟丹尼尔·伯努利提出了解决圣彼得堡悖论的新理论。他认为，心理价值（moral value）[1] 是人们行动的基础；心理价值并不与收益的多少成正比，而与原来拥有的财富有关——人们并不认为 1000 元收益在价值上必定是 100 元收益的 10 倍。他进一步假设，人们拥有一个关于财富的效用函数 $u(x)$；在衡量一场赌博的价值时，判断标准应该是期望效用值 $U=\sum_{i=1}^{n} p_i u(x_i)$，而不是期望值 $X=\sum_{i=1}^{n} p_i x_i$。

通过心理测试的方法，可以测出决策者对于不同收益和损失的效用值，并画出相应的效用曲线。作者曾在课堂上对学生做过如下测试。首先设定一个有风险的方案：选择这个方案，有一半的可能得到 1000 元，一半的可能没有收益，也就是收益为 0。显然，这个方案的期望收益是 500 元。如果设定得到 1000 元的效用为 1，没有收益的效用为 0，那么，该方案的期望效用是 0.5。然后设定若干个没有风险的方案，并且按照收益值由小到大的顺序依次提出供学生选择：

（1）有百分之百的把握获得 100 元；

（2）有百分之百的把握获得 200 元；

（3）有百分之百的把握获得 300 元；

---

[1] 国内不少文献将 moral value 译成“道德价值”。作为形容词，moral 一词既有道德的意思，又有精神和心理的意思。从上下文来看，将 moral value 译成“心理价值”比较合适。

（4）有百分之百的把握获得 400 元；

（5）有百分之百的把握获得 500 元；

（6）有百分之百的把握获得 600 元；

（7）有百分之百的把握获得 700 元。

如图 6.2 所示，效用曲线以收益值为横坐标，以效用值为纵坐标。在测试中，学生们表现出不同的风险态度。有的学生停留在方案（3）。这种人宁可稳拿 300 元，也不肯冒 50%失败的风险去争取更多收益，因而是风险厌恶的。在他们的心目中，稳拿 300 元的无风险方案和与有风险方案是等价的，它们的效用都是 0.5。于是就得到点 A（300，0.5），它是风险厌恶学生的效用曲线上的一个点。有的学生则停留在方案（7）。这种人是风险偏好的，他们宁可冒 50%失败的风险去争取更多的收益，也不愿选择稳拿少于 700 元的方案。在他们看来，稳拿 700 元的效用是 0.5，这和有风险方案的效用是等价的。于是就得到点 B（700，0.5），它是风险偏好学生的效用曲线上的一个点。经过反复测试，可以得到不同的点，并最终得到图 6.2 中的三条效用曲线。从曲线的切线斜率变化可以看出，风险厌恶者对损失比较敏感，而对收益的反应比较迟钝。风险偏好者对收益比较敏感，而对损失的反应比较迟钝。

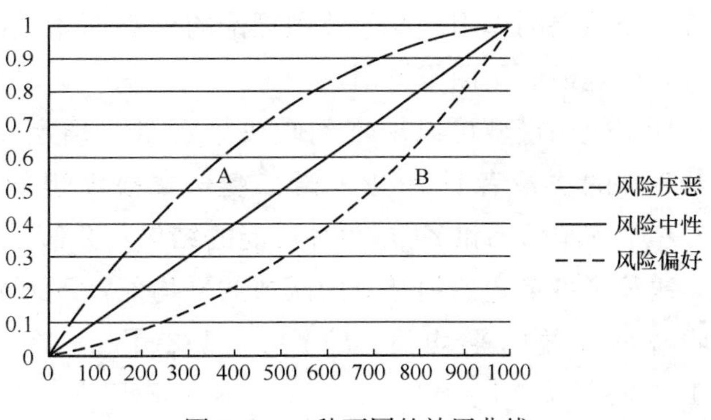

图 6.2 三种不同的效用曲线

以上分析表明，概率论和心理学是不确定性决策理论的两大理论基础。传统经济学通常假定，在不确定条件下——实际是在风险条件下——人们总是能够根据概率判断的原则，理性地或者比较理性地做出正确选择；而心理学和行为经济学的研究表明，传统经济学的理性假设具有系统偏差。心理学的研究成果拓展了经济学的研究视野，为经济学解释人类行为提供了新的工具。然而，在应用主流心理学的研究成果时，必须持谨慎的态度。首先，现代心理学从诞生之日起，就存在追随和模仿自然科学的倾向，试图用自然科学中实证的方法以及观察和实验的方法来研究人的心理和行为，以生物的、生理的或机械运动的形式来解释人类复杂的心理现象。这使得心理学本身具有较大的局限性。其次，主流心理学的理论和方法基本上是在西方的社会文化背景下发展起来的，难免会打上西方文化和价值观的烙印，这使它注定是“一种关于 19 世纪和 20 世纪西方人的心理学”（墨菲，1980，p. 615）。我国的历史、文化、政治和社会经济环境与主流心理学赖以发展的背景之间存在巨大的差异，因此，对主流心理学的成果，只能有条件地借鉴，切忌盲目照搬。

6.1.3 VNM 期望效用函数：一个“风险弓”的视角

由冯·诺依曼和摩根斯坦创建的期望效用模型，长期以来一直在不确定性决策领域占据主导地位。特别是在信息经济学和投资组合理论等研究领域，期望效用模型发挥着十分重要的作用。期望效用理论的核心理念是：人们的决策原则不是最大化期望收益，而是最大化期望效用。

期望效用模型可以用来刻画决策者对不确定性或风险的态度。根据期望效用理论，理性的决策者具有冯·诺依曼—摩根斯坦效用函数，也就是 VNM 效用函数 $U(\cdot)$。假设 Y_1 和 Y_2 是两种可能的结果，并假设得到 Y_1 和 Y_2 的概率均为 1/2，那么，决策者的期望效用是效用函数的平均值：$E[U(Y)]=1/2[U(Y_1)+U(Y_2)]$；而期望收益是收益的平均值：$E(Y)=1/2(Y_1+Y_2)$，相应的效用值为 $U[E(Y)]=U[1/2(Y_1+Y_2)]$。

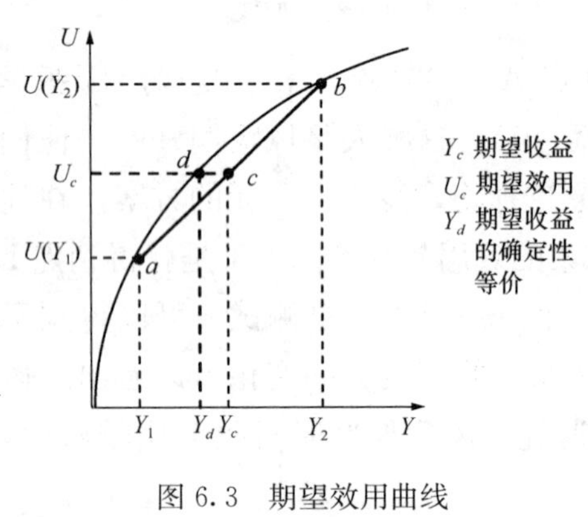

图 6.3 期望效用曲线

（资料来源：亨德里克斯，2007，p.134）

风险厌恶决策者的期望效用函数曲线如图 6.3 所示。随着收益值 Y 的增加，效用值 U 也增大；但是，U 的增加值却在逐步减少。这说明风险厌恶决策者的效用函数是凹函数。图中的线段 ab 及其上方弧线所组成的图形看起来像一张弓，不妨叫作“风险弓”。弓弦反映客观存在的不确定性或风险的大小：弓弦越长，随机结果的变动幅度越大（方差越大），风险也就越大。弓的弯曲程度则反映决策者主观上的风险厌恶程度：弓背越弯，决策者风险厌恶的程度越大。横坐标上的 $Y_c=1/2(Y_1+Y_2)$ 是期望收益，纵坐标上的 $U_c=1/2[U(Y_1)+U(Y_2)]$ 是随机结果 Y 的期望效用。

图 6.3 中横坐标上的 Y_d 被定义为随机结果 Y 的**确定性等价**（certainty equivalent），这是因为，Y_d 的效用和随机结果 Y 的期望效用都是 U_c。对于风险厌恶的决策者来说，确定性等价 Y_d 小于期望收益 Y_c。例如，在前面提到的课堂测试中，有的学生宁可稳拿 300 元，也不肯冒 50%失败的风险去争取更大的收益。在他们的心目中，稳拿 300 元和与有风险收益的期望值 500 元是等价的，它们的效用都是 0.5。在这个例子中，300 元就是有风险收益的确定性等价。确定性等价是对风险收益的一个估价。有了这个概念，最大化期望效用函数的问题就可以转化为最大化确定性等价的问题。

期望收益与确定性等价之差是**风险溢价**（risk premium），又叫作风险成本。在上面的例子中，风险溢价是 Y_c-Y_d。对于风险厌恶的决策者来说，风险溢价为正值；这可以理解为决策者为了规避风险而付出的代价。显然，风险溢价（风险成本）取决于两个因素：一是风险的大小（随机结果的方差，表现在图 6.3 中，就是线段 ab 的长度），二是决策者的风险态度（VNM 效用函数的凹性，表现在图 6.3 中，就是曲线的曲率）。

如果决策者是**风险偏好**（risk seeking）的，“风险弓”的弓背就位于弓弦的下方，效用函数是凸函数，风险溢价（风险成本）为负。如果决策者是**风险中性**（risk neutral）的，“风险弓”的弓背与弓弦合为一体，效用函数是线性的，风险溢价（风险成本）为零。

一般地讲，VNM 效用函数严格的凹性意味着

$$U(\sum_{i=1}^{n} p_i Y_i) > \sum_{i=1}^{n} p_i U(Y_i)$$

式中 p_i（$i=1, 2, \cdots\cdots, n$）是得到第 i 个随机结果的概率。如果效用函数 U 是二次可微的，风险厌恶等价于二阶导数 $U''<0$。**绝对风险规避系数**（coefficient of absolute risk aversion）$r=-U''(Y)/U'(Y)$，它是效用函数 U 的曲率的一个测度，又叫作**阿罗—普拉特测度**（Arrow—Pratt measure）。$r>0$，表示决策者风险厌恶，$r<0$，表示决策者风险偏好，$r=0$，表示决策者风险中性。可以证明，风险溢价的值是 $1/2r$ Var（Y），式中的 Var（Y）是 Y 的方差（迪克西特，2006，p. 115）。期望收益减去风险溢价，就可以得到随机结果 Y 的不确定性等价。

6.1.4　委托代理问题的一般性分析框架

经济学的问题一般都可归结为在一定约束条件下的最大化问题。最大化的对象和约束条件随着研究背景的变化而不同。然而，所有约束条件下的最大化问题都有一个共同的数学结构，反过来，这一数学结构又为分析问题提供了一个共同的经济学直觉（迪克西特，2006，p. 1）。委托代理委托的核心问题是风险的合理分配以及对代理人的有效激励。在委托代理模型中，委托人的问题是：在满足代理人**个人理性约束**（individual rationality constraint）和**激励相容约束**（incentive compatibility constraint）的前提下，设计一个合同，以最大化自己的期望效用（张维迎，1996，pp. 418—428）。委托人在设计合同时需要考虑两方面的因素：一是风险的合理分配，二是对代理人的有效激励。

背景材料：个人理性约束和激励相容约束（资料来源：张维迎，1996，p. 275）

个人理性约束又叫参与约束（participation constraint），它要求代理人接受合同时所能得到的期望效用不能小于其保留效用（reservation utility）或机会成本（opportunity cost），也就是不接受合同时所能得到的最大期望效用。激励相容约束又叫作自选择条件（self-selection condition），它要求代理人选择委托人所希望的行动时所能得到的期望效用，不小于其选择其他行动时所得到的期望效用。只有满足参与约束，代理人才可能接受合同；只有满足激励相容约束，代理人才有可能选择委托人所希望的行

动。满足参与约束的机制是可行的（feasible）；满足激励相容约束的机制是可实施的（implementable）。

在建立模型前，首先要对当事人的风险态度做出假设。一般的委托代理模型都假设委托人是风险中性的，其效用函数是线性的；代理人是风险厌恶的，其效用函数是凹函数。做出这种假设的主要依据是风险分散程度的不同：委托人往往同时从事多项业务（鸡蛋放在多个篮子里），单项业务的风险对其整体利益影响不大，因而委托人的风险能够得到分散；而代理人往往只从事一项业务（鸡蛋放在一个篮子里），该项业务的风险会造成其利益的较大波动，因而代理人的风险比较集中（亨德里克斯，2007，p. 93）。

6.1.4.1 决策顺序与信息结构

在委托代理关系中存在两种不同的选择行为：一是委托人选择代理人，并按一定方式付酬。委托人不能直接观察到代理人的行为，他需根据一定的合同向代理人支付与其行为结果相称的报酬。二是代理人选择自己的行动，代理人的行动既会影响自己的收益，也会影响委托人的收益。行动所产生的结果受随机因素（“自然”）的影响，不在代理人的完全掌控之中。

图 6.4 和图 6.5 描述了**完全或然合同**（complete contingent contract）中的决策顺序和信息结构，以及其中的参与约束和激励相容约束。所谓完全或然合同是指能够精确规定当事各方在未来所有可能的或然情况下如何行动的合同，是完全信息条件下的合同。以下两种情况满足完全信息的条件：一是委托人能够直接观察到代理人的努力水平；二是委托人只能观察到代理人的产出水平，而产出水平和努力水平之间有一种稳定的关系，因此，委托人能够从产出水平推断出代理人的努力水平。为简化起见，图 6.4 和图 6.5 中只列出了两种合同 $\{a, b\}$ 和 $\{c, d\}$，并且只给出了合同 $\{a, b\}$ 的决策顺序。完全或然合同中的变量是代理人努力水平的函数；这是因为，委托人能够观察到（或者根据产出水平精确推断出）代理人的努力水平。

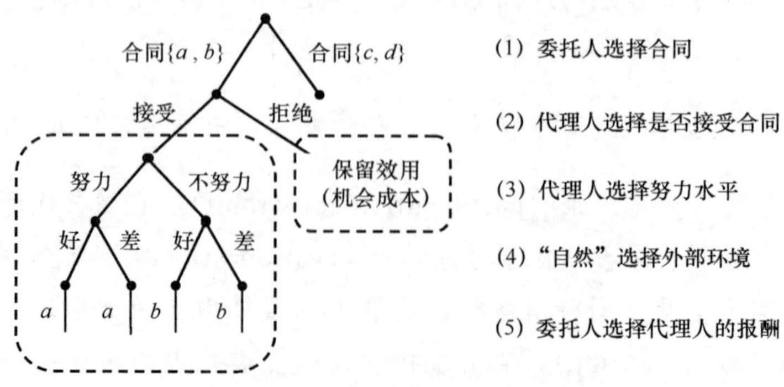

图 6.4　完全或然合同中的参与约束

（资料来源：亨德里克斯，2007，p. 98）

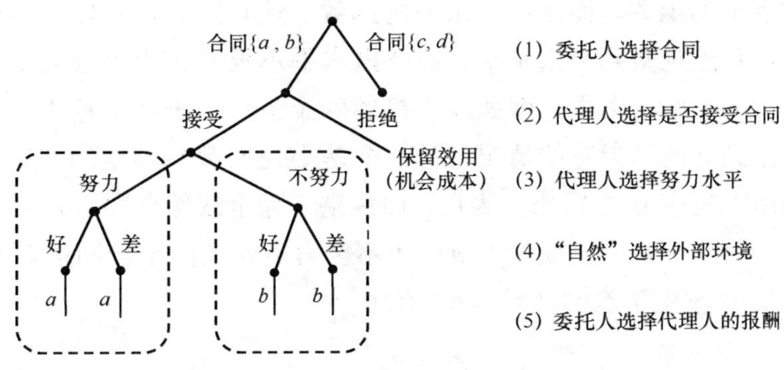

图 6.5　完全或然合同中的激励相容约束

（资料来源：亨德里克斯，2007，p. 95）

决策树中包括五个决策：

（1）委托人选择合同。这里，委托人选择了合同 $\{a, b\}$。

（2）代理人选择是否接受合同。如果不接受合同，决策过程终止，代理人可以从其他机会中得到保留效用。如果代理人接受合同，决策过程继续进行。参与约束要求，代理人从图 6.4 中左边虚线框内得到的收益不低于右边虚线框内的收益水平。

（3）代理人选择努力水平——努力或不努力。产出水平受代理人的努力水平和外部环境随机因素的影响。

（4）虚拟参与人“自然”决定外部环境，进而决定结果的好与差。假设 $p>0.5$，当代理人选择努力时，“自然”选择好结果的概率为 p，选择差结果的概率为 $1-p$；反之，当代理人选择不努力时，“自然”选择好结果的概率为 $1-p$，选择差结果的概率为 p。

（5）委托人选择对代理人的支付报酬。当代理人选择努力时，支付报酬 a，否则支付报酬 b（$a>b$）。显然，要想使代理人做出高水平努力的选择，图 6.5 中左边虚线框内的支付水平不能低于右边虚线框内的支付水平——这就是激励相容约束的要求。

在上述完全信息的条件下，“自然”的选择对代理人没有影响——无论“自然”做出何种选择，代理人只要努力，肯定能够得到 a，如果不努力，则肯定得到 b；而委托人的期望效用会受到来自“自然”和代理人两方面的影响。因此，在完全或然合同中，代理人不承担任何风险，而委托人承担了全部风险。

严格地讲，在完全或然合同中，当事双方之间的关系不是真正意义上的委托代理关系。因为根据前面的定义，委托代理关系只是在信息不对称的条件下才存在；而在完全或然合同中，所谓的代理人并不具备信息优势。因此，完全或然合同中当事双方之间的关系只是一种“准委托代理关系”。

图 6.6 描述了**完全合同**（complete contract）中的决策顺序和信息结构，以及其中的激励相容约束。所谓完全合同是指能够精确规定当事各方在未来所有可能的**可观察**的或然情况下如何行动的合同。在完全合同中，信息结构发生了变化——合同中的变

量不再是努力水平的函数，而是产出水平的函数。这是因为，委托人不能观察到代理人的努力水平，只能观察到产出水平；而产出水平不仅受代理人努力水平的影响，而且还受外部环境的影响。图中由虚弧线连接的两个节点，表示信息集。其中一个信息集是委托人观察到好的结果时的情况；另一个是委托人观察到差的结果时的情况。注意，完全合同用大写字母｛A，B｝表示，以区别于完全或然合同｛a，b｝。在完全或然合同中，变量 a 对应于努力，变量 b 对应于不努力；而在完全合同中，变量 A 对应于好的结果，变量 B 对应于差的结果（$A>B$）。

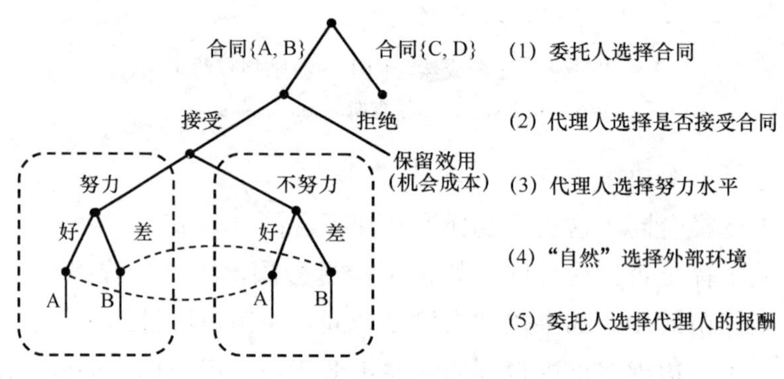

图 6.6　完全合同中的激励相容约束

（资料来源：亨德里克斯，2007，p. 100）

在这种条件下，由于信息是不完全的，委托人和代理人都要承担风险。逆向归纳分析的结果表明，在其他条件相同的情况下，与完全或然合同相比，代理人在完全合同中的期望效用保持不变，而委托人的期望效用有所下降——这说明信息不对称造成了效率损失（亨德里克斯，2007，p. 103）。效率损失可以归结于两方面的原因：一是客观上的风险，二是代理人主观上的风险厌恶。由于代理人是风险厌恶的，其期望工资因承担风险而有所提高（注意，这里说的是“工资”而不是“效用”，对于风险厌恶的代理人而言，工资和效用是不一样的），提高的数值等于委托人期望效用水平下降的幅度（注意，对于风险中性的委托人而言，期望效用水平和收入水平是一致的）——委托人付出了风险成本，代理人获得了风险溢价——这是信息优势给代理人带来的**信息租**（information rent）。

从效率的角度来看，上述完全合同委托代理模型的均衡结果是**次优**（second best, or next best）的（张维迎，1996，pp. 433—437）。在完全信息（完全或然合同）的条件下，委托人承担全部风险，代理人不承担任何风险。由于委托人是风险中性的，完全或然合同中的强激励是有效率的。而在信息不对称（完全合同）的情况下，合同只能建立在可观察变量（产出水平）的基础上，代理人需要承担一定风险——“自然”的选择会影响代理人的期望效用。因此，不完全信息条件下的最优合同是风险分配和行为激励之间的折中，前面所说的效率损失正是这种折中的后果。

前面讨论了完全或然合同和完全合同条件下的决策顺序和信息结构，以及其中的参与约束和激励相容约束问题。接下来的问题是：委托代理理论能否用于不完全合同？对于这个问题的答案应该是肯定的。诚然，在多数情况下，委托代理理论被划为完全合同理论的范畴[❶]（亨德里克斯，2007）；但是，也有的经济学家把委托代理理论应用于不完全合同理论（Bowles，2006）。在《企业理论与中国企业改革》一书中，张维迎（2000）把代理理论（包括代理成本理论与委托代理理论）划为不完全合同的范畴。如果我们把委托代理理论理解为"在代理人参与约束和激励相容约束得到满足的前提下，委托人效用最大化的问题"，该理论的应用范围就可以不限于完全合同的范畴。

总之，在信息对称的条件下，委托人能够观察到代理人的行动，通过强制性的合同就可以使代理人采取委托人所希望的行动，因而无须考虑代理人的激励相容约束。风险问题和激励问题能够得到独立解决。最优合同的均衡结果是帕累托最优的。代理人的支付与产出结果之间的关系由委托人和代理人的绝对风险规避系数的比例所决定（张维迎，1996，p. 412）。在信息不对称的条件下，强制性的合同失灵，委托人只能通过激励性的合同使代理人采取委托人所希望的行动，因而必须同时考虑代理人的参与约束和激励相容约束。最优激励合同要求代理人承担比信息对称条件下更大的风险，对于风险厌恶的代理人来说，这意味着更多的报酬。

6.1.4.2　激励强度与信息强度

假设风险中性的委托人和风险厌恶的代理人之间有一个完全合同。代理人的努力水平为 e，其努力成本为 $C(e)$。产出水平 Y 不仅取决于代理人的努力水平 e，还受不确定环境的影响：$Y=e+x$，其中 x 是数学期望为零的随机变量。委托人只能观察到产出水平 Y，不能观察到代理人的努力水平 e。合同规定，工资由固定工资和变动工资两部分组成：

$$w=\alpha+\beta Y=\alpha+\beta(e+x)$$

式中 α 是固定工资，β 是激励系数（$0\leqslant\beta\leqslant 1$）。委托人的效用函数为 $P(e)-w$，其中 $P(e)$ 是代理人努力水平为 e 时产出的价值。

上述合同中共有四个变量，其中努力水平 e 由代理人决定，随机变量 x 由"自然"决定，固定工资 α 和激励系数 β 由委托人决定。委托人的问题是：在同时满足代理人参与约束和激励相容约束的条件下，选择 α 和 β，最大化自己的期望支付。求解这个最大化问题，可以得到最优激励强度：

$$\beta=\frac{P'(e)}{1+r\mathrm{Var}(x)C''(e)}$$

式中 r 是代理人的风险规避系数，Var（x）是随机变量 x 的方差，方差越大，外部环境的不确定程度越高（亨德里克斯，2007，p. 104）。

---

❶　2016 年诺贝尔经济学奖的获得者本特·霍姆斯特罗姆（Bengt Holmström，1949—）就是完全合同理论和委托代理理论的代表。

从上面的表达式中可以看出，激励强度 β 的大小取决于两方面的因素：一是当事人的风险态度和能力，二是任务和环境的性质。首先，β 与 $P'(e)$ 正相关。$P'(e)$ 是产出价值的变化率，可以理解为产出价值对代理人努力水平的敏感程度。其次，β 与 r 和 Var（x）负相关。风险厌恶的代理人不喜欢收益水平的不确定性，其风险溢价不仅取决于主观上的风险厌恶程度（也就是风险规避系数 r），还取决于客观上不确定性的大小，也就是 x 的方差 Var（x）。最后，β 与 $C''(e)$ 负相关。$C''(e)$ 可以被解释为代理人对自己行为的判断力；一般来说，环境越简单，代理人对自己行为的判断力越强，$C''(e)$ 值就越小。就建设项目而言，一方面，不确定因素较强，作为代理人的承包商对自己行为的估计误差较大，因而 $C''(e)$ 较大；另一方面，利益相关者较多，搭便车的行为较为普遍，因而采用较弱的激励强度是比较合适的。

最优激励合同还可能受其他可观测变量的影响。假设除了产出水平 Y 之外，委托人还能观测到另一个期望值为 0 的随机变量 y，它可以理解为总体经济环境——y 值为正，说明条件有利，y 值为负，则说明条件不利。y 与代理人努力水平 e 无关，但是可能与外生变量 x 有关，进而对 Y 产生影响。这时的合同是：

$$w = \alpha + \beta(e + x + \gamma y)$$

式中的 γ 是一个系数，如果 $\gamma = 0$，代理人的工资与 y 无关。通过与前面类似的求解过程，可以得到考虑总体环境 y 时的最优激励强度：

$$\beta = \frac{P'(e)}{1 + r\mathrm{Var}(x + \gamma y)C''(e)}$$

式中 $\gamma = -\mathrm{Cov}(x,y)/\mathrm{Var}(y)$，$\mathrm{Cov}(x,y)$ 是 x 和 y 的协方差[1]（亨德里克斯，2007，pp. 119—120）。

由此可以得到信息强度原理（informativeness principle）：如果 y 和 x 不相关，协方差 $\mathrm{Cov}(x,y) = 0$，于是 $\gamma = -\mathrm{Cov}(x,y)/\mathrm{Var}(y) = 0$。也就是说，$y$ 不能提供任何有关 x 的信息，将 y 写进合同中是没有意义的。反之，如果 y 和 x 相关，合同中就包含变量 y。将 y 写入合同后，信息量的增加会降低不确定性。可以证明，将 y 写入合同后，一方面可以提高合同的激励强度和代理人分享的剩余份额，另一方面可以减少代理人承担的风险，最终取得减少代理成本的效果（张维迎，1996，pp. 438—439）。

委托人引入变量 y 是为了获得更多有关不确定因素 x 的信息，并且利用 y 值对代理人的努力水平 e 做出更好的估计。如果 y 和 x 正相关，则有 $\gamma < 0$，在此情况下，y 值得不到正面的评价—— $y > 0$ 可以理解为总体环境有利，任何给定的产出水平可能更多地反映了代理人遇到了相对有利的环境而不是付出了较大的努力，因此，产出水

---

[1] 协方差（covariance）$\mathrm{Cov}(x,y) = E\{[x-E(x)][y-E(y)]\} = E(xy) - E(x)E(y)$，又记作 σ_{xy}，是二维随机向量（x，y）的数字特征，用来刻画 x 和 y 取值间的相互关系。协方差为正，表明 x 和 y 呈同向变动的趋势；协方差为负，则表明 x 和 y 具有反向变动的关系。x 和 y 之间的相关系数 $\rho_{xy} = \frac{\sigma_{xy}}{\sqrt{\sigma_{xx}}\sqrt{\sigma_{yy}}}$，式中 σ_{xx}、σ_{yy} 分别代表 x 和 y 的方差（陈家鼎等，1980，pp. 116～120）。

平按 γy 的绝对值向下调整；反之，$y<0$ 可以理解为总体环境不利，产出水平按 γy 的绝对值向上调整。以一个班级的考试成绩为例，当平均分数是90分时，75分就不能算是好成绩，不应该奖励；而当平均分数是60分时，75分就是相当好的成绩了。如果 y 和 x 负相关，则有 $\gamma>0$。为了剔除总体环境的影响，也要做出相应的调整——当 $y>0$ 时，产出水平按 γy 的绝对值向上调整；反之，当 $y<0$ 时，产出水平按 γy 的绝对值向下调整。此时的调整方向与 x、y 正相关时的情况相反。

6.2　建设项目的垂直治理空间

建设项目的垂直治理可以归结为客户对一阶供应商的**激励问题**（incentive problem）；而激励问题又起因于专业化分工。比较优势定理（the law of comparative advantages）可以解释专业化分工的必要性和有效性（亨德里克斯，2007，pp. 5—6）。专业化分工不仅是提高劳动生产率的有力措施，而且是应对不确定性的有效方法（奈特，2006）。

背景材料：劳动分工的巨大优势（资料来源：斯密，2002，pp. 8—10）

在《国富论》的第一章，亚当·斯密以扣针制造业为例，说明了劳动分工的巨大优势："扣针的制造分为十八种操作。……我见过一个这种小工厂，只雇用十个工人，因此在这一个工厂中，有几个工人担任二三种操作。像这样一个小工厂的工人，虽很穷困，他们的必要机械设备，虽很简陋，但他们如果勤勉努力，……一人一日可成针四千八百枚。如果他们各自独立工作，不专习一种特殊业务，那末，他们不论是谁，绝对不能一日制造二十枚针，说不定一天连一枚针也制造不出来。他们不但不能制出今日由适当分工合作而制成的数量的二百四十分之一，就连这数量的四千八百分之一，恐怕也制造不出来。"

专业化分工一方面可以带来巨大的效益，另一方面会产生双边或多边的依存关系，进而产生激励问题和**协调问题**（coordination problem）（亨德里克斯，2007，pp. 8—9）。在这两类问题中，信息是至关重要的因素。当出现信息不对称并且存在利益冲突时，就会产生激励问题——拥有私人信息的一方有可能凭借信息优势损害他人的利益——这时需要通过适当的激励设计降低利益冲突的程度。协调问题也源于信息的短缺，但问题的实质是缺乏他人决策方面的信息（亨德里克斯，2007，p. 291）。专业化的发展程度最终取决于收益和成本的权衡。从理论上讲，当边际收益等于边际成本时，专业化达到最佳水平。

6.2.1　项目采购方式

表6.2列出了几种有代表性的**项目采购方式**（Project Procurement Route，PPR），

建筑业专业化分工的多样性和组织的复杂性由此可见一斑。建设项目的各种采购方式都是在一定历史条件下产生的，又随着社会经济发展和科学技术进步而变化。不同的建设项目采购方式具有不同的治理结构。在不同的采购方式中，有关各方的责权利配置不同。委托代理的层次越多，信息不对称的程度越大，激励问题也就愈加突出。反之，协调问题将成为主要矛盾。例如，传统的DBB模式以设计与施工相分离为特征。该模式中的委托代理关系可分为两个层次：在第一层次，业主是委托人，设计方和总承包商是两个相对独立的代理人；在第二层次，总承包商与分包商之间形成委托代理关系。DB模式将设计与施工合为一体。该模式中的委托代理关系可分为三个层次：在第一层次，业主是委托人，设计—建造公司是代理人；在第二层次，设计—建造公司是委托人，设计方和总承包商是两个相对独立的代理人；在第三层次，总承包商与分包商之间形成委托代理关系。由于该模式的层次较多，委托代理关系相对复杂，对代理人的激励问题成为主要矛盾。在CM模式中，业主、设计方和建设管理公司之间形成三位一体的关系。其中在风险型建设管理模式中，委托代理关系可分为两个层次：在第一层次，业主是委托人，设计方和建设管理公司是两个相互关联的代理人；在第二层次，建设管理公司和分包商之间存在委托代理关系。在代理型建设管理模式中，委托代理关系只有一个层次：业主是委托人，设计方、建设管理公司和承包商是相互关联的三个代理人。由于该模式的层次较少，委托代理关系比较简单，协调问题成为主要矛盾。

建设项目采购方式比较 表6.2

类型	示意图	合同关系	说明
传统的DBB模式 Design—Bid—Build 设计-招标-建造	业主 设计方 总承包商 自有力量 分包商	1. 业主与设计方签订设计合同，与总承包商签订施工合同。 2. 总承包商与分包商签订合同	1. 设计、招标、施工依次进行。 2. 业主是中心环节
DB模式 Design—Build 设计-建造	业主 设计-建造公司 设计方 总承包商 自有力量 分包商	1. 业主与设计—建造公司签订合同。 2. 设计—建造公司分别与设计方、总承包商签订合同。 3. 总承包商与分包商签订合同	1. 业主代表负责与设计—建造公司的沟通与协调。 2. 设计—建造公司是中心环节

续表

类型	示意图	合同关系	说明
CM 模式（一） Construction Management 风险型建设管理	业主 设计方　建设管理公司 分包商	1. 业主与设计方签订设计合同，与建设管理公司签订咨询服务合同和施工合同。 2. 建设管理公司与分包商签订合同（须经业主确认）。 3. 建设管理公司与设计方之间是协调关系	1. 业主、设计方和建设管理公司三位一体。 2. 分阶段发包，没有总承包商。 3. 建设管理公司是中心环节
CM 模式（二） Construction Management 代理型建设管理	业主 设计方　建设管理公司 承包商	1. 业主与设计方签订设计合同，与承包商签订施工合同，与建设管理公司签订咨询服务合同。 2. 建设管理公司与设计方之间是协调关系，与承包商之间也是协调管理关系	

近年来，公私合伙制（public—private partnerships，PPP）在基础设施建设领域得到广泛应用。PPP 有广义和狭义之分。广义的 PPP 泛指公共部门与私人部门为提供公共产品或服务而建立的各种合作关系，而狭义的 PPP 可以理解为一系列项目采购方式的总称，它包含 BOT（建设—运营—转交）、TOT（转交—运营—转交）、DBFO（设计—建造—融资—经营）等多种模式。狭义的 PPP 更加注重合作过程中的风险分担机制和项目的资金价值（王灏，2004）。从纵向一体化的角度来看，PPP 将建设项目的设计、施工和运营合为一体。从项目融资投资的角度看，PPP 把政府直接投资改为间接融资。PPP 的实质是私人部门参与提供公共产品或服务。把握住这个实质是正确理解 PPP 的关键所在。目前在国际上还没有形成关于 PPP 的统一的定义；有关国家和国际组织对 PPP 的分类多达十几种。如表 6.3 所示，世界银行根据五个方面的因素，将广义 PPP 分为六种类型。

世界银行的 PPP 分类　　**表 6.3**

PPP 类型	产权	经营和维护	投资	商业风险	合同期限
服务外包	公共部门	公共部门和私人部门	公共部门	公共部门	1—2 年
管理外包	公共部门	私人部门	公共部门	公共部门	3—5 年
租赁	公共部门	私人部门	公共部门	共同分担	8—15 年
特许经营	公共部门	私人部门	私人部门	私人部门	25—30 年
BOT/BOO	私人部门和公共部门	私人部门	私人部门	私人部门	20—30 年
剥离	私人部门或私人部门和公共部门	私人部门	私人部门	私人部门	永久

（资料来源：The World Bank，1997）

6.2.2 建设项目的合同类型

多数情况下，一种建设项目采购方式会涉及不同的委托代理关系。每种委托代理关系都需要合同来规范。建设项目常用的合同类型有：固定价格合同（fixed price contract，有时又叫作 lump-sum contract，即总价合同）、成本加费用合同（cost-plus fee contract）和实测数量合同（remeasurement contract）等。合同的类型影响经济交往的结构，并进一步影响当事人行为的均衡分布（Bowles，2004，p. 258）。如图 6.7 所示，不同的项目采购方式和不同的合同类型相结合，产生不同的项目治理结构和激励模式。这些模式中，没有“最好”，只有“最合适”。也就是说，应该根据当事人的风险态度和建设项目的实际条件，权衡利弊，选择合适的采购方式和合同类型。

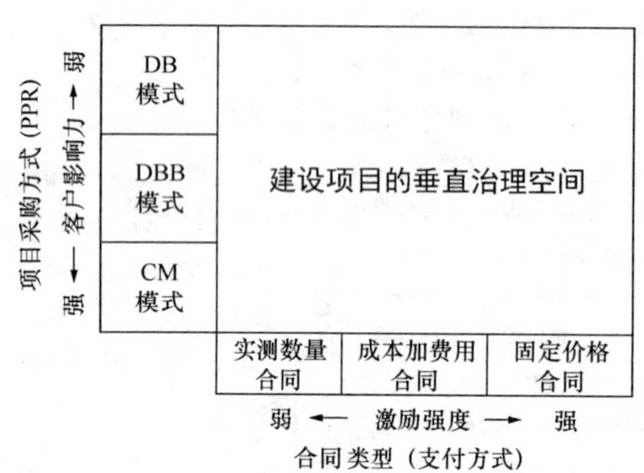

图 6.7 建设项目的垂直治理空间

（资料来源：Sha，2011）

需要指出，对于 DBB、DB、BOT 等模式，国外一般称之为项目采购方式；而在国内的文献中，不同的作者采用了不同的术语和称谓。不少作者把这些模式连同代建制一起统统叫作建设项目的管理模式，有的作者则把它们叫作建设工程交易模式，还有的作者把 BOT 等模式叫作建设项目的融资与合同管理模式。实际上，这些模式都属于项目治理的范畴。名不正则言不顺。为了理顺关系、规范研究，首先需要正名。把 DBB、DB、BOT 和代建制等模式叫作项目采购方式是比较合适的，这样可以与国际主流文献保持一致。更为重要的是，可以避免管理和治理之间的混淆。此外还要指出，无论从广义还是狭义的角度来看，PPP 都是一个大的概念范畴，而不是特定的某一种项目采购方式。因此，把 PPP 和 BOT、TOT、DBFO 等具体的项目采购方式在同一个层次上相提并论的做法是不合适的。

6.3 建设项目的垂直治理模型❶

治理问题的关键在于剩余控制权与剩余索取权的一致性；两者不对应会导致权利的残缺（费方域，2006）。谁最有积极性做出正确的决策，就应该让谁拥有控制权；拥有控制权的人应该是风险的承担者。每种治理结构都具有自己的权威程度（亨德里克

❶ 这一节的内容主要来自发表在 *Construction Management and Economics* 杂志和《项目管理技术》杂志上的文章（Sha，2011；沙凯逊等，2011）。

斯，2007，p. 231)。在不同的治理结构中，各方当事人的相对地位是不一样的。比如，在传统的 DBB 模式中，业主处于中心环节，理应承担激励和协调的主要职责；在 DB 模式中，设计—建造公司处于中心环节，是解决激励问题的关键所在；而在 CM 模式中，处于中心环节的建设管理公司是协调工作的主要力量。

背景材料：剩余控制权与剩余索取权

企业和建设项目都可以看作一系列合同的集合，这些合同又是不完全的，于是就产生了剩余权利，也就是剩余控制权和剩余索取权。前者是对合同中未能明确规定的事项进行决策的权利；后者是在合同履行之后取得剩余收益的权利，也就是从总产品中扣除所有签约要素的报酬之后的剩余利益的占有权。

6.3.1　不确定性、专用知识与信息成本

管理的决策理论学派认为，管理就是决策；而决策离不开信息的支持。如图 6.8 所示，决策所需要的信息与可获取信息之间的缺口是不确定性产生的根源，同时也可以作为不确定性的定义和测度标准。

如图 6.9 所示，根据产生的原因和可度量性的不同，广义的不确定性可以分为四种类型，即人为风险、自然风险、人为不确定性和自然不确定性。在图 6.9 中，上面一行是可度量的，包括人为风险和自然风险，这类问题属于风险决策的范畴。左侧一列是人为造成的，包括人为风险和人为不确定性，这类问题可以归结为信息不对称造成的委托代理问题。而自然不确定性，则可以看作是“自然”或虚拟参与人隐藏信息或隐藏行动的结果，并且这些结果是不可度量的。

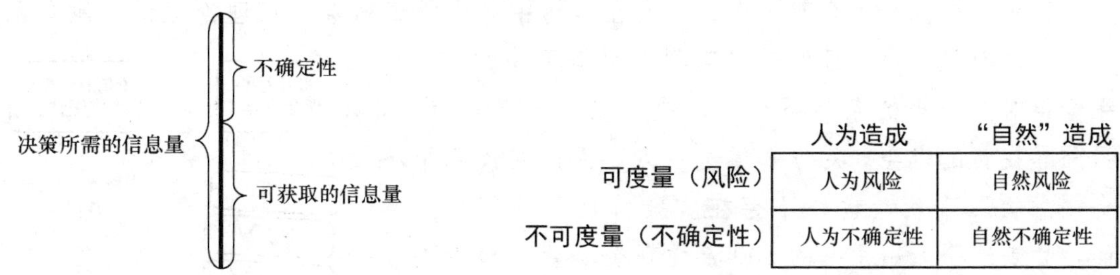

图 6.8　信息缺口：不确定性的定义与测度
（资料来源：Galbraith，1977）

图 6.9　不确定性方块图
（资料来源：沙凯逊等，2009）

根据奈特（2006）的理论，对于不确定性，专业化是较为有效的一种处理方法。专业注册师制度是针对不确定性，特别是自然不确定性的一种制度安排。由于建筑业所面临的自然不确定性是其他行业所没有的，因此面向建筑业的专业注册资格的种类要大大超过其他行业。如果说，不确定性是建设项目存在的重要理由，那么，以专业注册资格为代表的专用知识就是建设项目的核心要素。

如前所述，以期望效用模型为代表的不确定性决策理论实际上讨论的是风险决策的问题。在经典的委托代理模型中，委托人所能观察到的信息由代理人的行动和由“自然”提供的外部环境共同决定，而后者的概率分布是已知的。因此，在这些模型中，所谓的“不确定性”实际上也是作为风险来处理的。下面要建立的模型以奈特（2006）关于风险和不确定性的理论以及 Galbraith（1977）对不确定性的定义为依据，用可测度性（是否具有概率分布）作为区分风险和不确定性的标准；把专用知识作为解决不确定性问题的基本方法。在模型中，信息缺口（决策所需要的信息与可获取的信息之差）不仅用于衡量不确定性的大小，同时用于反映专用知识对于建设项目的重要程度。根据以上思路，可以将不确定性、专用知识和信息成本纳入委托代理关系的分析框架。

6.3.2 模型的基本假设

专用知识，特别是隐性知识（tacit knowledge），属于**人力资产专用性**（human asset specificity）的范畴。如前所述，专用性资产会导致交易成本的增加。首先，专用性资产使当事人之间的关系发生根本性转变——由互不依赖转变为相互依存；其次，当事人之间的分配对象由剩余改为**准剩余**（quasi surplus）——后者等于前者与沉淀投资之和；最后，专用性资产的投资者面临被其他当事人**“敲竹杠”**（hold up，索取高价，有时被译为“套牢”）的威胁，导致事后讨价还价的能力降低（亨德里克斯，2007，pp. 176—178）。

背景资料：资产专用性与“敲竹杠”问题

设想一个拥有 100 万元现金的人在市场中寻求投资机会。从理论上讲，他有无数个机会，而且在讨价还价时与谈判对手是平等的——如果觉得对方给出的条件不合适，他可以立即退出谈判，另外寻找新的机会。对方知道这一点，因此在谈判中不会刻意索取高价，也就不存在“敲竹杠”的问题。然而，如果这个人用手头的 100 万元现金购置一台专用设备（比如说一台挖掘机），事情就会发生很大变化——他的机会明显减少，谈判能力也明显减弱。这是因为，和 100 万元的现金资本相比，挖掘机的应用范围是十分有限的。如果觉得对方给出的条件不合适，他可以退出谈判，另寻机会，但是，新的机会是十分有限的。谈判对手就会利用这一点刻意索取高价，于是就产生了“敲竹杠”的问题。

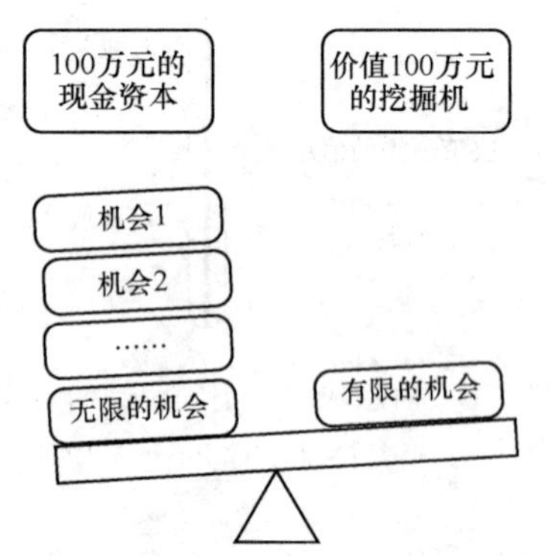

资产专用性导致谈判筹码减少，进而导致“敲竹杠”问题的产生

威廉姆森对治理结构进行比较分析，得出如图 6.10 所示的结论：市场适合于资产专用性较低的情况（$k < k_1$）；科层适合于资产专用性较高的情况（$k > k_2$）；混合结构只是在一定的资产专用性（$k_1 < k < k_2$）和较低的干扰频率条件下有效（Williamson，1991）。

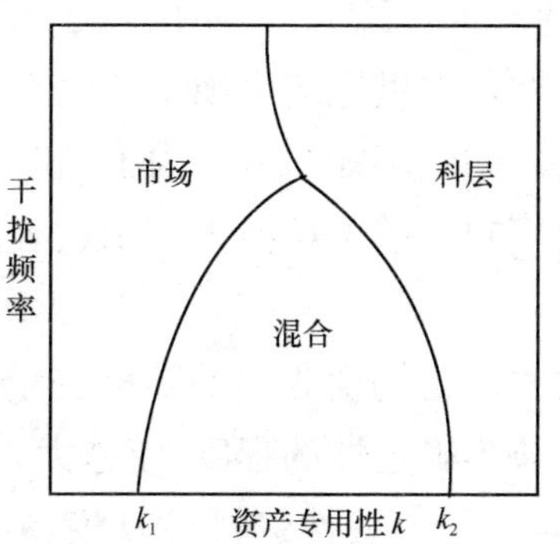

图 6.10　混合治理结构的有效空间

（资料来源：Williamson，1991）

按照上述结论，资产专用性很高的建设项目理应采用科层结构，而实际上采用的却是混合结构。在现实问题的挑战面前，有必要重新审视交易成本理论所做出的抽象与假设。分析治理结构的目标原本应该是生产成本和交易成本的最小化。而威廉姆森却忽略了生产成本。他的分析“完全集中于交易成本：既不考虑资产专用化带来的收益效果，也不考虑它所产生的生产成本的节约”（Williamson，1991，p. 282）。此外，尽管威廉姆森将资产专用性划分为场地、物质资产、人力资产、品牌资本、专用资产和时间专用性等六种类型，然而在分析过程中，他却“为简化起见，假设资产专用性的差异完全起因于物质和场地的性质”（Williamson，1991，p. 282）。威廉姆森之所以做出这样的处理，可能是因为其研究对象是重复进行的生产和交易的缘故（Turner and Keegan，2001；Turner，2004）。这些抽象与假设在带来分析便利性的同时，也产生了一定的局限性。建设项目是新颖、独特的一次性任务，信息缺口大。对于建设项目来说，处理不确定性所需的专用知识至关重要。这些特点与威廉姆森的假设条件之间有很大差别。在这种条件下选择治理结构，忽略生产成本而单独考虑交易成本的做法是否合适，这是一个值得讨论的问题。

应该看到，不确定性产生的压力有时会抑制有关当事人“敲竹杠”的积极性。如果信息缺口超过一定程度，不确定性对生产成本的影响可能会超过“敲竹杠”对交易成本的影响。因此，在资产专用性水平很高的情况下，混合结构也可能有效。就建设项目而言，当不确定性增加到一定程度，甲方“敲竹杠”的积极性降低，乙方纵向一体化的倾向也因此而减弱，因此，最终的选择就可能不是经典理论中所预期的科层结构，而是混合结构。由以上分析可以得出两个假设。

假设 1：较大的信息缺口（也就是较大程度的不确定性）要求较高的专业化水平，这意味着解决信息短缺问题所需的专用知识对于建设项目具有较高的重要性。

假设 2：当信息缺口达到一定程度，并且专用知识的比重超过一定程度时，建设项目采购方式的选择过程有可能不再沿着经典理论的预期方向发展，而是发生转折——相对于前面所说的根本性转变，这一转折或许可以叫作“二阶转变”。

6.3.3　模型的构建与求解

假设建设项目涉及两个当事人，一个是客户（委托人，甲方），一个是总承包商

（代理人，乙方）。委托人是风险中性的，代理人是风险厌恶的。考虑到专用知识的重要性，这里把建设项目的生产资料分为两类：一般性资料 G 和解决不确定性（信息短缺）的专用知识 K。为了同时将一般性资料 G 和专用知识 K 纳入模型，这里用非线性的柯布—道格拉斯生产函数表示项目的产出：

$$Y = K^{\gamma} G^{1-\gamma} + x$$

式中 x 是均值为零的随机变量，用来反映可测度的外部风险；γ 是信息缺口指数，用来反映不确定性的程度。γ 越大，专业知识 K 越重要。$\gamma=0$，专用知识 K 从模型中消失；$\gamma=1$，一般性资料 G 从模型中消失。这两种状态都不是我们所要讨论的，因此设定 $0<\gamma<1$。

甲方的可观测变量是项目的产出 Y，甲方给乙方的报酬是：

$$w = \alpha + \beta Y = \alpha + \beta(K^{\gamma} G^{1-\gamma} + x)$$

式中 α 是固定报酬，β 是激励系数。为满足激励相容约束，代理人需要选择为项目所付出的专用知识 K 和一般性资料 G，以最大化自己的期望效用。由此可以得到专用知识 K 和一般性资料 G 之间的比例关系，也就是专用知识比例系数：

$$\lambda = \sqrt{\frac{q\gamma}{p(1-\gamma)}}$$

式中 p 和 q 分别是专用知识 K 和一般性资料 G 的成本系数。
通过进一步求解，可以得到最优激励系数：

$$\beta^* = \frac{1}{1+\left(\frac{p}{\gamma}\right)^{\gamma}\left(\frac{q}{1-\gamma}\right)^{1-\gamma} r\mathrm{Var}(x)}$$

式中 r 是代理人的绝对风险规避系数，$\mathrm{Var}(x)$ 为随机变量 x 的方差。

6.3.4 比较静态分析

经济学模型中的变量可分为两类：内生变量和外生变量。内生变量又叫做决策变量（decision variable）；而作为给定条件的参数属于外生变量。所谓比较静态分析，就是分析外生变量的变化对内生变量的影响，以及最优解是如何随着参数的变动而变动的。这里所涉及的参数包括信息缺口指数 γ、专用知识 K 的成本系数 p 和一般性资料 G 的成本系数 q。

首先分析相关参数对“二阶转变”和项目采购方式的影响。如前所述，代理人为项目所付出的专用知识 K 和一般性资料 G 之间的比例，也就是专用知识比例系数是 $\lambda=\sqrt{\frac{q\gamma}{p(1-\gamma)}}$，这是代理人的激励相容约束所要求的。从这个表达式可以看出，专用知识比例系数 λ 随信息缺口指数 γ 的变化而变化；λ 是 γ 的函数，可表示为 $\lambda(\gamma;p,q)$。括弧中的分号用来区分自变量和参数：自变量 γ 位于分号的前面，参数 p、q 则在分号的后面。

图 6.11 给出了 λ 随 γ 的变化而变化的情况。横轴 γ 是信息缺口；γ 值越大，不确定性对生产成本的压力也就越大。纵轴 λ 是专用知识 K 和一般性资料 G 之间的比例；λ 值越大，专用知识 K 的比重就越大，代理人“敲竹杠”的压力也就越大。$\gamma=0$，说明没有信息缺口，因而也就没有不确定性，此时 $\lambda=0$，专用知识 $K=0$。随着 γ 的增加，λ 值越来越大，专用知识 K 的比重越来越大。$\gamma\rightarrow1$，说明信息缺口极大，这时 $\lambda\rightarrow\infty$，一般性资料 G→0。随着专用知识的相对成本系数 p/q 的增加，函数曲线向右偏移。这显示出参数 p、q 的变动带来的影响，也就是函数 $\lambda(\gamma;p,q)$ 的比较静态效应。

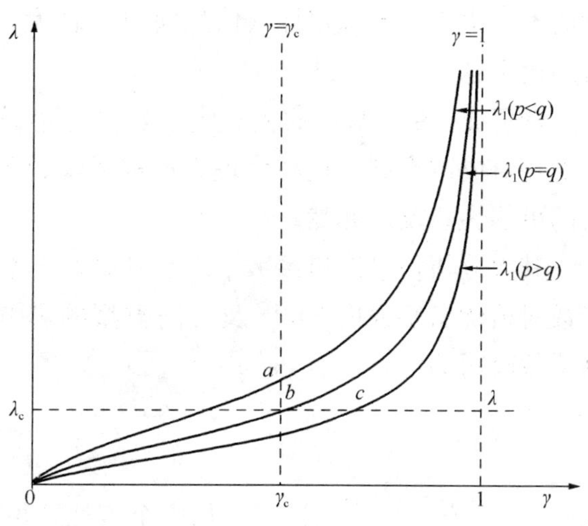

图 6.11 建设项目的二阶转变

根据前面的假设 2，设定两个临界值：$\gamma=\gamma_c$ 和 $\lambda=\lambda_c$。在图 6.11 中，发生“二阶转变”的空间由直线 $\gamma=\gamma_c$、$\gamma=1$ 和 $\lambda=\lambda_c$ 界定——比如，设定 $\lambda_c=1$，$\gamma_c=1/2$，于是曲线 λ_2（$p/q=1$）通过两条临界线 $\gamma=\gamma_c$ 和 $\lambda=\lambda_c$ 的交点。在这个区域之外（$0<\gamma<\gamma_c$ 或 $0<\lambda<\lambda_c$），“敲竹杠”问题对交易成本的影响是主要矛盾，对生产成本的影响可以忽略不计，选择治理结构按照威廉姆森的逻辑进行。而在这个区域之内，不确定性对生产成本的压力成为主要矛盾，在选择治理结构时，需要同时考虑生产成本和交易成本。

表 6.4 对图 6.11 给出的三种临界状态做出了比较。在 a 点处，“敲竹杠”压力大于不确定性压力，因此代理人掌握控制权的积极性较高，委托人介入的可能性较小；这种状态大致上对应于 DB 项目采购方式，即总承包模式。在 c 点处，不确定性压力大于“敲竹杠”的压力，因此代理人掌握控制权的积极性较低，委托人介入的可能性较大；这种状态大致上对应于 CM 项目采购方式。显然，只有 b 点同时满足两个临界条件，“敲竹杠”的压力和不确定性压力在这里大体上相当，这种状态大致上对应于传统的 DBB 项目采购方式。

三种临界状态的比较 **表 6.4**

状态	专用知识的相对成本系数	信息缺口指数	专用知识比例系数	项目采购方式
a	$p/q<1$	$\gamma=\gamma_c$	$\lambda>\lambda_c$	DB 模式
b	$p/q=1$	$\gamma=\gamma_c$	$\lambda=\lambda_c$	传统的 DBB 模式
c	$p/q>1$	$\gamma>\gamma_c$	$\lambda=\lambda_c$	CM 模式

由此可得到关于项目采购方式的两个命题。

命题 1：代理人在建设项目中投入的专业知识的比重由信息缺口和专用知识的相

对成本所决定。不确定性（信息缺口）越大，专用知识的相对成本越低，专用知识所占的比重越大。

命题 2：专用知识的相对成本是决定建设项目采购方式的重要因素。较低的专用知识相对成本有利于提高代理人承担风险、掌握控制权的积极性，从而降低委托人介入的可能性。反之亦然。

其次分析信息缺口系数 γ、专用知识成本系数 p 和一般性资料成本系数 q 这三个参数对最优激励强度 β^* 以及合同类型的影响。为了便于论述，将前面得到的最优激励系数改写为：

$$\beta^* = \frac{1}{1+\rho r \mathrm{Var}(x)}$$

式中 $\rho = \left(\frac{p}{\gamma}\right)^{\gamma}\left(\frac{q}{1-\gamma}\right)^{1-\gamma}$。从这个表达式可以看出，$\rho$ 随 γ 的变化而变化；ρ 是 γ 的函数，可表示为 $\rho(\gamma;p,q)$。括弧中的分号用来区分自变量和参数：自变量 γ 位于分号的前面，参数 p、q 则在分号的后面。可以证明，当 $\gamma^* = \frac{p}{p+q}$ 时，函数 $\rho(\gamma;p,q)$ 取得最大值 $\rho^* = p+q$。

图 6.12 给出了两种不同条件下，函数 $\rho(\gamma;p,q)$ 的曲线。由于最优激励系数 β^* 和 ρ 之间是负相关的关系，因此在 ρ 的极值点附近，给定风险的方差和代理人的风险态度，β^* 值较小，激励强度也较小。于是在 ρ 的极值点附近会形成一个用阴影表示的“弱激励区”。从图中可以看出，随着专用知识的相对成本系数 p/q 由小变大，“弱激励区”的位置从左向右移动——当 $p=1/2, q=1$ 时，“弱激励区”在 $\gamma=1/3$ 附近；当 $p=2, q=1$ 时，“弱激励区”在 $\gamma=2/3$ 附近。根据同样的道理可以推测，当 $p=q$ 时，“弱激励区”处于居中的位置。

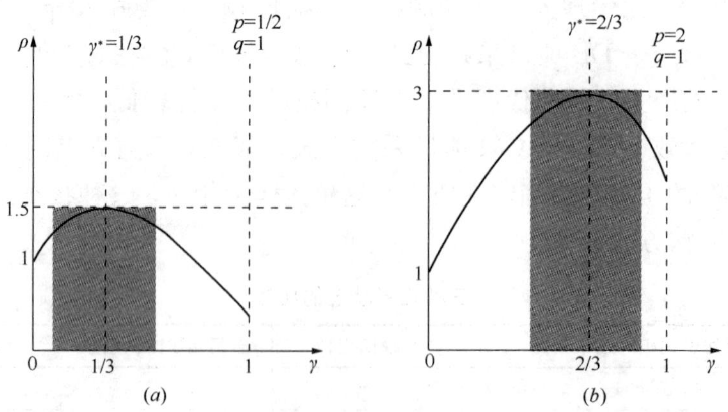

图 6.12 ρ 的极值点与弱激励区

由此可得到关于合同类型的两个命题。

命题 3：最优激励强度 β^* 和专用知识成本系数 p、一般性资料成本系数 q 负相关。

命题 4：在其他条件相同的情况下，给定一般性资料成本系数 p 和专用知识成本系数 q，在决定激励强度时，需考虑以下情况：

（1）当 p 明显小于 q 时，如果信息缺口很小，宜采用较弱的激励，否则采用较强的激励。

（2）当 p 明显大于 q 时，如果信息缺口很大，宜采用较弱的激励，否则采用较强的激励。

（3）当 p 与 q 大致相当时，如果信息缺口很大或是很小，宜采用较强的激励；否则采用较弱的激励。

6.3.5　小结

在一定意义上可以说，建设项目的存在是科层和市场治理失效的结果；而两者失效的主要原因又在于不确定性。按照奈特的逻辑，专业化是处理不确定性的有效手段，或者可以反过来说，不确定性导致专业化的产生和发展。按照威廉姆森的逻辑，资产专用性导致根本性转变的发生，并最终导致交易成本的增加。这里从建设项目的特殊性出发，修正了威廉姆森"在确定治理结构时可以忽略生产成本"的假设，将不确定性和信息成本纳入分析框架，用扩展后的委托代理模型分析了建设项目的采购方式和合同类型，得出以下结论：信息缺口和专用知识的相对成本系数是决定建设项目采购方式与合同类型的重要因素，它们不仅决定"二阶转变"发生的时机，而且决定"弱激励区"的分布。

总之，在决定建设项目的采购方式时，不仅要考虑乙方"敲竹杠"给交易成本带来的压力，还要考虑不确定性给生产成本带来的压力。在决定建设项目的合同类型时，需要同时考虑不确定性，以及一般性资料和专用知识的成本。

6.4　当事人的风险态度与建设项目的激励策略[1]

经济理论每一种研究范式的成功都在于它们所做出的抽象与假设，而这些抽象与假设不可避免地会产生一定的局限性（费方域，2006，p. 17）。如前所述，在委托代理理论中，一般假设委托人是风险中性的，其效用函数是线性的；代理人是风险厌恶的，其效用函数是凹函数。为了便于论述，下面把"委托人风险中性，代理人风险厌恶"的假设简称为"中性—厌恶"假设；并以此类推，把"委托人风险偏好，代理人风险厌恶"的假设简称为"偏好—厌恶"假设，如此等等，不一而足。

在多数情况下，基于"中性—厌恶"假设的模型具有较好的解释能力，因此在许多领域成为重要的分析工具。然而，现实中的当事人行为可能会出现与"中性—厌恶"

[1] 这一节的内容主要来自发表在《项目管理技术》杂志上的文章（华冬冬，沙凯逊，2011）。

假设不符的情况，这时就需要做出相应的修正。田厚平等人（2007）把参与人的风险偏好拓展到“委托人风险中性、代理人风险规避或风险中性”和“委托人风险规避、代理人风险中性或风险规避”等四种组合类型，研究了每种组合下的最优激励机制设计问题。然而，上述研究没有涉及当事人属于风险偏好的情况。这里从我国建设市场的实际出发，提出建设项目当事人风险态度多样性的命题，进一步放宽假设条件，引进风险偏好的假设，扩展委托代理模型的分析范围，并提出相应的激励策略。

6.4.1 建设项目当事人的风险态度多样性分析

由于我国建设市场的不成熟，加之激励机制中非经济因素的大量存在，建设项目当事人的行为偏离“中性—厌恶”假设的情况时有发生。首先，建设项目的甲方，特别是政府投资项目的甲方有时会表现出风险偏好的态度。在我国，地方政府扮演着“准市场主体的角色”（中国经济增长与宏观稳定课题组，2010）。地方官员的激励结构具有双重特征：他们一方面是“经济参与人”，另一方面是“政治参与人”。在政治晋升博弈中，参与人面临的是一个零和博弈：给定有限的晋升机会，一个人获得提升将直接降低另一人提升的机会。“官场”竞争的逻辑将深刻地改变由官员所主导的经济竞争的方式和内容（周黎安，2004）。在 GDP 拜物教盛行的地方和单位，关于“发展”的考量大于一切。在这种情况下，政府投资项目的建设单位往往表现出较强的机会主义行为和寻租倾向。在风险面前，当事人有可能表现出偏好而不是中性的态度。大量项目缺乏科学的论证，有的甚至不履行必要的程序而仓促上马。很难想象，风险中性或风险规避的当事人会如此鲁莽地决策。

背景资料：

据世界银行估算，1996 至 2005 年期间，我国因投资决策失误造成的损失至少为 2.4 万亿元。统计年鉴显示，1996 至 2005 年期间，我国投资项目失误率接近投资项目总数的 50%。2003 年对使用国债建设资金的 526 个城市基础设施项目的审计表明，在已建成的 320 个项目中，有 32 个项目基本没有投入运营，18 个长期处于试运营或非正常运行状态，69 个已经运营的项目没有达到当年设计生产能力。有 34 个项目存在较为严重的损失浪费问题（庞永师等，2009）。

其次，建设项目的乙方，特别是大型国有施工企业的决策者有时会表现出风险中性甚至风险偏好的态度。下面的例子就很有说服力。

背景资料：

中国铁建 2010 年 10 月 25 日发布公告称，该公司承建的沙特阿拉伯王国麦加轻轨项目发生 41.53 亿元人民币的巨额亏损。造成这一严重后果的原因固然有很多，而承包方在应对风险方面的失误则是致命的。这原本是一个商业项目，却被铁道兵出身的承包方视为“不讲条件，不讲价钱”的政治工程。首先，在施工条件异常困难、合同条款和报价与实际严重不符的情况下，该项目没有采用投标，而是采用了议标的方式。其次，该项目采用 EPC＋O&M（engineering procurement construction operation and management）总承包模式，而在签约时却只有概念性设计。最后，在变更索赔尚未落实的情况下，为了保证项目按时竣工，公司从全系统 15 家单位调集人员驰援现场，不计成本地展开会战（赵笛，2010）。这种反常的态度和行为最终使中国铁建公司蒙受惨重的损失。

无独有偶，2011 年 7 月 29 日，国资委有关负责人向记者证实，中国海外工程总公司（以下简称中海外）牵头的波兰高速公路项目因严重亏损，正面临巨额索赔。2009 年 9 月，中国中铁旗下的两家全资子公司（中海外和中铁隧道）联合上海建工集团及波兰德科玛有限公司组成中海外联合体，中标波兰 A2 高速公路中最长的两个标段，总里程 49 公里。这是我国建筑业正式承担的首个欧盟国家的建筑工程。因为波兰 2012 年 6 月和乌克兰联合举办欧洲足球杯，招标时要求必须在 2012 年 5 月 31 日前建成通车。然而，该项目于 2011 年 5 月中旬，因拖欠分包商工程费用而被迫停工。此时工期已过大半，而工程量只完成不到 20%。波兰高速公路管理局公开宣布解除与中海外联合体签署的承包协议。2011 年 6 月初，中海外总公司最终决定放弃该工程，因为如果坚持做完，中海外联合体可能因此亏损 6.94 亿美元（约合 25.45 亿元人民币）。业主方则给联合体开出了 7.41 亿兹罗提（约合 17.51 亿元人民币）的赔偿要求和罚单，外加三年内禁止其在波兰市场参与招标的惩罚。此次失败的原因比较复杂；但主要原因在于中海外的风险态度。当时波兰政府对该项目的预算为 28 亿兹罗提，而中方报价只为 13 亿兹罗提，仅是波兰方面预算的 46%。中海外波兰事件只是中国建筑企业“走出去”过程中一个“交学费”的典型案例。在一位熟悉国际工程承包法律纠纷的律师看来，“中海外不是第一个，肯定也不会是最后一个。”（倪伟峰等，2011）

以上分析表明，在一定条件下，建设项目的当事人有可能不服从“中性—厌恶”的假设，而是表现为“偏好—厌恶”或“中性—偏好”的风险态度。因此，有必要放宽“中性—厌恶”的假设，在新的条件下求解委托代理模型。

6.4.2　不同风险假设条件下的委托代理模型

在简化的委托代理模型中，一般设代理人的努力水平为 e；产出变量 $Y = e + x$，其中 x 是均值为零，方差为 σ^2 的随机变量，用来表示外生的不确定因素。委托人只能观察到产出水平 Y，不能观察到代理人的努力水平 e。线性合同中的工资由固定报酬 α 和变动报酬 βY 两部分组成：

$$w = \alpha + \beta Y = \alpha + \beta(e + x)$$

式中，β是激励系数（$0 \leqslant \beta \leqslant 1$），$\beta = 0$表示代理人不承担风险，$\beta = 1$则表示代理人承担全部风险（张维迎，1996，p. 431）。下面就在三种不同的当事人风险态度假设条件下，求解这一模型。

6.4.2.1 基于“中性—厌恶”假设的模型

在多数情况下，“中性—厌恶”的假设成立。在此条件下，委托人具有线性的效用函数；只需考虑委代理人的风险溢价。假设代理人具有不变的绝对风险规避特征，其绝对风险规避系数为$\rho_a > 0$。在此条件下的最优激励系数是：

$$\beta^* = \frac{1}{1 + b\rho_a\sigma^2}$$

式中b为代理人努力的成本系数。在等号右边的分式中，分母的值大于0而小于1，因此$0 < \beta^* < 1$，这说明代理人肯定要承担一部分风险，但不是全部风险。（张维迎，1996，pp. 432—435）。

6.4.2.2 基于“偏好—厌恶”假设的模型

前面所说的缺乏科学论证的政府投资项目的情况符合“偏好—厌恶”的假设。在此条件下，需要同时考虑委托人和代理人的风险溢价。假设风险偏好的委托人的绝对风险规避系数为$-\rho_p < 0$，风险规避的代理人的绝对风险规避系数为$\rho_a > 0$。在此条件下的最优激励系数是：

$$\beta^* = \frac{1 - b\rho_p\sigma^2}{1 - b\rho_p\sigma^2 + b\rho_a\sigma^2}$$

表6.5给出了不同参数条件下，目标函数的凹凸性以及相应的激励策略。可以看出，在“偏好—厌恶”的假设条件下，随着参数条件的改变，目标函数会由凹函数转变为凸函数。由凹到凸的临界点是$b\rho_p\sigma^2 = 1 + b\rho_a\sigma^2$，也就是$\rho_p - \rho_a = 1/b\sigma^2$。如果$\rho_p - \rho_a < 1/b\sigma^2$，说明代理人对风险的厌恶起支配作用；如果$\rho_p - \rho_a > 1/b\sigma^2$，则说明委托人对风险的偏好占据主导地位；而在临界点处，这两种态度所发挥的作用取得均衡。

“偏好—厌恶”假设条件下的参数条件与激励策略　　表6.5

参数条件		目标函数的性质	最优解	对代理人的激励策略
$b\rho_p\sigma^2 < 1 + b\rho_a\sigma^2$	$1 < b\rho_p\sigma^2 < 1 + b\rho_a\sigma^2$	凹函数	$\beta^* < 0$	不承担任何风险 外加鼓励措施
	$b\rho_p\sigma^2 = 1$		$\beta^* = 0$	不承担任何风险
	$0 < b\rho_p\sigma^2 < 1$		$0 < \beta^* < 1$	承担部分风险
$b\rho_p\sigma^2 = 1 + b\rho_a\sigma^2$		线性函数		不承担任何风险
$b\rho_p\sigma^2 > 1 + b\rho_a\sigma^2$		凸函数	$0 < \beta^* < 1$ （极小值）	不承担任何风险

需要说明的是，在以下两种情况下，表 6.5 中给出的最优解不能作为最优激励系数。

（1）当 $1 < b\rho_p\sigma^2 < 1 + b\rho_a\sigma^2$ 时，最优激励系数为负值。这说明，即使代理人不承担任何风险（$\beta^* = 0$），也无法满足最优激励合约的要求。为了帮助风险厌恶的代理人克服畏惧感，除了不让他承担项目的任何风险，还要通过其他额外的手段对其加以鼓励。

（2）如果 $b\rho_p\sigma^2 > 1 + b\rho_a\sigma^2$，目标函数为凸函数，$\beta^*$ 为极小值，并且 $0 < \beta^* < 1$。在闭区间 [0，1] 内，目标函数在 $\beta = 0$ 处取得最大值。这时，可行的激励策略是不让代理人承担任何风险。

此外，如果 $b\rho_p\sigma^2 = 1 + b\rho_a\sigma^2$，目标函数就成为线性函数，而且是减函数。在闭区间 [0，1] 内，目标函数在 $\beta = 0$ 处取得最大值。因此，可行的激励策略也是不让代理人承担任何风险。以上分析表明，在其他条件相同的情况下，“偏好—厌恶”假设条件下的激励强度要低于“中性—厌恶”假设条件下的激励强度。

接下来分析相关参数对最优激励强度 β^* 的影响。容易证明，最优激励系数 β^* 与代理人的努力成本系数 b 以及外界的不确定性因素的方差 σ^2 负相关。为了更加直观地分析当事人的绝对风险规避系数 ρ_a 和 $-\rho_p$ 对最优激励系数的影响，不妨把反映客观条件的努力成本系数 b 以及外界不确定性因素的方差 σ^2 的乘积 $b\sigma^2$ 标准化为 1，这样，最优激励系数就可以写作 $\beta^* = \dfrac{1-\rho_p}{1-\rho_p+\rho_a}$。从图 6.13 可以看出，如果 $0 < \rho_p < 1$，最优激励系数 β^* 与代理人的绝对风险规避系数 ρ_a 负相关，与委托人的绝对风险规避系数 $-\rho_p$ 正相关（β^* 与 ρ_p 负相关）。

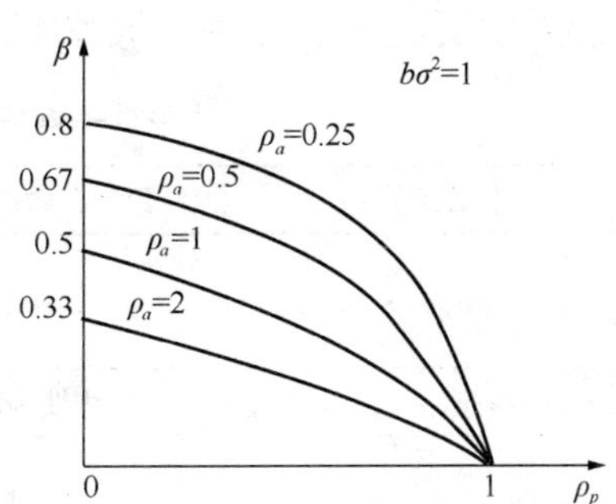

图 6.13 “偏好—厌恶”假设条件下当事人的风险态度与最优激励系数

在基于“偏好—厌恶”假设的模型中，双方当事人的效用函数都是非线性的。因此，该模型比基于“中性—厌恶”假设的模型更具普遍性。比如，令委托人的绝对风险规避系数 $-\rho_p = 0$，上面的最优激励系数就变为 $\beta^* = \dfrac{1}{1+b\rho_a\sigma^2}$。显然，后者是前者的一个特例。然而，不管假设条件如何变化，委托代理模型的基本思想不会改变。因此，在其他假设条件下求解最优激励系数，无须从头做起，只需要在上述模型的解的基础上，根据当事人的性质进行适当的变换，就可以得到相应的最优激励系数和可行的激励方案。

6.4.2.3 基于“中性—偏好”假设的模型

在前面所说的中国铁建公司的案例中，当事人的风险态度符合“中性—偏好”的假设。设风险偏好的代理人的绝对风险规避系数为 $-\rho_a < 0$。在此条件下的最优激励

系数是：

$$\beta^* = \frac{1}{1 - b\rho_a\sigma^2}$$

显然，显然，β^* 与代理人努力成本系数 b 和外界不确定性因素的方差 σ^2 正相关，而与代理人的绝对风险规避系数 $-\rho_a$ 负相关（β^* 与 ρ_a 正相关）。表 6.6 给出了不同参数条件下，目标函数的凹凸性以及相应的激励策略。如果 $0 < b\rho_a\sigma^2 < 1$，则有 $\beta^* > 1$，这说明，即使代理人承担全部风险（$\beta^* = 1$），也无法满足最优激励合同的要求。为了抑制风险偏好的代理人的冒险冲动，除了让他承担项目的全部风险，还要通过其他额外的手段对其施加压力。如果 $b\rho_a\sigma^2 = 1$，目标函数变成线性函数，而且是增函数。在闭区间 [0，1] 内，目标函数在 $\beta = 1$ 处取得最大值。因此，可行的激励策略也是让代理人承担全部风险。如果 $b\rho_a\sigma^2 > 1$，此时的目标函数为凸函数，β^* 为极小值，并且 $\beta^* < 0$。目标函数在 $\beta = 1$ 处取得最大值。因此，可行的激励策略是让代理人承担全部风险。以上分析表明，在其他条件相同的情况下，“中性—偏好”假设条件下的激励强度要高于“中性—厌恶”假设条件下的激励强度。

“中性—偏好”假设条件下的参数条件与激励策略 **表 6.6**

参数条件	目标函数的性质	最优解	对代理人的激励策略
$0 < b\rho_a\sigma^2 < 1$	凹函数	$\beta^* > 1$	承担全部风险 外加抑制措施
$b\rho_a\sigma^2 = 1$	线性函数	$\beta^* = 0$	承担全部风险
$b\rho_a\sigma^2 > 1$	凸函数	$\beta^* < 0$ （极小值）	承担全部风险

6.4.3 小结

抽象与假设是理论分析的起点。起点上差之毫厘，结论上就有可能谬以千里。因此，对于任何研究工作来说，一定要正确把握好抽象与假设这一关键环节。在运用经典模型时，一定要认真考虑其中的假设条件与所研究的具体对象之间是否一致的问题。

前面的比较静态分析表明，引进风险偏好的假设，会使目标函数的凹凸性随着参数条件的改变而改变，从而显著提高激励策略的复杂性。在“委托人风险偏好，代理人风险厌恶”假设条件下，要求的激励强度较低，有些时候为了帮助代理人克服畏惧感，除了不让他承担项目的任何风险，还要通过其他手段对其加以鼓励。而在“委托人风险中性，代理人风险偏好”的假设条件下，要求的激励强度较高，有些时候为了抑制代理人的冒险冲动，除了让他承担项目的全部风险，还要通过其他手段对其施加压力。

实际生活中许多看似非理性的行为，只要放在特定的背景条件下，就不难给出合理的解释。在前面所说的例子中，政府投资项目中盲目乐观的决策者以及中国铁建公司表现出来的不可理喻的行为，正是在某些风险态度支配下理性选择的结果。在我国建设项目的当事人身上表现出来的“中性-偏好”、“偏好-厌恶”等风险态度，在很大程度上可以归结为非经济因素的影响。对于政府投资项目和大型国有企业的决策者来说，的确存在经济和政治的双重激励；在有些情况下，政治激励的作用甚至要超过经济激励。如何在委托代理模型中同时考虑这两方面的因素，是一个值得进一步探讨的问题。

6.5　结　　论

这一讲重点分析了建设项目的垂直治理，即建设单位（甲方）和项目法人（乙方）之间的委托代理关系。首先介绍了委托代理理论的基本概念和模型；然后从项目采购方式和合同类型两个维度出发，分析了建设项目的垂直治理空间。接下来从建设项目的特殊性出发，对威廉姆森在治理结构分析中所采用的简化处理方法做出修正，提出“二阶转变”的假设。将不确定性和信息成本纳入分析框架，用委托代理模型分析建设项目的采购方式和合同类型。静态比较分析的结果表明，信息缺口和信息的相对成本系数是决定建设项目治理结构和报酬结构的重要因素，它们不仅决定“二阶转变”发生的时机和项目采购方式，而且决定“弱激励区”的分布与合同的最优激励强度。

在委托代理理论中，一般假设委托人是风险中性的，其效用函数是线性的；代理人是风险厌恶的，其效用函数是凹函数。在多数情况下，基于“中性-厌恶”假设的模型具有较好的解释能力。由于我国建设市场的不成熟，加之激励机制中非经济因素的大量存在，建设项目当事人的行为偏离“中性-厌恶”假设的情况时有发生，这时就需要做出相应的修正。引进风险偏好的假设，会使目标函数的凹凸性发生改变，从而显著提高激励策略的复杂性。

前面介绍的垂直治理模型的基本思想是：在满足代理人的参与约束和激励相容约束的前提下，最大化委托人的期望效用。这个模型隐含了一个假设，即“正常的”委托人不存在道德风险问题。而我国建设市场中的许多矛盾和问题都是由甲方行为不规范所造成的。实际上，甲方的风险态度和行为不仅影响甲方和乙方之间的关系，还会影响到建筑企业对项目经理的管控与激励。如何规范甲方行为的问题将放到第 8 讲中去讨论。

参考文献

1. 伯利，米恩斯（2005）现代公司与私有财产，中译本，甘华鸣，罗锐韧，蔡如海译，北京：商务印书馆.
2. 陈家鼎，刘婉如，汪仁观（1980）概率统计讲义，北京：人民教育出版社.

3. 迪克西特（2006）经济理论中的最优化方法，冯曲，吴桂英译，上海：上海人民出版社.
4. 费方域（2006）企业的产权分析，上海：上海三联出版社.
5. 亨德里克斯（2007）组织的经济学与管理学，中译本，胡雅梅，张学渊，曹利群译，北京：中国人民大学出版社.
6. 华冬冬，沙凯逊（2011）当事人的风险态度与建设项目的激励策略，项目管理技术，**9**（10），21—25.
7. 厉以宁，秦宛顺（1985）现代西方经济学概论，北京：北京大学出版社.
8. 刘建洲（1993）不确定性经济学的发展及其对西方经济学的影响，华中理工大学学报（社会科学版），（1），22—27.
9. 墨菲（1980）近代心理学历史导引，中译本，林方，王景和译，北京：商务印书馆.
10. 奈特（2006）风险、不确定性与利润，中译本，安佳译，北京：商务印书馆.
11. 倪伟峰，谷永强，姚伟涛（2011）中海外波兰欠费用致多工程搁浅亏数十亿，新世纪周刊，（29）36—48.
12. 庞永师，蒋莎莎，王亦斌（2009）政府偏好对公共建设项目决策的影响，广州大学学报（社会科学版），**8**（5），25—28.
13. 钱德勒（1987）看得见的手：美国企业的管理革命，中译本，重武译，北京：商务印书馆.
14. 沙凯逊（2013）建设项目治理，北京：中国建筑工业出版社.
15. 沙凯逊，华冬冬，徐聪（2011）一个建设项目垂直治理的委托代理模型，项目管理技术，**9**（5）28—34.
16. 沙凯逊，宋涛，亓霞，华冬冬（2009）从不确定性看建设项目的治理逻辑，山东建筑大学学报，**11**（4），283—287.
17. 斯密（2002）国民财富的性质和原因的研究（上册），中译本，郭大力，王亚南译，北京：商务印书馆.
18. 田厚平，刘长贤，吴萍（2007）非对称信息下参与人不同风险偏好组合的委托代理问题，管理工程学报，**21**（3）24—28.
19. 王灏（2004）PPP的定义和分类研究，都市快轨交通，**17**（5），23—27.
20. 张维迎（1996）博弈论与信息经济学，上海：上海三联出版社.
21. 张维迎（2000）企业理论与中国企业改革，北京：北京大学出版社.
22. 赵笛（2010）中国铁建沙特轻轨项目面临41亿巨亏，http://www.sina.com.cn，2010-10-26.
23. 周黎安（2004）晋升博弈中政府官员的激励与合作，经济研究，（6），36—40.
24. 中国经济增长与宏观稳定课题组（2010）后危机时代的中国宏观调控，经济研究，（11），4—20.
25. Bowles, S.（2004）*Microeconomics: Behavior, Institutions and Evolution*, Princeton University Press, Princeton.
26. Galbraith, J. R.（1977）*Organization design*, Addison-Wesley, Reading.
27. Machina, M.（1987）*Decision-making in the presence of risk*, Science, **236**（4801），537—543.
28. Sha, K. X.（2011）Vertical governance of construction projects: an information cost perspective, *Construction Management and Economics*, **29**（11），1137—1147.
29. The World Bank（1997）*Selecting an Option for Private Sector Participation*, Washington D. C. USA.

30. Turner, J. R. (2004) Farsighted project contract management: incomplete in its entirety, *Construction Management and Economics*, **22** (1), 75—83.

31. Turner, J. R. and Keegan, A. (2001) Mechanisms of governance in the project-based organization: roles of the broker and steward, *European Management Journal*, **19** (3), 254—267.

32. Williamson, O. E. (1991) Comparative economic organization: the analysis of discrete structural alternatives, *Administrative Science Quarterly*, **36** (2), 269—296.

第 7 讲　建设项目的水平治理：一个联盟博弈的视角

- □ 合作博弈的基本分析单位是联盟，建设项目本身也是一个联盟。用合作博弈的理论和方法研究建设项目供应链中各种当事人之间的关系，是一种恰当的技术路径。
- □ 联盟博弈的理论和方法主要涉及以下内容：一方面要把“蛋糕”做得足够大，从而实现联盟的外部稳定；另一方面要把“蛋糕”分得足够公平，从而实现联盟的内部稳定。
- □ 核、夏普里值与核仁是联盟博弈的三种解的概念，分别体现了不同的公平观，即基于交易收益的公平观、多劳多得的公平观和罗尔斯的平均主义公平观。它们在存在性、唯一性和空间分布上具有不同的特性。
- □ 在建设项目水平交易的三人联盟博弈中，重置成本受参与人的禀赋(技术能力、信息能力、融资能力)和决策环境(项目的复杂程度、市场成熟度、融资渠道、社会习俗)的影响；这些因素共同决定了参与人及其联盟的谈判能力。通过引入重置成本的概念，可以将谈判能力内生化。
- □ 在研究建设项目的稳定性时，需要充分考虑解析方法与公平观的一致性。在多数情况下，凭“常识”和直觉制定的收益分配方案与联盟博弈中的公平观不相符。

作为临时性的多边组织，建设项目的成员通过相互依存的资产与能力的合作，达到整合资源、节约成本、创造价值的目的(Winch，2001)。由此产生的项目租金(project rent)是建设项目存在的主要理由；项目租金的分配则是项目治理的核心内容(沙凯逊，2008)。第 6 讲从委托代理的角度讨论了建设项目的垂直治理，也就是业主对一阶供应商(first-tier suppliers)的激励和风险分担问题。这一讲则从联盟博弈的视角研究建设项目的水平治理，研究对象是一阶供应商之后当事人之间的合作关系。

根据当事人之间是否可以达成具有约束力的协议，博弈可分为合作博弈和非合作博弈。非合作博弈论的重点是个体理性和个人最优决策，合作博弈则强调集体理性、效率和公平(张维迎，1996，p. 5)。实际上，在博弈论发展的初始阶段，合作博弈受到了比非合作博弈更多的重视。20 世纪 70 年代，随着信息经济学的发展，非合作博弈论在经济学研究领域占据了主导地位；相比之下，合作博弈论在这一时期的研究与应用都显得不够活跃。进入 21 世纪之后，在经济全球化的背景下，合作博弈论再次引起人们的重视，进入了新的快速发展阶段。合作博弈的基本分析单位是**联盟**(coalition)，建设项目本身也是一个联盟，用合作博弈理论的思想和方法研究建设项目供应链中各种当事人之间的合作关系，是一种恰当的技术路径。

这一讲的结构安排如下：首先简要介绍联盟博弈的基本要素和基本类型。然后较为详细地介绍可转移效用的常规联盟博弈的三种解的概念——核、夏普里值与核仁。最后通过引入重置成本的概念，将影响参与人谈判能力的主要因素内生化，把建设项目的水平交易抽象为可转移效用的三人联盟博弈，针对不同的条件建立相应的联盟博弈模型并且进行求解与分析。

7.1 联盟博弈简介

对于社会经济发展和人类进步而言，竞争与合作就像一枚硬币的两面，是同等重要的。在资源有限的情况下，合作可以视为物质资本和人力资本的替代性资源(黄少安，韦倩，2011)。一般说来，与不合作相比，当事人之间的合作会产生较大的收益，即所谓“一加一大于二”的效果，这部分额外的收益是合作带来的剩余，也就是**组织租金**(organizational rent)。对于“理性的”当事人来说，如果没有组织租金，就没有合作的理由，因此，组织租金是合作的必要条件。然而，仅有组织租金是不够的，如果对组织租金的分配不公，当事人之间未必能够达成合作的协议。因此，联盟博弈的研究内容主要涉及以下两个方面：一是组织租金的确定，二是组织租金的分配。也就是说，一方面要把“蛋糕”做得足够大，从而实现联盟的外部稳定；另一方面要把“蛋糕”分得足够公平，从而实现联盟的内部稳定。

研究联盟博弈，不能把追求个体利益最大化作为出发点。这是因为，如果联盟中的每个人都追求利益最大化，就无法达成一个合作协议。因此，联盟博弈的均衡结果，是某种势均力敌的稳定状态；这种稳定状态可以在一定程度上反映每个参与人的禀赋和权力。

利用合作博弈理论来研究组织租金的形成与分配，有三种可供选择的技术路径。一是建立联盟博弈(coalitional games)模型，二是建立谈判博弈(bargaining games)模型，三是建立无限次重复博弈(infinitely repeated games)模型。在谈判博弈和无限次重复博弈中，参与人通过威慑达成有约束力的协议。从方法论的角度来看，这两种博弈属于能够实现合作结果的非合作方法的范畴(董保民等，2008，p. 9)。

在企业理论的研究领域，青木昌彦(2005)较早地构建了基于谈判博弈的分析框架，对现代公司制企业的制度结构和效率特征进行比较分析。青木昌彦把企业看作是股东和雇员形成的联盟，两者共同构成企业特质性资源，形成组织租金，并通过合作博弈共同分享，从而达到一种组织均衡。组织均衡的实现，同时决定了管理政策和组织租金的内部分配。青木昌彦在不同的历史、法律、政治和经济条件下，论述和比较了股东主权、共同治理和法人管理主义等不同模式中雇员(工会)和股东、管理者的集体谈判，参与管理的方式和效率，从而使企业的合作博弈理论成为比较企业制度分析的一个一般性框架。然而，该框架没有将影响谈判能力的诸多因素内生化，致使企业权力和租金分配都是外生的，这严重影响了模型的解释能力。针对这一问题，卢周来(2009)引入“重购成本”的概念，较好地解决了谈判能力的内生化和计量问题。应该指出的是，这两个模型都是在纳什谈判模型的基础上发展起来的，只涉及劳方(雇员)和资方(股东)两个参与人。此外，纳什谈判模型中的效用是序数效用，排除了人际间的效用比较。因此，对纳什解的公平性是存在质疑的(Bowles，2004，p. 177)。

近年来，联盟博弈理论在其他领域也得到广泛应用；涉及成本分配技术的改进(鲍新中，刘小军，2009)，区域产业结构的优化(王光净等，2010)，公私合伙制(public—private partnerships，PPP)的分析(张万宽，2008)，以及社会经济网络的形成机制(李峰等，2010)等。令人遗憾的是，在绝大多数的研究中，联盟博弈的特征函数都是外生给定的。这种简化处理的方法使模型的洞察力和说服力大打折扣，因而存在较大的改进空间。

7.1.1 联盟博弈的基本要素

对联盟博弈的讨论离不开集合的运算。表 7.1 给出了几个有关集合运算的符号。在下面的讨论中会用到这些符号。

有关集合运算的几个符号　　表 7.1

运算符	含　义
$A\subseteq B$	A 是 B 的子集(集合 A 的所有元素同时都是集合 B 的元素)
$A\subset B$	A 是 B 的真子集(A 是 B 的子集，且 A 不等于 B)
$A\cup B$	A 与 B 的并集(以属于 A 或属于 B 的元素为元素的集合)
$A\cap B$	A 与 B 的交集(以属于 A 且属于 B 的元素为元素的集合)
$A\setminus B$	A 与 B 的差集(以属于 A 而不属于 B 的元素为元素的集合)
$\lvert S\rvert$	集合 S 的基数，也就是该集合中元素的个数

设想一个联盟博弈。集合 $N=\{1,2,\cdots\cdots,n\}$ 是由全体参与人组成的**总联盟**(grand coalition)。包括空集 $\varnothing$ 和 N 本身在内，集合 N 共有 2^n 个子集(如表 7.2 所示，三人联盟博弈有 $2^3=8$ 个子集)。这些子集构成联盟博弈空间 2^N 。为简便起见，后面把总联盟 N 中的小联盟 S 简称为联盟。联盟 S 是总联盟 N 的子集，可以表示为 $S\subseteq N$ 。联盟 S 的价值是 $v(S)$ 。联盟博弈的价值空间是一个 n 维实数空间 R^N (如图 7.1 所示，三人联盟博弈的价值空间是三维实数空间)。**特征函数**(characteristic function)反映了联盟博弈空间和联盟价值空间之间的映射(mapping)关系。参与人的支付向量 $x=(x_1,x_2,\cdots,x_n)$ 又称**支付配置**(payoff allocation)；其中的元素 x_i 是参与人 $i(i=1，2，\cdots，n)$ 从对价值 $v(S)$ 的分配中获得的收益。每个支付配置代表了一种分配方案。为了便于

阅读和理解，下面的讨论都是限于三人博弈的范围，并且尽量用图解的方式来替代数学解析的方法。

为了直观地了解联盟博弈的基本要素，下面用一个三人博弈的例子来做具体说明。如表 7.2 所示，表的左侧是联盟博弈的各个子集 S；右侧是联盟博弈的特征函数 $v(S)$ 。显然，三个参与人联合起来形成总联盟会取得较大的收益，从而产生组织租金——这正是当事人合作的前提。

一个三人联盟博弈的特征函数　　**表 7.2**

S	$v(S)$	S	$v(S)$
∅	0	{1，2}	0
{1}	0	{1，3}	0
{2}	3	{2，3}	0
{3}	0	{1，2，3}	5

接下来的问题是，如何分配总联盟的收益，使得每个参与人都觉得“公平”与“合算”，从而都有积极性选择合作而不是背离。和非合作博弈理论一样，合作博弈理论也是建立在“参与人理性”的假设条件的基础之上。因此，在正式讨论联盟博弈的解的概念之前，先要交代两个有关理性的概念。满足个**体理性**(individual rational)的分配方案能够使每个参与人的支付不低于个人单干时的收益水平。满足**集体理性**(group rational)的分配方案能够使参与人的支付总和等于总联盟的价值，也就是参与人恰好能将合作所带来的收益分配完毕，没有剩余。因此，满足集体理性的配置是“有效的”(efficient)分配方案。

在联盟博弈中，同时满足个体理性和集体理性的支付向量的集合叫作**分配集**(imputation set)。如果存在能够使总联盟稳定的分配方案，那么，这个方案(支付向量)一定在这个分配集之中。图 7.1 给出了表 7.2 所示的三人联盟博弈的分配集：三角形 ABC 是一个等值面；等值面上的任何一点 $x(x_1,x_2,x_3)$ 都代表一个支付向量或分配方案(x_1 、x_2 和 x_3 分别是三个参与人的支付)，满足 $x_1+x_2+x_3=5$ ；也就是说，这个分配方案能够使合作所带来的收益恰好被参与人分配完毕，没有剩余，因而满足集体理性。用阴影表示的三角形 BDE 是三角形 ABC 的一部分，对于其中的任何一点 $x(x_1,x_2,x_3)$，都有 $x_1\geqslant 0$ ，$x_2\geqslant 3$ ，$x_3\geqslant 0$ ；也就是说，这个分配方案使每个参与人的支付都不低于个人单干时的收益水平，因而满足个人理性。由于三角形 BDE 中的任何一点(支付向量)都同时满足个体理性和集体理性，因此，三角形 BDE 就是这个三人博弈的分

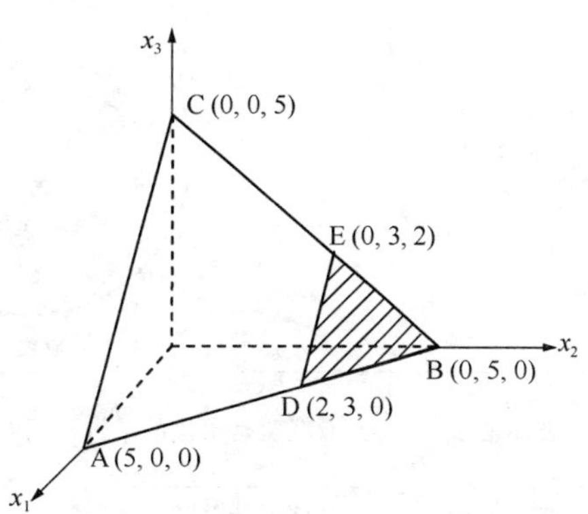

图 7.1　三人联盟博弈的分配集
(资料来源：董保民等，2008，p. 21)

配集。

7.1.2 联盟博弈的分类

从是否考虑合作成本的角度出发，联盟博弈可分为**常规联盟博弈**(canonical coalitional game)和**联盟形成博弈**(coalition formation game)。如表 7.3 所示，常规联盟博弈只考虑合作带来的收益，不考虑合作时可能发生的成本。对于总联盟中的任意两个联盟(它们的交集为空集)来说，这两个联盟中的所有参与人组成的新联盟的价值不会小于原先两个联盟的价值之和——这种性质就是所谓的超可加性(supper-additivity)。既然形成较大的联盟不会对现有联盟中的任何成员带来任何损失，那么，肯定会形成由全体参与人组成的总联盟——这就是常规联盟博弈的基本假设。常规联盟博弈所要研究的主要问题是如何保持总联盟的稳定性。常规联盟博弈最常用的表达形式是特征型(characteristic form)。特征函数形式的 n 人博弈可以定义为一个组合(N, v)，其中 N 是参与人的集合，v 是特征函数(亨德里克斯，2007，p. 23，p. 242)。在常规联盟博弈中，联盟 S 的价值只受其成员的影响，而与差集 $N \setminus S$ 中的成员(也就是总联盟中除了联盟 S 以外的其他成员)结构无关(Saad *et al.*，2009)。与常规联盟博弈不同，联盟形成博弈需要同时考虑合作的收益和成本，此时的联盟博弈往往不具备超可加性，总联盟不一定是最优的结构。联盟形成博弈的核心问题是如何形成一个合适的联盟结构。

联盟博弈的两大类型 表 7.3

博弈类型	常规联盟博弈	联盟形成博弈
示意图	1 4 3 2	4 1 3 2
基本假设	总联盟是最优的结构，因而肯定可以形成总联盟	总联盟不一定是最优的结构，因而不一定能够形成总联盟
核心问题	如何保持总联盟的稳定性	如何形成合适的联盟结构
表达方式	用特征型表达	不用特征型表达

(资料来源：Saad *et al.*，2009，p. 79)

从效用是否可以转移的角度考虑，联盟博弈又可划分为**可转移效用的联盟博弈**(coalitional game with transferable utility)和**不可转移效用的联盟博弈**(coalitional game with non-transferable utility)。为简便起见，在下面的讨论中把可转移效用称为 TU，把不可转移效用称为 NTU。TU 的概念由冯·诺依曼和摩根斯坦(Neumann and Morgenstern，1944)提出。TU 的性质意味着价值 $v(S)$ 所代表的效用可以在联盟成员之间进行任何形式的分配。这里只讨论 TU 常规联盟博弈。为简便起见，在下面的讨论中，有时把 TU 常规联盟博弈称为 TU 联盟博弈，有时简称为联盟博弈。

7.2　常规联盟博弈的几种解的概念

TU 联盟博弈(N, v)的解是一个分配集(同时满足个体理性和集体理性的支付向量的集合)。注意，这句话反过来并不成立。也就是说，分配集不一定就是 TU 联盟博弈的解。在图 7.1 中，三人联盟博弈的分配集是三角形 BDE。分配集中的元素(也就是上述三角形中的点)同时满足个体理性和集体理性，元素之间不存在占优关系，但是共同占优于其他的分配(库恩，2004，p. 333)。求解 TU 联盟博弈涉及两方面的问题，一是总联盟的稳定性，二是总联盟的公平性；前者是要找到一个支付向量或分配方案，使得所有参与人都没有离开总联盟的意愿，后者是对总联盟的收益进行评估，确定公平的分配标准。

TU 联盟博弈涉及多种解的概念(solution concept)，它们大体上可分为三种类型：(1)**核**(core)和稳定集(stable set)，它们的基础是分配占优(imputation dominance)。(2)**夏普里值**(Shapley value)和 B—C 权力指数(Banzhaf—Coleman power index)等估值方法，它们的基础是当事人的期望边际贡献(expected marginal contribution)。(3)谈判集(bargaining set)、内核(kernel)与**核仁**(nucleolus)，它们都强调当事人之间的势均力敌，因此，一般把它们划为联盟博弈中的第三种类型；其中谈判集以异议(projection)和反异议(counter-projection)的概念为基础，内核与核仁则是建立在过剩值(excess)和盈余(surplus)的概念基础之上(杨荣基等，2007)。也有人把谈判集视为谈判博弈的一部分，把它们放到合作博弈的非合作方法中去讨论(董保民等，2008，pp. 197—202)。这里只介绍三种解的概念：核、夏普里值和核仁。

7.2.1　核

核是最早出现的联盟博弈的解的概念。它是同时满足个体理性、集体理性和**联盟理性**(coalitional rational)的支付向量的集合。如前所述，个体理性从参与人个体的角度出发，要求每个参与人的支付不低于个人单干时的收益水平。集体理性从总联盟的角度出发，要求总联盟创造的收益得到充分利用，被全部分配完毕，没有剩余。联盟理性则是从联盟的角度出发考虑问题，要求使总联盟中每个联盟的成员都对分配方案感到满意，不至于离开总联盟。

联盟成员对分配方案的满意程度(或不满意程度)，可以用过剩值来衡量。对于 n 人联盟博弈(N, v)中的联盟 S，支付向量 $x\,(x_1, x_2, \cdots\cdots, x_n)$ 的过剩值是：

$$e(x, S) = v(S) - \sum_{i \in S} x_i$$

它是联盟 S 的价值与联盟成员在分配方案 x 下的支付总和之间的差值。如果过剩值 $e(x,S)>0$，说明在分配方案 x 的条件下，联盟 S 的价值 $v(S)$ 在分配之后还有剩余。也就是说，分配方案 x 不能使联盟成员尽享由他们所创造的价值 $v(S)$。显然，该分配方案不能使联盟成员感到满意。在这种情况下，联盟成员就有可能脱离总联盟 N，另外单独组建联盟 S。

对联盟理性的判定又叫作独立性检验（stand-alone test）。如果过剩值 $e(x,S)>0$，意味着分配方案 x 没有通过独立性检验，于是该分配方案不满足联盟理性。一个支付向量（分配方案）x 处于核中的充分必要条件是：它对于所有联盟的过剩值都是负数或零（Saad *et al.*，2009，p. 84）。需要说明的是，当过剩值 $e(x,S)$ 是负数时，并不意味着联盟成员能够获得超出联盟价值 $v(S)$ 的收益——这时的 $e(x,S)$ 表示联盟 S 的成员拒绝分配方案 x 时所蒙受的损失。

从以上分析可以看出，核是由能够满足一系列不等式的支付向量组成的集合。一般地，给定 TU 联盟博弈（N，v）和一个支付向量 x，可以通过线性规划来确定该博弈的核。然而，计算工作量会随参与人数量的增加而成指数倍地增加，很快就变得不可计算了（李昭智，1984）。三人联盟博弈的核可以用单纯形的方法来求解。图解的方法至少有两个优点。一是简单，可以省去繁杂的不等式运算。二是直观明了，有助于加深对核的概念的理解。

背景材料：

单纯形（simplex）是指在一定空间内，由直线段形成的最简单的封闭图形。二维空间中的单纯形是三角形。左图中的单纯形是高度为 1 的正三角形 ABC。D 是其中的任意一点。从 D 点到 AB、BC 和 CA 的垂直距离分别是 x、y 和 z。设三角形的边长为 a，于是，正三角形 ABC 的面积为 $1/2a$；这也是三角形 ADB、BDC 和 CDA 的面积之和。也就是 $1/2ax+1/2ay+1/2az=1/2a(x+y+z)$。由此可得 $x+y+z=1$。也就是说，从单纯形中任一点到它的三个边的垂直距离之和为 1。这是一个十分有用的性质。

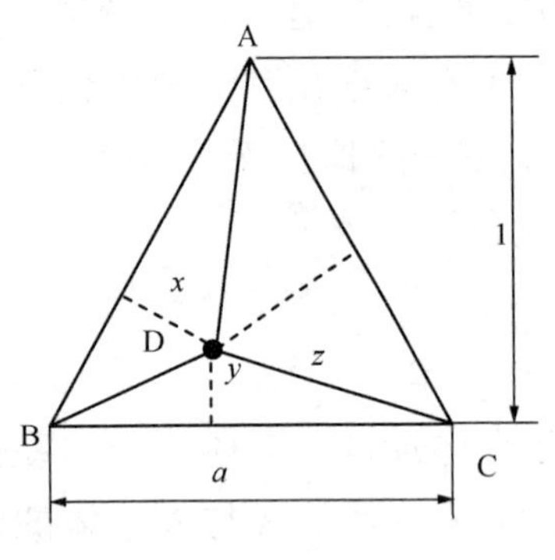

下面是通过单纯形的方法求解核的一个例子。考虑一个只有三个人的社会。假设在这个社会中，如果三人同心协力，组成一个总联盟，就能创造出 1 个单位的财富，实现社会福利最大化。如果其中两人合作，组成一个联盟，而另一人单干，那么，两人组成的联盟可以创造并分享 α 个单位的财富（$1/2<\alpha<1$），而单干的人不能获得财富。于是这个联盟博弈的特征函数可写作：

$$v(N)=1,\ v(\{1\})=v(\{2\})=v(\{3\})=0$$

$$v(\{1,2\}) = v(\{1,3\}) = v(\{2,3\}) = \alpha$$

这个联盟博弈可以用图 7.2 中的单纯形来求解。单纯形中的每一个点 x 都代表一种分配方案，x_1、x_2 和 x_3 是该点到三个边的垂直距离，分别代表三个参与人的支付水平。

首先考虑个体理性和集体理性，确定联盟博弈的分配集。对于单纯形中所有的点，$x_1 \geqslant 0$，$x_2 \geqslant 0$，$x_3 \geqslant 0$ 这三个条件都成立，满足个体理性——分配方案使得每个参与人的收益不低于个人单干时的收益水平。对于单纯形中的所有点，$x_1 + x_2 + x_3 = 1$ 也都成立，满足集体理性——分配方案使得总联盟所创造的财富恰好被分配完毕，没有剩余。由于单纯形中所有的点都同时满足个体理性和集体理性，因此，这个单纯形就是联盟博弈的分配集。

其次进行独立性检验，找出所有满足联盟理性的分配方案（支付向量）。在三人联盟博弈中，共有 $2^3 = 8$ 个联盟。除了总联盟和空集之外，需要对 6 个联盟（3 个单人联盟，三个双人联盟）进行独立性检验。对于单人联盟来说，对于单纯形中所有的点，都有 $x_1 \geqslant 0 = v(\{1\})$，$x_2 \geqslant 0 = v(\{2\})$，$x_3 \geqslant 0 = v(\{3\})$，因此都满足联盟理性。对于双人联盟来说，则要求同时满足以下三个条件：(1) $x_1 + x_2 \geqslant \alpha$，(2) $x_2 + x_3 \geqslant \alpha$，(3) $x_3 + x_1 \geqslant \alpha$。

从图 7.2 中可以看出，等值线 $x_2 + x_3 = \alpha$ 在水平方向上把单纯形一分为二，形成一个三角形和一个等腰梯形；梯形内所有的点都满足条件（1）。同样的道理，等值线 $x_1 + x_2 = \alpha$ 和 $x_3 + x_1 = \alpha$ 分别在与水平线成 120°角和 60°角的方向上对单纯形做出切割，形成两个等腰梯形，这两个梯形中所有的点都分别满足条件（2）和条件（3）。因此，如果存在同时满足以上三个条件的点，这些点一定是在三个等腰梯形的交集之中。随着 α 的增大，三条等值线的位置会逐渐向它们所对应的底边方向平移。针对不同的 α 值，会出现以下三种情况：

（1）如图 7.2（1）所示，当 $1/2 < \alpha < 2/3$ 时，三条等值线都位于单纯形的三个顶点和重心之间，因此，三条等值线围成的三角形（阴影部分，也就是上面所说的三个等腰梯形的交集）中所有的点都同时满足 $x_1 + x_2 \geqslant \alpha$、$x_2 + x_3 \geqslant \alpha$ 和 $x_1 + x_3 \geqslant \alpha$，也就是满足联盟理性。此时的核是一个由无数支付向量组成的实数集。

（2）如图 7.2（2）所示，当 $\alpha = 2/3$ 时，三条等值线 $x_1 + x_2 = 2/3$、$x_2 + x_3 = 2/3$ 和 $x_1 + x_3 = 2/3$ 相交于单纯形的重心（上面所说的三个等腰梯形的交集），只有这一点满足联盟理性，这时的核只包含一个支付向量，也就是 (1/3，1/3，1/3)。

（3）如图 7.2（3）所示，当 $2/3 < \alpha < 1$ 时，三条等值线都位于单纯形的重心和三条边之间，因此，单纯形中的任何一点都无法同时满足 $x_1 + x_2 \geqslant \alpha$、$x_2 + x_3 \geqslant \alpha$ 和 $x_1 + x_3 \geqslant \alpha$，因而无法满足联盟理性。这时的核是一个空集。三条等值线线围成的三角形（阴影部分）是“影子核”（shadow core）（其中所有的点同时满足 $x_1 + x_2 \leqslant \alpha$、$x_2 + x_3 \geqslant \alpha$ 和 $x_1 + x_3 \leqslant \alpha$）。既然核是空集，总联盟就无法保持稳定。

综上所述，从理性的角度来看，TU 联盟博弈的核是同时满足个体理性、集体理

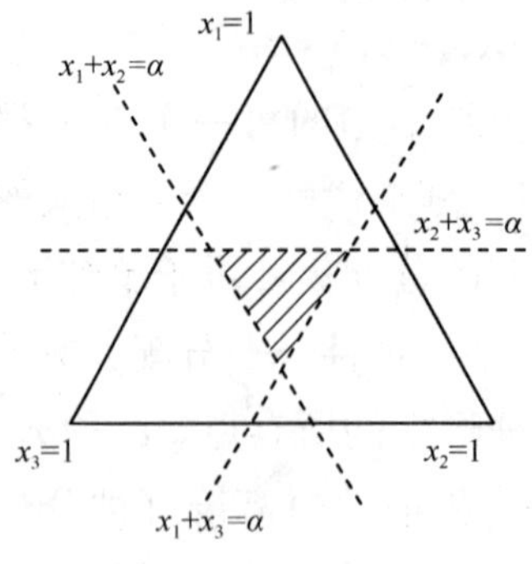

(1) $1/2<\alpha<2/3$

三条等值线围成的三角形（阴影部分）中的所有点都满足联盟理性，此时的核是一个由无数支付向量组成的实数集。

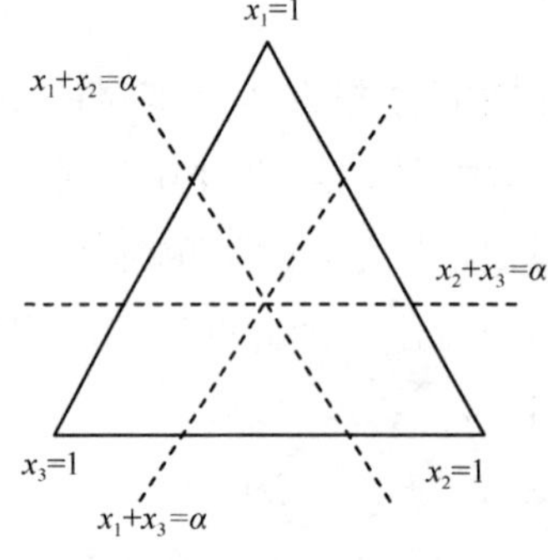

(2) $\alpha=\dfrac{2}{3}$

三条等值线相交于单纯形的重心，只有这一点满足联盟理性，这时的核只包含一个支付向量，也就是（1/3, 1/3, 1/3）。

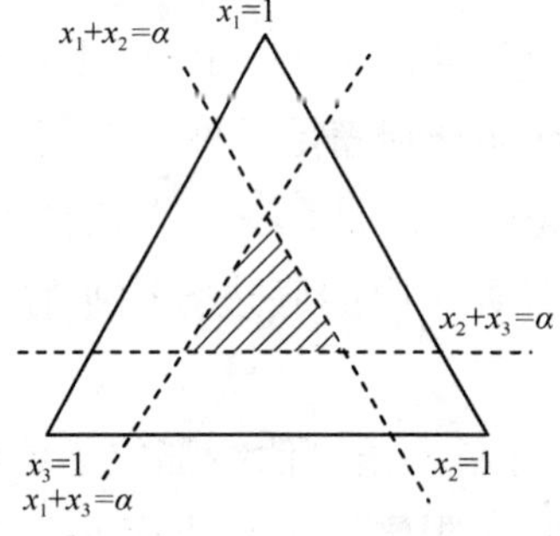

(3) $2/3<\alpha<1$

单纯形中的所有点都无法满足联盟理性，此时的核是一个空集。三条等值线围成的三角形（阴影部分）是“影子核”。

图 7.2　三人联盟博弈的核

性和联盟理性的支付向量的集合。从稳定的角度来看，核是同时满足间接外部稳定性和间接内部稳定性的支付向量的集合。从几何性质的角度来看，核是凸的闭集。核中的配置不会被其他任何联盟推翻；只要参与人的利益分配在核中进行，就可以确保总联盟的稳定。

然而，联盟博弈的核有可能是空集。如果核是空集，就无法找到一种有关各方都能够接受的利益分配方案，总联盟也就不会稳定；因此，判断核是否为空集的问题就成为总联盟稳定性研究的关键。邦达列瓦和夏普里根据线性规划中的对偶理论证明了B—S 定理（Bondareva—Shapley theorem）。该定理给出了 TU 联盟博弈核非空的充要条件：一个博弈的核是非空的，当且仅当该博弈是平衡的（balanced）。B—S 定理表明，“核非空”与“平衡博弈”是两个等价的概念。为了简单起见，有关平衡博弈的内容在这里不再展开。

有些时候，只要确定了博弈的类型，就可以判定 TU 联盟博弈的核是否是空集。首先来看凸博弈（convex game）。凸博弈的直观含义是，参与人对某个联盟的边际贡献（也就是有该参与人的联盟价值与没有该参与人的联盟价值之差）不会随着联盟规模的扩大而减少。可以证明，对于联盟博弈来说，凸博弈是平衡的，因而具有非空的核，但是，这个结论反过来说并不一定成立；平衡博弈不一定是凸博弈。也就是说，凸博弈只是核非空的充分条件。其次来看简单博弈（simple game）。如果一个联盟博弈的特征函数只取值 0 和 1，并且单人联盟的价值为 0，总联盟的价值为 1，这种联盟博弈便是简单博弈。简单博弈常用来描述投票选举的情况。价值为 1 的联盟被称为“胜利联盟”，价值为 0 的则被称为“失利联盟”。简单博弈的核非空的充要条件是：存在具有否决权的参与人（veto player）或否决人（谢识予，2008，p. 364；Saad *et al*.，2009，p. 82）。最后来看常和本质博弈。常和博弈，又叫非零和博弈，是指各参与人的支付之和是一个非零的常数。如果在一个联盟博弈中，总联盟的价值大于所有单人联盟的价值之和，该博弈便是本质博弈。可以证明，常和本质博弈的核是空集（谢识予，2008，p. 366）。

总之，对于 TU 联盟博弈来说，超可加性是核非空的必要条件；凸博弈（合作是关于规模报酬非递减的博弈）是核非空的充分条件；平衡博弈是核非空的充要条件。对于简单博弈来说，否决人的存在是核非空的充要条件。常和本质博弈的核一定是空集。当然，对于三人联盟博弈来说，核是否为空集的问题就要简单得多——通过图解的方法可以做到一目了然。

7.2.2　夏普里值

在利用核的概念求解联盟博弈时，会出现以下两个问题：（1）核是空集，（2）核是由无数个支付向量组成的实数集。此外，有些时候核中的支付配置方案对某些参与人是不公平的（Saad *et al*.，2009，p. 83）。针对这些问题，夏普里在研究多人合作对策问题时提出了一种新的方法。这种方法既可以体现多劳多得的分配原则，也可以反映个体在集体中的重要程度。按照夏普里的思路，收益的分配既不是平均分配，也不是根据投入的比例分配，而是根据参与人对联盟的边际贡献进行分配。

夏普里通过公理化的方法，提出了后来被称为夏普里值的解的概念。需要指出的是，这里的“值”是一个分配方案（支付向量），与前面所说的联盟的“价值”（一个实数）是两个不同的概念。为了得到一个具有唯一性的解，夏普里首先提出了一组公理：

（1）有效性公理（efficiency axiom），也就是前面所说的集体理性，它要求把总联盟的收益全部分配完毕，不留剩余。

（2）对称性公理（symmetry axiom）又称匿名性公理（anonymity axiom），它要

求平等地对待贡献相同的人。参与人的支付取决于他对联盟的贡献，而与他的称谓或在联盟中的位次无关。

（3）虚拟性公理（dummy axiom），它要求对于没有对联盟做出贡献的参与人（虚拟参与人），不给予任何支付。

（4）可加性公理（additivity axiom）又称集成性公理（aggregation axiom），它要求任何两个独立的博弈组合而成的博弈的值等于原先两个博弈的值之和。

夏普里证明，在 TU 联盟博弈（N，v）的博弈空间 2^N 和 n 维实数空间 R^N 之间，存在着同时满足有效性、对称性、虚拟性和可加性公理的唯一的映射 $\varphi(v)$。也就是说，对于 TU 联盟博弈（N，v）来说，夏普里值 $\varphi(v)$ 是 n 维实数空间 R^N 中唯一满足以上四个公理的支付向量或分配方案。

求解夏普里值的基本原理是：一个参与人的支付应该等于他对每一个他所参与联盟的边际贡献的数学期望值。通过计算这个数学期望值，可得到夏普里值 $\varphi(v)$ 分配给参与人 i 的支付：

$$\varphi_i = \Sigma_{S\subseteq N, S\supseteq i} \frac{|S-1|!(n-|S|)!}{n!}[v(S)-v(S\setminus i)]$$

式中 N 是总联盟，$|S|$是联盟 S 中参与人的个数，$v(S)$ 是联盟 S 的价值。求和符号 $\Sigma_{S\subseteq N, S\supseteq i}$ 说明，S 是总联盟中所有不包含参与人 i 的联盟。为简便起见，这里省略了公式的推导过程。

卜面举例说明夏普里值的计算方法。考虑一个三人联盟博弈（N，v），总联盟 $N=\{1,2,3\}$；空集的价值是 $v(\varnothing)=0$；单人联盟的价值是 $0\leqslant v(\{i\})\leqslant 1,(i-1,2,3)$；双人联盟的价值是 $0\leqslant v(S)\leqslant 1,(|S|=2)$；总联盟的价值是 $v(N)=1$。根据上面的计算公式，可以算出第一个参与人的夏普里值：

$$\begin{aligned}\varphi_1 =& \frac{(1-1)!(3-1)!}{3!}[v(\{1\})-v(\varnothing)]+\frac{(2-1)!(3-2)!}{3!}[v(\{1,2\})-v(\{2\})]\\ &+\frac{(2-1)!(3-2)!}{3!}[v(\{1,3\})-v(\{3\})]+\frac{(3-1)!(3-3)!}{3!}\\ &[v(\{1,2,3\})-v(\{2,3\})]\\ =&\frac{1}{3}+\frac{1}{6}[2v(\{1\})-v(\{2\})-v(\{3\})+v(\{1,2\})+v(\{1,3\})-2v(\{2,3\})]\end{aligned}$$

按照同样的方法，可以算出其余两个参与人的夏普里值：

$$\varphi_2 =\frac{1}{3}+\frac{1}{6}[2v(\{2\})-v(\{3\})-v(\{1\})+v(\{1,2\})+v(\{2,3\})-2v(\{1,3\})]$$

$$\varphi_3 =\frac{1}{3}+\frac{1}{6}[2v(\{3\})-v(\{1\})-v(\{2\})+v(\{1,3\})+v(\{2,3\})-2v(\{1,2\})]$$

一般来说，夏普里值与核并无关联。但在有些条件下，联盟博弈的夏普里值位于核中。可以证明，n 人联盟博弈（N，v）的夏普里值位于核中的充要条件是：该博弈是完全凸博弈。这时，夏普里值就是核的几何重心（董保民等，2008，p. 45）。这时的解，既具有核的稳定性，又具备夏普里值的公平性。

7.2.3　核仁

和夏普里值一样，核仁也是具有唯一性的 TU 联盟博弈的解的概念。如果说，夏普里值体现了多劳多得的公平观，那么，核仁反映了罗尔斯的平均主义（equalitarianism）公平观。这种公平观主张所谓的"最大最小原则"（maxi-mini rule）。也就是说，在考虑社会福利最大化的问题时，把在社会中处于最不利地位的成员的福利是否最大作为判断标准（高东苗，2010）。在联盟博弈中，核仁的概念正是体现了这种思想：如果能够找到一个支付向量或分配方案，它不仅同时满足个体理性和集体理性，而且使满意程度最低的联盟的满意程度实现最大化，那么，该支付向量便是核仁。在"最大最小原则"下，核仁是唯一的最佳分配方案。

背景资料：众说纷纭话"公平"

经济学中的公平理论凝聚了诸多思想家的智慧，其中影响较大的流派有功利主义（utilitarianism）的公平观、古典自由主义公平观和罗尔斯主义（rawlsianism）公平观。如下面的分析所示，公平是一个社会历史范畴，因此不存在永恒不变的公平。

功利主义不考虑个人行为的动机与手段，只考虑行为结果对最大幸福值的影响。根据边沁的"最大幸福"（maximum happiness）原则，任何正确的行动和政治方针都必须做到产生最多数人的最大幸福，并将痛苦缩减到最少，在必要时，甚至可以牺牲少部分人的利益来满足最多数人的最大幸福（边沁，2000）。

福利经济学的功利主义认为，社会福利水平等于社会所有成员的效用之和，一个社会应追求社会总效用的最大化，收入均等是实现社会福利最大化的重要手段。古典自由主义强调自由市场秩序中的机会平等，认为市场机制是实现社会公平的根本保障。

罗尔斯主义对机会平等和结果公平这两个方面都给予足够的重视，但首先强调结果公平。罗尔斯将其正义理论体系概括为两大原则，一是自由平等原则，二是机会公正和差别原则二者的结合。差别原则是使社会中最不利的成员获得最大利益。他认为，在坚持机会公正平等、地位和职位开放的基础上，运用差别原则，从社会中甄别出最少受惠者，使之得到补偿，这样才能使穷人和社会不幸者的生活条件得到最大的改善，逐步缩小社会的不平等（罗尔斯，1988，pp. 61—62）。

7.2.3.1　关于"三妻分产"的思想实验

在第 3 讲"制度与博弈"中提到的"三妻分产"博弈涉及一场财产纠纷。富翁在婚书中向他的三个妻子许诺，他死后将给第一个妻子 100 个单位的遗产，给第二个妻子 200 个单位的遗产，给第三个妻子 300 个单位的遗产（遗产的单位用金币计）。但是，人们在富翁死后清算遗产的时候发现，他的财产不够 600 枚金币，只有 100 枚、200 枚或者 300 枚金币。这时的问题是：这三个妻子各应分得多少金币？

从直观上看，富翁的遗产似乎应该按照婚书中约定的比例（1∶2∶3）进行分配，拉比（古代犹太人中的智者）提出的解决方案有些“不合常理”。奥曼和马斯库勒从博弈论的角度证明，这个分配方案正是三人联盟博弈的核仁解（Aumann and Maschler, 1985）。不难想象，古代犹太人没有博弈论作为理论支持，也没有核仁解的概念，但是有理由相信，“三妻分产”的分配方案是在一定的社会伦理法则支配下不断试错的结果。这里所说的“一定的社会伦理法则”应该与“最大最小原则”有关。为了加深对核仁概念的理解，有必要从拉比的视角重新审视这个案例。

首先考虑三个妻子及其联盟的谈判能力。富翁在婚书中所许诺的遗产数量反映了各个妻子的禀赋。每个妻子及其联盟的谈判能力不仅与个人禀赋有关，还受富翁留下的实际遗产数量的影响。这里以实际遗产为 200 枚金币的情况为例，分析个人禀赋、实际遗产数量和谈判能力之间的关系。为了方便起见，下面用数字 1、2 和 3 作为三个妻子的编号，用两位数 12、13 和 23 分别表示三个双人联盟。现在考虑 1 和 23 之间的谈判过程。全部遗产 200 枚金币在满足 1 的需求（100 枚金币）之后，还有 100 枚金币的剩余；但是，200 枚金币无法满足 23 的需求（500 枚金币），更不可能留下剩余。因此，在谈判中 1 有可能做出 100 枚金币的让步，而 23 不会做出让步，这意味着 23 拥有 100 枚金币的谈判筹码。通过类似的推理，可以得到三种情况下三个妻子及其联盟的谈判筹码。在联盟博弈的语境中，这些谈判筹码就是联盟的价值：

（1）当遗产为 100 枚金币时，$v(\{1\})=v(\{2\})=v(\{3\})=0$，$v(\{1,2\})=v(\{1,3\})=v(\{2,3\})=0$，$v(\{1,2,3\})=100$。

（2）当遗产为 200 枚金币时，$v(\{1\})=v(\{2\})=v(\{3\})=0$，$v(\{1,2\})=v(\{1,3\})=0$，$v(\{2,3\})=100$，$v(\{1,2,3\})=200$。

（3）当遗产为 300 枚金币时，$v(\{1\})=v(\{2\})=v(\{3\})=0$，$v(\{1,2\})=0$，$v(\{1,3\})=100$，$v(\{2,3\})=200$，$v(\{1,2,3\})=300$。

接下来通过思想实验来还原古代犹太人的推断过程。由于只有三个参与人，可以采用单纯形的方法进行“沙盘推演”。如图 7.3 所示，假设三个人最初分别位于单纯形

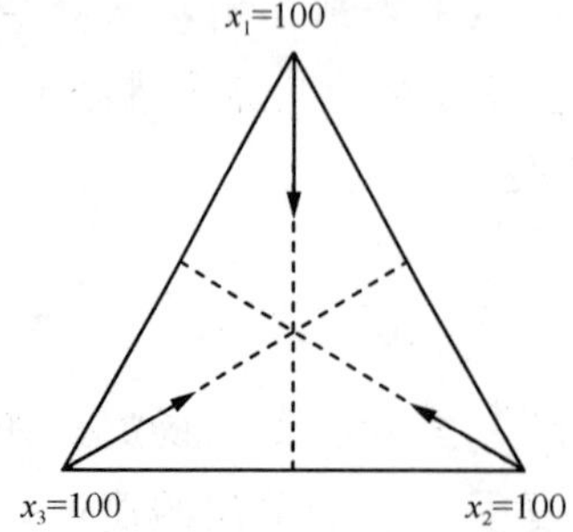

图 7.3 关于“三妻分产”的思想实验（遗产为 100 枚金币）

的三个顶点，这意味着一人获得全部遗产，其余两人一无所获。这种方案对于第一个人来说似乎是最好的；但是，这个人很快就会发现，由于其他两人的强烈反对，这个方案是不可能实现的。要想达成有约束力的协议，必须开展谈判；而谈判的本质就是做出妥协与让步。接下来的问题是：由谁做出让步？让步到何处为止？从下面的分析可以看出，谈判是复杂的——从各方所做出的让步程度来看，谈判可分为对称谈判和非对称谈判；从谈判的进程来看，谈判可分为一阶段谈判和两阶段谈判。

当遗产为 100 枚金币时，三个双人联盟的力量都很弱（$v(\{1,2\}) = v(\{1,3\}) = v(\{2,3\}) = 0$），任何一个双人联盟都不会对另外一人造成压力，因此，三人必须做出同样程度的让步，也就是沿着图 7.3 中的箭头方向相向而行，直到三个箭头汇合到一点为止。这个点就是单纯形的几何中心——在联盟博弈的语境中，它既是核仁（满足“最大最小原则”），又是夏普里值（满足“多劳多得”的公平观）。三位妻子各自得到 100/3 枚金币。显然，在这种情况下三人的让步是对称的，谈判过程只有一个阶段。

当遗产为 200 枚金币时，谈判过程分两个阶段，而且谈判中的让步是非对称的。这时双人联盟 12 和 13 的力量很弱（$v(\{1,2\}) = v(\{1,3\}) = 0$），不能使 3 和 2 做出让步；而 23 的力量很强（$v(\{2,3\}) = 100$），23 与 1 之间有数值为 100 的“压力差”，足以迫使 1 做出让步。在这一轮谈判中，由于 1 的让步，得到如图 7.4 所示的等腰梯形。在联盟博弈的语境中，这个等腰梯形是博弈的核。为了在等腰梯形中找到大家都认可的唯一的分配方案，思想实验还要继续下去。在第二阶段的谈判中，由于 23 和 1 之间的“压力差”已被耗尽，三人之间处于相对平等的状态。为了取得大家都能接受的分配方案，三人都需要做出让步——首先，在垂直方向上，等值线 $x_2 + x_3 = 100$ 和单纯形的底边 x_2x_3 相向而行，最终停留在等腰梯形的中位线。然后，在水平方向上，2 和 3 相向而行，最终停留在等腰梯形中位线的中点 γ（50，75，75）——这就是联盟博弈的核仁。

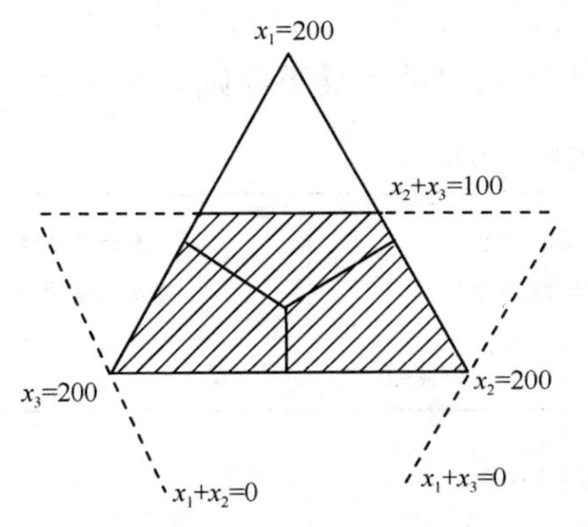

特征函数

$v(\{1\})=v(\{2\})=v(\{3\})=0$

$v(\{1,2\})=v(\{1,3\})=0$

$v(\{2,3\})=100$

$v(\{1,2,3\})=200$

阴影部分（等腰梯形）为核，核仁γ（50, 75, 75)位于等腰梯形中位线的中点，既不是等腰梯形的几何中心；也不等于夏普里值$\left(33\frac{1}{3}, 83\frac{1}{3}, 83\frac{1}{3}\right)$。

图 7.4　关于“三妻分产”的思想实验（遗产为 200 枚金币）

当遗产为300枚金币时，双人联盟的谈判能力各不相同：$v(\{1,2\})=0)$，$v(\{1,3\})=100$，$v(\{2,3\})=200$。在这种情况下，谈判也需要分两个阶段完成，而且谈判中的让步也是非对称的。在第一轮的谈判中，23与1之间的“压力差”是200，13与2之间的“压力差”是100。因此，1和2都需要造成相应程度的让步，而3无须做出让步。如图7.5所示，第一轮谈判的结果是一个平行四边形，也就是联盟博弈的核。在第二阶段的谈判中，由于三人之间的“压力差”已被耗尽，大家处于相对平等的状态。为了取得大家都认可的唯一的分配方案，三人都需要做出让步——等值线 $x_2+x_3=200$ 和单纯形的底边 x_2x_3 相向而行；等值线 $x_1+x_3=100$ 和单纯形的侧边 x_1x_3 相向而行。最终得到的核仁 γ(50，100，150）位于平行四边形的重心。这时的夏普里值与核仁重合。

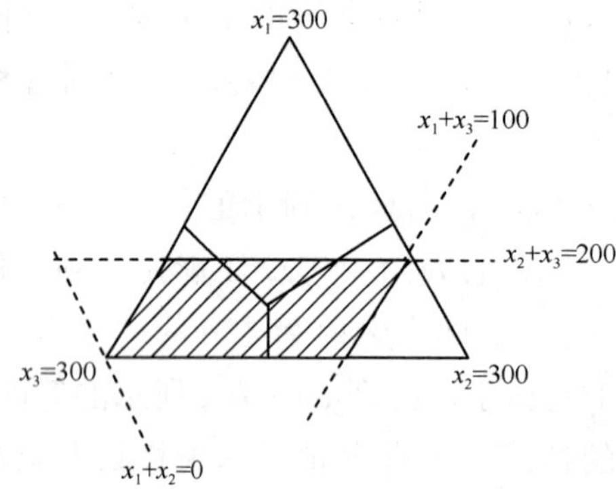

特征函数

$v(\{1\})=v(\{2\})=v(\{3\})=0$

$v(\{1,2\}=0$

$v(\{1,3\}=100$

$v(\{2,3\}=200$

$v(\{1,2,3\})=300$

阴影部分（平行四边形）为核，核仁γ (50, 100, 150) 位于平行四边形的重心；等于夏普里值(50, 100, 150)。

图7.5　关于“三妻分产”的思想实验（遗产为300枚金币）

有关“三妻分产”的思想实验结果表明，联盟博弈的解实际上是当事人在一定的主客观条件下让步和妥协的结果。表7.4列出了三种情况下的直觉解（按照1∶2∶3的比例进行分配）和拉比解（上述思想实验的结果）。显然，两者之间存在较大差异。造成这种差异的原因在于，直觉解是按照个人禀赋来分配遗产；而古代犹太人在设计分配方案时，不仅考虑禀赋，而且考虑遗产的实际数量。在比拉看来，个人禀赋不等于谈判能力。这一观念“无意中”与两千多年后的“最大最小原则”相吻合。

“三妻分产”的解决方案　　**表7.4**

遗产数量	第一个妻子（谈判能力弱）		第二个妻子（谈判能力中）		第三个妻子（谈判能力强）	
	直觉解	拉比解	直觉解	拉比解	直觉解	拉比解
100	50/3	100/3(＋)	100/3	100/3(＝)	150/3	100/3(－)
200	100/3	50（＋）	200/3	75（＋）	100	75（－）
300	50	50（＝）	100	100（＝）	150	150（＝）

注：(＋)表示拉比解大于直觉解；(－)表示拉比解小于直觉解；(＝)表示拉比解等于直觉解。

7.2.3.2　核仁的求解

一般来讲，根据“最大最小原则”求解核仁的过程可分为两步。第一步，确定满意程度最低的联盟，也就是“最不满意联盟”。第二步，确定使“最不满意联盟”感到最满意的分配方案。前面已经说过，在 n 人联盟博弈 (N, v) 中，对于给定的分配方案或支付向量 x，联盟 S 的成员的不满意程度可以用过剩值 $e(x,S)=v(S)-\Sigma_{i\in S}x_i$ 来衡量。因此，可以用过剩值来甄别“最少受惠者”。过剩值 $e(x,S)$ 越大，联盟 S 的成员对分配方案 x 的不满意程度越高（满意程度越低），拒绝该分配方案的意愿就越强烈；反之，他们对分配方案 x 的满意程度就越高。当过剩值为负数时，$e(x,S)$ 表示联盟 S 的成员拒绝分配方案 x 所蒙受的损失。

对于给定的分配方案或支付向量 x，每个联盟都有一个过剩值；而总联盟 N 有 2^n 个子集；因此，对于每一个支付向量案 x 来说，都存在 2^n 个过剩值。这些过剩值可以用一个 2^n 维向量 $\theta(x)=(\theta_1(x),\theta_2(x),\cdots\cdots,\theta_k(x)\cdots\cdots,\theta_{2^n}(x))$ 来表示。向量 $\theta(x)$ 中的各个分量根据过剩值的大小按降序排列（确切地说，是按非升序排列）—— $e(x,S)$ 最大（也就是满意程度最低）的联盟排在最前面，$e(x,S)$ 最小（也就是满意程度最高）的联盟排在最后面。如果在联盟博弈的分配集 I（同时满足个体理性和集体理性的支付向量的集合）中存在一个支付向量 γ，对于任何其他的支付向量 $x(x\neq\gamma)$，按照字典编纂的方式（lexicographically）进行比较时[1]，都有 $\theta(\gamma)\prec_{\text{lex}}\theta(x)$（式中的符号 $\prec_{\text{lex}}$ 表示“字典编纂式地小于”），那么，向量 γ 便是该联盟博弈的核仁。核仁 γ 代表的分配方案能够使满意程度最低的联盟的满意程度实现最大化，从而在罗尔斯的差别原则的意义上保证总联盟的稳定性。

综上所述，核仁的求解过程可以归结为下面的规划问题：

$$\min_{x\in I}\max_{S\subseteq N}e(x,S)。$$

该规划的求解过程包括以下步骤：首先在分配集 I 中找出能够使过剩值最大的联盟（即“最不满意联盟”）的过剩值最小的支付向量。如果这个支付向量是唯一的，那么，该支付向量便是联盟博弈的核仁；否则，就要找出能够使过剩值第二大的联盟（即“第二不满意联盟”）的过剩值最小的支付向量。以此类推，直到找到唯一的满足条件的支付向量为止。不难想象，当参与人的数目较大时，上述规划问题的求解将十分复杂。

三人博弈的情况则比较简单。考虑一个三人联盟博弈 (N, v)，总联盟 $N=\{1,2,3\}$，其价值 $v(N)=1$；空集的价值是 $v(\varnothing)=0$；单人联盟的价值是 $v(\{i\})=0(i=1,2,3)$；双人联盟的价值是 $0\leqslant v(S)\leqslant 1(|S|=2)$。如表7.5所示，对于每一个分配方

---

[1] 设有两个向量 $y=(y_1,y_2,\cdots\cdots,y_k)$ 和 $z=(z_1,z_2,\cdots\cdots,z_k)$，如果存在一个整数 $l\in(1,2,\cdots\cdots,k)$，使得 $y_1=z_1$，$y_2=z_2$，……，$y_{l-1}=z_{l-1}$，$y_l<z_l$，那么就说向量 y 字典编纂式地小于向量 z，并且记作 $y\prec_{\text{lex}}z$。

案 x 来说都有 $2^3=8$ 个过剩值。

三人博弈中分配方案 x 的过剩值 **表 7.5**

$e(x,\varnothing)=0$	
$e(x,N)=v(N)-x_1-x_2-x_3=0$	
$e(x,\{1\})=v(\{1\})-x_1=-x_1$	单人联盟的过剩值之和 $E_1=e(x,\{1\})+e(x,\{2\})+e(x,\{3\})=-1$
$e(x,\{2\})=v(\{2\})-x_2=-x_2$	
$e(x,\{3\})=v(\{3\})-x_3=-x_3$	
$e(x,\{1,2\})=v(\{1,2\})-x_1-x_2$	双人联盟的过剩值之和 $E_2=e(x,\{1,2\})+e(x,\{1,3\})+e(x,\{2,3\})$ $=v(\{1,2\})+v(\{1,3\})+v(\{2,3\})-2$
$e(x,\{1,3\})=v(\{1,3\})-x_1-x_3$	
$e(x,\{2,3\})=v(\{2,3\})-x_2-x_3$	

在这个三人博弈中，双人联盟的强弱对核仁的分布会产生较大影响。首先看双人联盟的力量很弱，也就是任何一个双人联盟的价值都不大于 1/3 的情况：$v(\{1,2\})\leqslant 1/3$，$v(\{1,3\})\leqslant 1/3$，$v(\{2,3\})\leqslant 1/3$。在这种条件下，可以证明：

（1）除空集和总联盟之外，过剩值最大的联盟（即“最不满意联盟”）只能是单人联盟而不是双人联盟。于是，求解核仁的规划问题可以简化为

$$\min_{x\in I}\max[e(x,\{1\}),e(x,\{2\}),e(x,\{3\})]。$$

（2）对于核仁 γ 来说，三个单人联盟的过剩值是相等的，也就是 $e(\gamma,\{1\})=e(\gamma,\{2\})=e(\gamma,\{3\})$。由于单人联盟的过剩值之和 $E_1=e(x,\{1\})+e(x,\{2\})+e(x,\{3\})=-1$，由此可得到博弈的核仁 $\gamma_1=\gamma_2=\gamma_3=1/3$。显然，此时的核仁 γ 与单纯形的几何中心重合。

其次看双人联盟的力量很强，也就是任何两个双人联盟的价值之和都不小于 1 的情况：$v(\{1,2\})+v(\{1,3\})\geqslant 1$，$v(\{1,2\})+v(\{2,3\})\geqslant 1$，$v(\{1,3\})+v(\{2,3\})\geqslant 1$。在这种条件下，可以证明：

（1）除空集和总联盟之外，过剩值最大的联盟（即“最不满意联盟”）只能是双人联盟而不是单人联盟。于是求解核仁的规划问题可以简化为

$$\min_{x\in I}\max[e(x,\{1,2\}),e(x,\{1,3\}),e(x,\{2,3\})]。$$

（2）对于核仁 γ 来说，三个双人联盟的过剩值是相等的：$e(\gamma,\{1,2\})=e(\gamma,\{1,3\})=e(\gamma,\{2,3\})$。由于双人联盟的过剩值之和 $E_2=v(\{1,2\})+v(\{1,3\})+v(\{2,3\})-2$，由此可得到博弈的核仁

$$\gamma_1=\frac{1}{3}+\frac{1}{3}[v(\{1,2\})+v(\{1,3\})-2v(\{2,3\})]$$

$$\gamma_2=\frac{1}{3}+\frac{1}{3}[v(\{1,2\})+v(\{2,3\})-2v(\{1,3\})]$$

$$\gamma_3=\frac{1}{3}+\frac{1}{3}[v(\{1,3\})+v(\{2,3\})-2v(\{1,2\})]$$

此时的核仁 γ 位于表示双人联盟价值的三条等值线围成的三角形的几何中心。把

这三个式子与计算夏普里值的三个公式相比较，可以发现在双人联盟的力量很强的三人联盟博弈中，夏普里值 φ 位于单纯形的几何中心 $w\left(\frac{1}{3},\frac{1}{3},\frac{1}{3}\right)$ 与核仁 γ 连线的中点。

对于三人联盟博弈来说，利用图形求解是简单而直观的方法。高度为 1 的单纯形是上述三人联盟博弈的分配集（对于其中的任何一点 x，都满足个体理性和集体理性，也就是同时满足以下条件：$x_1 \geqslant 0$，$x_2 \geqslant 0$，$x_3 \geqslant 0$；$x_1 + x_2 + x_3 = 1$）。核仁 γ 位于分配集中，并且满足“最大最小原则”。图 7.6 给出双人联盟力量很强的两种情况。在图 7.6（1）中，$v(\{1,2\}) = 0.8$，$v(\{1,3\}) = 0.3$，$v(\{2,3\}) = 0.7$，核为非空；由三条等值线围成的三角形就是博弈的核。在图 7.6（2）中，$v(\{1,2\}) = 0.85$，$v(\{1,3\}) = 0.45$，$v(\{2,3\}) = 0.8$，核为空集；由三条等值线围成的三角形是博弈的“影子核”。在以上两种情况下，三条等值线围成三角形，核仁 γ 位于这个三角形的几何中心。

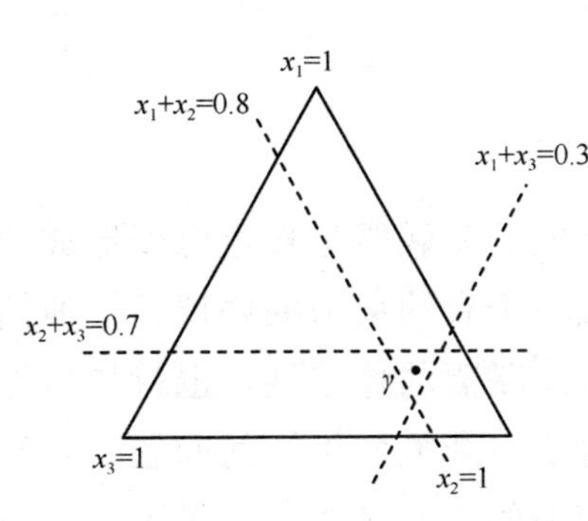

（1）特征函数

$v(\{1,2,3\})=1$

$v(\{1\})=v(\{2\})=v(\{3\})=0$

$v(\{1,2\})=0.8$

$v(\{2,3\})=0.7$

$v(\{1,3\})=0.3$

核是由三条等值线围成的三角形。核仁 $\gamma\left(\frac{0.7}{3},\frac{1.9}{3},\frac{0.4}{3}\right)$ 位于核的几何中心。夏普里值 $\varphi\left(\frac{1.7}{6},\frac{2.9}{6},\frac{1.4}{6}\right)$ 位于单纯形的几何中心 $w\left(\frac{1}{3},\frac{1}{3},\frac{1}{3}\right)$ 与核仁 γ 连线的中点，不在核中。

$x_1=1$
$x_1+x_2=0.85$
$x_1+x_3=0.45$
$x_2+x_3=0.8$
γ
$x_3=1$
$x_2=1$

（2）特征函数

$v(\{1,2,3\})=1$

$v(\{1\})=v(\{2\})=v(\{3\})=0$

$v(\{1,2\})=0.85$

$v(\{2,3\})=0.8$

$v(\{1,3\})=0.45$

核是空集。三条等值线围成的三角形是“影子核”。核仁 $\gamma\left(\frac{0.7}{3},\frac{1.75}{3},\frac{0.55}{3}\right)$ 位于“影子核”的几何中心。夏普里值 $\varphi\left(\frac{1.7}{3},\frac{2.75}{3},\frac{1.55}{3}\right)$ 位于单纯形的几何中心 $w\left(\frac{1}{3},\frac{1}{3},\frac{1}{3}\right)$ 与核仁 γ 连线的中点，不在“影子核”中。

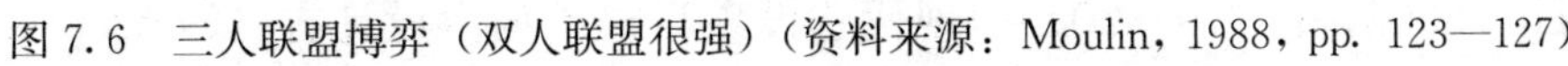

图 7.6　三人联盟博弈（双人联盟很强）（资料来源：Moulin，1988，pp. 123—127）

如果双人联盟的力量有的很强，有的很弱，例如 $v(\{1,2\}) = 0.4$，$v(\{1,3\}) = 0.9$，$v(\{2,3\}) = 0.2$，则会出现图 7.7 的情况。核是由三条直线 $x_1 + x_2 = 0.4$、$x_2 + x_3 = 0.2$、$x_1 + x_3 = 0.9$ 以及单纯形的一边 $x_2 = 0$ 围成的梯形。核仁 γ(0.575，0.05，

0.375）位于梯形中位线的中点。夏普里值 $\varphi\left(\frac{2.9}{6}, \frac{0.8}{6}, \frac{2.3}{6}\right)$ 不在核中。

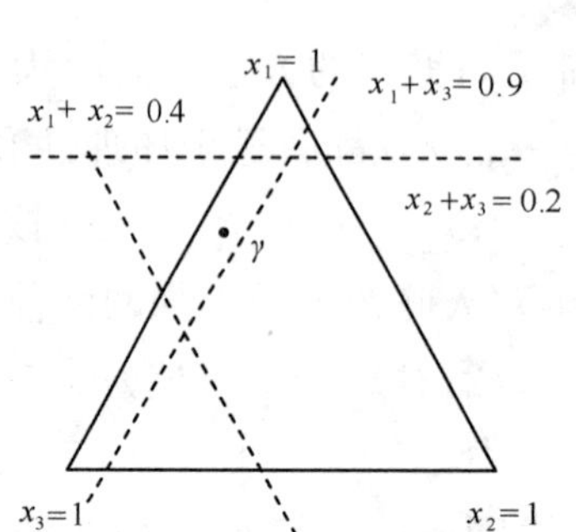

特征函数

$v(\{1,2,3\})=1, v(\{1\})=v(\{2\})=v(\{3\})=0$

$v(\{1,2\})=0.4$

$v(\{2,3\})=0.2$

$v(\{1,3\})=0.9$

核是由三条等值线以及单纯形的一边 $x_2=0$ 围成的梯形。核仁 $\gamma(0.575, 0.05, 0.375)$ 位于梯形中位线的中点。夏普里值 $\varphi(\frac{2.9}{6}, \frac{0.8}{6}, \frac{2.3}{6})$ 不在核中。

图 7.7　三人联盟博弈（双人联盟有的很强，有的很弱）

（资料来源：Moulin，1988，pp. 123—127）

7.2.4　小结

常规联盟博弈的基本假设是：由全体参与人组成的总联盟是肯定可以形成的。然而，如果参与人感到分配方案不公平，就无法形成一个有约束力的协议，使他们参与联盟。对核、夏普里值与核仁的求解，都是围绕着总联盟的稳定性，也就是对组织租金分配的公平性展开的。然而，对“公平”的理解是一个见仁见智的问题。合作博弈与非合作博弈的不同，就在于合作博弈没有一个统一的解的概念。这是因为，没有哪个解能够符合所有人对“公平”的理解。核、夏普里值与核仁这三种解的概念源自不同的公平观，因而在存在性、唯一性和空间分布上具有不同的特性（详见第 3 讲中的表 3.4，TU 联盟博弈的三种解的概念）。它们都可以用来解释 TU 联盟博弈的稳定性，各有长处和局限性，而且相互联系。可以证明，如果 TU 联盟博弈的核是非空的，其核仁一定位于核中（董保民等，2008，p. 47；Saad *et al.*，2009，p. 84）。在满足可加性公理的条件下，夏普里值与核仁重合（董保民等，2008，p. 49）。如果夏普里值与核仁都在核中并且重合，那么，无论从哪种公平观的角度来衡量，TU 联盟博弈都是稳定的。

7.3　基于建设项目 3C 结构的联盟博弈模型[1]

Winch（2002，pp. 19—20）把现代建设项目抽象为由设计方（Conception）、施工方（Construction）和控制方（Control）组成的 3C 结构。根据这一思路，我们可以把建设项目的水平交易抽象为三人 TU 联盟博弈；用 $N=\{1,2,3\}$ 表示参与人集合。特

[1] 这一节的内容主要来自《项目管理技术》杂志上发表的文章（沙凯逊，2011）。

征函数受参与人的禀赋和决策环境等因素的影响；这些因素共同决定了参与人的谈判能力。为了深入理解建设项目水平交易中当事人之间的合作关系，下面的模型引入了重置成本的概念，将参与人的谈判能力内生化。

7.3.1　重置成本、谈判能力与联盟博弈的价值

在对联盟博弈解的概念的基础性研究中，参与人的谈判能力一般是外生给定的。这样做可以简化分析过程，而且无损于理论的正确性。然而，在对某一特定问题的具体分析中，如果仍然外生给定谈判能力，就无法揭示参与人的地位和作用，以及参与人之间的相互影响，结果只能是隔靴搔痒。因此，对建设项目联盟博弈的研究，必须从谈判能力的内生化开始。

新古典经济学中的一般均衡（瓦尔拉均衡），是指市场上所有商品的供给和需求相等，也就是市场出清（market clearing）的状态。此时的均衡是帕累托最优的；所有的人都是价格的接受者。然而，这只是一种现实生活中并不存在的理想状态。相比较而言，在信息不对称的条件下，通过相机续约（contingent renewal）的内生执行（endogenous enforcement）策略实现的均衡能够较好地反映要素市场中的实际情况。这种非出清条件下的均衡有以下特点：(1) 帕累托无效，买卖双方都存在改进的空间；(2) 市场不出清，有些卖方无法进入交易，只能得到保留支付（reservation payoff）；(3) 进入交易的卖方能够获得高于保留支付的收益，高出的那部分收益便是均衡租金；(4) 买方是价格制定者（Bowles，2004，pp. 256—257）。

在建筑市场中，由于供大于求而造成的非出清现象普遍存在。对某一建设项目而言，假设参与人 $i(i=1,2,3)$ 不参与该项目，可以获得保留支付 w_i ；这时项目联盟就需要以 $\overline{w_i}$ 的代价寻找新的参与人，$\overline{w_i}$ 就是参与人 i 的**重置成本**（replacement cost）。在市场不出清的情况下，重置成本大于保留支付，即 $\overline{w_i}>w_i$。重置成本越高，说明参与人的可替代性程度越低，对其他参与人施加成本的能力就越强，其谈判能力也就越强（卢周来，2009）。

在建设项目的 3C 结构中，参与人的谈判能力取决于两方面的因素：一是参与人的禀赋，二是市场的供求状况。一般来讲，在同样的市场条件下，参与人的禀赋条件越好，其重置成本越高。此外，参与人的重置成本还受项目复杂程度的影响。对于普通的建设项目来说，很容易在建筑市场中找到合作伙伴，这意味着参与人的可替代性较高，重置成本较低；而对于复杂的建设项目，情况正好相反，某些高禀赋的参与人因“奇货可居”而具有较强的谈判能力。由此可见，参与人的禀赋有绝对和相对之分：绝对禀赋反映了参与人的自身条件，相对禀赋则要同时考虑参与人的绝对禀赋以及市场的供求状况。重置成本可以用来表示参与人的相对禀赋。为了揭示参与人在建设项目 3C 结构中的地位和作用，以及参与人之间的相互影响，在构建联盟博弈模型时，需要将重置成本内生化。

在联盟博弈中，联盟 S 的价值 $v(S)$ 就是它所能保证的支付水平，也反映了该联盟的谈判能力。从前面的分析来看，在建设项目的三人联盟博弈中，一个联盟的谈判能力不仅取决于参与人的禀赋（技术能力、信息能力和融资能力），还受决策环境（项目的复杂程度、市场成熟度、融资渠道和社会习俗）等因素的影响。重置成本正是这些因素的综合体现。假设项目联盟（总联盟）所创造的支付为 1，参与人 i 的重置成本 $0 < \overline{w}_i \leqslant 1$，我们可以通过下面的式子来确定建设项目联盟博弈的特征函数：$v(S) = \max(0, 1 - \Sigma_{i \in N \setminus S} \overline{w}_i)$，式中的运算符 $i \in N \setminus S$ 表示总联盟中除去联盟 S 的联盟的成员。

7.3.2 建设项目三人联盟博弈的求解与分析

利用图形求解三人联盟博弈的核与核仁是简单而直观的方法。图 7.8 到图 7.13 给出了六种重置成本条件下，建设项目三人联盟博弈的特征函数以及核、核仁与夏普里值。在图 7.8 所示的"三高"状态中，三人的重置成本相同 $\left(\frac{1}{4}\right)$，都等于 1。这时的核包含无数个分配方案，整个单纯形都满足个体理性、集体理性和联盟理性，核仁位于核的几何中心，且等于夏普里值。

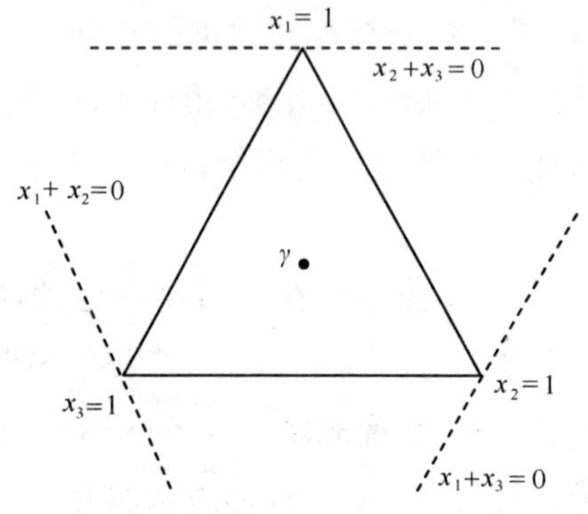

重置成本 $\overline{w}_1 = \overline{w}_2 = \overline{w}_3 = 1$
特征函数
$v(\{1\}) = v(\{2\}) = v(\{3\}) = 0$
$v(\{1, 2\}) = v(\{1, 3\}) = v(\{2, 3\}) = 0$
联盟博弈的解
整个单纯形 为核；核仁 $\gamma(\frac{1}{3}, \frac{1}{3}, \frac{1}{3})$ 位于核的几何中心，且等于夏普里值 φ。

图 7.8 "三高"状态下的建设项目三人联盟博弈

在图 7.9 所示的临界状态中，三人的重置成本相同，并且都等于 $\frac{1}{3}$。这时，核只

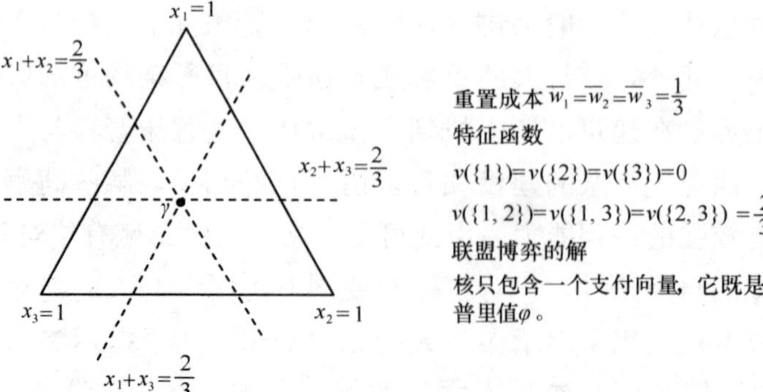

重置成本 $\overline{w}_1 = \overline{w}_2 = \overline{w}_3 = \frac{1}{3}$
特征函数
$v(\{1\}) = v(\{2\}) = v(\{3\}) = 0$
$v(\{1, 2\}) = v(\{1, 3\}) = v(\{2, 3\}) = \frac{2}{3}$
联盟博弈的解
核只包含一个支付向量，它既是核仁，也等于夏普里值 φ。

图 7.9 临界状态下的建设项目三人联盟博弈

包含一个支付向量；三条直线 $x_1+x_2=\frac{2}{3}$、$x_1+x_3=\frac{2}{3}$ 和 $x_2+x_3=\frac{2}{3}$ 相交于一点 $\gamma\left(\frac{1}{3},\frac{1}{3},\frac{1}{3}\right)$，它既是核仁，也等于夏普里值。

在图 7.10 所示的“三低”状态中，三人的重置成本相同 $\left(\frac{1}{4}\right)$，都小于 $\frac{1}{3}$。这时的核为空集；三条直线 $x_1+x_2=\frac{3}{4}$、$x_2+x_3=\frac{3}{4}$ 和 $x_1+x_3=\frac{3}{4}$ 围成的三角形是“影子核”。核仁位于“影子核”的几何中心，且等于夏普里值。由于核是空集，总联盟无法保持稳定。这也从反面说明，在不确定性和复杂程度很低，因而重置成本很低的情况下，客户（甲方）没有必要采用项目这种组织形式。

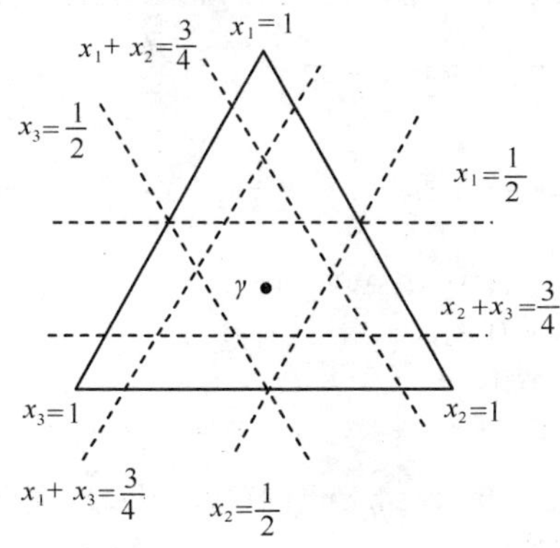

重置成本 $\overline{w}_1=\overline{w}_2=\overline{w}_3=\frac{1}{4}$

特征函数

$v(\{1\})=v(\{2\})=v(\{3\})=\frac{1}{2}$

$v(\{1,2\})=v(\{1,3\})=v(\{2,3\})=\frac{3}{4}$

联盟博弈的解

核是空集。核仁 $\gamma\left(\frac{1}{3},\frac{1}{3},\frac{1}{3}\right)$ 位于“影子核”的几何中心，且等于夏普里值 φ。

图 7.10　“三低”状态下的建设项目三人联盟博弈

在图 7.11 所示的“一低两高”的状态中，两人的重置成本相同 $\left(\frac{2}{3}\right)$，另一人的重置成本 $\left(\frac{1}{3}\right)$ 明显低于这两方。这时，重置成本较低的参与人的支付水平低于其他两方。根据直觉，项目收益似乎应按照参与人的重置成本的比例（1∶2∶2）进行分配，然而，根据罗尔斯的平均主义的公平观（核仁），分配比例是 $\frac{1}{6}:\frac{5}{12}:\frac{5}{12}$；根据多劳多得

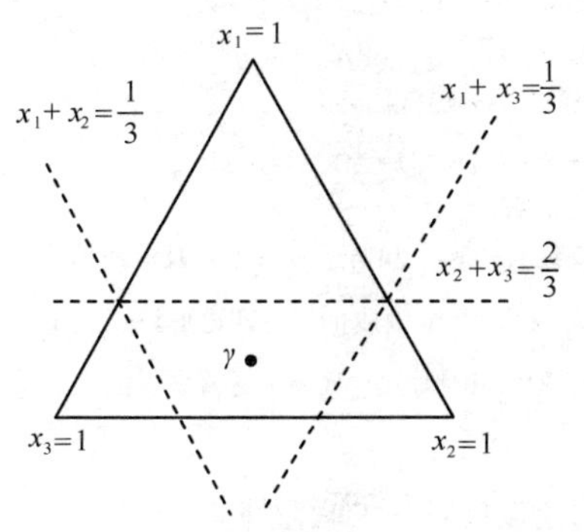

重置成本 $\overline{w}_1=\frac{1}{3}$，$\overline{w}_2=\frac{2}{3}$，$\overline{w}_3=\frac{2}{3}$

特征函数

$v(\{1\})=v(\{2\})=v(\{3\})=0$

$v(\{1,2\})=v(\{1,3\})=\frac{1}{3}$，$v(\{2,3\})=\frac{2}{3}$

联盟博弈的解

核是由直线 $x_1+x_2=\frac{1}{3}$、$x_1+x_3=\frac{1}{3}$ 和 $x_2+x_3=\frac{2}{3}$，以及单纯形的一边 $x_1=0$ 围成的梯形；核仁 $\gamma\left(\frac{1}{6},\frac{5}{12},\frac{5}{12}\right)$ 位于梯形中位线的中点；夏普里值 $\varphi\left(\frac{2}{9},\frac{7}{18},\frac{7}{18}\right)$ 在核中。

图 7.11　“一低两高”状态下的建设项目三人联盟博弈

的公平观（夏普里值），分配比例是 $\frac{2}{9}:\frac{7}{18}:\frac{7}{18}$。由 $\frac{1}{6}<\frac{1}{5}<\frac{2}{9}$ 可知，按照核仁分配，重置成本较低的参与人的支付水平低于凭“直觉”分配的水平；而按照夏普里值分配，则高于凭“直觉”分配的水平。

在图 7.12 所示的“一高两低”的状态中，两人的重置成本相同 $\left(\frac{1}{3}\right)$，另一人的重置成本 $\left(\frac{2}{3}\right)$ 明显高于这两人。这时，重置成本较高的参与人的支付水平应该高于其他两人。根据直觉，项目收益似乎应按照参与人的重置成本的比例（2 : 1 : 1）进行分配；根据罗尔斯的平均主义的公平观（核仁）和多劳多得的公平观（夏普里值），分配比例是 $\frac{5}{9}:\frac{2}{9}:\frac{2}{9}$。由 $\frac{5}{9}>\frac{1}{2}$ 可知，无论按照核仁分配，还是按照夏普里值分配，重置成本较高的参与人的支付水平都高于凭“直觉”分配的水平。

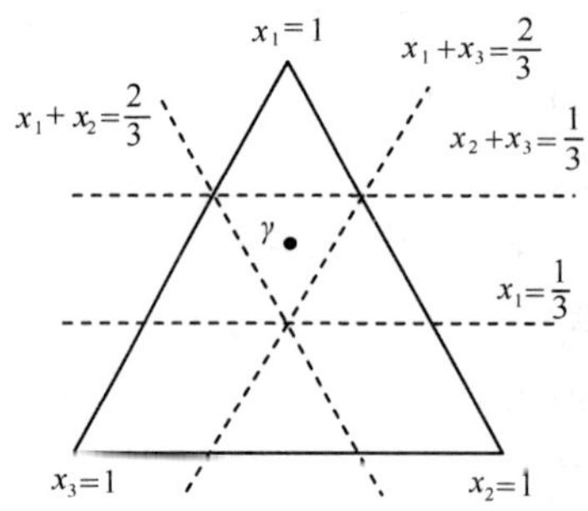

重置成本 $\overline{w}_1=\frac{2}{3}$, $\overline{w}_2=\frac{1}{3}$, $\overline{w}_3=\frac{1}{3}$
特征函数
$v(\{1\})=\frac{1}{3}$, $v(\{2\})=v(\{3\})=0$
$v(\{1,2\})=v(\{1,3\})=\frac{2}{3}$, $v(\{2,3\})=\frac{1}{3}$
联盟博弈的解
核是由直线 $x_1+x_2=\frac{2}{3}$、$x_1+x_3=\frac{2}{3}$ 和 $x_2+x_3=\frac{1}{3}$ 围成的三角形；核仁 $\gamma(\frac{5}{9},\frac{2}{9},\frac{2}{9})$ 位于核的几何中心，且等于夏普里值 φ。

图 7.12　“一高两低”状态下的建设项目三人联盟博弈

在图 7.13 所示的“高中低并存”的状态中，三人的重置成本之间存在明显差异，分别为 $\frac{1}{3}$、$\frac{2}{3}$ 和 1。此时，无论是根据核仁还是夏普里值进行分配，都与“直觉”相吻合：项目收益的分配比例是 $\frac{1}{6}:\frac{1}{3}:\frac{1}{2}$。

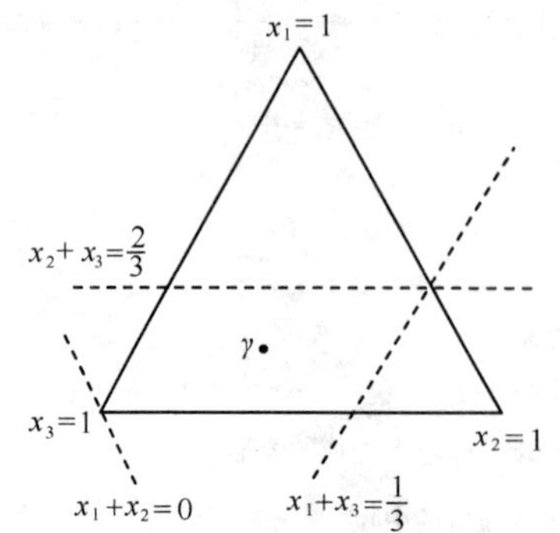

重置成本 $\overline{w}_1=\frac{1}{3}$, $\overline{w}_2=\frac{2}{3}$, $\overline{w}_3=1$
特征函数
$v(\{1\})=v(\{2\})=v(\{3\})=0$
$v(\{1,2\})=0$, $v(\{1,3\})=\frac{1}{3}$, $v(\{2,3\})=\frac{2}{3}$
联盟博弈的解
核是由直线 $x_1+x_3=\frac{1}{3}$ 和 $x_2+x_3=\frac{2}{3}$，以及单纯形的两个边 $x_1=0$ 和 $x_2=0$ 围成的平行四边形；核仁 $\gamma(\frac{1}{6},\frac{1}{3},\frac{1}{2})$ 位于核的几何中心，且等于夏普里值 φ。

图 7.13　“高中低并存”状态下的建设项目三人联盟博弈

7.4 结　　论

这一讲从联盟博弈的角度审视建设项目的水平治理问题。在研究中我们把项目联盟看作是合作博弈的均衡结果，把决策者处理信息的能力以及寻找合作伙伴的方式作为决定治理结构的重要影响因素。作为市场非出清条件下的产物，重置成本可以用来反映建设项目参与人的相对禀赋。一般来说，项目的复杂性和不确定性越强，建设市场中符合条件的参与人越少，参与人的重置成本就越高。通过引入重置成本的概念，我们将谈判能力内生化。在此基础上建立的联盟博弈模型，能够较好地解释参与人的相对禀赋和项目联盟的稳定性，以及利益分配之间的关系。

前面只对几种特殊情况进行了解析，而现实情况是千变万化的；尽管如此，我们还是可以从中得出一些有益的启示。第一，重置成本是影响联盟博弈格局的决定性因素。从核（基于交易收益的公平观）的角度来看，重置成本越大，项目联盟越稳定；博弈的核随着重置成本的下降而缩小（如图 7.8 和图 7.9 所示，核从整个单纯形缩小到一点）；当不确定性的影响微不足道，进而使重置成本降低到一定程度时，联盟博弈的核成为空集，总联盟失去稳定性，项目这种组织形式也就失去了存在的意义——这也从反面证明，不确定性和复杂性是建设项目存在的主要理由。第二，核、夏普里值与核仁这三种解的概念体现了不同的公平观。因此，在研究建设项目的稳定性时，需要充分考虑解析方法与公平观的一致性，选择合适的方法。例如，夏普里值比较适合于多劳多得公平观深入人心的地方；而在罗尔斯的平均主义观念盛行的场合，核仁是比较合适的方法。第三，在多数情况下，凭直觉制定的建设项目收益分配方案，貌似公平，实则不然。这是因为，人们的直觉往往与上述公平观不相符。因此，在研究建设项目的稳定性时，需要充分考虑解析方法与公平观的一致性。第四，在一定条件下，三种不同的公平观可以取得一致，此时，建设项目的稳定性最佳。

由于受篇幅的限制，这里没有讨论重置成本的估算问题，而这一问题对于建设项目水平治理的深入研究是至关重要的，因此有必要在今后做这方面的专题研究。最后应该指出，上述联盟博弈模型没有考虑合作时发生的成本问题。实际上，合作成本属于交易成本的范畴；而一个没有交易成本的经济社会，犹如没有摩擦力的物质世界，是不现实的。如果要将合作成本纳入建设项目水平治理的研究领域，需要借助联盟形成博弈的理论和方法。

参考文献

1. 鲍新中，刘小军（2009）合作博弈理论对成本分配技术的改进，工业工程，**12**（2），68—71.
2. 边沁（2000），道德与立法原理导论，中译本，时殷弘译，北京：商务印书馆.
3. 董保民，王运通，郭桂霞（2008）合作博弈论，北京：中国市场出版社.

4. 高东苗（2010）最大最小化原则：功利主义和公平的社会契约，北京科技大学学报（社会科学版），(3) 162—168.

5. 亨德里克斯（2007）组织的经济学与管理学，中译本，胡雅梅，张学渊，曹利群译，北京：中国人民大学出版社.

6. 黄少安，韦倩（2011）合作与经济增长，经济研究，(8)，51—64.

7. 库恩（2004）博弈论经典，中译本，韩松等译，北京：中国人民大学出版社.

8. 李峰，李莉，沈惠璋，刘尚亮（2010）合作博弈与社会经济网络形成，现代管理科学，(1)，60—62.

9. 李昭智（1984）NP-完全问题浅谈，天津理工大学学报，(1)，27—33.

10. 卢周来（2009）合作博弈框架下企业内部权力的分配，经济研究，(12)，106—118.

11. 罗尔斯（1988）正义论，中译本，何怀宏等译，北京：中国社会科学出版社.

12. 青木昌彦（2005）企业的合作博弈理论，中译本，郑江淮等译，北京：中国人民大学出版社.

13. 沙凯逊（2008）从管理到治理：建设项目理论演进探析，建筑经济，(6)，12—14.

14. 沙凯逊（2011）基于联盟博弈的建设项目水平治理分析，项目管理技术，**9** (11)，21—25.

15. 王光净，杨继君，刘仲英（2010）基于合作博弈的区域产业结构优化模型，工业工程与管理，**15** (1)，53—58.

16. 谢识予（2008）经济博弈论（第三版），上海：复旦大学出版社.

17. 杨荣基，彼得罗相，李颂志（2007）动态合作尖端博弈论，北京：中国市场出版社.

18. 张维迎（1996）博弈论与信息经济学，上海：上海三联出版社.

19. 张万宽（2008）公私伙伴关系的理论分析——基于合作博弈与交易成本的视角，经济问题探索，(5)，125—130.

20. Aumann, R. J. and Maschler, M. (1985) Game-theoretic analysis of a bankruptcy problem from the Talmud, *Journal of Economic Theory*, **36** (2), 195—213.

21. Bowles, S. (2004) *Microeconomics: Behavior, Institutions and Evolution*, Princeton University Press, Princeton.

22. Moulin, H. (1988) *Axioms of cooperative decision making*, Cambridge University Press, New York.

23. Neumann J. Von and Morgenstern, O. (1944) *Theory of Games and Economic Behavior*. Princeton, University Press, Princeton, NJ.

24. Saad, W., Han, Z., Debbah, M., Hjørungnes, A. and Basar, T. (2009) Coalitional game theory for communication networks, *IEEE Signal Processing Magazine*, **26** (5), 77—97.

25. Winch, G. M. (2001) Governing the project process: a conceptual framework. *Construction Management and Economics*, **19** (8), 799—808.

26. Winch, G. M. (2002) *Managing Construction Projects: An Information Processing Approach*, Blackwell Science, Oxford.

第 8 讲　针对项目经理的治理：一个共同代理的视角

- □ 建筑企业对项目经理的激励问题不同于一般企业对车间主任的激励问题。后者可以归结为双边委托代理问题，前者则属于“一仆二主”的共同代理问题。
- □ 与传统的双边委托代理模型相比，标准的共同代理模型只是增加了一个委托人，然而，参与人之间的关系却发生了实质性的变化——由双边关系变为“多边关系”，由此导致合约外部性以及显示原理的失效。
- □ 共同代理问题可以归结为纵向激励和横向协调问题，其中涉及到三种效应，一是代理人的“寻租效应”，二是委托人之间的“共谋效应”，三是当事人之间的“制衡效应”。对这三种效应的比较和分析，应该成为研究共同代理问题的主线。
- □ 建筑企业对项目经理的激励并没有一定之规，而是要针对不同的情况采取不同的策略。在选派项目经理和制定激励方案时需要考虑的因素有：建设项目的规模和复杂程度、建设单位在签约时的表现、项目经理以往的表现、项目采购方式以及当地的市场环境等。
- □ 建设单位的不当行为会加剧项目经理的机会主义倾向。建设单位的行为规范问题，最终可以归结为项目法人的定位以及剩余控制权与剩余索取权的合理配置问题。对政府投资和非政府投资两种类型的建设项目采取“一手抓、一手放”的方针，对前者有利于减少腐败行为和工程质量事故，对后者有利于提高效率。

如前所述，治理问题产生的根源在于当事人交互式依存关系带来的复杂性。治理的主要任务是处理好各种利益相关者之间的关系，营造一个良好的制度环境（也就是所谓的“关系场”），使人们有积极性做正确的事情（Sha，2016）。建设项目的生产和交易涉及多种关系。前面两讲分别从委托代理和联盟博弈的角度讨论了建设项目的垂直治理和水平治理。垂直治理的研究对象是客户与一阶供应商（first-tier suppliers）之间的关系。水平治理的研究对象是一阶供应商之后供应链中各种当事人之间的关系（Winch，2001）。这一讲以共同代理的解释逻辑为主，研究建筑企业与项目经理之间的关系，也就是针对项目经理的治理问题。

项目经理对于建设项目来说是至关重要的。根据国家标准《建设工程项目管理规范》GB/T 50326—2006，以下简称为《规范》），建设工程项目管理应“全面实行项目经理责任制”；项目经理“由法定代表人任命”，是“企业法定代表人在建设工程项目上的授权委托代理人”❶；“项目经理责任制的核心是项目经理承担实现项目管理目标责任书确定的责任”；项目管理目标责任书“由法定代表人或其授权人与项目经理协商制定”（编写委员会，2006，pp. 488—495）。显然，建筑企业的绩效水平在很大程度上取决于项目经理的能力和态度。

凡是存在委托代理关系的地方都存在激励不相容、责任不对等和信息不对称的问题。就建筑企业和项目经理的关系而言，两者的效用函数不同会导致激励不相容；对经营后果的责任不对等会使项目经理产生机会主义的行为倾向；信息不对称则会使项目经理有可能通过混淆成本构成、隐瞒收入水平等方式攫取项目的剩余，侵害企业的权益。由于建设项目“游离”于建筑企业之外，项目经理往往会有一种“将在外君命有所不受”的心态。如何通过有效的治理结构来规范项目经理的行为，这是建筑企业所面临的重大课题。

由于建筑企业和建设项目之间存在着耦合关系，针对项目经理的治理问题不仅涉及建筑企业和项目经理，而且涉及第三方——建设单位。三者之间存在着“一仆二主”的复杂关系，这使得经典的委托代理理论难以奏效，因此需要采用新的视角和方法。

这一讲的结构安排如下：首先简要介绍共同代理理论的基本概念和方法，为下面的分析做准备；然后分析建筑企业对建设项目经理的激励问题并提出相应的策略；最后分析我国建设单位的行为现状，并针对项目法人缺失问题和对不同类型建设项目的分类治理问题提出若干建议。

8.1 共同代理理论简介

本书的第 6 讲介绍了单任务的双边委托代理关系（bilateral principal—agent relationship）：一个委托人将某一项任务托付给一个代理人，由于两者的利益不一致，信息不对称，代理人有可能偏离委托人利益最大化的方向。为了让代理人讲真话、不偷懒，委托人需要向代理人提供足够的激励。由此派生出一些不同的模型，比如，逆向选择模型所要解决的是代理人事前隐藏信息的问题；而代理人事后隐藏信息或行动的问题则要由道德风险模型来解决。这些模型可以为许多重要的经济现象提供富有弹性的研究框架。然而，现实生活中的委托代理关系没有这么纯粹和简单，而是普遍存在着两个或两个以上委托人试图影响同一个代理人的现象，例如，多个制造商选择同一个零售商作为销售代理，几家银行同时向一家企业贷款，多个政府机构对同一家企业进行规制，以及多个国家针对一家跨国公司的税收竞争等等。理论研究和实践应用的

❶ 这里的授权委托代理人（authorized agent）是法律术语，是法定代理人（statutory agent ）的对称。前者根据委托授权而产生，后者根据法律规定而产生。

结果表明，委托人与代理人的数量对委托代理关系的性质具有实质性的影响。如表 8.1 所示，经过三十多年的发展，对委托代理关系的研究已经从以经典的双边委托代理（一个委托人、一个代理人）扩展到复杂的多边合约（多个委托人、多个代理人）。在集中式合约中，除了双边代理之外，还有多代理人的集中式合约（例如，在拍卖市场中，一个拍卖者面对多个竞拍者）。在多边合约中，除了用实线表示的纵向关系（委托人对代理人的激励）之外，还存在用虚线表示的横向关系（委托人之间的协调）。纵向激励问题与横向协调问题相互交织在一起，使研究工作愈加复杂，也更具挑战性。

委托代理模型：从双边代理到复杂的多边合约　　表 8.1

集中式合约（centralized contracting）	双边代理（bilateral agency）	一个委托人 一个代理人
	多代理人的集中式合约	一个委托人 多个代理人
多边合约（multi-contracting）	共同代理（common agency）	多个委托人 一个代理人
	复杂的多边合约	多个委托人 多个代理人

共同代理（common agency）属于多边合约（multi-contracting）的范畴，它可以简单地理解为“多个委托人、单一代理人、单一代理事务”的委托代理关系（刘有贵，蒋年云，2006）。一个比较经典的定义是：个人（代理人）的行为选择影响的不止一个人，而是多个人（委托人），这些委托人对各种可能行为的偏好往往是相互冲突的，这种情况就是“共同代理”（Bemheim and Whinston，1986，p. 923）。

8.1.1　基本模型与发展脉络

标准的共同代理模型包括两个委托人和一个代理人；每个委托人同时独立地（非合作地）向代理人提出一个合同。每个委托人都试图影响代理人的决策。除了委托人和代理人之间的信息不对称、利益不一致之外，共同代理模型中还增加了一个新的因素——互为对手的委托人之间的竞争与合作。

对共同代理理论的系统性研究是从 20 世纪 80 年代中期开始的。1985 年，美国斯坦福大学的伯恩海姆（Bemheim）和西北大学的惠斯顿（Whinston）共同发表了一篇具有开创性意义的文章（Bemheim and Whinston，1985）。他们对企业产品销售代理问题的研究结果表明，共同代理在本质上可以看作是一种间接机制，这种机制可以促进委托人之间的共谋（collusion）。1986 年，这两位作者又提出了一个更具一般性的共同代理模型（Bemheim and Whinston，1986）。该模型以道德风险问题为背景。模型中包括多个委托人和一个代理人，所有的参与人都是风险中性的。由此得出的主要结论是：（1）总起来看，机制的实施总是有效的（成本最小化），（2）非合作行为导致有效的行动选择的充要条件是：委托人之间的共谋能够在最优的成本水平实施最优的行动。简言之，在一定条件下，委托人之间的共谋能够导致有效的结果。

以上基本模型所得出的结论引起了学界的极大兴趣。此后的理论研究主要沿着以下几个方向展开：一是共同代理博弈均衡的特征分析；二是多委托人环境下的激励机制设计原理研究；三是委托人的竞争与合作对激励的影响分析；四是代理人面临多任务情况时的激励问题研究（于立宏，管锡展，2005）。随着研究工作的深入进行，基本模型中的假设条件也被逐步放松：从委托人任务同质性到异质性，从静态到动态，朝着更贴近现实的方向推进（王小芳，管锡展，2004）。在法国图卢兹大学的马赫蒂摩（Martimort）和美国芝加哥大学的斯托尔（Stole）等人的共同努力下，多委托人激励理论的分析框架现已基本形成（Stole，1991；Martimort，1992；Martimort and Stole，2001；Martimort and Stole，2002；Martimort，2009）。

共同代理理论框架的构建为多个领域的研究提供了新的视角和方法。近年来，在应用层面上的相关文献涉及多个国家对跨国公司的税收竞争问题（Olsen and Osmundsen，2011）、西方议会中的院外游说活动问题（Martimort，2009）、多家银行向同一客户贷款时的信用风险问题（Bennardo *et al.*，2015）、政府机构设置中的集权与分立的权衡问题（陈健，胡家勇，2013）、政府的规制结构与腐败防范问题（Hemsley，2016）、企业的研发外包问题（Billette de Villemeur and Versaevel，2017）等。这些研究在纵向上涉及国家、产业、组织以及个人等不同层次，在横向上涵盖了政治、经济、社会等不同领域。在我国建设项目治理的研究领域，共同代理的理论和方法也得到了初步应用，涉及建设项目经理的授权赋能问题（孙春玲等，2012）、业主对项目管理公司的激励问题（张光宇，李长春，2014）、代建制模式中政府投资单位、使用单位和代建单位三者之间的关系问题（石磊，刘安琪，2015）等内容。

8.1.2 研究维度与研究空间

对共同代理的研究涉及以下不同的维度。第一个维度涉及代理人对合同的选择方式——全部接受或拒绝（all-or-nothing）*vs.* 部分接受。在传统的双边委托代理模型中，代理人对委托人提出的合同只有两种选择，要么接受，要么拒绝。而在共同代理模型中，代理人有了更多的选择：全部接受、部分接受和全部拒绝。

首先看一个与政府规制有关的例子。两个政府机构（委托人）从不同的角度对同一家企业（代理人）进行规制；其中第一个机构所关心的是企业的产出水平，第二个机构的规制对象是企业造成的污染。面对政府的规制，这家企业只有两种选择：要么同时接受两个政府机构的规制，要么同时拒绝（这意味着企业离开它所从事的行业或者干脆关门大吉）。伯恩海姆和惠斯顿（Bemheim and Whinston，1986）把这种“要么全部接受、要么全部拒绝”的代理方式称为**内在共同代理**（intrinsic common agency）[1]。

另一个例子涉及企业的产品销售问题。两家生产厂商（委托人）生产不同的产品，它们通过非线性定价（nonlinear pricing）[2] 的策略向同一家零售商（代理人）提出产品销售合同。在这种情况下，零售商可以同时接受这两家企业的合同，也可以单独接受其中一家的合同。伯恩海姆和惠斯顿（Bemheim and Whinston，1986）把这种代理方式称作**授权共同代理**（delegated common agency）。授权共同代理在旅游业和金融保险业普遍存在（Bemheim and Whinston，1986；王小芳，管锡展，2004）。在上述产品销售的例子中，如果零售商单独接受一家生产厂商的合同，就会导致排他性交易或独占交易（exclusive dealing）。因此，独占交易可以看作是授权共同代理的一种特殊情况。实际上，在对独占交易的研究中，共同代理博弈模型发挥了十分重要的作用（黄建军，2012）。

非内在共同代理（non-intrinsic common agency）可以看作是介乎于内在共同代理和授权共同代理之间的另一种特殊情况（Calzolari and Scarp，1999）。在授权共同代理中，委托人可以针对代理人的不同选择——接受或拒绝其他委托人提出的合同——设计一个合同菜单，并通过这种方式来影响代理人是否接受其他合同的决策。而在非内在共同代理中，每个委托人只能向代理人提供一种合同（而不是合同菜单），不能根据代理人对其他委托人的合同的选择情况改变自己的合同；代理人可以对合同做出自由选择——全部接受、部分接受或者全部拒绝。

第二个维度与信息不对称的时间特征有关——事前隐藏信息 *vs.* 事后隐藏信息或隐藏行动。在信息经济学中，这两种不同性质的问题需要用不同的博弈模型来处理。关于逆向选择和信息甄别的共同代理的分析框架涉及事前的信息不对称，也就是代理人事前隐藏信息的情况。关于道德风险的共同代理的分析框架涉及事后的信息不对称，也就是代理人事后隐藏信息或隐藏行动的情况。

需要说明的是，在有关共同代理的分析中，有时会涉及完全信息（也就是信息对称）的情况（Martimort，2007）。在这种情况下，当事人之间的关系不是严格意义上的“委托代理”关系。之所以会出现这种情况，是因为在共同代理中，互为对手的委托人之间存在着协调问题。如果这个问题解决不好，即便在完全信息条件下，也会导致多重均衡和效率损失。

第三个维度涉及合同信息对于委托人的公开程度——公开 *vs.* 非公开。在合同中

---

[1] 国内的相关文献多把 intrinsic common agency 译为“内生型共同代理”。这里翻译成“内在共同代理”是基于以下考虑：共同代理（common agency）中的“共同”（common）一词是与“排他”（exclusive）相对立的。显然，all-or-nothing 的这种选择方式是共同代理的内在要求——如果不采用这种方式，代理人有可能只接受一个委托人的合同，这时的合同就是排他合同了。

[2] 在这种定价方式下，消费者对某一商品或服务支付的价格同购买的数量不成线性比例。这方面的例子包括数量折扣和数量补贴等方式。

有一些需要由委托人控制的行动。如果这些行动是所有委托人都能看到并且能够证实的，共同代理就是**公开代理**（public agency），否则就是**非公开代理**（private agency）。前面提到的第二个例子属于公开代理。这是因为每一家生产厂商可都能够看到并证实另一家生产厂商对零售商的销售数量。而在前面提到的第一个例子中，第一个政府机构只能了解并证实与企业产出水平有关的信息，第二个政府机构只能了解并证实与企业污染水平有关的信息。因此它们只能根据自己掌握的私人信息对企业进行规制。这就是非公开代理的情况。与公开代理相比，在非公开代理的条件下，签约的可能性较小，合同的不完全性较强。而在公开代理的条件下，委托人之间的协调较为容易进行（Martimort，2007）。

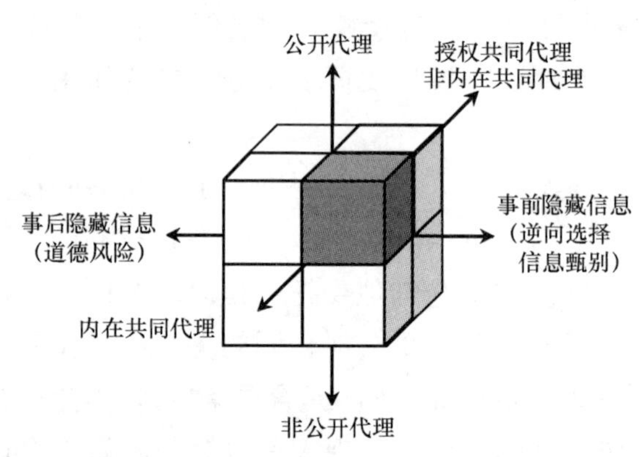

图 8.1　共同代理的研究空间：三个维度与八个象限

如图 8.1 所示，以上三个维度将共同代理的研究空间划分为八个象限。每个象限对应于一个特定的研究领域。例如，图中用深色表示的象限的研究对象是：事前隐藏信息的公开的内在共同代理。与其他象限相比，这个象限的问题相对比较简单。在利用共同代理模型分析相关问题时，首先要解决好定位问题：（1）代理人对合同的选择方式，是内在共同代理还是授权共同代理；（2）信息不对称的时间特征，是事前隐藏信息还是事后隐藏信息；（3）合同信息对于委托人的公开程度，是公开代理还是非公开代理。只有这样，才能避免文不对题和“张冠李戴”的现象。

8.1.3　机制设计与授权原理

在共同代理的研究领域，激励理论和机制设计理论占有十分重要的地位。机制设计理论由赫尔维茨（Hurwicz）创立，经过马斯金（Maskin）和迈尔森（Myerson）等人的发展，现已成为现代经济分析的一种重要方法❶。机制设计理论主要采用博弈论的方法，但两者的思路存在差异。博弈论的基本思路是：在给定博弈规则的条件下，推断参与人可能采取的行动和均衡结果。而机制设计所要解决的问题是：给定一个目标，如何设计一种博弈规则（机制）来实现这一目标。从研究内容来看，机制设计属于具有委托代理关系的不完全信息静态博弈的范畴。

激励相容和显示原理（revelation principle）是机制设计理论的两大基石。所谓激

❶ 利奥尼德·赫尔维茨（Neonid Hurwicz，1917—2008）是俄裔美籍经济学家，埃里克·马斯金（Eric Maskin，1950—）和罗杰·迈尔森（Roger Myerson，1951—）是美国经济学家。他们三位因在创立和发展机制设计理论方面所做出的重要贡献而共同获得 2007 年诺贝尔经济学奖。

励相容，是指委托人所设计的机制能够使代理人有积极性讲真话、不偷懒。为了做到这一点，委托人必须给代理人一定的激励补偿，代理人由此获得信息租金。显示原理为最优机制的设计提供了一条捷径——它使得机制设计者在搜寻最优机制时，可以把注意力集中在“直接机制”这个较小的范围之内。

背景资料：

贝叶斯纳什均衡、机制设计与显示原理（资料来源：张维迎，1996）

在 1967 年以前，人们对不完全信息博弈的解析是无能为力的，这是因为，当一个参与人不知道他在与谁博弈时，博弈规制是没有意义的。海萨尼[1]（Harsanyi，1967）通过引入虚拟参与人“自然”这个角色，把不完全信息静态博弈转换为完全但不完美信息博弈，也就是静态贝叶斯博弈。这就是所谓的“海萨尼转换”。

在贝叶斯博弈中，“自然”首先随机决定参与人的类型（type）。参与人的策略和效用都是这个随机变量的函数，因而都是类型依存（type contingent）的。类型是参与人的私人信息。每个参与人知道自己的类型，不知道别人的类型，但知道类型上的联合分布，从而能对其他参与人的类型做出先验的分布判断。在博弈中，每个参与人根据自己的类型、条件概率和其他参与人的策略来决定自己的策略。所谓贝叶斯纳什均衡，就是使所有参与人期望效用最大化的策略组合。

委托人在机制设计中的任务是决定一个配置函数，使自己的期望效用最大化。典型的机制设计是一个三阶段不完全信息博弈：（1）委托人设计一个机制（合同、激励方案）。（2）代理人同时选择接受或拒绝委托人提出的方案。如果代理人选择拒绝，他得到外生给定的保留支付。（3）选择接受机制的代理人按照机制的规则进行博弈。

机制是一套博弈规则。代理人需要根据规则发出消息（message，例如拍卖中的报价）；实现的消息决定配置结果（例如，拍卖中由谁得到拍卖品，支付的价格是多少）。根据消息空间（message space）的性质，机制可以分为直接机制和间接机制。例如，现实中的拍卖机制一般都是间接机制——拍卖者不是让买者直接报告自己的类型（拍卖品对买者的价值，也就是买者对拍卖品的实际估价），而是问买者愿意出多少价格，而买者的报价是其类型的函数。反之，如果拍卖者让买者直接报告个人的类型，这就是直接机制——这时代理人的策略空间等同于类型空间。

由于配置函数依赖代理人发出的消息，而消息本身又依赖于代理人的类型，因此，不论委托人设计何种机制，配置函数最终依赖于代理人的类型向量。委托人可以选择任何一个满足参与约束，同时满足激励相容约束的机制。这个机制可以是间接机制，也可以是直接机制。从机制设计者的角度来看，消息空间的维度越小越好。显示原理

---

[1] 约翰·海萨尼（John C. Harsanyi，1920—2000）是匈牙利裔美籍经济学家。由于在博弈论的发展及其在经济学领域的应用中所做出的开创性贡献，他在 1994 年和纳什、泽尔腾共同获得诺贝尔经济学奖。

告诉我们，对于任何贝叶斯博弈的任何贝叶斯纳什均衡来说，都可以找到与之相对应的某个激励相容的直接机制。也就是说，任何一个机制（比如一级密封拍卖机制或二级密封拍卖机制）所能达到的配置结果都可以通过一个（讲真话）的直接机制实现。根据这一原理，迈尔森（Myerson，1979）把对最优机制的搜寻范围从一般的消息空间缩小到了代理人的类型空间，从而大大降低了机制设计的复杂程度。

显示原理在双边委托代理的研究领域得到了广泛的应用。然而，在处理共同代理问题时，它的适用性受到了挑战。首先，代理人在多个委托人之间扮演着关联者的角色，而在许多情况下，这个角色在直接交流博弈（direct communication game）中并不存在。其次，委托人可能会诱使代理人向其他委托人说谎，这可能会使真实均衡（truthful equilibrium）❶ 无法存在。再次，把注意力集中在直接交流博弈中的真实均衡，可能会将一些由均衡外消息❷所支持的均衡排除在外（Martimort and Stole，2002）。说到底，显示原理失效的原因可以归因于共同代理中的"多边关系"，以及由此产生的交流空间的复杂性。

针对以上挑战和问题，人们提出了不同的解决办法。其中的一种思路是放弃直接显示机制，转而把注意力集中在间接机制集合中的子集。马赫蒂摩和斯托尔（Martimort and Stole，2002）指出，问题的关键不是交流空间（communication space，也就是前面所说的消息空间）的性质，而是委托人向代理人提供的选择方案的集合。有鉴于此，他们把单个委托人条件下的**税收原理**（taxation principle）❸ 扩展为多边合约条件下的**授权原理**（delegation principle）。

授权原理和税收原理都是用分散的选择菜单（间接机制）来取代直接交流机制。从这个意义上讲，它们都是显示原理（直接机制）的逆向原理。根据显示原理，机制设计者在寻找最优机制时，可以把注意力集中在代理人的类型空间。而根据授权原理，在研究多委托人条件下的均衡问题时，可以把注意力集中在合约变量的分散式菜单的策略空间——从代理人的角度来看，交流本身没有价值，只有交流所产生的与支付有关的结果才是重要的，因此，可以用分散的选择菜单来取代交流。这样，在显示原理失效的情况下，授权原理依然可以在一定程度上减少共同代理问题的复杂程度。

8.1.4 合约外部性与均衡结果分析

经济学中的**外部性**（externality）是指"那些生产或消费对其他团体强征了不可

❶ 共同代理博弈通常都有若干个均衡结果，其中有一个是真实均衡。在真实均衡中，每个委托人的贡献表（contribution schedule）都是按照各自的支付函数来安排的。

❷ 我们将在下一节介绍均衡外消息这个概念。

❸ 税收原理指出，对于任何一种讲真话的直接机制，都存在一种相关的税率表或选择菜单可供代理人选择，并且会得到同样的均衡结果（Guesnerie，1981；Rochet，1985）。

补偿的成本或给予了无须补偿的收益的情形。”（萨缪尔森，诺德豪斯，1996，p. 263）外部性可分为负外部性（成本制造者没有支付成本，例如，化工厂排放废水给周围居民带来负面影响）和正外部性（收益创造者没有获得收益，例如，科研成果，特别是基础性的研究成果被他人无偿使用）。市场失灵和“搭便车”问题都与外部性有很大关系。传统上，解决外部性问题主要通过以下两种途径。一是政府干预。例如，对排污企业征收税款（庇古税[1]），对基础研究项目提供补贴。二是采取合并的方法，将外部性问题内部化。例如，通过企业兼并，纵向一体化能使一定的外部性问题内部化。科斯提出了解决外部性的新思路：通过创造一个外部性市场来交易所有权。科斯指出，如果满足下列条件：（1）产权得到明确的界定；（2）讨价还价是有效率的（没有交易成本）；那么在外部性条件下，当事人之间的讨价还价将导致有效的资源配置方案。

共同代理中的**合约外部性**（contractual externalities）缘于委托人之间的非合作行为。考虑两家零售商（委托人）和一个制造商（代理人）之间的共同代理博弈。制造商向这两家零售商提供中间产品，零售商把一个单位的中间产品转换成一个单位的成品，然后销往市场。每个委托人向代理人提出非线性价格合同，合同中包含一些由这个委托人控制的行动变量。这些合约变量不仅出现在代理人的效用函数中，也出现在其他委托人的目标函数中。所谓直接外部性，就是指一个委托人的合约变量直接影响其他委托人的支付的情况。而间接外部性是指一个委托人通过代理人影响其他委托人的情况。

一个内在共同代理的博弈过程包括以下步骤：

（1）由“自然”决定代理人的类型 θ。在非对称信息条件下，θ 是代理人的私人信息。而在完全信息条件下，它是所有参与人的共同知识。

（2）两个委托人各自独立地向代理人提出非线性的价目表。非线性价目表内包含多种选项，因此可以看作是一种合同菜单。在纯策略（而不是混合策略）均衡中，代理人只能在每个委托人提供的合同菜单选项中选择一项，那些未被选择的选项就是所谓的“均衡外选择”或“非均衡选择”（out-of-equilibrium choice）[2]。

（3）代理人决定同时接受或同时拒绝委托人提出的两个合同。

（4）如果代理人同时拒绝这两个合同，他将得到外生的保留效用。如果同时接受这两个合同，他就要决定为两个委托人提供的中间产品的数量。

在授权共同代理中，须将步骤（3）改为：代理人决定接受一个委托人的合同、两个委托人的合同，或者拒绝所有的合同。

在不同条件下，这个模型会产生不同的均衡结果。下面是有关直接外部性的几个分析结论（Martimort and Stole，2001）：

---

[1] 英国经济学家庇古在 1920 年出版的《福利经济学》一书中主张，当存在外部不经济效应时，政府应当向企业征税。这种政策建议后来被称为庇古税（普雷斯曼，2000，p. 204）。

[2] 与此相关的术语还有均衡外报价（out-of-equilibrium offer）和均衡外消息（out-of-equilibrium message）等。

（1）在内在共同代理、完全信息的条件下，非线性价格具有承诺[1]的价值，因而会加剧委托人之间的竞争。此时博弈模型具有多重均衡的结果：任何一个介于古诺双寡头模型解和完全竞争模型解之间的结果都可以作为均衡结果。

（2）在授权共同代理、完全信息的条件下，均衡外消息可以使委托人之间竞争足够“软”，进而使直接机制下的激烈竞争被共谋的结果所取代。在这种情况下，上述内在共同代理博弈模型的均衡产量仍然是均衡结果，不过，剩余的分配不同于内在共同代理的情况。

（3）在非对称信息条件下，非线性价格的承诺价值会有所削弱。在这种情况下，内在共同代理的均衡集的规模有所缩减。

有关直接外部性的分析结果还表明，合同信息对于委托人的公开程度也会对均衡结果产生影响。例如，在完全信息的条件下，非公开的内在共同代理同时面临着两个问题，一是均衡的多样性，二是系统性的效率低下。而公开的内在共同代理在恢复效率的同时，会使多重均衡的问题更加严重。

此外，信息不对称与合约外部性造成的扭曲与委托人任务的性质有关。例如，在逆向选择（事前隐藏信息）的非公开的内在代理中，间接外部性可能会带来不同的后果：如果委托人的任务是相互替代的，为了吸引代理人为自己工作，委托人会提高激励强度，这时的合约外部性是正向的。而当任务互补时，每个委托人都希望搭其他委托人的“便车”，结果导致较低强度的激励合同，这时的合约外部性是负向的（Martimort，2007）。

以上分析表明，多边合约会带来新的交易成本，其均衡结果往往是（事中）无效的。接下来的问题是：既然如此，为什么在有些时候人们会选择共同代理，而不采用集中式合约呢？为了回答这个问题，需要在第三优（the third best）[2] 的环境中考察合约的效率问题。在现实世界中，每一项制度安排都有其比较优势，同时不可避免地具有局限性。尽管在多数情况下，共同代理存在多重均衡和效率损失的问题，然而在某些条件下，共同代理的整体效果会好于集中式合约。例如，在政府机构对企业实施监管的案例中，由于不同机构之间存在相互监督和制约，致使每个机构都不会轻易接受企业的贿赂，从而导致社会成本的减少和的社会福利的改善（Martimort，2007）——这可能是政府监管采用多个机构（委托人）而不是一个机构（委托人）的原因之一。再比如，有研究表明，对于复杂的大型项目而言，控制权的分离（多个委托人）是预防腐败的一种有效途径（Hemsley，2016）。

---

[1] 承诺（commitment）是指使参与人的威胁策略变得可信的行动。例如，西楚霸王项羽用“破釜沉舟”的举动向敌方表明一种可置信的威胁，这就是一种承诺行动。

[2] 根据黄有光教授提出的第三优理论，最优世界（无扭曲，无信息成本和行政成本）和次优世界（有扭曲，信息成本和行政成本可以忽略）实际上并不存在。虽然次优被认为是“最优可行的”（optimal feasible），但如果考虑行政管理的费用和信息的不足，它实际上既不是最优的，也不是可行的。真正可行的最优者，应该是所谓的“第三优”——由于现实世界同时存在扭曲和信息成本，因此称为第三优世界更为恰当。

8.1.5　小结

与双边委托代理模型相比，标准的共同代理模型只是增加了一个委托人，然而，参与人之间的关系却发生了实质性的变化——由双边关系变为“多边关系”。一方面，两个委托人的目标函数中都含有对方的合约变量，因此导致合约的直接外部性。另一方面，这些合约变量还会出现在代理人的效用函数中，代理人在与一个委托人签约时，其私人信息中不仅包含了他本人的类型，而且包含了其他委托人提出的激励方案的信息，由此导致合约的间接外部性以及显示原理的失效。

共同代理问题可以归结为纵向激励和横向协调问题，其中涉及三种效应。一是代理人的“寻租效应”：代理人会利用自己的信息优势来攫取信息租金。二是委托人之间的“共谋效应”：如果委托人之间能够形成共识，相互合作，就可以迫使代理人采取有利于委托人共同利益的行动。三是当事人之间的“制衡效应”：委托人之间的相互监督和制约会减少代理人对个别委托人行贿的可能性。对这三种效应的比较和分析，应该成为研究共同代理问题的主线。

在利用共同代理模型分析相关问题时，首先要解决好基本定位问题，也就是在图 8.1 中找到相应的象限。除此之外，还要厘清以下关系：（1）委托人的性质，是同质还是异质；（2）任务的性质，是互补还是替代；（3）合同的形式，是线性的还是非线性的；（4）签约的时间特征，是同时进行的还是序贯的。如果在一个模型中同时考虑以上所有因素，问题将变得十分复杂，以至于陷入无解的困境。因此有两种可供选择的技术路径：一是根据具体的研究对象，对现有理论模型做出必要的修正或扩展，二是在现有理论模型分析结论的基础上进行定性分析。对于复杂性很强的问题来说，采用第二条技术路径的效果可能会更好。

8.2　建筑企业对项目经理的激励

如前所述，建设项目属于企业间（inter-firm）组织的范畴，它可以看作是市场中类似于企业的组织，也就是所谓的“准企业”。由于建设项目的特殊性，建筑企业对项目经理的激励不同于一般企业对车间主任的激励——后者属于企业内部上下级关系的范畴；而对于前者来说，除了要考虑建筑企业和项目经理之间的上下级关系之外，还要考虑建设单位的影响。因此，讨论对项目经理的激励问题，需要从项目经理、建筑企业和建设单位之间的“一仆二主”关系入手。

8.2.1　建设项目中的“一仆二主”关系

建筑企业与项目经理之间的关系属于企业内部上下级之间的科层关系。从表面上看，这种关系与一般企业与车间主任之间的关系相类似，但在实际上并不这么简单。

首先，与一般企业中的车间主任相比，项目经理的责任和权力要大得多。根据《建筑施工企业项目经理资质管理办法》（建建［1995］1号），项目经理“应该按照建筑施工企业与建设单位签订的工程承包合同，与本企业法定代表人签订项目承包合同”；不仅“在工程项目施工中处于中心地位，对工程项目施工负有全面管理责任”，而且可以“以企业法定代表人的代表身份处理与所承担的工程项目有关的外部关系，受委托签署有关合同”。考虑到项目经理部不具备法人资格与企业签订承包合同，《规范》用项目管理目标责任书取代了项目承包合同；尽管如此，项目经理依然具有相当大的权限。特别是在项目经理部的组建、材料采购、专业分包和劳务队伍选用等方面，项目经理拥有很强的话语权。

其次，项目经理部兼有成本中心和利润中心的作用。在管理会计中，成本中心和利润中心都属于责任中心的范畴；前者只对成本负责；后者既对成本负责，又对收入和利润负责。利润中心本身又可分为两种类型：自然利润中心具有完全经营决策权，人为利润中心具有部分经营权。在建筑产品的生产过程中，企业无疑要承担利润中心的角色，项目则被定位为一次性的成本中心（施炯，2009）。作为企业与项目之间的“耦合器”，项目经理部不仅拥有相对独立的生产经营决策权，不仅要对成本负责，而且要承担许多与收入和利润有关的职责。合同变更、设计变更、签证计量和索赔过程的复杂性和不确定性，客观上给项目经理部提供了相当大的操作空间。因此，项目经理部不仅要对成本负责，而且要部分地对收入和利润负责，实际上承担了人为利润中心的责任。

总之，由于建筑项目的分散性、流动性、复杂性和不确定性，企业不得不把相当大的决策权让渡给项目经理；与此同时，在权责划分、信息沟通、激励与控制等方面带来一系列新的问题。项目经理责任制的实施效果取决于项目管理目标责任书的执行情况；而目标责任书的执行效果不仅取决于企业与项目经理部之间的关系，还受到建设单位的影响。由于以上原因，建筑企业对项目经理的激励问题要远比一般企业对车间主任的激励问题复杂。

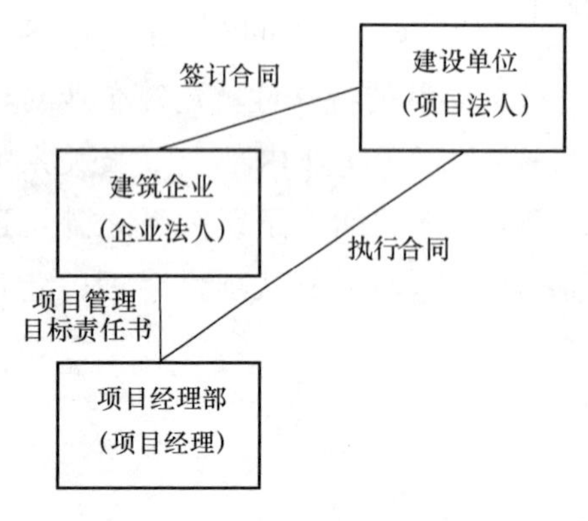

图8.2　建设项目中的“一仆二主”关系

一般的委托代理模型只涉及一个委托人和一个代理人。例如，在公司治理中，企业所有者是委托方，经理是代理方。而建筑企业对项目经理的激励问题则要复杂得多。由于建筑企业和建设项目之间存在耦合关系，对项目经理的激励问题不仅涉及建筑企业和项目经理，而且涉及第三方——建设单位。如图8.2所示，在建设单位（甲方）与建筑企业（乙方）之间、建筑企业与项目经理之间以及建设单位与项目经理之间存在三种委托代理关系。第一种关系以甲乙双方签订的施工合同为基础，属于建设项目垂直治理的范畴。由于甲方是委托人，乙方是代理人，甲方比乙方“高出一头”。第二种关系以项目管理目标责任书为基础，属于公司治理的范畴。建筑企业和项目经理部同在一条垂直线上，这说明两者之间的上下级关系。第三种关系，也就是建设单位和项目经理之间的委托代理关系，是在执行施工合同的过程中产生的。这样，项目经理与建筑企业（企业法人）和建设单位（项目法人）之间就形成了“一仆二主”的复杂关系❶。

在“一仆二主”的共同代理模型中，建筑企业的问题是：在充分考虑建设单位的影响作用，并且满足项目经理的参与约束和激励相容约束的前提下，选择一个激励合同（目标责任书），以最大化自己的期望效用函数。解决这一问题的关键在于“寻租效应”、“共谋效应”和“制衡效应”之间的权衡。

“寻租效应”是信息成本的函数。信息成本越高，“寻租效应”越明显，对代理人的激励也就应该越弱。在讨论信息成本时，充分统计量的概念是十分重要的，它可以用来确定哪些观测变量应该进入目标责任书。在新古典经济学的完全竞争的市场条件下，参与人的行为都被总结在价格之中，价格就是充分统计量。在我们讨论的问题中，建筑企业不可能也没有必要掌握项目经理的全部信息，只需掌握数量有限的必要信息，就可以监控项目经理的行为；这些必要信息就是充分统计量，也就是充分信息。一般来说，充分信息中所要求的变量数目越少，信息成本就越低。

“共谋效应”取决于委托人之间的合作程度。委托人之间的合作程度越高，“共谋效应”就越明显，对代理人的激励也就应该越强。就建设项目而言，建筑企业和建设单位之间的关系在很大程度上取决于项目采购方式和合同类型，而信息缺口和信息的相对成本系数是决定建设项目治理结构和报酬结构的重要因素（沙凯逊等，2011）。需要强调指出的是，在一般情况下，由于建设单位（甲方）是委托人，建筑企业（乙方）是代理人，甲方总比乙方“高出一头”，两者之间存在“位势差”。这种位势差越小，“共谋效应”越强。例如，在传统的设计—招标—建造（DBB）模式和设计—建造（DB）模式中，甲方乙方之间的对手关系容易产生机会主义的行为倾向，进而削弱“共谋效应”；而在建设管理（CM）模式中，业主、设计方和建设管理公司之间形成三位一体的关系，有利于营造“同心同德”的氛围，进而增强“共谋效应”。

“一仆二主”关系中的“制衡效应”取决于三方之间的力量对比和信息结构。三方之间越是势均力敌，信息越是通畅，“制衡效应”就越强。在建设项目的实施过程中，建设单位有可能“收买”项目经理，在合同变更、设计变更、签证计量和索赔等环节弄虚作假，侵害建筑企业的利益。因此，这里的重点是防范建设单位和项目经理之间的串通与共谋。

---

❶ 如果换一个角度来看，三者之间还存在着“一主二仆”的关系，也就是一个委托人（建设单位）与两个代理人（建筑企业和项目经理）之间的委托代理关系。由于这一讲的研究内容是对项目经理的激励问题，因此这里只分析“一仆二主”关系。

建筑企业对项目经理的激励问题还受市场环境的影响。在前面的理论分析中隐含了一个假设，即市场是充分竞争的，市场中的所有参与人都是平等的。然而，我国建筑市场的实际情况却并非如此。如前所述，当前我国建筑市场的基本格局可以概括为：甲方强、乙方弱、第三方不公。由于项目法人缺位、利益主体的关系失衡，压级压价、垫资施工和拖欠工程款等违规行为已经成为压在建筑企业头上的“三座大山”。这些因素不仅扩大了甲乙方之间的位势差，削弱了“共谋效应”，而且为项目经理与企业讨价还价的行为提供了借口——一旦项目出现亏损，企业很难判断，究竟是外部环境的原因，还是项目经理部的问题。环境的复杂性导致充分信息中外生变量数目的增加，企业监督项目经理部的成本增加，进而导致“寻租效应”的增强。在“共谋效应”不强而“寻租效应”不弱的情况下，剥夺项目经理部的经营自主权就成为一种合乎逻辑的选择。

背景材料：

在很长一段时间内，中建总公司实行“项目经理管项目”模式。由于对项目经理部的管理失控，项目的亏损面一度超过八成，甚至出现过“由 45 个人办的 45 件事，造成损失 9 亿元、潜亏 2 亿元”的严重事件。针对这种情况，该公司从 2001 年开始推行“法人层次管项目”模式，把财务和人员调配权全部集中到法人层面，进而又取消了三级企业的独立财务系统。通过逐步收回项目经理对人、财、物的控制权，该公司形成了“三大集中”的管理模式，即资金财务集中管理，劳务分包集中招标和大宗物资集中采购。通过“变法”，该公司迅速扭亏为盈，超过九成的项目都是盈利的，只有不到 5%的项目出现政策性亏损（苏京鳄，2009）。

8.2.2 影响因素与激励策略

下面的分析将表明，在共同代理博弈模型的语境中，对建设项目中“一仆二主”关系的分析是一个十分复杂的问题。

（1）就代理人对合同的选择方式而言，由于项目经理不可能在两个委托人之间进行自由选择，这里的选择方式应该是内在共同代理。与授权共同代理相比，内在共同代理的情况比较简单。

（2）就代理人信息不对称的时间特征而言，存在两种可能性：在选择项目经理时，存在事前隐藏信息的问题；在激励项目经理执行施工合同时，存在事后隐藏行动的问题。

（3）就合同信息对于委托人的公开程度而言，应该是非公开代理——这是因为两个委托人都不能掌握对方对项目经理进行管控的全部信息。与公开代理相比，非公开代理的情况更加复杂。

（4）就委托人的性质而言，两个委托人的差异体现在以下两个方面。第一，建设单位（甲方）和建筑企业（乙方）之间是委托代理关系，甲方比乙方“高出一头”。第二，这两个委托人与项目经理相互之间的了解程度也有很大差异：项目经理和建筑企业之间存在重复博弈关系，可以通过多个项目加深相互了解；而项目经理与建设单位之间的关系是一次性的，只限于某个建设项目的实施阶段。与同质的委托人相比，异质委托人之间开展合作的难度更大。

（5）就任务的性质而言，建筑企业和建设单位之间是互补关系。合约外部性使得两个委托人产生相互“搭便车”的倾向。

（6）就合同的形式而言，两个委托人与项目经理之间的合同（激励方案）都是非线性的。建筑企业和项目经理之间的合同（项目管理目标责任书）虽然是显性的，但是涉及多方面的内容，因而不是线性的。建设单位和项目经理之间的“合同”不仅是隐性的，而且是动态变化的。实际上，这些“合同”是建设单位在施工合同的执行过程中对项目经理的激励方案，涉及合同变更、设计变更、签证计量和索赔等内容。

（7）就签约的时间特征而言，应该属于序贯签约——首先是建设单位与建筑企业签订施工合同；然后是建筑企业和项目经理签订项目管理目标责任书；最后才是项目经理执行施工合同，与建设单位产生委托代理关系。与同时签约相比，序贯签约的情况更加复杂。

模型的本质在于对现实世界的抽象与简化。博弈模型的优势在于它的洞察力，而不是处理细枝末节的能力。在针对项目经理的治理问题中，建设单位（甲方）和建筑企业（乙方）之间的委托代理关系和“一仆二主”的共同代理关系交织在一起。对于这样的复杂问题，与其建立一个面面俱到的模型，不如采用定性分析的方法。相比之下，后者更能抓住问题的本质。

为了形成针对项目经理有效治理，需要抑制“寻租效应”，增强“共谋效应”和“制衡效应”。在选派项目经理和制定激励方案时，建筑企业需要考虑以下两个因素：一是建设项目的性质，二是建设单位（甲方）的类型。建设项目有大小、繁简之分。一般来说，项目的规模越大、越复杂，信息成本就越高，“寻租效应”也就越明显，反之亦然。建设单位可以大致分为“鸽派”和“鹰派”两种类型。一般来说，建筑企业与“鸽派”建设单位开展合作的难度较小，“共谋效应”和“制衡效应”比较明显；反之亦然。把以上两个维度结合起来，可以得到四种情景类型：Ⅰ型（复杂项目、“鹰派”甲方）、Ⅱ型（复杂项目、“鸽派”甲方）、Ⅲ型（简单项目、“鹰派”甲方）和Ⅳ型（简单项目、“鸽派”甲方）。表 8.2 给出了这四种不同情景下的治理难度、对项目经理的要求以及目标责任书的激励强度。在第一种情况下，治理的难度最大，建筑企业一方面要选派业务能力和自律能力最强的项目经理，另一方面要加强对项目经理的约束和监控。而在第四种情况下，建筑企业和项目经理的压力都较小，这时可赋予项目经理较多的自主权以提高生产效率。

针对项目经理的治理：四种不同的情景　　表 8.2

情景类型	Ⅰ型 复杂项目 “鹰派”甲方	Ⅱ型 复杂项目 “鸽派”甲方	Ⅲ型 简单项目 “鹰派”甲方	Ⅳ型 简单项目 “鸽派”甲方
抑制“寻租效应”的难度	＋＋	＋	0	－
增强“共谋效应”的难度	＋＋	0	＋	－
增强“制衡效应”的难度	＋＋	＋	＋	－
对项目经理业务能力的要求	＋	＋	0	0
对项目经理自律能力的要求	＋＋	0	＋	0
目标责任书的激励强度	－	0	＋	＋＋

注：“＋＋”表示很强，“＋”表示强，“0”表示一般，“－”表示弱。

此外，建筑企业在选派项目经理和制定激励方案时，还要考虑当地的市场环境和项目的采购方式。如前所述，在设计—招标—建造（DBB）、设计—建造（DB）和建设管理（CM）几种模式中，在第三种情况下甲方对项目的介入程度越高。一般说来，在其他条件相同的情况下，市场环境越好，甲方对项目的介入程度越高，针对项目经理的治理难度就越小，反之亦然。

8.2.3　小结

建筑企业对项目经理的激励问题不同于一般企业对车间主任的激励问题。后者可以归结为“单一委托人、单一代理人、单一事务”的双边委托代理问题，前者则属于“一仆二主”的共同代理问题。

在确定对项目经理的激励强度时，建筑企业需要考虑两方面的因素。一是委托人之间，也就是建筑企业与建设单位的合作与制衡带来的正面效应；二是代理人，也就是项目经理凭借信息优势造成的负面的“寻租效应”。如果正面效应足够大，“寻租效应”足够小，建筑企业可以采取较强的激励强度，赋予项目经理足够的自主权，同时承担相应的风险。反之，如果正面效应不强而“寻租效应”不弱，建筑企业则应该采取较弱的激励强度，适当收权。如此看来，建筑企业对项目经理的激励并没有一定之规，而是要因地制宜，随机应变，针对不同的情况采取不同的策略；需要考虑的因素有：建设项目的规模和复杂程度、建设单位在签约时的表现、项目经理以往的表现、项目采购方式以及当地的建筑市场环境等。

《规范》的初衷是“进一步深化和加强项目经理责任制，规范项目管理行为，加快项目管理方式与国际接轨”（编写委员会，2006，p.1）。然而，从目前我国建筑市场的实际情况来看，项目经理责任制的实施效果并不理想。一方面是因为甲乙方之间的位势差过大，导致“共谋效应”和“制衡效应”不足；另一方面是因为，建筑企业监督项目经理的信息成本过高，导致“寻租效应”过强。为了实现“项目管理方式与国际接轨”的目标，首先需要创造出“与国际接轨”的市场秩序。

8.3　规范建设单位行为：一个项目治理的视角[1]

从建筑企业对项目经理激励的角度来看，建设单位的不当行为会加剧项目经理的机会主义倾向。从建设单位（甲方）和建筑企业（乙方）关系的角度来看，甲方具有先动优势（first-move advantage），从而造成与乙方之间的策略不对称（strategic asymmetry）（Bowles，2004，p. 249—250）；建筑市场中的关系失衡往往可以从建设单位身上找到原因。因此，有必要重点研究建设单位的行为规范问题。规范市场主体行为的工作可以分解为三个层次：一是加大惩处力度，提高违规成本，使市场主体不敢违规；二是强化约束和监督，提高违规的风险和难度，使市场主体不能违规；三是合理配置责权利关系，减少寻租空间，使市场主体不想违规；其中第三个层次最为关键，它是从源头上解决问题的根本之策，也是项目治理所要解决的主要问题（沙凯逊，孙晓冰，2009）。

8.3.1　建设单位行为的现状分析

建筑市场中的关系失衡、市场主体行为失范已经严重影响了企业的盈利能力和行业的健康发展。从建设项目有关各方的关系来看，当前我国建筑市场的基本状态可以描述为：处于强势地位的甲方、处于弱势地位的乙方和有失公允的第三方（刘倩等，2008）。一般认为，产业结构不合理是造成这一局面的主要原因；实际上，甲方的行为失范问题更加值得重视。据国家有关部门统计和执法检查表明，建筑市场检查出来的问题中，建设单位/业主的违规行为占七成以上（吴锐等，2004）。项目控制权与剩余索取权的不对应是甲方行为不规范的深层次原因；由此产生的压级压价、垫资施工和拖欠工程款等违规行为已经成为压在建筑企业头上的“三座大山”。

背景资料：

2007年，北方某城市建委以提高施工企业盈利能力为主题，通过召开建筑企业和项目部两级座谈会、发放调查问卷、调查表等形式进行专项调研。在调查中，有75%的企业认为建设单位存在的问题是影响企业利润最主要的因素。具体表现为以下五个方面。

（1）拖欠工程款。所有被调查的企业认为，拖欠工程款对企业利润造成严重影响。政府要求对农民工的工资拖欠问题在3天内解决，对劳务分包企业的拖欠款问题在一星期内解决，而建设单位拖欠建筑企业工程款问题的解决却遥遥无期。工程款拖欠时间一般在一年到五年，许多项目工程款已形成坏账死账。此外，部分建设单位以物抵

---

[1] 这一节的内容主要来自发表在《项目管理技术》杂志上的文章（沙凯逊，孙晓冰，2009）。

款，变相克扣施工单位的应得款项。例如，某建筑企业在 1994 年承担的某项工程被拖欠的工程款 1870 万元，到 2007 年仍未全部收回，建设单位不仅不支付利息，反而要求建筑企业“让利”180 万元。

(2) 垫资施工。企业垫资施工的程度越来越高，前几年垫资强度一般到工程进度达到正负零的水平，现在则增加到主体完成一半甚至到主体封顶。大量流动资金被长期占用，银行利息使企业不堪重负。

(3) 压级压价。94.4%的企业认为，建设单位压级压价对建筑企业利润造成严重影响。建设单位在招标过程中普遍存在压级压价的问题，部分建设单位甚至在招标过程中设置陷阱诱使建筑企业低于成本价中标。例如，某建筑企业承担的某项工程总造价为 7700 万元，签订合同后才发现，由于施工图上没有明确说明，有 700 多万元的试桩费用没有包含在内。

(4) 过度肢解分包工程。88.3%的企业认为，过度肢解分包对施工单位的利润率产生了严重影响。多数情况下，总承包企业只负责主体结构施工，利润空间被大大压缩；另一方面，还要担负分包施工的工期、质量、安全等一系列责任。例如在某项工程中，仅楼梯工程就被肢解分包给 4 家企业，在装饰阶段，整个工地有 40 多家分包企业，总包企业协调管理的难度可想而知。

(5) 工程审计中存在的问题。一是建设单位为了达到削减结算额或是延长决算时间的目的，违反规定对工程进行重复审计。二是审计时间太长，迟迟不能决算。例如，某建筑企业承担的某项工程整个工期才用了 5 个月的时间，而结算却用了 3 年，审计持续了 2 年，剩余工程款要用 7 年的时间才能全部收回（刘倩等，2008）。

项目治理是建筑市场有效运行的微观基础，建设单位是占据主导地位的市场主体。然而，恰恰在建设项目治理和建设单位的行为规范方面，我国的建筑法规体系存在“瓶颈”与“短板”。急需研究解决的问题有两个，一是项目法人的缺失问题，二是对不同类型建设项目的分类治理问题。

8.3.2 建设项目法人的定位问题

首先需要搞清楚建设单位、业主、使用单位和建设项目法人之间的联系与区别。建设项目是由若干个法人单位组成的临时性的联盟（coalition）。联盟内不同企业的短期利益是相同的，而长期利益是不同的，它们之间的关系是市场交易关系，而不是科层关系。项目联盟不是独立的经济实体。所谓项目法人，实际上相当于前面所说的建设项目 4C 结构体系中的客户（Client），也就是建筑交易中的甲方。“客户”、“甲方”和“建设单位”是同义词，在不同的语境中可以互相替换。在不同的项目采购方式中，项目法人可能是投资方，可能是业主或用户，也可能是代建单位或项目管理公司。

其次要把财产所有权和项目所有权区别开来。财产所有权与产权是等价的概念；

而项目所有权则是项目的剩余权利。建设项目治理的关键在于剩余控制权与剩余索取权的一致性，也就是说，项目联盟内的各个方面都应该是责、权、利的统一体。拥有控制权的人应该是风险的承担者；谁最有积极性做出正确的决策，就应该让谁拥有控制权。反过来讲，剩余控制权与剩余索取权的不对应就会导致权利的残缺（费方域，2006；沙凯逊等，2004）。

最后来看我国建设项目法人的实际定位情况。1996 年 4 月，国家计委颁布了《关于实行建设项目法人责任制的暂行规定》，这标志着建设项目法人责任制的正式推行。然而，这项制度只是局限于国有单位经营性基本建设大中型项目和国家重点建设项目；至于其他类型的建设项目，现有的建设程序仍然默认并实行“使用单位就是建设单位，就是项目法人”的传统模式（张伟，朱宏亮，2007）。把建设单位与业主或使用单位混为一谈的做法，不仅在理论上会产生歧义，在实践中也会带来许多麻烦，造成建设项目法人的模糊与缺位。特别是在推行代建制的过程中，代建单位的项目法人地位没有法律保障，使用单位的权力过大，在很大程度上影响了代建制的质量和效率（潘灿菊，2008）。项目法人的缺位和非项目法人的越位，已经成为建设项目治理的瓶颈问题，急需通过立法加以解决。

第一，要通过立法明确建设单位的内涵：建设单位，在私人投资项目和特许经营权融资建设项目中是指投资人；在政府投资项目中，如采用自建模式是指使用单位，如采用工程指挥部模式是指工程指挥部，如采用组建项目法人模式是指项目公司，如采用代建制模式是指代建单位。

第二，要通过立法解决建设项目法人的定位问题。这个问题涉及以下三点。一是建设项目法人的权利与义务：建设项目法人依法独立享有有关建设项目的民事权利能力和承担民事义务，依法对建设项目的建设资金、建设工期、工程质量、生产安全、环境保护等进行管理。二是建设项目法人的设立和法人执照管理。建设项目法人执照是项目法人依法行使权利的依据，也是区分项目法人和非项目法人的标志。由建设单位申请设立登记和办理建设项目法人执照，是确认项目法人地位的必要步骤。三是建设项目法人的终止。项目是一种临时性的组织，建设项目一旦结束，项目法人自然也就不复存在。在不同的治理模式下，建设项目的生命周期不同，需要做出明确的界定。

8.3.3　对不同类型建设项目的分类治理问题

按照投资来源的不同，建设工程项目可分为政府投资项目和非政府投资项目两大类型。在我国的固定资产投资中，政府投资项目一直占有很大的比重。2008 年，为应对国际金融危机，我国政府重新启用积极的财政政策，提出了由 4 万亿投资计划支持的十项措施，其中绝大部分是政府的公共投资项目。这是在有效需求不足、进出口贸易萎缩条件下的次优选择。从目前的情况来看，经济增长主要依靠投资拉动的格局在短期内难以改变（沙凯逊等，2009）。

政府投资项目中，作为客户的地方政府的行为特别值得关注。实证研究表明，在分权体制的财政激励和政治激励下，地方政府在我国经济成长中更多的是扮演了“企业家”的角色，而不是非经济性公共物品提供者的角色（傅勇，2010）。在政府投资项目中，建设单位/业主往往表现出较低的耐心程度（较小的贴现因子）。一般建设项目的首要任务是保证项目的效率；而对政府投资项目而言，在很多情况下，预防腐败和减少工程质量事故成为主要矛盾，为此不得不以牺牲效率作为代价。

公共选择理论认为，政府及其官僚与其他社会组织、机构一样，也是谋求自身特殊利益的利益集团（林光彬，2002）。许多国家在政府投资项目的治理方面，都是从本国的实际出发，综合考虑信息成本与代理成本之间以及监督成本与渎职犯罪后果之间的关系，在不同的历史条件下采取了不同的治理措施（Winch，2001；沙凯逊等，2003）。

背景资料：

针对严重的腐败问题，意大利政府在 1994 年至 1998 年间先后颁布了三项法令，重新规范了政府投资项目的招标问题。新法令的一项重要内容是强调设计与施工的分离，不仅设计过程与施工过程要分离，设计人员与施工人员也要分离。这样做的目的主要是为了增加透明度，保证建设项目严格按照规定的程序进行。由于“设计—施工”（*appalto—concorso*）的承包方式被严格限制在一些特殊的建设项目，建筑企业无法过多地介入建设项目的设计工作（沙凯逊，邓晓红，2001）。

在日本，私人项目和公共项目有不同的管理办法。私人项目主要采用总价包干（lump-sum）的合约形式，公共项目采用设计与施工分离的方式（沙凯逊等，2003）。

2005 年 9 月，中国土木工程学会组织赴美国和加拿大考察建筑市场规范业主行为的法规及实务。考察报告指出，美国的政府投资工程仍然主要采用传统的所谓三角方式，即业主分别与设计机构和承包商签订设计合同与施工合同，业主直接对设计和施工工作进行管理（中国土木工程学会，2009）。

从以上背景资料中可以看出，为了提高公开性和透明度，保证严格的建设程序，美国、日本、意大利等国在政府投资项目中都主张采用设计与施工分离的方式。尽管这样做会带来部分成本的增加，但是，与贪污腐败和工程质量事故造成的损失相比，还是合算的。

我国现行的法律法规对政府投资和非政府投资两类不同性质的建设项目的界定不够明确，一方面不利于对政府投资项目的规制，另一方面不利于非政府投资项目效率的提高。在交易成本存在的条件下，不同的产权结构和治理模式会产生不同的效率。对政府投资和非政府投资两种类型的建设项目，应该采取“一手抓、一手放”的方针。也就是说，对于前者，不仅要在招投标和监理等方面做出强制性的规定，而且要对项目的实施进行强制性的监控。比如做出以下规定：经营性政府投资项目应当采用项目法人责任制模式或特许经营权融资建设模式；公益性（非经营性）政府投资项目应当采用代建制模式或政府集中采购模式；政府投资项目应当采用设计和施工相分离的模式。这样做，虽然会导致部分成本的增加，但是可以有效减少寻租和腐败，总起来看还是值得的。而对于后者，不必做出如此严格的限制，而是应该给予充分的自由度。例如，不一定采用公开招标的方式，而是采用关系型合约的方式，从而使市场主体之间保持长期稳定、相互信任和良性互动的合作关系。

8.4　结　　论

这一讲从共同代理的角度讨论了针对项目经理的治理问题，还从项目治理的角度讨论了建设单位的行为规范问题。之所以把这两个问题放到一起讨论，是因为建设单位的行为在很大程度上可以决定建筑企业对项目经理的激励效果。

共同代理理论固然是对传统委托代理理论的扩展与深化，但是并没有从根本上改变委托代理理论的基本逻辑。这个基本逻辑是：在委托人与代理人目标函数不一致、信息不对称的前提下，在满足代理人的参与约束和激励相容约束的条件下，设计最优契约，使代理人的努力水平符合委托人的利益。

由于建设单位的影响，建筑企业对项目经理的激励问题要比一般的公司对车间主任的激励问题复杂得多。从共同治理的角度来看，在确定对项目经理的激励强度时，建筑企业需要同时考虑正面的“共谋效应”、“制衡效应”和负面的“寻租效应”。由于同时存在扭曲和信息成本，建筑企业的激励方案不可能做到“最优”，能够达到“第三优”的水平就相当不错了。

在建筑市场的诸多矛盾中，对建设项目的治理是主要矛盾。在建设项目的诸多利益主体中，建设单位是矛盾的主要方面。抓住了项目治理这个主要矛盾以及建设单位这个矛盾的主要方面，就是抓住了纲，就可以做到纲举目张。建设单位的行为规范问题，最终可以归结为项目法人的定位以及剩余控制权与剩余索取权的合理配置问题。在建设项目中明确设立项目法人，有利于做到产权明晰、政企分离和政事分离。公共建设项目是腐败行为频繁发生的领域，也是拖欠工程款和农民工工资的重灾区，因而是整顿和规范建筑市场秩序工作的重中之重。对政府投资和非政府投资两种不同类型的建设项目采取“一手抓、一手放”的方针，对前者有利于减少腐败行为和工程质量事故，对后者有利于提高效率。

从目前我国建筑市场的实际情况来看，由于利益主体关系失衡，大多数建设项目的“共谋效应”和“制衡效应”不敌“寻租效应”。建筑企业之所以对项目经理普遍采取弱激励的策略，原因就在于此。项目合伙制（project partnering）和项目联盟（project alliancing）等关系型项目交付安排（relational project delivery arrangements），也可以看作是旨在减少甲乙方之间的位势差、增强“共谋效应”而做出的制度安排

(Lahdenperä，2012)；而这些正是下一讲所要讨论的主要话题。

参考文献

1. 编写委员会（2006）建设工程项目管理规范实施手册（第二版），北京：建筑工业出版社.
2. 陈健，胡家勇（2013）政府机构设置：集中还是分立，河北经贸大学学报，**34**（4），42—46.
3. 费方域（2006）企业的产权分析，上海：上海三联出版社.
4. 傅勇（2010）财政分权、政府治理与非经济性公共物品供给，经济研究，（8），4—15.
5. 黄建军（2012）从极端到综合：独占交易理论新进展，产经评论，（1），35—42.
6. 林光彬（2002）社会等级制度与“三农”问题，读书，（2），30—34.
7. 刘倩，杨杰，沙凯逊（2008）建筑企业的盈利能力：调研与思考，建筑经济，（1），17—19.
8. 刘有贵，蒋年云（2006）委托代理理论述评，学术界，（1），69—78.
9. 潘灿菊（2008）浅谈代建制相关政策法规的完善，建筑，（2），36—38.
10. 普雷斯曼（2000）思想者的足迹：五十位重要的西方经济学家，中译本，陈海燕，李倩，陈亮译，南京：江苏人民出版社.
11. 萨缪尔逊，诺德豪斯（1996）经济学（第 12 版）中译本，萧琛等译，北京：北京经济学院出版社.
12. 沙凯逊，邓晓红（2001）欧盟建筑交易制度比较研究：启发与思考，建筑经济，（3），19—22.
13. 沙凯逊，华冬冬，徐聪（2011）一个建设项目垂直治理的委托代理模型，项目管理技术，**9**（5）28—34.
14. 沙凯逊，孙晓冰（2009）规范建设单位行为：一个项目治理的视角，项目管理技术，**7**（10）13—17.
15. 沙凯逊，宋涛，赵锦锴，殷涛（2003）从美日两国的历史经验看建设交易制度创新，建筑经济，（3），10—12.
16. 沙凯逊，宋涛，赵锦锴，殷涛（2004）从非对称信息看建设市场的整顿和规范，建筑经济，（1），82—85.
17. 沙凯逊，杨杰，孙晓冰（2009）建筑业：“闹冬”里转型正当时，建筑经济，（2），43—45.
18. 石磊，刘安琪（2015）三方代建模式下共同代理问题研究，工程管理学报，**29**（2）91—95.
19. 施炯（2009）我国建设工程项目管理的发展历程和趋势探析，建筑经济，（5），27—30.
20. 苏京鳄（2009）中建总公司：法人层次管项目，90%盈利，建筑，（1），10—21.
21. 孙春玲，张华，李贺，宋红（2012）基于共同代理框架的项目经理授权赋能研究，建筑经济，（6），31—34.
22. 王小芳，管锡展（2004）多委托人代理关系——共同代理理论研究及其最新进展，外国经济与管理，**26**（10）10—14.
23. 吴锐，李世蓉，任玉珑（2004）政府投资项目中业主行为不规范原因的经济学分析，建筑经济，（2），31—33.
24. 于立宏，管锡展（2005）多委托人激励理论：一个综述，产业经济研究，（13）54—63.
25. 张光宇，李长春（2014）基于共同代理的业主方项目管理激励制度探讨，建筑经济，**35**（11），46—49.
26. 张伟，朱宏亮（2007）政府投资项目代建制与相关法规体系协调的研究，建筑经济，（10），9—12.
27. 张维迎（1996）博弈论与信息经济学，上海：上海三联出版社.
28. 中国土木工程学会（2009）美国、加拿大建筑市场规范业主行为对我国的启发，中国建筑装饰网，http：//www. ccd. com. cn，2009-2-20.

29. Bennardo, A., Pagano, M. and Piccolo, S. (2015) Multiple-bank lending, creditor rights and information sharing, *Review of Finance*, **19** (2), 519—570.

30. Bernheim, B. D. and Whinston, M. D. (1985) Common marketing agency as a device for facilitating collusion, *The RAND Journal of Economics*, **16** (2), 269—281.

31. Bernheim, B. D. and Whinston, M. D. (1986) Common agency, *Econometrica*, **54** (4), 923—942.

32. Billette de Villemeur, E. and Versaevel, B. (2017) One lab, two firms, many possibilities: on R&D outsourcing in the biopharmaceutical industry, *MPRA Paper*, No. 76903.

33. Bowles, S. (2004) *Microeconomics: Behavior, Institutions and Evolution*, Princeton University Press, Princeton.

34. Calzolari, G. and Scarpa, C. (1999) Non-intrinsic common agency, *SSRN Electronic Journal*, DOI: 10.2139/ssrn. 200558, 1—17.

35. Guesnerie, R. (1981) On taxation and incentives: further remarks on the limits to redistribution, *University of Bonn Discussion Paper*, 89.

36. Harsanyi, J. (1976) Games with incomplete information played by 'Bayesian' players, Part I, The basic model, *Management Science*, **14** (3), 159—182.

37. Hemsley, P. (2016) Corruption and optimal regulation under common agency, *EconomiA*, **17** (2), 199—209.

38. Lahdenperä, P. (2012) Making sense of the multi-party contractual arrangements of project partnering, project alliancing and integrated project delivery, *Construction Management and Economics*, **30** (1), 57—79.

39. Martimort, D. (1992) Multi-principaux avec anti-selection, *Annales d'Économie et de Statistique*, (28), 1—37.

40. Martimort, D. (2007) Multi-contracting mechanism design, *Advances in Economic Theory Proceedings of the World Congress of the Econometric Society*, eds. Blundell, R., Newey, A. and Persson, T., Cambridge University Press.

41. Martimort, D. and Stole, L. (2001) Contractual externalities and common agency equilibria, *Advances in Theoretical Economics*, **3** (1), 1037—1037.

42. Martimort, D. and Stole, L. (2002) The revelation and delegation principles in common agency games, *Econometrica*, **70** (4), 1659—1673.

43. Martimort, D. and Stole, L. (2009) Market participation under delegated and intrinsic common agency games, *The RAND Journal of Economics*, **40** (1), 78—102.

44. Myerson, R. (1979) Incentive-compatibility and the bargaining problem, *Econometrica*, **47** (1), 61—73.

45. Olsen, T. E. and Osmundsen, P. (2011) Multinationals, tax competition and outside options, *Journal of Public Economics*, **95** (11—12), 1579—1588.

46. Rochet, J. C. (1985) The taxation principle and multi-time Hamilton—Jacobi equations, *Journal of Mathematical Economics*, **14** (2), 113—128.

47. Sha, K. X. (2016) Understanding construction project governance: an inter-organizational perspective, *International Journal of Architecture, Engineering and Construction*, **5** (2), 117—127.

48. Stole, L. (1991) Mechanism design under common agency, mimeo, University of Chicago.

49. Winch, G. M. (2001) Governing the project process: a conceptual framework, *Construction Management and Economics*, **19** (7), 799—808.

第9讲　关系治理与行业自律：一个非正式制度安排的视角

- □ 对于建设项目治理来讲，正式制度和非正式制度安排有如鸟之两翼、车之双轮，两者缺一不可。如果说正式合同是对当事人的刚性约束，关系合同是对当事人的柔性约束，那么，行业自律则是当事人的自我约束。
- □ 关系型建筑合约可以概括为一种刻意不完全、基本上自我执行的制度安排，其重点在于事后的3R，即再谈判（renegotiation）、利益再调整（realignment）和项目效率的恢复（restoration）。
- □ 建设项目中的"关系"因素是与生俱来的。在"关系台阶"上，以DBB（设计—招标—建造）和DB（设计—建造）等传统项目采购方式为代表的准关系合同和以PP（项目合伙制）、FA（框架性协议）和PPP（公私合伙制）等协作性制度安排为代表的"真"关系合同分别位于一阶和二阶的位置。前者属于合同治理的范畴；后者属于关系治理的范畴。
- □ 制度环境是关系型建筑合约的"赋能者"。当前我国建筑市场和建筑专业体制都不够完善，建设项目当事人之间信任与沟通的基础不够牢固。在某些"赋能者"本身严重"失能"的情况下，关系型建筑合约在我国的实施效果就会大打折扣。
- □ 建筑专业体制属于社群治理的范畴。如果说市场是基于价格信号的"看不见的手"，政府是基于规制的"看得见的手"，那么，建筑专业体制则可以看作是基于自律的"第三只手"。该体制的比较优势可以弥补市场和政府的不足，在行业自律中发挥独特的作用。
- □ 我国建筑专业体制的转型升级需要着重解决好以下问题：一是淡化官办色彩以还原独立本色，二是简化资质管理以增强职业操守。三强化项目治理以持守无偏立场。

前面三讲从正式合同的角度介绍了建设项目的垂直治理、水平治理和针对项目经理的治理问题。而在现实中，建设项目治理既涉及正式制度，又涉及非正式制度安排。随着工程实践和相关理论的发展以及外部环境的变化，人们对于建设项目的认识不断深化。越来越多的人意识到，对于建设项目治理来讲，正式制度和非正式制度安排有如鸟之两翼、车之双轮，两者缺一不可。在一定条件下，非正式制度安排比正式制度更加富有效率，并且成本更低（Baker *et al*.，2002）。

这一讲从非正式制度安排的角度讨论建设项目的治理问题，也就是关系治理和行业自律的问题。首先介绍关系合同和关系治理的基本原理，分析我国建筑业推行关系合同的机遇和挑战。然后从社群治理的角度分析建筑专业体制对行业自律机制的促进作用，简要介绍发达国家建筑业在提升职业道德标准、改造专业教育培训体系、发挥政府引领作用等方面的最新进展。最后就如何解决专业组织的定位、专业人士的操守和专业服务的公正性等问题提出若干建议。

9.1　关系合同与关系治理

关系合同（relational contract）[1] 的概念来源于美国法学家麦克尼尔（Macneil）提出的**关系合同理论**（relational contract theory）。麦克尼尔把合同放到社会和关系的背景中来考察，强调社会关系对于合同乃至合同法的影响作用。他认为，合同反映了“与预测交换的未来的过程有关的当事人之间的关系”[2]（麦克尼尔，1994，p. 4）。这句话有两层含义：第一，合同是当事人之间的一种关系；第二，需要把当下的交换放到未来去考虑。在麦克尼尔看来，“交换”不再是新古典经济学中的离散性（discrete）交易[3]，而是作为社会学意义上的交换。这种交换所涉及的也不仅是“合意”这一种因素，而是包括命令、身份、社会功能、血缘关系、官僚体系、宗教义务、风俗习惯等多种因素。这些因素使得合同成为涵盖多种关系的一种连续过程。因此在时间的维度上，麦克尼尔的合同不再仅是一次性交易，而是指向未来的长期性合作；在空间的维度上，也不再局限于“合意”这一点，而是涉及交换得以发生的各种社会关系。关系合同的运行不仅依赖于对结构的事前约定和理性规划，还依赖于某些社会过程和社会规则。

关系治理（relational governance）是指“包含特定关系的资产（relationship-specific asset），同时具备高度组织间信任的企业之间的交易”（Zaheer and Venkatraman，1995，p. 374）。这种企业之间长期稳定的关系是一种半垂直的非正式关系。关系治理包含结构与过程两个维度。结构维度是指组织之间的准纵向一体化（vertical quasi-integration），过程维度是指组织之间的联合行动（joint action）。经验分析表明，信任、资产专用性、不确定性与互惠性投资等因素共同影响关系治理的结构与过程（Zaheer

---

[1] 在相关文献中有时会同时出现 relational contract 和 relational contracting 这两个词汇。前者是名词，后者是动名词。它们在英文中的区别是不言自明的；在中文的语境中则要有所区别。为了避免混淆，本书把前者翻译成“关系合同”（强调合同本身），把后者翻译成“关系型合约”（强调一种动态的合同关系）。

[2] 这句话的英文原文是 relations among parties to the process of projecting exchange into the future。其中 projecting exchange into the future 的意思是“把当下的交换放到未来去考虑”；这里译为“预测交换的未来”。

[3] 国内有的文献将 discrete transaction 译成“个别性交易”或“分立性交易”。在这种交易中，当事人之间除了单纯的物品交换外不存在任何关系。也就是说，每笔交易是可清算的，不同的交易之间没有关联。

and Venkatraman，1995）。

关系治理是一种自我执行（self-enforcing）的机制；它包含大量非正式制度安排的因素，诸如企业间的长期依存关系、共同的期望、联合行动和程序上的公平等（Geyskens *et al*.，2006）。关系治理既包括经济性治理，也包括社会性治理。经济学家主要关注合作所能带来的期望支付——这是关系治理的理性依据。社会学家所关注的则是，在相互信任的交往过程中所形成的共同的价值观和情感基础（Geyskens *et al*.，2006）。在国内，有人从范式的高度出发，把基于正式合同的项目治理称为“合同范式”，把基于关系合同的项目治理称为“关系范式”；认为前者是“硬性”的治理，后者是“软性”的治理（杜亚灵，尹贻林，2012）。

9.1.1 协作性制度安排与关系型建筑合约

由于建设项目的不确定性、生产过程的碎片化、组织间的对抗性关系和频频发生的合同风险等原因，建筑业的生产效率远低于其他许多行业（Rahman and Kumaraswamy，2002）。在新的历史条件下，经济全球化、政策法规体系的变革、私人投资的扩张、建筑服务化（servitization of construction）的发展趋势以及越来越多的大型复杂项目，特别是跨部门、多阶段的基础设施项目带来了新的挑战（Hartmann *et al*.，2010；Gottlieb and Jensen，2012；Henisz *et al*.，2012），促使建筑业寻求并采用新的项目治理模式。在过去的几十年里，协作性制度安排在建筑业受到普遍重视，并在实践中形成了多种模式，如项目合伙制（project partnering，PP）、战略合伙制（strategic partnering，SP）、项目联盟（project alliancing，PA）、战略联盟（strategic alliancing，SA）、一体化项目交付（integrated project delivery，IPD）、框架协议（framework agreements，FA）、公私合伙制（public—private partnerships，PPP）与合资（joint venture，JV）等。这些模式都可划归到**“关系型合约”**（relational contracting，RC）的名下。

背景材料：关系型项目交付安排（RPDA）的三种形式（资料来源：Lahdenperä，2012）

项目合伙制（PP）、项目联盟（PA）和一体化项目交付（IPD）这三种模式都属于关系型项目交付安排（relational project delivery arrangement，RPDA）。这些模式有利于建设项目的利益相关者建立相互信任的合作关系，促进沟通与协调、共享资源与信息、化解冲突与争端，变利益对抗为合作共赢，因此成为建设项目理论研究与应用的新热点。

项目合伙制（PP）的核心理念是相互信任与承诺，关键在于合伙协议书（partnering charter）和分层决策（decision ladder）机制。这种模式是有关各方通过一系列的项目合作而形成的长期战略合作关系。最早的PP项目可以追溯到1988年，当时美国陆军工程兵部队（US Army Corps of Engineers）在阿拉巴马州William Bacon Oliver

大坝工程中首次采用了这种模式，旨在营造一种积极的、避免争议的气氛，通过团队合作与协商，在不同组织间定义共同目标、改善沟通、形成合作解决问题的态度。PP 模式在工期、成本、质量、索赔及争端解决等方面都具有明显的正面效果，因而得以在世界范围内推广。英国建筑业在 1995 年引进了这种模式。在 20 世纪 90 年代中后期，该模式在澳大利亚、新加坡、中国香港等国家和地区得到推广应用。

项目联盟（PA）的核心理念是风险共担、利益共享，关键在于具有连带责任的多边合同（multi-party contract with joint liability）。最早的 PA 项目出现在石油行业。1992 年，英国石油（PB）公司在北海石油项目中首次采用了这种模式，旨在抵御项目所面临的高风险。PA 模式在 1994 年被引进澳大利亚的石油和天然气工程项目，然后在欧洲大陆得到推广应用。1997 年，建设领域第一个采用 PA 模式的项目出现在澳大利亚。到目前为止，已有数百个建设项目采用 PA 模式，其中绝大多数是公路、铁路、水利等基础设施的建设项目。

一体化项目交付（IPD）的核心理念是多种专业人士的早期参与和一体化。该模式的特点是，若干个具有互补性质的企业组合在一起，通过连带及个别责任（joint and several liability）机制，相互负责，并且对客户负责。相对于前两种模式而言，IPD 模式出现的时间较晚。2005 年，美国加利福尼亚州萨特健康中心（Sutter Health）的建设项目首次采用 IPD 模式。IPD 模式多用于医疗保健设施和医院的建设项目。

图 9.1 给出了 PP、PA 和 IPD 三种模式产生与发展的时空分布。从中不难看出，

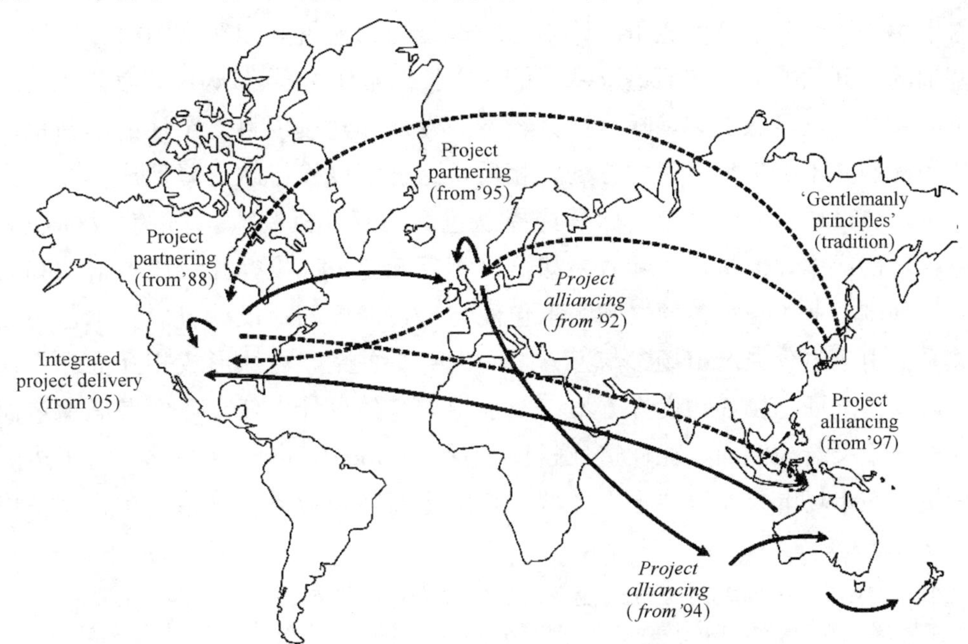

图 9.1　不同形式的关系型项目交付安排（RPDA）的产生、推广与互动

（资料来源：Lahdenperä，2012）

说明：1. 实线表示模式的推广，虚线表示理念的传播；2. 正体字表示建筑业，斜体字表示其他行业。

从模式推广的角度来看（如实线所示），美国、英国和澳大利亚扮演了策源地和集散中心的角色；而从理念传播的角度来看（如虚线所示），日本的管理理念和西方的“绅士原则”（Gentlemanly Principles）是其主要的文化根源。RPDA的诸多核心理念，如相互尊重和善意、开放和积极的沟通以及对改进的承诺等，都可以从全面质量管理、精益生产等理论和实践中找到自己的源头。

实际上，在建筑业早已存在关系治理的因素。例如，日本的传统文化强调人与人之间的长期合作。日本企业中的终身雇佣制和集体决策制就充分体现了以“和”为核心的价值观念。受传统文化观念和社会习俗的影响，日本建筑业的多数分包商在与总承包商的博弈中选择了合作。分包商在历史上一直处于从属地位，他们十分注重保持并发展与总承包商的长期业务联系。实际上，这种合作关系确实能给他们带来利益（Reeves，2002）。在“制造商—供应商”关系分析中，这种因长期合作产生的利益被称为“关系租金”（relational rent）。

如果说，日本建筑业重视企业间的长期合作关系是因为受文化传统影响的缘故；那么，关系治理在英国受到重视，则是形势变化带来的结果。传统上，英国建筑业以专业化分工、竞争性投标、详细的合同文本、详细的图纸和细节说明为特征。这种体制明确规定了建筑市场中各种参与人的权利、义务和责任，可以有效地减少腐败行为，保证工程质量，因而被世界各国所效仿。然而，事情正在发生戏剧性变化：当我国建筑业着手引进这种基于高度竞争的体制之时，英国的建筑业却在试图放弃以最低投标价为基础的公开招投标，转而追求基于信任的长期合作关系（Lorch，姜阵剑，2003）。

英国建筑业已经意识到，随着社会经济的发展和建设项目复杂性的不断提高，高度竞争的体制并不能带来真正的好处；相反，这种制度安排缺乏降低成本的动力。从理论上讲，建设项目的公开招投标是选择承包商的有效机制[1]。竞争性投标理应给业主带来较低的成本，但是，实际效果却恰恰相反：竞争性投标导致成本增加和效率降低，并且加剧了业主与承包商之间、承包商与分包商之间、设计单位与承包商之间的对手关系。由于过分强调市场参与各方之间的对手关系，往往形成相互推卸责任而不是共担风险的局面。例如，设计方不仅要承担本身的设计责任，还要考虑承包商在施工中的机会主义行为倾向，往往造成过度设计（Winch，2000）。此外，由于边际贡献难以衡量，在市场上只能以“平均贡献”来确定商品和劳务的价格，在这种平均原则

[1] 招标投标有两个基本功能，一是揭示信息，二是减少代理成本。对于公共项目而言，招标投标还可以有效地减少腐败行为。在一级密封投标（firs-price sealed bid，公开招标，密封投标，报价最低者中标）模型中，每个投标者不知道其他投标者的真实生产成本，只知道其概率分布，这种情况下的博弈结果是贝叶斯均衡（Bayesian equilibrium）。可以证明，每个投标人的投标报价依赖于他的实际生产成本，贝叶斯均衡报价高于生产成本，投标报价与实际生产成本之间的差异随总投标人数的增加而减少。如果参加竞争的人足够多，每个交易者都不可能通过说假话对交易结果产生很大影响，在这种情况下，尽管信息是不对称的，接近瓦尔拉均衡或帕累托最优的资源配置还是可以实现的（张维迎，1996，pp. 258—261）。

下，“劣币驱逐良币”，高质量的商品和劳务就会被低质量的商品和劳务赶出市场。

英国建筑业的变革始于上世纪末，重点是改变建筑业供应链内部及供应链与业主之间的关系，建立信任和长期合作的关系。新的合作关系产生了新的采购方式和付款方式。变革中产生的一种治理模式是合伙制。两家或多家公司为了相互的目标共同努力工作来改善业绩——这还是解决纠纷并不断做出改进的一种新办法。合伙的几家公司为达到这些目标协同工作，它们之间不再是对手关系。由所有的参与公司共同分享项目的成功，如果项目失败，则共担风险，因此，促使项目成功是每家参与公司的共同目标。合伙关系依赖于非常简洁的协议而不是复杂的合同。有时采取对所有参与方公开账目的会计制度，也就是说，承包商必须将真实成本公开，并努力降低成本（Winch，2000；Lorch，姜阵剑，2003）。

实证研究表明，关系治理与正式合同之间确实存在互补关系。在风险较大的复杂交易中，正式合同和非正式合同共同发挥作用，会产生较好的交易绩效——明确的合同条款和纠纷解决程序，再加上灵活的关系治理，会使合同的履行更加顺畅（Poppo and Zenger，2002）。

9.1.2　关系型建筑合约的研究现状

随着实践的发展，对于关系型建筑合约的理论研究也取得了长足的进步。现有的文献表明，研究工作采用了以下理论视角和方法：

• 新古典经济理论（Tennant and Fernie，2012）；

• 交易成本经济学和博弈论（Jeffries and Reed，2000；Poppo and Zenger，2002；Lu *et al.*，2015）；

• 关系合同理论（Chan *et al.*，2010），

• 社会学和心理学（Henisz *et al.*，2012），

• 社会网络分析（Pryke and Pearson，2006），

• 活动理论（activity theory）（Hartmann and Bresnen，2011），

• 话语性制度主义（Gottlieb and Jensen，2012），

• 维特根斯坦的家族相似性（family-resemblance）哲学（Yeung *et al.*，2012），以及

• 服务主导（service-dominant）的方法（Jacobsson and Roth，2014）。

与此同时，也有不少研究者通过实证的方法来解释应用关系合同的动力与障碍，以及影响关系合同的关键成功要素（critical success factors，CSF）。这方面的研究包括：

• 定性的案例研究（Rahman and Kumaraswamy，2002；Rahman *et al.*，2007；Chan *et al.*，2010；Dewulf and Kadefors，2012；Gottlieb and Jensen，2012），

• 定量的案例研究（Pryke and Pearson，2006；Doloi，2009；Suprapto *et al.*，

2015；Ning and Ling，2015），

• 合同治理与关系治理之间比较研究（Poppo and Zenger，2002；Lu *et al*.，2015；Bygballe *et al*.，2015），

• 不同的关系型项目交付安排模式之间的比较研究（Lahdenperä，2012），以及

• 不同国家和地区之间的比较研究（Pryke and Pearson，2006；Ling *et al*.，2014）。

尽管取得了长足的进步，对关系型建筑合约的研究仍然存在很大的发展空间。首先，对关系型建筑合约的概念和定位还存在不同的看法。多数文献认为，（1）关系合同，也就是非正式合同，是与正式合同相对应的一个概念，因而和正式合同处于同一个层次；（2）与正式合同相类似，关系合同也是通过一些具体模式实现的。例如，Chan *et al*.（2010）认为，关系合同包括项目合伙制（PP）、战略合伙制（SP）、项目联盟（PA）、战略联盟（SA）、公私合伙制（PPP）与合资（JV）等六种类型。再比如，Lahdenperä（2012）把关系型项目交付安排（RPDA）划分为以下三种模式，即项目合伙制（PP）、项目联盟（PA）和一体化项目交付（IPD）。显然，这些模式都是关系合同的具体表现形式和下属类型。然而，在有的文献中，关系合同被“升格”到高于正式合同的层次。例如，Henisz *et al*.（2012）认为，关系型建筑合约需要三个制度“支柱”的支撑，它们分别是规制性（regulative）“支柱”、规范性（normative）“支柱”和认知性（cognitive）“支柱”；而正式合同就包含在规制性“支柱”之内。这样一来，关系合同就被置于正式合同之上。而在有的文献中，关系合同又被“降格”，和一些下属的具体模式相提并论。例如，Jacobsson and Roth（2014，p. 420）认为，“客户—供应商之间的合作关系可以通过关系型合约（RC）、项目联盟（PA）、战略联盟（SA）、一体化项目交付（IPD）以及合伙制等方式来实现”，这种表述把关系合同与它的下属类型放在同一个层次上。第二，如前所述，项目治理可分为垂直治理和水平治理；和垂直治理一样，水平治理也可以采用关系合同的方法。例如，在日本，大多数专业分包商都愿意和某一个总承包商保持长期稳定的合作关系（Reeves，2002）。然而，从目前关系型建筑合约的文献来看，研究工作主要集中于业主与总承包商之间的关系；鲜有水平治理中关系合同的研究。第三，有些实证研究的样本空间有限，因此，它们的可信程度是成问题的。实证研究的另一个问题是，在某些特定条件下得出的研究结论不可避免地具有局限性，有时甚至会出现相互矛盾的现象。比如，在关系治理和正式合同的关系问题上，就存在不同的看法。一种观点认为，正式合同与关系治理互为替代品。另一种观点则认为，关系治理与正式合同之间的关系是互补关系。再比如，一般认为，信任是关系合同的核心。更有人指出，信任机制对于关系治理，就像价格机制对于市场、权威机制对于企业一样，是不可或缺的（徐忠爱，2008）。然而，澳大利亚的一项实证研究表明，“对于项目的成功来说，信任和信用的作用有限，甚至没有什么作用”（Doloi，2009，p. 1108）。这一结论印证了 Jeffries and Reed

（2000）的观点："过多的信任如同过少的信任一样，都是有害的。"由此可见，为了得到有意义的研究结论，必须从当地的实际条件出发，从社会构建的角度对关系合同加以考察和分析（Hartmann and Bresnen，2011）。

9.1.3　理解关系型建筑合约[1]

理解关系合同，需要从合同理论的"死亡"与复兴谈起。1974 年美国法学家吉尔莫出版了令学界震惊的《合同的死亡》一书。他在该书的开头就写道："合同和上帝一样，已经死亡。"（Gilmore，1974，p. 3）需要指出的是，这里被宣告"死亡"的并不是合同本身，而是 19 世纪末、20 世纪初在美国流行的合同法理论体系，也就是只关注合同的表达形式、忽略合同关系整体环境的法律形式主义（legal formalism）（Gilmore and Collins，1995）。实际上，在经济活动中，合同无处不在，并且在不断变化和发展之中——例如，众包（crowdsourcing）就是互联网时代出现的新的合同形式。因此，所谓"合同死亡"的说法，只不过是对法学界理论与实践严重脱节的一种描述而已。实际上，"合同死亡"的说法反而会激发起新的研究热情。正如日本学者内田贵（2005）所说："尽管合同被宣告死亡，却带来了合同法的复兴。"如图 9.2 所示，在 20 世纪七八十年代出现的合同理论的复兴可分为两个方面：一是法学界的研究工作（Macaulay，1985；Macneil，1974a，1974b，1978，1980，1983，1987），二是新制度经济学所做出的贡献（Jensen and Meckling，1976；Fama and Jensen，1983a，1983b；Williamson，1985；Grossman and Hart，1986）。合同理论在这两个方面所取得的成果都可以为关系型建筑合约领域的研究提供有益的启发。

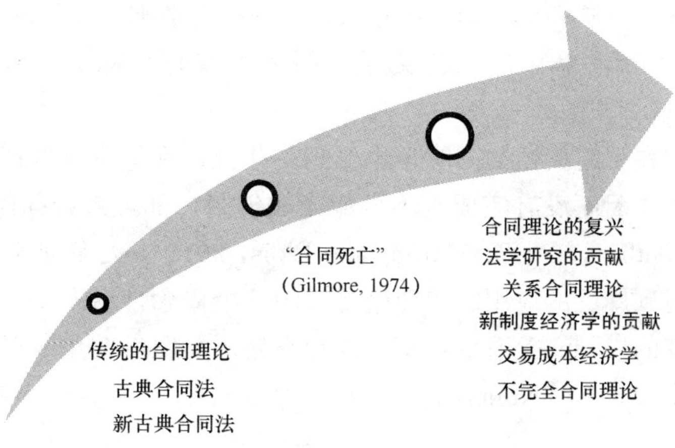

图 9.2　合同理论的"死亡"与复兴

[1] 这一节的内容主要来自发表在 International Journal of Architecture, Engineering and Construction 上的文章（Sha，2016b）。

9.1.3.1 法学界对关系型合约的认识

在许多人认为传统的合同法理论没有发展前途的时候，麦克尼尔扮演了反潮流的角色。他既没有站在“合同死亡”学派一边，也没有盲目支持传统合同的原则，而是从社会学的角度对合同这一古老的话题给予新的阐释，提出了“关系合同”的概念，发展了新的理论。关系合同理论把关系作为基本分析单位，把各种社会关系作为研究工作的切入点。该理论可以概括为以下几点：

• 合同不应被看作是离散的交易，而应被看作是一种关系，一种“已经交易、正在交易或者期望在今后交易的人们之间的关系”（Macneil，1987，p. 272）。

• 关系通常由其内部价值和更为广泛的社会经济因素所维系。因此，即便是一笔简单的交易——比方说，某个司机偶然在新泽西州高速公路上的加油站加了一次油——也可以被认为是涉及更为广泛的社会和经济背景（Macneil，1978）。

• 合同由以下四个原始根源派生而来：一是专业化和分工，二是选择的意识，三是关于过去、现在与未来的自觉意识，四是社会矩阵（Macneil，1974b）。

• 合同无处不在，这是因为几乎在任何地方都会有交换，并且只要有交换就会有合同。

• 合同在关系的深度方面存在很大差异。任何合同都与“关系谱系”的某一个位置相对应。这个“关系谱系”包括各种关系，从特别强的关系（例如长期的雇佣关系）到“近乎离散”的关系（例如商品的现货交易）。

• 关系由一整套规范（norm）所支配，这里的规范是指“将团体成员结合在一起，并且用来指导、控制和调整恰当的合意行为的行动准则”（Macneil，1980，p. 38）。由于规范的重要作用，麦克尼尔的关系合同理论有时被称为“基于规范的理论”（Mouzas and Blois，2013）。

关系合同理论在引起关注的同时，也受到一些批评和指责。批评者认为，该理论过分关注环境因素，因而没有完成也不可能完成创制一部关系合同法的任务（Eisenberg，2002；McKendrick，2002；Mouzas and Blois，2013）。尽管如此，关系合同理论还是在多个领域得到广泛的应用。该理论提供的一个概念性启发是：关系合同不应被看作是“固定不变的权利义务清单，而应该看作是环境发生变化或遇到困难时进行再谈判和调节的一个起点。”（Kimel，2007，p. 250）

9.1.3.2 新制度经济学对关系型合约的认识

在对关系合同的研究中，新制度经济学采用了不同的视角和方法。在关系合同理论的语境中，虽然有些合同的关系较强，有些合同的关系较弱，但是，几乎所有的合同都是关系型的（Macneil，1983，p. 342）；而在新制度经济学的语境中，威廉姆森（Williamson，1985，p. 15）指出：“企业、市场和关系型合约是重要的经济制度”。这种表述本身就意味着，关系型合约是企业与市场的混合物，或者是准纵向一体化（Zaheer and Venkatraman，1995）。这里的“关系型合约”主要是指长期的合同，它们通常是由不太正式的关系规范来治理的（Klein，2005）——而这正是建设项目的情况。因此可以说，建设项目中的“关系”因素是与生俱来的。

交易成本理论是新制度经济学的重要组成部分。该理论把交易作为基本分析单位，并且主张组织是重要的。这种方法十分重视合同的作用，并认为任何与合同有关的问题都可以从节约交易成本的角度来解释（Williamson，1985）。这里的核心问题是“以一种区别性（主要是节约交易成本）的方式将具有不同属性的交易与具有不同成本和能力的治理结构组合在一起”（Williamson，1991b，p. 79）。该理论的基本模型可以用一个函数来表达，函数的因变量是组织的形态，自变量则是交易的几个基本属性，包括资产专用性、不确定性和交易频率等，其中资产专用性的影响最大（Williamson，1991a）。交易成本经济学有一个与关系合同密切相关的性质，这就是它特别重视通过私人制序（private ordering）而不是法院裁定（court ordering）来调停事后的合同关系（Williamson，1985）。

不完全合同理论是新制度经济学的另一个重要分支。该理论把合同权利分为特定权利和剩余权利，并且重点关注剩余权利的有效配置，旨在实现决策功能与剩余权利的合理匹配（Grossman and Hart，1986）。这种理论认为，所有权就是对剩余权利的购买，并且主要根据剩余索取权在控制代理问题方面的比较优势来解释各种组织形态存在的理由（Grossman and Hart，1986；Fama and Jensen，1983b）。不完全合同理论提供的一个概念性启发是：任何合同的签订与执行都是有成本的；合同的实际效果取决于其成本与效益的平衡。

9.1.3.3　对关系型建筑合约的概念化

建设领域的合作关系并不是新鲜事物，因为建设项目本身就是一种联盟——通过这种临时性的组织，若干个法律上独立的企业将其资源、能力和知识组合在一起，为客户提供定制的建筑产品（Winch，1989；Sha，2016a）。建设项目以不完全的长期合同为特点，属于市场和企业的混合物。因此，建设项目这种组织形式本身就包含了许多“关系”的成分。

根据前面几小节的分析，我们可以说，无论从关系合同理论的角度，还是从新制度经济学的角度出发，所有的建设合同都可以看作是“关系合同”。然而，当前关系型建筑合约的相关文献所讨论的内容主要是协作性制度安排，而不是传统的建设项目采购方式。于是，在建设项目领域就存在两种类型的“关系合同”。一种是以 DBB（设计—招标—建造）和 DB（设计—建造）等传统的建设项目采购方式为代表的准关系合同，一种是以 PP（项目合伙制）、FA（框架协议框架）和 PPP（公私合伙制）等协作性制度安排为代表的“真”关系合同（以下简称为关系合同）。如图 9.3 所示，准关系

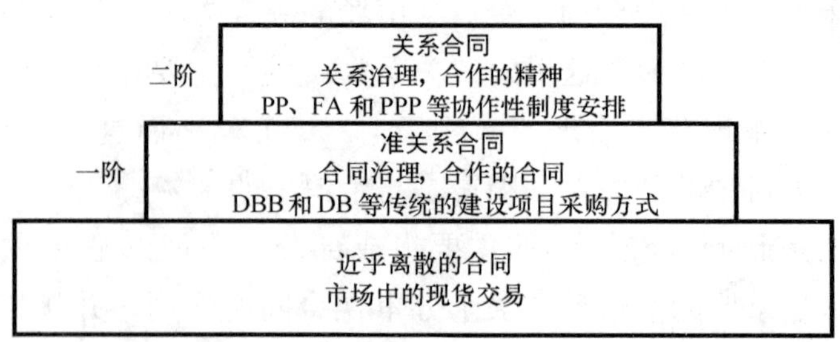

图 9.3　关系型建筑合约的两种类型：关系合同 *vs*. 准关系合同

合同和关系合同分别位于“关系台阶”的一阶和二阶的位置。前者属于合同治理的范畴，是一种“合作的合同”，一种需要依靠法律来维系的公事公办的关系；而后者属于关系治理的范畴，是一种“合作的精神”，一种无须法律约束的“你情我愿”的关系（Tennant and Fernie，2012）。

以上两种类型的合同都是不完全的。但是，前者的不完全性主要是由客观上交易的不确定性以及主观上当事人的有限理性所造成的，因而是不得已而为之；而后者的不完全性是刻意造成的，这种不完全性使当事人拥有事后进行机动的余地（Macneil，1978；Jeffries and Reed，2000）。更为重要的是，准关系合同是具备法律效力的，也就是说，如果出现违约的现象，当事人就可以诉诸法庭；而关系合同基本上是自我执行的——关系型合约尽管包含了一些可以由第三方实施的成分，但是，对于其中的一些实质性内容来说，第三方“无法验证合同义务是否得到履行”（Brown *et al*.，2004，p. 747）。在有限理性、自利和机会主义行为的假设条件下，关系型建筑合约可以概括为一种刻意不完全、基本上自我执行的制度安排，其重点在于事后的 3R，即再谈判（renegotiation）、利益再调整（realignment）和项目效率的恢复（restoration）。

9.1.3.4　推行关系型建筑合约的决定性因素

把关系合同与准关系合同区分开来，不仅有利于深入理解建设项目的关系治理，而且可以使分析和讨论更加清晰和简单。例如，根据麦克尼尔的观点（Macneil，1978），信任、相互利益和共同目标往往被作为关系型建筑合约的主要影响因素（Chan *et al*.，2010；Hartmann and Bresnen，2011）。然而，建设项目本身就是市场中类似于企业的组织（Sha，2016a），也就是 Eccles（1981）所说的准企业；建设项目治理的目的就是使法律上独立的项目参与方为了共同的目标而在一起工作（Sha，2016a），因此，作为准关系合同（传统项目采购方式）的必要条件，后面的两个因素（相互利益和共同目标）已经在项目治理领域得到充分的分析和研究。有鉴于此，下面就没有必要重复分析相互利益和共同目标这样的因素，而应把关系型建筑合约的特殊性作为重点研究对象。

一个建设项目可以通过若干种不同的方式来组织实施，包括准关系合同和关系合同，它们各自拥有下属的具体模式。采用哪一种模式更合适？问题的答案与项目的所在环境有关，并最终取决于所选方法的成本与效益之间的平衡。如表 9.1 所示，理论研究与实证研究的结果表明，关系型建筑合约的效率是若干因素的函数。这些因素分布在两个维度上：一是建设项目本身的性质，二是所谓的“赋能者”（enabler）——也就是用来支持战略目标实施的“组织的、文化的、技术的和人力资源的一些做法”（Project Management Institute，2013，p. 36）。

推行关系型建筑合约的决定性因素　　**表 9.1**

维度	因　素
建设项目的性质	**期限** 由于预测方面的困难，商品或服务供应的合同期限越长，购买者就越不可能，实际上也越不希望对要求他方所做的事情做出明确的规定（Coase，1937，p. 391）。 大多数关系合同都是发生在期限长、不确定性强的合同中（Macneil，1978）。 **复杂性** 项目的复杂程度与签约各方之间的关系保持状况、合作状况以及合同的灵活性成正相关关系（Ning and Ling，2015）。 **公共项目 *vs.* 私人项目** 在采用关系合同时，公共项目通常会受到更多的约束，这是因为（甲乙双方之间的）密切关系可能会招致腐败的指控（Ling *et al.*，2014）。 与私人项目相比，讨价还价和自由选择合作伙伴的机会在公共项目中会受到更多的限制（Dewulf and Kadefors，2012）
赋能者	**文化背景** 协作性工作实践的效果极大地受限于制度性假设所赖以存在的环境（Tennant and Fernie，2012）。 那些使亚洲企业高效运转的社会、经济和文化前提（如合伙制、网络关系和公司间相互依存关系等）绝不会与（新古典经济学中的）个人主义、工具主义和均衡概念产生共鸣（Biggart and Hamilton，1998）。 一般认为，合伙制的发展是以源于日本的实践为基础的（Lahdenperä，2012）。 日本建筑承包商之间合作共存的伦理观念在一定程度上根植于 18 世纪封建时期形成的“协力会”（*nakama*）的历史传统之中（Reeves，2002）。 **经济发展模式与当地市场条件** 把合伙制看作是局地出现的、社会构建的一种实践可能是比较合适的（Hartmann and Bresnen，2011）。 在代理人发生变更时，与自由市场经济国家（如英国和美国）相比，协调市场经济国家（如法国、德国和日本等）采用关系合同的可能性更大（Henisz *et al.*，2012）。 2008 年英国急剧的经济衰退已经使许多建筑客户重新评价公司的采购策略，结果使建筑业（放弃协作性制度安排的变革）“恢复原状”（Tennant and Fernie，2012）。 **制度环境** 合伙制与政府政策和法律框架的变化有很大关系。合伙制的核心作用是打破了作为项目治理活动平台的既有规则制度环境的平衡（Gottlieb and Jensen，2012）。 **建筑专业体制** 专业人士及其组织通过局部的互动形成专业社群。在这个社群中，信誉、信任、信息和知识的交换以及合意惯例的形成是必不可少的（Sha，2013）。 **信任** 信任及其基本规范行为是自我执行的保证，这是一种比（正式）合同和垂直一体化效率更高、成本更低的一种替代性方法（Poppo and Zenger，2002）。

续表

维度	因素
赋能者	信任大体上应该是关系合同和队伍构建的核心（Rahman *et al.*，2007）。 合同治理机制（如控制与监督系统）需要由关系机制（如信任与认知一致性）来补充（Hartmann *et al.*，2010）。 在存在资产专用性的情况下，信任允许较大的选择治理结构的灵活性（Jeffries and Reed，2000）。 关系治理与信任相互关联，后者能够改善组织间的交易绩效（Poppo and Zenger，2002）。 过多的信任如同过少的信任一样，都是有害的。低组织信任和关系合同是相容的（Jeffries and Reed，2000）。 对合作的商业激励（如框架性协议）表现为今后的业务量，这种激励支持"基于互惠的合作"，未必是因为组织间彼此信任的缘故（Tennant and Fernie，2012）。 对于项目的成功来说，信任和信用的作用有限，甚至没有什么作用（Doloi，2009，p. 1108）。 **沟通与交流** 交流是关系合伙制成功的唯一关键因素（Doloi，2009）。 在业务人员的例会中，合同各方当事人内在化的、多年养成的工作方式就变得明显起来（Hartmann and Bresnen，2011）

从新制度经济学的角度来看，表 9.1 中的"赋能者"大致上与威廉姆森提出的四个制度层次相对应，它们分别是：(1) 社会基础或文化基础，(2) 基本制度环境，(3) 治理制度，(4) 短期的资源配置（Williamson，2000）。值得指出的是，表中列出的各种观点基本上是一致的，对信任则存在不同的看法；而信任又往往被看作是关系合同的关键所在。对信任的不同看法可能要归因于不同的研究背景。这个事实再次提醒我们，研究关系型建筑合约必须坚持具体问题具体分析的原则，一切从实际出发，而不是简单套用现成的理论。

9.1.4 我国建筑业推行关系型合约的机遇和挑战❶

SWOT 分析，即"优势—劣势—机遇—威胁"态势分析，是最常用的战略分析方法之一。SWOT 分析的步骤通常是：识别内部因素（优势与劣势）和外部因素（机遇和挑战）；选择并评价其中的重要因素；对内外因素之间的关系做出判别。SWOT 矩阵包括四个象限，分别代表四种策略：(1) SO（优势—机遇）策略；(2) WO（劣势—机遇）策略；(3) ST（优势—威胁）策略；(4) WT（劣势—威胁）策略。这里采用 SWOT 的思路和方法，分析我国建筑业推行关系合同的机遇和挑战。图 9.4 给出了关系型建筑合约自身的内部因素和我国建筑业推行关系型建筑合约的外部条件。

首先分析内部因素之间的关系。应该指出，关系型建筑合约的优势与劣势不是绝对的；其比较优势会随着制度环境的变化而变化。为了对关系型建筑合约的优劣做出评价，首先要考察我国建筑业的发展环境。

长期以来，政府主导的基本建设投资一直是我国经济发展的主要驱动力。以 2008

❶ 这一节的内容主要来自发表在 International Journal of Architecture，Engineering and Construction 上的文章（Sha，2016b）。

年应对国际金融危机的一揽子计划为例，在四万亿元的投资总额中，有 38%以上的资金被用于公共基础设施建设。国家的“十三五”发展规划已经确定了 6.5%以上的年均增长率，这意味着在今后一段时期内将会有更多的建设项目。除了传统的基础设施建设项目之外，近年来中央政府又推出了新的建设计划，旨在稳定经济增长，消化钢铁、水泥等行业的过剩产能。2015 年 8 月，国务院办公厅发布了两个通知，一是《关于推进城市地下综合管廊建设的指导意见》，二是《关于推进海绵城市建设指导意见》。根据这两个通知，到 2020 年，要建成一批具有国际先进水平的地下综合管廊并投入运营；城市建成区 20%以上的面积要达到海绵城市的目标要求；到 2030 年，这个比例要达到 80%以上。据估计，仅地下综合管廊建设这一项计划就会带来四千亿至五千亿元的投资。这两个通知还强调指出，无论是地下管廊还是海绵城市建设，都要积极推 PPP 和特许经营等模式，吸引社会资本的广泛参与（胡健，2015；吴荻，2015）。在地方层面，各级政府对基建投资项目表现出更大的热情，因为这些项目能够快速改变城市面貌，进而突显地方官员的政绩。在这种情况下，遍布各地的大兴土木就不足为奇了。

	优势（S）	劣势（W）
内部因素	1. 程序灵活性带来的效率 2. 由于和谐的工作方式而降低的交易成本 3. 作为价值共同创造者的客户的深度介入 4. 较强的限制机会主义行为的能力	1. 在当事人之间培养和维系关系的成本 2. 由于弹性安排造成的寻租空间 3. 由当事人之间的密切关系所带来的公司合谋的可能性
	机遇（O）	**挑战（T）**
外部因素	1. 越来越多的大型复杂基础设施项目 2. 由于公共财政资源不足导致PPP 模式的广泛应用 3. 儒家倡导的传统道德观念，如“和为贵”，“己所不欲勿施于人”等	1. 各级政府在经济活动中的强势作用 2. “权大于法”的思维习惯 3. 由于产权不明、责权不清所造成的公共项目客户行为不规范 4. 建筑市场不成熟 5. 建筑专业体系不完善

图 9.4　我国建筑业推行关系合同的 SWOT 分析

背景材料： 令世人震惊的中国式大拆大建（资料来源：陈阳，2016）

2016 年 8 月 26 日，为了给建设中的地铁 2 号线让路，江西省南昌市一座 500m 长的立交桥在数小时内被拆除。68 台挖掘机同时作业的场面令人叹为观止。这座刚刚服役 24 年的立交桥在一夜之间被夷为平地，不仅使当地居民感到不可思议，也让世界感到震惊。一位英国《每日邮报》的读者在看了相关报道后，在网上发表了以下评论：“在英国，这种事情需要一年到一年半的时间才能完成!”

总之，目前我国到处都是雄心勃勃的开发计划和基础设施建设项目，这些项目大都面临着工期紧迫、资金短缺的问题，对私人资本表现出强烈的需求。PPP 模式正是在这种背景下在我国得以迅速推广的[1]。因此，对内部因素的分析结果是：目前在我国，关系型建筑合约的优势超过劣势。实际上，我国建筑业确有一些关系合同的成功案例（梁永宽，2012）。

背景材料：我国建设项目关系合同管理的一个成功案例（资料来源：梁永宽，2009）

茂名乙烯改扩建工程项目的规模为 100 万吨/年，概算投资约为 75 亿元。2004 年 6 月 30 日乙烯裂解炉开始打桩，2006 年 7 月 28 日乙烯装置完成中间交工，高密度聚乙烯装置投料试车，同年 8 月 8 日聚丙烯装置投料试车，9 月 28 日乙烯装置投料试车。

该项目具有工期紧、建设与生产相交叉的特点，因此采用了业主项目经理负责制的治理模式。业主方茂名石化公司组建项目经理部，全面负责项目建设期间的组织和管理，以及进度、费用、质量、合同和 HSE（Health Safety and Environment）等“五大控制”。项目经理部下设职能齐全的部门：设计管理部负责项目的设计管理以及总体院与专业院之间的协调；项目控制部负责招标、合同策划和管理，并负责工程概算、预算和结算等项工作；施工管理部负责施工组织和现场调度；生产准备部负责项目生产准备和投料试车，组织工程竣工验收等。

该项目强调信任与合作，绝大部分管理工作都是由业主方负责，旨在通过统一的协调与合作提高管理效率和项目绩效。大部分装置都采用专业分包的方式，只有部分装置采用 EPC 总承包，聘请监理公司实施工程监理。项目合同多采用框架式的约定方式，有的工程甚至开工后还没有签订正式合同。乙烯裂解等主要装置都没有明确的合同价，只是原则上约定，工程结算总价不超过批复概算的工程费。在聚丙烯装置的 EPC 总承包合同中约定的结算价为：在批复的项目概算的基础上降低 3 个百分点；合同不约定工程量清单，以设计最终出图为准。其他大部分子项目以施工图预算加签证的结算方式为主，把签证的权力授予现场监理，最终由业主相关部门审定。合同控制报告分为周报、月报和专项报告，及时处理有关变更事宜。处理工程最终结算的原则是：业主在不超过主管部门批复的限额内，尽量满足承包商的要求。

该项目比原计划提前 11 天投料试车。建设成本共节约两亿多元，使生产成本大幅度降低。新增每吨乙烯生产能力的投资约为 1.2 万元，远低于国内同类项目 2.5 万—4 万元/的水平。从整体上看，该项目的成本控制和进度控制达到国内先进水平，但也存在一些问题。例如，项目投产后的一段时期内，曾出现非计划的抢修；设备方面也暴露了一些问题。分析结果表明，建设过程中的抢工期和业主方控制过度是造成这些问

[1] 在 2013 年底召开的全国财政工作会议上，PPP 以“政府和社会资本合作模式”的名义被正式提出，会议期间还别开生面地套开了一个关于 PPP 的研讨会。2014 年 9 月，财政部发出《关于推广运用政府和社会资本合作模式有关问题的通知》，随后又相继颁布《政府和社会资本合作模式操作指南（试行）》、《PPP 项目合同指南（试行）》、《关于规范政府和社会资本合作合同管理工作的通知》和《政府和社会资本合作项目财政承受能力论证指引》等一系列文件。在财政部公布 30 个 PPP 示范项目以后，不少省份陆续推出了省级层面的 PPP 项目。由此可以清晰看出 PPP 模式在我国加速发展的轨迹。

题的主要原因。

接下来分析外部因素，也就是我国推行关系型建筑合约的机遇和挑战之间的关系。如前所述，以 PPP 模式为代表的关系型建筑合约在我国具有巨大的发展潜力。然而，下面的一些不利因素会严重制约关系型建筑合约的顺利实施。一是市场经济还不成熟。目前的经济体制在许多方面还不够完善，核心问题是政府对资源的直接配置过多，不合理的干预太多。产能过剩、城市病严重、耕地占用过多、地方债风险、生态环境破坏等问题，很大程度上都与政府干预过多有关。二是法治不健全。有法不依、执法不严、违法不究甚至知法犯法的现象时有发生，背后则是"权大于法"的传统思维在作祟。三是建筑市场中的关系失衡。政府不仅是政策的制定者，也是公共项目的业主。大量事实表明，建筑市场中的信任缺失和秩序混乱，在很大程度上要归因于地方政府在公共项目建设中的违规行为（刘倩等，2008）。

背景材料：由 BT 模式引发的拖欠工程款诉讼案（资料来源：栗泽宇，2015）

在地方建设资金短缺的大背景下，"建设—移交"（Build-Transfer，BT）模式受到地方政府的青睐，大量社会资本通过这一途径进入市政设施和保障房建设等领域，一方面为解决资金短缺、推动基础设施建设做出了贡献，另一方面造成沉重的债务负担。2013 年中期的统计数据表明，由 BT 模式造成的债务高达 1.5 万亿元，占全部地方债务的 8%，仅次于银行贷款所占比例。由于 BT 模式在我国缺乏法规约束，运作不够规范，近年来已暴露出诸多问题。

2015 年 1 月，为索要高达 9 亿元的拖欠工程款，素有"中国最大包工头"和"中国式 BT 鼻祖"之称的严介和旗下的太平洋建设集团对 6 个地方政府提起诉讼，涉及河北、云南、湖南、贵州、山东和贵州等省份的 15 个项目。严介和在接受媒体专访时表示，这是向其他地方政府发出一个信号，它们总共欠了太平洋建设高达 500 亿元的工程款。

造成这些拖欠工程款主要原因是 BT 模式；而太平洋建设集团本身也是依靠 BT 模式发展起来的。1996 年严介和垫资 5000 万元帮助江苏宿迁市政府建设一条市府大道，由此开创了中国式的 BT 模式。此后，他将 BT 模式迅速复制到全国各地，太平洋建设集团也得以迅速扩张。2015 年，以太平洋建设为主体的"苏太华系"再次入选《财富》世界 500 强，位居中国私营实体企业之首，全球建筑行业私企第一。

据后续报道，在提起诉讼的几个月后，太平洋建设集团已与 4 个地方政府达成了总额约 7 亿元的和解协议。严介和在一次新闻发布会上表示："我们的诉讼给相关地方政府造成了巨大压力，这意味着法治确实管用。我看到了中国的很大希望。"

前面对"赋能者"的分析表明，关系型建筑合约的实施需要良好的制度环境来保证。当前我国建筑市场和建筑专业体制都不够完善，建设项目当事人之间信任与沟通的基础不够牢固。在某些“赋能者”本身严重“失能”的情况下，关系型建筑合约在我国的实施效果就会大打折扣。因此，对外部因素的分析结果是：目前在我国推行关系型建筑合约的挑战超过机遇。

9.1.5 小结

关系型建筑合约代表了一种新的思维方式。它的出现和发展在很大程度上要归因于传统的建设项目采购方式，也就是准关系合同的效率低下。随着建设项目规模的不断扩大，复杂性不断提高，以及制度环境的不断变化，越来越多的人认识到，建设项目参与各方之间的合作关系可以创造新的商机，这是市场、正式合同或纵向一体化所难以做到的。

建设项目以高度定制的长期合同为特征，因此它本身就包含了许多“关系”的成分。在建设项目的语境中研究关系合同，需要把准关系合同与关系合同区分开来。准关系合同属于合同治理的范畴，主要考虑事前的机制设计；而关系合同属于关系治理的范畴，主要关注事后的3R，即再谈判（renegotiation）、利益再调整（realignment）和项目效率的恢复（restoration）。

关系合同与准关系合同各有自己的优点和局限性，它们的签订与执行都是需要付出成本的。因此，协作性制度安排的优劣取决于建设项目自身的性质，以及若干赋能者的情况，这些赋能者涉及文化背景、基本制度环境、项目治理、项目管理以及组织之间、个人之间的关系。

关系型建筑合约可以被理解为一种内嵌于历史和当地环境的实践活动。因此，在分析关系型建筑合约的适用性时，需要充分考虑建设项目的社会、经济、文化背景和制度环境。SWOT分析表明，关系型建筑合约在我国同时面临着巨大的机遇和挑战；挑战是如此严峻，以至于潜力和优势无法被充分发挥出来。关系型建筑合约的成功实施有赖于建筑市场的成熟和建筑专业体制的完善。政府不仅是立法者和政策制定者，还是最大的建设项目客户；关系型建筑合约的成功实施，关键在于政府转变职能，处理好政府与市场、第三方的关系。

如前所述，关系型建筑合约包含了项目合伙制、项目联盟、框架协议等多种形式。每一种形式都有自己的特点，适用于不同的场合。由于篇幅的限制，这里没有详细讨论这些具体的模式。实际上，具体到每一种模式，都有许多问题值得专门研究。在这方面已经有大量的研究成果，并且有新的文献不断出现。感兴趣的读者可阅读并跟踪相关文献。

9.2 建筑专业体制与行业自律

是否具备健全的行业自律机制是衡量一个经济是否健康、成熟的重要标志。与关系型建筑合约相比，行业自律是一种更“软”的非正式制度安排。如果说正式合同是对当事人的刚性约束，关系合同是对当事人的柔性约束，那么，行业自律则是当事人的自我约束。建筑业的行业自律，要求市场参与人遵守诺言、实践成约、自觉克服机会主义的行为倾向。从博弈论的角度看，行业自律是市场参与者长期动态重复博弈的结果。行业自律既属于道德范畴，又属于经济范畴。作为市场与政府之间的第三个制度性变量，建筑专业体制在激励机制和信息机制方面具有比较优势。

现代社会是陌生人社会和合同社会，在很多情况下，市场交易都具有一次性博弈的性质；而且，合同不可能穷尽所有可能发生的情况，因而是不完全的。因此，自律机制单靠市场这只看不见的手是无法形成和完善的。政府管制可以在一定程度上解决市场机制自身的缺陷，但同时会带来垄断和成本过高的问题；而垄断又是产生寻租和腐败的重要根源。建筑专业体制以专业人士为主体，以自身信誉为保证，以信息服务为主要活动内容。建筑专业体制在行业内所营造的“熟人共同体”，有助于克服市场参与人之间的不信任。更为重要的是，这种体制是凭借自身的信誉和服务获取利益而不是凭借垄断地位去寻租。这些特点决定了建筑专业体制可以在建筑行业自律机制的形成和发展中发挥其独特的作用。

背景材料：熟人社会与“无主体熟人社会”（资料来源：吴重庆，2011）

费孝通先生曾把中国农村称为“熟人社会”。这种社会有以下三个特点。一是舆论压人。在传统的乡村里，血缘和地缘合一，频密的互动带来信息的对称状态，舆论的发生与传播总是快速而广泛。熟人社会里的所谓“民风淳朴”，与其说是个体自觉践履道德规范的产物，毋宁说是“熟人社会”里道德舆论压力的结果。二是“面子”有价。不同于“陌生人社会”的无情冷漠，熟人社会充满人情味，好面子。为什么面子值钱？因为在封闭的社会空间里，社会资源有限，要有所作为，就需要“有头有脸”。三是“社会资本”可累积。美国社会学家科尔曼指出，“社会资本是生产性的，是否拥有社会资本，决定了人们是否可能实现某些既定目标”。在一定意义上讲，熟人社会里每个人所拥有的“关系”，就是他的“社会资本”。

自20世纪80年代以来，由于农村的主体成员常年离土离乡，“熟人社会”逐渐转化为“无主体熟人社会”；结果造成舆论失灵，“面子”贬值和社会资本流散。当前乡村中出现的大量纠纷，基本上都可以从“无主体熟人社会”的行为逻辑中得到解释。

9.2.1　对建筑专业体制的理论探析[1]

经过二百多年的发展历程，建筑专业体制如今走到了一个转折关头（Hughes and

---

[1] 这一节的内容主要来自《建筑经济》杂志上发表的文章（沙凯逊，孙晓冰，2014a）。

Hughes，2013）。在新的历史条件下，构建"新型专业化"（New professionalism）的任务被提上了议事日程。实际工作千头万绪，理论研究需要先行一步。首先要搞清楚建筑专业体制存在的理由。只有解决好"为什么"的问题，明白该体制的合理性和必要性，才不会失去信心。其次要搞清楚该体制的本质属性和内在逻辑。只有解决好"是什么"的问题，明白应该坚持什么和摒弃什么，才不会迷失方向。

9.2.1.1 从不确定性看建筑专业体制的必要性

建筑专业体制最早出现在第一次工业革命时期的英国。由于在保证工程质量、降低交易费用等方面发挥了很好的作用，这种体制被世界各国所仿效，并在二战结束后的一段时期里达到了"神话般的黄金时代"（Duffy and Rabeneck，2013）。20 世纪 70 年代石油危机之后，特别是进入 21 世纪以来，在经济自由化、信息革命和资源环境问题的多重挑战面前，发达国家的建筑专业体制出现明显的下滑趋势。在这种情况下，就出现了"专业和专业组织在今天是否依然重要"的问题（Hughes and Hughes，2013）。回答这个问题，需要从专业体制存在的理由入手。在这方面，奈特的分析框架具有很好的启发性（Knight，1921）❶。按照奈特的分析逻辑，可度量的"不确定性"叫作风险，而真正的不确定性是不可度量的。对于不确定性来说，专业化是较为有效的一种处理方法。由于建筑业所面临的自然不确定性是其他行业所没有的，因此面向建筑业的专业注册资格的种类要大大超过其他行业。

随着世界步入信息时代，人们获取和处理信息的能力得到空前提高。于是有人会问：专业体制是否还有必要继续存在？答案应该是肯定的。一方面，像 BIM（building information modeling）之类的信息系统固然能够解决许多问题，但是，说到底，它们不具备专业体制所特有的应对不确定性的能力，只能发挥"辅助"的作用。另一方面，自然资源枯竭、生态环境恶化、南北差距加大等矛盾日益突出，使整个国际社会变得更加脆弱，面临更多的不确定性，对专业体制提出新的更高的要求。因此，专业体制不仅有必要继续存在，而且需要进一步发展和完善。

9.2.1.2 从 RICS 看建筑专业体制的本质属性

建筑专业体制以专业人士为主体。对专业人士的角色定位存在不同的看法❷；然而，大多数文献都认为，专业人士应该具备以下基本素质（Duffy and Rabeneck，2013；Hughes and Hughes，2013；Connaughton and Meikle，2013）：一是必要的专业

---

❶ 奈特在这方面的论述，详见第 5 讲 5.2 节，建设项目存在的理由。

❷ 关于建筑专业人士及其组织的定义包括：（1）客户（甲方）与建筑业之间的居间代理人（Duffy and Rabeneck，2013），（2）平衡商业需求和公共利益的独立顾问（Twinn，2013），（3）参与建成环境的设计、开发、运营和维护的所有专业人士和利益相关者集团（Hartenberger *et al.*，2013），（4）参与建筑物的建设、管理、出租和估价，以及为这些服务提供材料和技术支持业务的任何个人和团体（Janda and Parag，2013）。

知识和技能。它们使专业人士能够在不确定的条件下发挥独特的作用。二是相应的执业资格和身份认同。市场进入壁垒具有信息甄别的作用。取得专业人士资格或行业协会成员的身份无异于获得一枚“社会印章”。三是严格的职业道德和伦理规范。它们以公正和公开为特征，有助于在行业内培养信任，增进合作。四是明确的服务导向。高举为公共利益服务的旗帜，有助于赢得社会的认可与尊重。

建筑专业体制以专业组织为核心。专业人士的素质不是与生俱来的个人禀赋，而是在专业组织营造的制度环境下经过长期学习和实践形成的。这里以英国皇家特许测量师学会（RICS）为例来说明这个问题。作为独立的专业组织，RICS 有四个战略目标：一是对行业的规制和提升，二是制定并保持最高的教育和资质标准，三是通过严格的伦理规范来保护客户和消费者的利益，四是为政府和企业提供公平、可靠的建议、分析和指导。RICS 遵循两项基本原则。一是为公共利益服务的原则。在 1881 年获取皇家特许状时，RICS 就做出了为公共利益服务的承诺。此后，RICS 一直恪守这一承诺，并把它作为核心原则。二是自律的原则。RICS 拥有严格的内部监督与检查制度，其内部规则和标准不仅完全符合现有的法律法规，而且在有些方面会高于政府的要求。凭借这些目标和原则，RICS 为其成员营造了良好的制度环境，其自身也取得了非凡的成就，从最初的 20 名成员发展到现在的 10 万名会员，成为世界顶级的建筑专业组织。

从 RICS 可以看出，建筑专业体制的精髓在于它的独立性、利他性和自律性。首先，保持独立性，而不是依附于任何其他组织和利益集团，可以使专业人士在决策时持守公平的立场。其次，利他性使专业体制有别于市场。这是因为，无论是职业道德、伦理规范，还是为公共利益服务，都属于利他的范畴；而根据新古典经济学，市场参与人都是利己的；“在完美竞争的条件下，道德在市场没有用武之地”（Gauthier，1986，p. 93）。最后，自律性使专业体制有别于政府。这是因为，自律意味着自我约束、遵守诺言和实践成约，而政府的科层体制以他律为基本特征。

根据新制度经济学，经济治理可分为市场、政府和社群三种基本形式。以上分析表明，专业体制属于社群治理的范畴。如果市场是基于价格信号的“看不见的手”，政府是基于规制的“看得见的手”，那么，建筑专业体制则可以看作是基于自律的“第三只手”。

9.2.1.3　从社群治理看建筑专业体制的比较优势

市场调节、政府干预和社群治理各具优势和不足。在现代经济治理中，三者不可偏废。如图 9.5 所示，市场调节机制从一元调节到二元调节，进而发展到三角增进机制，反映了市场经济从简单到复杂、从低级到高级的演进过程。在市场经济的“古典阶段”，以市场为主的一元调节机制曾经使“资产阶级在它的不到一百年的阶级统治中所创造的生产力，比过去一切世代创造的全部生产力还要多，还要大”（马克思，恩格

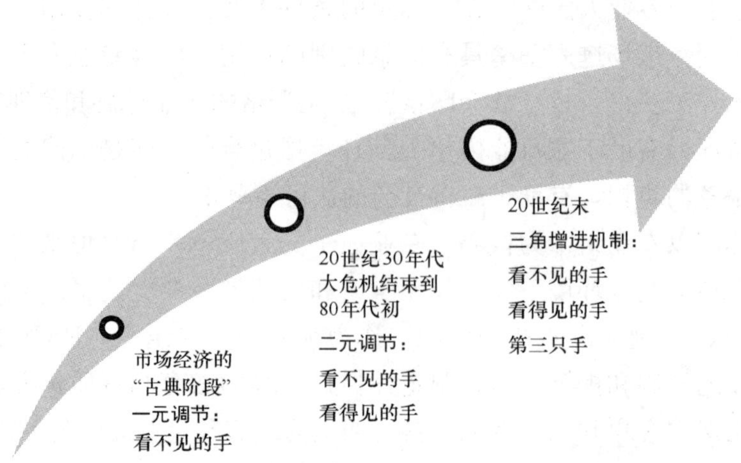

图 9.5 市场经济从简单到复杂、从低级到高级的演进过程

斯，1964）。然而，市场失灵的出现"破坏了看不见的手的理论所假定的完全竞争的田园诗般的画面"（萨缪尔逊，诺德豪斯，1996）。从 20 世纪 30 年代大危机结束到 80 年代初，计划经济体制和政府干预大行其道，在创造非凡业绩的同时，又出现了政府失灵的问题。市场失灵和政府失灵的同时存在，给社群治理带来了发展空间。

所谓社群，就是频繁进行直接交往的一群人（Bowles，2004，p. 474）。在博弈论的语境中，"频繁的直接交往"就是动态重复博弈。对"囚徒困境"的分析结果表明，在一次性博弈中，由于个人理性与集体理性之间的矛盾，个人效用最大化行为未必导致社会福利最优。如果说，完美竞争条件下的市场是一个"陌生人社会"，那么，社群可以看作是"熟人社会"：其成员之间的交往是频繁发生的，并且基本上都不是匿名的。正是这种直接的重复交往，使博弈双方有可能走出囚徒困境。一方面，频繁的交往可以降低信息成本，增进成员之间的相互了解。另一方面，为了在今后免受惩罚，社会成员会在当下表现出较强的合作愿望。无名氏定理（folk theorem）表明，如果重复博弈的可能性足够大并且参与人有足够的耐心（贴现因子足够大），那么，理性的参与人即使在本性上不是合作型的，也有积极性克服短期机会主义行为，建立乐意合作的声誉，最终取得双赢/多赢的结果（张维迎，1996，pp. 363—374）。

作为市场和政府之外的第三种力量，建筑专业体制的比较优势主要表现在以下几方面：

- 基于长远预期的激励机制。使市场参与人能够预期到博弈能长期重复进行下去，与未来的长期收益相比，眼前的利益是第二位的，从而产生合作与自律的积极性。明晰的产权是人们追求长远利益的主要动力。

- 基于声誉信息的约束机制。通过客观、准确和公开的声誉信息，使诚实守信者受到褒奖，使投机取巧者名誉扫地直至绳之以法，为自己的不良行为付出代价，从而促使市场参与人自觉约束自己的机会主义行为。

• 基于信息反馈的强化合作机制。在信息不完全但信息成本足够低的情况下，通过"边做边学"（learning by doing）的信息反馈，可以促进参与人之间的合作。

• 基于行业规范和职业道德的养成机制。使市场参与人通过意识形态的"教化"，从思想上重视自己的声誉，恪守职业道德，从而形成良好的竞争环境。

这些优势可以归因于社群中重复博弈中所形成的局部信息和来自同行的压力（沙凯逊等，2003）。

9.2.1.4　小结

建筑专业体制既有优势，也有局限性。市场、政府和建筑专业体制之间的关系是相辅相成的互补关系。建筑专业体制的独立性、利他性和自律性可以弥补市场和政府的不足。反过来，市场和政府的比较优势又是建筑专业体制所缺少的。现代建筑业的发展，需要三者形成合力，而不是相反。

由于社会经济条件和制度环境等方面的原因，建筑专业体制在我国的发展历程不同于发达国家。在发达国家，建筑专业体制主要是在市场的驱动下，自下而上地发展起来的。例如，RICS 肇始于 1868 年 20 名工料测量师在伦敦一家酒店开的一次会，在 13 年之后才获取皇家特许状。而在我国，建筑专业体制是在政府推动下，自上而下地发展起来的。制度演化具有路径依赖的特性。发展具有中国特色的建筑专业体制，必须把专业体制的一般性规律和我国的特殊性有机地结合在一起。这在理论上和实践上都有很大的挑战性，同时也为创新提供了巨大的空间。

9.2.2　建筑专业体制的发展趋势❶

在建筑业的现代化进程中，建筑专业体制发挥了独特优势。然而，随着西方经济进入"后现代"的发展阶段，它正面临着前所未有的挑战，进而引发一系列的反思与变革。

9.2.2.1　新时期呼唤新型专业化

在新的历史时期，建筑业需要承担可持续发展的新任务。可持续建筑要求做到"既满足当代人的需要，又不对后代人满足其需要的能力构成危害"（UN World Commission on Environment and Development，1987）。实际上这是当代人对后人的一种承诺，涉及代际博弈（inter-generational games）。在这方面首先需要回答的问题是：谁来代表并且保护后代人的利益？市场做不到这一点。这是因为，根据新古典经济学，市场是不讲道德的（Gauthier，1986）。政府应该这样做，但是有两方面的局限性。一是政府官员的短视行为。二是双重身份的尴尬：作为公共利益的"管家"，政府有责任

❶ 这一节的内容主要来自《建筑经济》杂志上发表的文章（沙凯逊，孙晓冰，2014b）。

着眼于未来，而作为大型项目的投资者，它又有尽快实现投资收益的冲动（Bonham，2013）。建筑专业体制在代表公共利益方面具有得天独厚的优势，理应在可持续建筑领域发挥重要的作用。然而，该体制正面临着巨大挑战，在此重任面前显得力不从心。

首先是来自新自由主义经济范式的挑战。该范式强调自由竞争，反对国家干预；以产权私有化、完全市场化和政府职能最小化为基本政策主张。在它的冲击和影响下，专业知识和专业服务的“商品化”趋势越来越明显，面临着从独立的第三方异化为市场附庸的危险：“短期主义、官僚体制和政府外包已经侵蚀了建筑专业体制。问责制正在取代信任关系，规制和制度正在取代伦理规范和职业道德，剩下的事情则由市场来处理。”（Bordass and Leaman，2013）

其次是来自信息革命的挑战。在工程建设领域，以 BIM（building information modeling）为代表的新技术表现出巨大的优势和发展潜力，正在酝酿一次新的革命。随着信息透明度的提高，客户变得越来越“专业”，专业人士面临着被边缘化的危险（Jaradat *et al*.，2013）。

最后是来自组织变革的挑战。许多专业服务企业采用全球化和多元化的发展战略，正在不断扩大规模；治理结构也从传统的专业合伙制（P2 模式，professional partnership）改为有限责任公司。对商业利益的过分关注，以及对公司的“规范化”管理，使专业服务企业“去专业化”(de-professionalization）的倾向越来越明显（Connaughton and Meikle，2013）。

新任务和新挑战呼唤新型专业化。为了遏制建筑专业体制的下滑趋势，发达国家正在进行深刻反思，并且采取一系列措施提升职业道德标准，改造专业教育培训体系，发挥政府的引领作用，努力使老体制焕发出新的生机和活力。

9.2.2.2 提升职业道德标准

道德标准是专业体制的伦理基础。在时间的维度上，责任伦理可分为事前的责任（responsibility）和事后的问责（accountability）。前者解决“应该做什么和怎么做”的问题；后者解决“做错了事应该承担什么责任”的问题。在责任对象的维度上，责任伦理可分为由低到高的三个层次：为客户负责，为社会负责和为后代人负责（Hill *et al*.，2013）。这两个维度构成了专业体制的伦理空间。

新型专业化要求为后代人负责。但是从目前的情况来看，专业组织的道德标准中都没有这方面的要求。以建筑专业体制的发源地英国为例，做得最好的土木工程师协会（ICE）和皇家特许测量师学会（RICS）都处于责任伦理的中间层次：前者把为公共利益服务作为首要责任，后者做出了为公共利益服务的承诺；而其他专业组织基本上处于最低层次，把为客户服务放在首位。有人认为，“把为客户服务放在首位”的标准太低——这一点“连理发师都能达到”（Hill *et al*.，2013）。更加糟糕的是，在与客户意见发生冲突的情况下，有时连最低层次的标准也未必能达到。

为了提升专业伦理水平和职业道德标准，发达国家采取了以下措施。一是提出了类似于希波克拉底誓言❶的伦理框架。该框架包含以下十项内容（Bordass and Leaman，2013）：

（1）目光远大，做社会及其资源，乃至整个地球的管家；

（2）除了对客户尽义务之外，只做正确的事情；

（3）通过开放和坦诚的合作，建立信任关系；

（4）在设计、项目的实施和使用之间建立联系，着眼于结果；

（5）（工作完成后）不要离开，要提供跟进与售后服务；

（6）对工作绩效进行评估和反省，反馈所发现的问题；

（7）从行动中学习并且能承认错误，公开地分享知识；

（8）将实践、产业、教育、研究和政策制定结合在一起；

（9）向假设和标准提出挑战，不隐瞒自己不知道的东西；

（10）了解环境和约束条件，创造持久的价值，不急于做出选择。

二是在行业协会和高校之间保持一种“健康的张力”，以提高专业伦理和职业道德的教育水平。三是在制度上进一步强化专业人士的进入壁垒和退出机制。四是在组织上加强专业组织之间的整合。例如，英国在2007年成立了绿色建筑委员会（GBC）。这个跨专业的组织将英国皇家建筑师师学会（RIBA）、皇家特许建造学会（CIOB）等专业组织和大量的学术机构、企业整合在一起，有利于形成共同的理论规范和行为准则。

9.2.2.3　改造专业教育培训体系

教育培训是专业体制的知识基础。从目前的情况来看，在能力培养、职业态度、行为和伦理等方面，行业协会认可的专业课程体系和教育培训方法不能适应新型专业化的要求。一是缺少系统的整体规划，二是专业划分过细，三是行知脱节，四是人文社科方面的内容不足。

在改造建筑专业教育培训体系的过程中，发达国家借鉴现代医学教育的经验，采取了以下改进措施。一是在纵向上加强实践、科研、教学和培训等环节之间的联系与合作，逐步形成产学研一体化的教育培训模式。二是在横向上的跨学科整合，强调价值链和集体责任，突破单一学科的界限，开展多科教育（MPE，multi-professional ed-

---

❶　该誓言以两千四百多年前古希腊医生希波克拉底的名字命名，体现了所有医生共同的伦理规范和行为准则。下面是该誓言的一个版本：“我要遵守誓约，矢忠不渝。对传授我医术的老师，我要像父母一样敬重，并作为终身的职业。对我的儿子、老师的儿子以及我的门徒，我要悉心传授医学知识。我要竭尽全力，采取我认为有利于病人的医疗措施，不能给病人带来痛苦与危害。我不把毒药给任何人，也决不授意别人使用它。尤其不为妇女施行堕胎手术杀害生命。我要清清白白地行医和生活。无论进入谁家，只是为了治病，不为所欲为，不接受贿赂，不勾引异性。对看到或听到不应外传的私生活，我决不泄露。如果我能严格遵守上面誓言时，请求神祇让我的生命与医术得到无上光荣；如果我违背誓言，天地鬼神一起将我雷击致死。”

ucation)[1]。三是采用基于问题的学习模式（PBL，problem-based learning）[2]。这种教学模式以问题为基础，以学生为主体，在辅导教师的参与下，围绕某一专题或案例，以小组讨论的方式进行教学。剑桥大学的实践证明，这种模式有利于课程体系的融会贯通。四是师徒培训模式。在英国，ICE 和 RIBA 等专业组织都开始推行这种模式，以帮助大学毕业生在两年的时间内实现由实习生到初级专业人士的转变。五是通过专业竞赛提高学生的综合能力。欧美国家在以上几个方面都已经有许多成功的案例（Hartenberger *et al.*，2013）。

9.2.2.4 发挥政府的引领作用

新型专业化离不开市场和政府的支持与互动。政府应该并且能够发挥引领作用。作为立法者，政府一方面通过政策法规和行政指令发挥直接的推动作用，另一方面通过合理设置经济杠杆发挥间接的调控作用，将外部成本内部化，利用市场机制抑制外部不经济性。直接推动和间接调控双管齐下，共同促进范式转换。此外，作为公共项目的客户，政府可以通过提出新的设计和施工标准，影响和改变专业人士及其组织的思维方式和工作习惯，进而形成新的文化氛围。反过来，新范式和新文化又会促进政府的工作，改善政府的行为方式。政府、市场和建筑专业体制三者之间相辅相成，形成合力，可以取得很好的成效。在这方面，美国总务署（GSA）的经验很有说服力（Bonham，2013）。

GSA 是美国政府的“大房东”。它拥有 9600 座、面积为 3290 万平方米的房产供政府机构租用，同时负责联邦政府公共建筑的设计、建设、维护和管理等事务。GSA 在推行绿色建筑的过程中，一是严格执行有关建筑节能和环境保护的政策法规、政府指令和技术规范；二是率先采用绿色建筑评价体系 LEED[3]，并且不断提高认证等级：从 2003 年的认证级提高到 2006 年的银色级，再到 2010 年的金色级；三是注重与专业组织和专业服务企业的合作，形成良性互动。

丹佛法院大楼的建设项目是一个成功的案例。该项目的建筑面积为 2.9 万平方米，预算造价为 8500 万美元，由著名的建筑设计事务所 HOK 公司设计。项目本身取得了明显的成效，同时产生了很好的示范带头作用，因而被誉为“可持续的典范”。下面是该项目的绿色计划进程表：

- 1992 年，美国政府颁布能源政策法，为该项目的绿色计划提供了明确的法律依

---

[1] 这种教学方式在 1980 年被世界卫生组织（WHO）列为优先采用的方法。2003 年英国提出了一种两年制的医学研究生培养方案。不管将来从事什么专业，所有学生都采用同一种教学计划。除了基本的医学知识外，教学计划中还包括时间管理、信息技术和团队合作等内容。

[2] 该模式由美国神经病学教授 Barrow 在 1969 年提出，在 1993 年爱丁堡世界医学教育高峰会议上得到推荐，目前已成为国际上流行的医学教学方法。

[3] LEED（Leadership in Energy and Environmental Design）由五个方面，若干指标构成，满分是 110 分，包括四个认证等级：白金（80 分以上）、金（60—79 分）、银（50—59 分）和认证级（40—49 分）。

据；

• 1994 年，GAS 与 HOK 签署了设计合同；同年，GAS 推出卓越设计（Design Excellence）计划，并把该项目作为样板工程；

• 1998 年，GAS 推出卓越施工（Construction Excellence）计划；同年，美国绿色建筑委员会（USGBC）推出 LEED1.0，该项目是 12 个首批 LEED 试验项目之一；

• 2001 年，GSA 总结经验并加以推广，提出“可持续的最佳实践清单”；

• 2002 年，项目竣工；

• 2005 年，HOK 出版了具有里程碑意义的《HOK 可持续设计指导手册》，在业界产生很大影响；

• 2009 年，该项目取得 LEED 银色认证。

从上面的进程表可以看出，政府、政府客户（GAS）、专业组织（USGBC）和专业服务企业（HOK）有机地结合在一起，充分发挥了各自的优势，同时促进了自身的发展；GAS 在整个过程中发挥了核心纽带作用。因此有人认为，在建筑节能减排新技术的推广应用方面，像 GAS 这样的政府客户是“理想的实验室”（Bonham，2013）。

9.2.2.5　小结

200 多年前，在工业革命带来的巨大压力下，建筑专业体制应运而生。如今，为了适应新任务，迎接新挑战，发达国家提出了发展新型专业化的构想，进行了有益的探索，取得了初步成效。职业道德标准和专业教育培训体系是新型专业化的两大支柱。政府是引领新型专业化发展的重要力量。提升职业道德标准，一方面需要在观念的层面上形成新的伦理框架，另一方面需要在实践的层面上加强制度建设和组织建设。改造专业教育培训体系，需要在纵向上促进产学研一体化，在横向上进行跨学科整合，采取多种措施，培养新型专业化所需要的专业技能、职业态度和思维方式。发挥政府的引领作用，需要政府、政府客户、专业组织和专业服务企业之间形成良性互动，只有这样，才能取得事半功倍的效果。

我国的建筑专业体制只有 20 多年的历史。如果说，发达国家面临的问题是如何遏制住建筑专业体制下滑的趋势，那么，我们所要解决的问题则是如何使建筑专业体制尽快成熟起来。问题的性质虽然不同，但是两者之间存在不少共性。在发展具有中国特色的建筑专业体制时，我们需要并且可以从发达国家学到许多有价值的经验。

9.2.3　我国建筑专业体制的整体转型[1]

当前，我国正在着力打造“经济升级版”，以转变政府职能为突破口，深化改革，正确处理政府和市场、社会的关系：把“市场能做的事交给市场，社会能办的事分给

[1] 这一节的内容主要来自《建筑经济》杂志上发表的文章（沙凯逊，孙晓冰，2014c）。

社会，政府该管的管好”（李克强，2013）。这为建筑专业体制提出了新的要求，也带来了难得的转型机遇。

9.2.3.1 整体转型势在必行

从世界范围来看，建筑专业体制的出现可以归因于第一次工业革命带来的压力和动力；而我国的建筑专业体制则是经济改革和对外开放的结果。如表 9.2 所示，经过 20 多年的发展，我国的建筑专业体制已经初具规模（住房和城乡建设部，2013），并且发挥了积极的作用。但是，一些制度性瓶颈的存在严重制约了它的发展。一是浓厚的官办色彩，导致专业组织的独立性缺失，二是资质管理和市场准入的制度缺陷，造成专业人士的伦理意识淡漠。三是建设项目法人缺位，致使专业服务的立场失偏。分析表明，我国建筑专业体制的主要矛盾是政府、市场和建筑专业体制之间的关系失衡；矛盾的主要方面在于政府（Sha，2013）。要解决这些问题和矛盾，仅靠局部的调整与变革难以奏效。整体转型是我国建筑专业体制在新时期的内在需求。转型的目的是使建筑专业体制真正成为市场和政府之外的第三种力量，保持其独立、利他和自律的秉性，发挥其应有的独特优势。为了实现这一目标，需要着重解决好以下问题：一是淡化官办色彩以还原独立本色，二是简化资质管理以增强职业操守。三强化项目治理以持守无偏立场。

建筑业国家注册专业资格一览 表 9.2

专业资格类别	设立时间	注册人员数量	备 注
监理工程师	1992 年 6 月	128 715	1997 年正式实施
建筑师	1994 年 9 月	22 173（一级）	分为一级和二级
房地产估价师	1995 年 3 月	38 000	
造价工程师	1996 年 8 月	52 267	1998 年正式实施
结构工程师	1997 年 9 月	32 397（一级）	分为一级和二级
岩土工程师	1997 年 9 月	10 923	分为一级和二级
化学工程师	1997 年 9 月	3 706	分为一级和二级
城市规划师	1999 年 4 月	14 597	2000 年正式实施
建造师	2002 年 12 月	282 637（一级）	分为一级和二级
公用设备工程师	2003 年 1 月	16 878	
电气工程师	2003 年 3 月	12 940	
物业管理师	2005 年 11 月	—	

资料来源：住房和城乡建设部（2013）

9.2.3.2 淡化官办色彩以还原独立本色

专业组织是建筑专业体制的核心。独立性是专业组织的灵魂。丧失了独立性，专业组织就失去了存在的必要。我国专业组织的最大问题是缺少独立性。以注册建筑师为例，《注册建筑师条例》和《注册建筑师条例实施细则》均由政府制定；管理委员会委员由政府聘任；考试、注册和执业工作由政府部门的直属事业单位负责。政府的作用是如此之大，以至于专业组织微不足道、可有可无。正因为如此，尽管《注册建筑师条例》第六条规定"可以组建注册建筑师协会"，我国至今没有全国性的注册建筑师协会。其他专业领域虽然成立了全国性的专业组织，但是普遍存在独立性不足的问题。

专业组织和政府部门分别属于社群治理和科层治理的范畴。以专业组织之名行政府管控之实，不仅会失去社群治理的比较优势，而且在某些方面还不如单纯的科层治理。这方面已经有不少教训。例如，当初作为社会公正的重要符号而大力发展的中介组织，在不少地方和领域异化为腐败的温床，甚至蜕变为新的社会腐败主体（汪宛夫，2009）。

还原独立本色，关键在于专业组织的重新定位。要使专业组织真正做到姓"专"不姓"官"，成为市场经济"三角结构"中独立的第三方，而不是政府的附属机构。一是要利用简政放权的机会，重新审视建筑专业体制，提出"升级版"的组织架构和职能划分。二是要建立健全各级各类专业组织，没有成立的要尽快成立起来，已经成立的要加强制度建设。三是要积极创造条件，让专业组织在专业人士的教育培训、考试、注册和执业等方面发挥实质性的主导作用。

9.2.3.3　简化资质管理以增强职业操守

专业人士是建筑专业体制的主体。专业人士需要做到德才兼备。职业操守是专业人士安身立命之本；而我国建筑专业人士在这方面的表现令人担忧。有人通过考试取得执业资格后，自己不去营业，而是把执业资格租售给某些单位，供申报资质时弄虚作假之用。"专业人士"专业精神之缺失，由此可见一斑。这种现象不能简单归咎于个人，而要从制度上找原因。我国建筑业目前有两种资质：个人资质和企业资质。个人取得资格证书后，须受聘于一个企业后方可申请注册；企业资质是市场准入的判断标准。这种制度安排看似严密，实际上却在两方面造成寻租空间：一是企业私下对资质审批部门开展"公关"，二是"专业人士"公然向企业租售执业资格。在执业资质异化为"商品"的同时，职业操守也降到了底线之下。

适当简化资质管理有利于增强职业操守而不是相反。在建设市场准入方面，多数发达国家对企业资质没有要求；日本和香港只是在政府投资项目采购时，才对企业资质提出要求。实践证明，这些"宽松"的做法不仅效率高，而且有利于公平竞争。

正面教育固然重要，消除寻租的制度根源更重要。提升职业道德需要从资质管理制度改革做起，要逐步把资质管理的重点转移到对个人执业资格的管理上来。可借鉴日本和香港的做法，只在政府投资项目采购中对企业资质提出要求。实际上，在处理施工合同纠纷时，最高人民法院已经倾向于淡化企业资质的作用，把建设工程质量作为主要标准（孙尚云，2007）。此外，还要发挥专业组织的作用，提高自我监督和自我管理的能力。要建立违规“黑名单”制度，坚决杜绝出售或出租执业资格的现象，把敢于拿自己执业资格开玩笑的人清除出局。

9.2.3.4 强化项目治理以持守无偏立场

专业服务是建筑专业体制的价值所在。公正无偏是专业服务的基本准则。如果立场失偏，专业服务的价值就会大打折扣，甚至成为负值。当前我国建筑市场的基本情况可以描述为：处于强势地位的甲方、处于弱势地位的乙方和有失公允的第三方（刘倩等，2008）。专业人士和专业组织往往屈从于强势一方，导致立场失偏。

一般认为，产业结构不合理是造成这一局面的主要原因。实际上，甲方的行为失范问题更加值得重视。据国家有关部门统计和执法检查表明，建筑市场检查出来的问题中，建设单位/业主的违规行为占70%以上（吴锐等，2004）。在建设项目的诸多利益主体中，建设单位是矛盾的主要方面（沙凯逊，孙晓冰，2009）。因此，解决专业服务的立场失偏问题，需要从规范建设单位的行为做起。

规范建设单位行为，关键在于项目治理。要在建设项目中明确设立项目法人，做到产权明晰、政企分离和政事分离；解决项目法人缺位、非项目法人越位以及代建制项目中使用单位权力过大等问题。此外，还要在产业重组中加强政策引导，提高产业集中度，形成合理的比例关系。要充分发挥产业政策和经济杠杆的作用，引导和鼓励企业从自身的实际出发，准确定位。要完善市场准入和清出制度，缓解过度竞争的局面。

9.2.3.5 小结

由于历史的原因，我国“初级版”的建筑专业体制难免带有计划经济的烙印。该体制目前的基本状况是发展有余而规范不足；既不能满足发展社会主义市场经济的要求，也不能适应国际竞争的新形势。体制上先天不足的问题只能通过深化改革来解决。

建筑专业体制转型的重点在于解决专业组织的定位问题、专业人士的操守问题和专业服务的公正问题。表面上看，许多问题是专业人士和专业服务企业造成的，实际上，制度上的缺陷才是根本原因。因此，转型应该着眼于制度创新。突破了制度性瓶颈，“升级版”的建筑专业体制就有了基础；技术层面上的问题就不难解决了。

整体转型需要整体思维和统揽全局的顶层设计。转型中涉及政府机构改革和职能调整、建设市场准入和执业资质管理制度改革、产业结构调整等一系列问题。这些问题不是专业体制本身所能解决的，需要纳入建筑业改革的整体框架中统筹考虑。整体转型的关键在于克服既有模式的惯性和既得利益的阻力，简政放权，放松规制。这是“中国经济升级版”的题中应有之义，不仅需要壮士断腕的决心和勇气，还需要坚忍不拔的努力。

9.3 结　　论

这一讲从关系治理和社群治理的角度讨论了建设项目治理中的非正式制度安排问题。建设项目的关系治理主要通过协作性制度安排，也就是关系型建筑合约来实现；社群治理则主要通过专业人士及其组织，也就是建筑专业体制而付诸实践。与关系合同相对应的是准关系合同，也就是传统的建设项目采购方式；与社群治理相对应的是市场和政府。无论是关系合同与准关系合同之间，还是市场、政府与建筑专业体制之间的关系都是相辅相成的互补关系。

如前所述，对信任在关系治理中的作用问题存在不同的看法。尽管如此，本书的作者坚持认为，信任是关系治理的重要基础。交易各方之间的相互信任，可以降低签约的繁琐程度与交易成本，同时在不确定的环境里保持充分的灵活性。如果交易各方相互信任，就没有必要在合同中对未来的行动及其后果做出详尽的描述，而是可以通过合同之外的关系来协调各方的利益。一方面，信任能缓解交易各方对机会主义行为的担心，减少缔约成本和监督成本。另一方面，作为一种基础性的独特机制，信任可以通过互动式的因果关系来交流和分享信息。反过来看，如果信任程度不高，交易各方在签订合同时，就不得不按照“先小人，后君子”的原则行事，“把丑话说在前面”，对未来可能发生的各种事情及其后果做出详尽的规定。在这个意义上，可以说，正式合同的根源在于交易各方之间的信任不足。由于正式合同本身传递了一种对合作者不信任的信号，因而有可能诱发而不是抑制机会主义行为。有些时候，正式合同不但起不到预想的作用，还会对合作产生消极影响（程金伟，费方域，2010）。

从博弈论的角度来看，关系治理和社群治理都属于重复博弈的范畴。博弈不仅是参与人选择行动的过程，而且是参与人不断修正主观判断即先验概率的过程。一般情况下，交易各方很难通过“一锤子买卖”建立起充分的信任关系。俗话说得好，路遥知马力，日久见人心。关系合同中的信任需要时间的检验。同样，在社群治理中，基于长远预期的激励机制和基于声誉信息的约束机制也需要以交易各方的长期交往为基础。信息成本是不完全信息动态博弈中的一个重要因素。由于信息的不完全性，一种行动要起到传递信息的功能，行为者必须为此付出足够的成本。

前面三讲从正式合同的角度介绍了建设项目的垂直治理、水平治理和针对项目经理的治理。这一讲又从非正式制度安排的角度讨论了关系治理和行业自律的问题。关系型建筑合约是面向建设项目的，因而属于微观的范畴；而建筑专业体制是建筑交易体制的一部分，属于中观的范畴。根据威廉姆森提出的制度的四层次分析框架，治理是在一定的制度环境下进行的（Williamson，2000）。对于建设项目治理来说，建筑交易体制是其最直接的制度环境。一个完善的制度环境应该保证在市场竞争中讲真话的人不吃亏，使讲假话、投机取巧的人受到约束和惩罚。改革开放以来，我国在建设领域的制度建设取得了很大进展。然而，建筑市场的混乱局面表明，我国的建筑交易体制还有待完善，在理论和实践方面还有许多亟待研究和解决的问题。这些问题正是第10讲所要研究的内容。

参考文献

1. 陈阳（2016）68 台挖掘机一起上阵，24 年立交桥一晚上被拆，http：//www. nanhuazaobao. net/a/sh/2016/ 0828 /6348. html，2016-09-09.
2. 杜亚灵，尹贻林（2012）公共项目管理绩效改善研究的范式变革，工程管理学报，**26**（1），39—44.
3. 程金伟，费方域（2010）重复博弈下的研发联盟治理模式，现代管理科学，（12）16—17.
4. 胡健（2015）地下综合管廊建设：撬动四五千亿投资，http：//www. chinanews. com/house/2015/04-15/ 7208211. shtml，2016-10-09.
5. 李克强（2013）中国将给世界传递持续发展的讯息，人民网，http：//finance. people. com. cn/，n/2013/0909/ c1004-22860309. html，2013-09-09.
6. 栗泽宇（2015）最大包工头严介和讨薪：状告地方政府拖欠工程款，http：//finance. sina. com. cn/chanjing /gsnews/20150123/223221385768. shtml，2013-09-09.
7. 梁永宽（2009）委托代理理论下的建设项目治理机制——基于南海石化项目与茂名乙烯改扩建项目的案例研究，建筑经济，（5），83—86.
8. 梁永宽（2012）合同与关系——项目管理成功之道，北京：世界图书出版公司 .
9. 刘倩，杨杰，沙凯逊（2008）建筑企业的盈利能力：调研与思考，建筑经济，（1），17—19.
10. 马克思，恩格斯（1964）共产党宣言，中译本，中共中央马克思恩格斯列宁斯大林著作编译局译，北京：人民出版社 .
11. 麦克尼尔（1994）新社会契约论，中译本，雷喜宁，潘勤译，北京：中国政法大学出版社 .
12. 内田贵（2005）契约的再生，中译本，胡宝海译，北京：中国法制出版社 .
13. 萨缪尔逊，诺德豪斯（1996）经济学（第 12 版）中译本，萧琛等译，北京：北京经济学院出版 .
14. 沙凯逊，孙晓冰（2009）规范建设单位行为：一个项目治理的视角，项目管理技术，**7**（10），13—17.
15. 沙凯逊，孙晓冰（2014a）对建筑专业体制的理论探析，建筑经济，**35**（3），10—12.
16. 沙凯逊，孙晓冰（2014b）发达国家建筑专业体制改造提升的经验启示，建筑经济，**35**（4），5—7.
17. 沙凯逊，孙晓冰（2014c）从“经济升级版”看我国建筑专业体制的整体转型，建筑经济，**35**（5），15—17.
18. 沙凯逊，赵锦锴，宋涛，殷涛（2003）建筑业的民间机构与行业自律，土木工程学报，**36**（9），106—110.
19. 孙尚云（2007）试议我国建筑业资质管理制度存在的问题及其解决思路，中国律师网，09http：//www. china-lawyering. com/luntan7/post/421. asp，2007-08-03/2013-10-16.
20. 汪宛夫（2009）中介腐败症与“药方”，瞭望，（24），23—26.
21. 吴重庆（2011）从熟人社会到“无主体熟人社会”，读书，（1），19—25.
22. 吴荻（2015）国务院发文推进海绵城市建设：2020 年达标 20%，http：//www. guandian. cn/article/20151016 /166666. html，2016-10-09.
23. 吴锐，李世蓉，任玉珑（2004）政府投资项目中业主行为不规范原因的经济学分析，建筑经济，

(2)，31—33.

24. 徐忠爱（2008）公司和农户缔结的超市场契约及其治理的信任机制，南京农业大学学报（社会科学版），**8**（3），51—57.
25. 张维迎（1996）博弈论与信息经济学，上海：上海三联出版社.
26. 住房和城乡建设部（2013）人员资格查询，http：//www. mohurd. gov. cn/wbdt/ryzgcx/index. html，2013-07-20.
27. Baker，G.，Gibbons，R. and Murphy，K. J.（2002）Relational contracts and the theory of the firm，*Quarterly Journal of Economics*，**117**（1），39—81.
28. Biggart，N. W. and Hamilton，G. G.（1998）On the limits of a firm-based theory to explain business networks：the Western bias of neo-classical economics，in Segal—Horn S.（Eds.），*The Strategy Reader*（141—160），Blackwell，Oxford.
29. Bonham，M. B.（2013）Leading by example：new professionalism and the government client，*Building Research and Information*，**41**（1），77—94.
30. Bordass，B. and Leaman，A.（2013）A new professionalism：remedy or fantasy? *Building Research and Information*，**41**（1），1—7.
31. Bowles，S.（2004）*Microeconomics：Behavior，Institutions and Evolution*，Princeton University Press，Princeton.
32. Brown，M.，Falk，A. and Fehr，E.（2004）Relational contracts and the nature of market transactions，*Econometrica*，**72**（3），747—780.
33. Bygballe，L. E.，Dewulf，G. and Levitt，R. E.（2015）The interplay between formal and informal contracting in integrated project delivery，*Engineering Project Organization Journal*，**5**（1），22—35.
34. Chan，A. P.，Chan，D. W. and Yeung，J. F.（2010）*Relational Contracting for Construction Excellence：Principles，Practices and Case Studies*，Spon Press，Abingdon.
35. Coase，R. H.（1937）The Nature of the Firm，*Economica*，**4**（16），386—405.
36. Connaughton，J. and Meikle，J.（2013）The changing nature of UK construction professional service firms，*Building Research and Information*，**41**（1），95—109.
37. Dewulf，G. and Kadefors，A.（2012）Collaboration in public construction—contractual incentives，partnering schemes and trust，*Engineering Project Organization Journal*，**2**（4），240—250.
38. Doloi，H.（2009）Relational partnerships：the importance of communication，trust and confidence and joint risk management in achieving project success，*Construction Management and Economics*，**27**（11），1099—1109.
39. Duffy，F. and Rabeneck，A.（2013）Professionalism and architects in the 21st century，*Building Research and Information*，**41**（1），115—122.
40. Eccles，R. G.（1981）The quasifirm in the construction industry，*Journal of Economic Behavior and Organization*，**2**（4），335—357.
41. Eisenberg，M. A.（2002）. Relational Contracts，in Beatson，J. and Friedmann，D.（Eds.），*Good Faith and Fault in Contract law*（291—304），Clarendon Press，Oxford.
42. Fama，E. F. and Jensen，M. C.（1983a）Separation of ownership and control，*Journal of Law and Economics*，**26**（2），301—325.

43. Fama, E. F. and Jensen, M. C. (1983b) Agency problems and residual claims, *Journal of Law and Economics*, **26** (2), 327—349.

44. Gauthier, D. (1986) *Morals by Agreement*, Clarendon Press, Oxford.

45. Geyskens, I. , Steenkamp, Jan-Benedict E. M. and Kumar, N. (2006) Make, buy, or ally: a transaction cost theory meta-analysis, *Academy of Management Journal*, **49** (3), 519—543.

46. Gilmore, G. (1974) *The death of contract*, Ohio State University Press, Columbus.

47. Gilmore, G. and Collins, R. K. L. (1995) The death of contract, *Social Science Electronic Publishing*, (5), 260—261.

48. Gottlieb, S. G. and Jensen, J. S. (2012) Making sense of partnering: discourses, governance and institutional change, *The Engineering Project Organization Journal*, **2** (3), 159—170.

49. Grossman, S. J. and Hart, O. D. (1986) The costs and benefits of ownership: A theory of vertical and lateral integration, *The Journal of Political Economy*, **94** (4), 691—719.

50. Hartenberger, U. , Lorenz, D. and Lützkendorf, T. (2013) A shared built environment professional identity through education and training, *Building Research and Information*, **41** (1), 60—76.

51. Hartmann, A. and Bresnen, M. (2011) The emergence of partnering in construction practice: an activity theory perspective, *The Engineering Project Organization Journal*, **1** (1), 41—52.

52. Hartmann, A. , Davies, A. and Frederiksen, L. (2010) Learning to deliver service-enhanced public infrastructure: balancing contractual and relational capabilities, *Construction Management and Economics*, **28** (11), 1099—1109.

53. Henisz, W. J. , Levitt, R. E. and Scott, W. R. (2012) Toward a unified theory of project governance: economic, sociological and psychological supports for relational contracting, *Engineering Project Organization Journal*, **2** (1—2), 37—55.

54. Hill, S. , Lorenz, D. , Dent, P. and Lützkendorf, T. (2013) Professionalism and ethics in a changing economy, *Building Research and Information*, **41** (1), 8—27.

55. Hughes, W. and Hughes, C. 2013 Professionalism and professional institutions in times of change, *Building Research and Information*, **41** (1), 28—38.

56. Jacobsson, M. and Roth, P. (2014) Towards a shift in mindset: partnering projects as engagement platforms, *Construction Management and Economics*, **32** (5), 419—432.

57. Janda, K. B. and Parag, Y. (2013) A middle-out approach for improving energy performance in buildings, *Building Research and Information*, **41** (1), 39—50.

58. Jaradat, S. , Whyte, J. and Luck, R. (2013) Professionalism in digitally mediated project work, *Building Research and Information*, **41** (1), 51—59.

59. Jeffries, F. L. and Reed, R. (2000) Trust and adaptation in relational contracting, *The Academy of Management Review*, **25** (4), 873—882.

60. Jensen, M. and Meckling, M. (1976) Theory of the firm: managerial behavior, agency costs and ownership structure, *Journal of Financial Economics*, **3** (4) 305—360.

61. Kimel, D. (2007) The Choice of paradigm for theory of contract: Reflections on the relational model, *Oxford Journal of Legal Studies*, **27** (2), 233—255.

62. Klein, P. G. (2005) The Make-or-buy decision: lessons from empirical studies, in Ménard, C. and

Shirley, M. M. (Eds.), *Handbook of New Institutional Economics* (435—464), Springer, Dordrecht.

63. Knight, F. H. (1921) *Risk, Uncertainty and Profit*, Houghton Mifflin Company, Boston.

64. Lahdenperä, P. (2012) Making sense of the multi-party contractual arrangements of project partnering, project alliancing and integrated project delivery, *Construction Management and Economics*, **30** (1), 57—79.

65. Ling, F. Y. Y., Ong, S. Y., Ke, Y. J., Wang, S. Q. and Zou, P. (2014) Drivers and barriers to adopting relational contracting practices in public projects: Comparative study of Beijing and Sydney, *International Journal of Project Management*, **32** (2), 275—285.

66. Lorch, R., 姜阵剑 (2003) 英国建筑业的战略经验，建筑经济，(5), 18—22.

67. Lu, P., Guo, S. P., Qian, L. M., He, P. and Xu, X. Y. (2015) The effectiveness of contractual and relational governances in construction projects in China, *International Journal of Project Management*, **33** (1), 212—222.

68. Macaulay, S. (1985) An empirical view of contract, *Wisconsin Law Review*, 465—482.

69. Macneil, I. R. (1974a) Restatement (second) of contracts and presentiation, *Virginia Law Review*, **60** (4), 589—610.

70. Macneil, I. R. (1974b) The many futures of contracts, *Southern California Law Review*, **47** (3), 691—816.

71. Macneil, I. R. (1978) Contracts: Adjustments of long-term economic relations under classical, neoclassical, and relational contract law, *Northwestern University Law Review*, **72** (6) 854—905.

72. Macneil, I. R. (1980) *The New Social Contract*, Yale University Press, New Haven, CT.

73. Macneil, I. R. (1983) Values in contract: internal and external, *Northwestern University Law Review*, **78** (2), 340—418.

74. Macneil, I. R. (1987) Relational contract theory as sociology: A reply to professors Limberg and de Vos, *Journal of Institutional and Theoretical Economics*, **143** (2), 272—290.

75. McKendrick, E. (2002) The Regulation of long-term contracts in English law, in Beatson, J. and Friedmann, D. (Eds.), *Good Faith and Fault in Contract law* (305—333), Clarendon Press, Oxford.

76. Mouzas, S. and Blois, K. (2013) Contract research today: where do we stand? *Industrial Marketing Management*, **42** (7), 1057—1062.

77. Ning, Y. and Ling, F. Y. Y. (2015) The effects of project characteristics on adopting relational transaction strategies, *International Journal of Project Management*, 33 (**5**), 998—1007.

78. Poppo, L. and Zenger, T. (2002) Do formal contracts and relational governance function as substitutes or complements, *Strategic Management Journal*, **23** (8), 707—725.

79. Project Management Institute (2013) *Organizational Project Management Maturity Model* (OPM3), 3rd Edition, Project Management Institute, Inc., Newtown Square, PA, USA.

80. Pryke, S and Pearson, S. (2006) Project governance: case studies on financial incentives, *Building Research and Information*, **34** (6), 534—545.

81. Rahman, M. M. and Kumaraswamy, M. M. (2002) Culture change initiatives: needs for the Hong Kong construction industry, *Proceedings of the Conference on Re-engineering Construction*, April

2002，Hong Kong，ACMA，CIOB (HK) & HKIE，52—63.

82. Rahman，M. M.，Kumaraswamy，M. M. and Ling，F. Y. Y. (2007) Building a relational contracting culture and integrated teams，*Canadian Journal of Civil Engineering*，**34** (1)，75—88.

83. Reeves，K. (2002) Construction business system in Japan：general contractors and subcontractors，*Building Research and Information*，**30** (6)，413—424.

84. Sha，K. X. (2013) Professionalism in China' s building sector：an economic governance perspective，*Building Research and Information*，**41** (6)，742—51.

85. Sha，K. X. (2016a) Understanding construction project governance：an inter-organizational perspective，*International Journal of Architecture，Engineering and Construction*，**5** (2)，117—127.

86. Sha，K. X. (2016b) Relational contracting in China' s building sector：potentialities and challenges，*International Journal of Architecture，Engineering and Construction*，**5** (4)，207—216.

87. Suprapto，M.，Bakker，H. L. M. and Mooi，H. G. (2015) Relational factors in owner-contractor collaboration：The mediating role of teamworking，*International Journal of Project Management*，**33** (6)，1347—1363.

88. Tennant，S. and Fernie，S. (2012) The commercial currency of construction framework agreements，*Building Research and Information*，**40** (2)，209—220.

89. Twinn，C. (2013) Professionalism，sustainability and the public interest：what next? *Building Research and Information*，**41** (1)，123—128.

90. UN World Commission on Environment and Development (1987) *Our Common Future/Brundtland Report*，Retrieved September 23，2016，from http：//www. answers. com/topic/brundtland-report.

91. Williamson，O. E. (1985) *The Economic Institutions of Capitalism：Firms，Markets，Relational Contracting*，Free Press，Collier Macmillan，London.

92. Williamson，O. E. (1991a) Comparative economic organization：the analysis of discrete structural alternatives，*Administrative Science Quarterly*，**36** (2)，269—296.

93. Williamson，O. E. (1991b) Strategizing，economizing，and economic organization，*Strategic Management Journal*，**12** (S2)，75—94.

94. Williamson，O. E. (2000) The new institutional economics：taking stock，looking ahead. *Journal of Economic Literature*，**38** (3)，595—613.

95. Winch，G. M. (1989) The construction firm and the construction project：A transaction coat approach，*Construction Management and Economics*，**7** (3)，331—345.

96. Winch，G. M. (2000) Institutional reform in British construction：partnering and private finance，*Building Research and Information*，**28** (2)，141—55.

97. Yeung，J. F，Chan，A. P. and Chan，D. W. (2012) Defining relational contracting from the Wittgenstein family-resemblance philosophy，*International Journal of Project Management*，30 (**2**)，225—239.

98. Zaheer，A. and Venkatraman，N. (1995) Relational governance as an interorgannizatonal strategy：an test of the role of trust in economic exchange，*Strategic Management Journal*，**16** (5)，373—392.

第 10 讲　建筑交易体制变迁的分析与比较：一个演化博弈的视角

- 生物进化论和经典博弈论是演化博弈论的两个理论渊源。演化稳定策略（ESS）和复制者动态是演化博弈论的两种主要分析工具。前者可以为演化稳定性提供“静态”的概念性分析，后者可以用来解释个体的动态适应性。
- 从新制度经济学演化学派的角度出发，建筑交易体制可以视为建筑市场中各种参与人之间长期的、未经协调的、带有偶然性的行动后果。
- 贪婪者—分享者—中庸者三人博弈模型可以揭示建筑交易体制演化均衡的某些特征；可以解释多重均衡、路径依赖和对初始条件的敏感性，以及帕累托无效结果的长期存在。该模型的分析结果与相关领域比较研究的结果有很好的一致性。
- 从总体上看，我国的建筑交易体制仍处于其生命周期的初级阶段。早期改革的不彻底性，传统体制的强大惯性，以及建筑市场中各方关系的不平衡，导致了我国建筑业的低水平均衡。要走出这种帕累托无效状态，唯有坚持市场化改革的正确方向，坚持理论创新和制度创新。
- 在现实中，没有“最优的”，只有“最合适的”建筑交易体制。制度的形成和发展有赖于文化的滋养。如果说，发达国家的先进经验在科学性层面和技术性层面具有国际化的特征，那么，在文化性层面，必须考虑本土化的问题，也就是如何适应所在国家和地区的文化传统的问题。

前面几讲讨论了建设项目的垂直治理、水平治理、针对项目经理的治理和关系治理。这些不同形式的治理活动都是在一定的制度环境下进行的。这一讲从演化博弈的视角研究建筑交易体制的变迁问题。**建筑交易体制**（construction business system，在英国又叫 contracting system）是建设项目和建筑企业最直接的制度环境，是一种“高度结构化的关系集合”和“制度化的利益集合”，具有划分角色，明确责任、权利和义务，提供激励约束机制的功能（Winch，2000a）。健全的建筑交易体制会产生有效的激励和良好的合约关系，规范建筑市场秩序，增进合作，降低风险，减少交易费用，进而改善建设项目业绩，提高建筑业的竞争力和整体效益。反之，不良的建筑交易体制会带来冲突的利益关系和机会主义行为，最终导致建筑市场秩序混乱和腐败现象，酿成重大事故（Bologna and Nord，2000；Reeves，2002；Piteroforte and Miller，2002；

Sha，2004）。

说到国家交易体制，人们往往会联想到瑞士的银行业、比利时的巧克力制造业、意大利的时装业和日本的汽车工业所特有的竞争优势。对于行业的竞争优势或劣势，仅从地理位置和自然资源禀赋条件等方面分析是不够的，需要从历史和制度的角度出发，做出合理的解释（Winch，2010，p. 24）。

这一讲以演化博弈论的解释逻辑为主，揭示建筑交易体制变迁的内在机理。首先简要介绍演化博弈论的基本概念和方法。然后将建筑交易体制内生化，建立贪婪者—分享者—中庸者三人博弈模型以解释建筑交易体制的产生原因和发展规律。接下来对不同国家建筑交易体制比较研究的成果进行梳理和归纳，验证博弈模型的分析结果和实际演化过程的一致性。最后对我国建筑交易体制的变迁做出简要的回顾总结并对今后的制度创新提出若干建议。

10.1　演化博弈论的基本概念和方法

如图 10.1 所示，生物进化论和经典博弈论是演化博弈论的两个理论渊源。20 世纪 60 年代，生态学家开始运用博弈论的思想和方法来解释生态现象，并创立了演化博弈论。然而，当初把演化博弈论引入经济学领域时曾引起很大争议——经济学和经典博弈论的研究对象是完全理性的人，而动植物的进化毫无理性可言，两者之间存在很大的差异。随着心理学研究的发展以及有限理性概念的提出，这一矛盾得到缓和，越来越多的经济学家应用演化博弈理论来解释经济现象并且取得了明显进展。

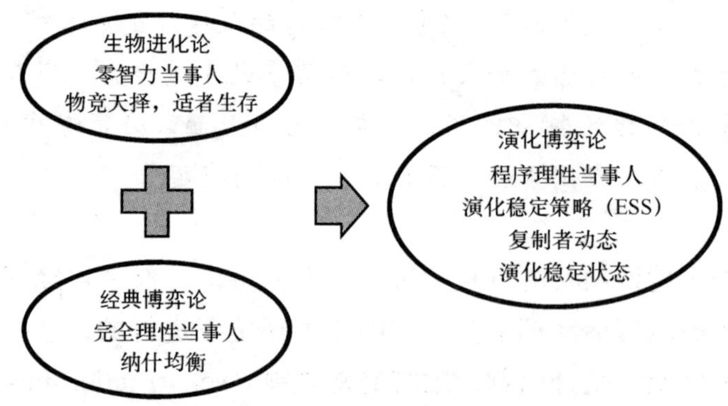

图 10.1　演化博弈论的理论渊源和主要分析工具

背景资料：达尔文的生物进化论

生物进化论和细胞学说、能量守恒与转化定律一起，被誉为 19 世纪自然科学的三大发现，也被视为马克思主义哲学产生的自然科学基础。1859 年，英国生物学家达尔文在《物种起源》一书中提出了生物进化的自然选择学说。“自然选择”意味着生物进化不需要上帝或是外来智慧的设计，而是依靠自然的力量来完成。进化论的基本观点可以概括为：(1) 遗传和变异。所有生物都有变异特性，世界上没有两个完全相同的生命个体。(2) 过度繁殖。生物都有过度繁殖的倾向，而生物种群的规模却相对稳定，这说明新生的后代中只有少数个体能够存活下来。(3) 生存竞争。由于生存空间和食物是有限的，生命个体必须为生存而斗争。(4) 适者生存。所谓"适者"，就是指具有能适应环境的有利变异的个体。正如达尔文所说，生存下来的物种不是最强壮的，也不是最聪明的，而是最能够适应变化的。

1896 年，我国近代启蒙思想家严复的著名译作《天演论》问世。这本书是在英国生物学家赫胥黎的《进化论与伦理学》的基础上完成的。"物竞天择，适者生存"的思想使处于"知识饥荒"的知识界如获至宝，当时就产生了轰动效应，并且影响了以后的几代人。

在演化博弈的分析框架中，参与人是适应性当事人（adaptive agent）（Bowles，2004，p. 60），这种当事人的理性既不是生物进化模型中的零智力，也不是经典博弈论中的完全理性，而是依靠经验法则（rule of thumb）进行决策的程序理性（procedural rationality）（亨德里克斯，2007，p. 17）。演化博弈分析关注的焦点不是**个体**（individual），而是**种群体**（population）的行为规则（Bowles，2004，p. 60）。从演化博弈的角度来看，建筑交易体制是不同策略之间的演化适应性（evolutionary adaptation）的均衡结果。

演化稳定策略（ESS，evolutionarily stable strategy）和**复制者动态**（replicator dynamic）是演化博弈论的两种主要分析工具。前者可以为演化稳定性提供"静态"的概念性分析（McKenzie，2009），后者可以用来解释个体的适应性（fitness），也就是后代成活率的变动情况。

10.1.1　演化稳定策略

ESS 的概念最早由英国生态学家梅纳德·史密斯和美国遗传学家普莱斯提出。他们在研究中发现，动物个体之间常常为各种资源（包括食物、栖息地和配偶等）展开竞争或合作，但竞争或合作不是杂乱无章的，而是按一定行为方式（即策略）进行的。他们在 1973 年《自然》杂志发表的《动物冲突的逻辑》一文中给出了如下定义："ESS 是这样一种策略，如果种群体的大多数成员都采取这种策略，那么，就不存在一种具有突变特征的策略，能够产生更高的生殖适应性"（Maynard Smith and Price，1973，p. 15）。换言之，如果某个种群体的所有成员都采取 ESS，它就可以抵御采取其他策略的个体的入侵。利用这一概念，梅纳德·史密斯和普莱斯解释了在同一种动物之间的"有限战争"中，本质上是自私的个体能够和平共处甚至相互合作的现象。

从本质上说，ESS 是对纳什均衡的一种扩展或改进。纳什均衡是一种策略组合

(strategy profile)——例如囚徒困境博弈中的策略组合（坦白，坦白）——其中每个参与人的策略都是对该组合中其他策略的最优反应。而 ESS 是一种策略，是对其本身的最优反应。ESS 可以是纯策略（参与人在其策略空间中选取唯一确定的策略），也可以是混合策略（参与人采取的不是唯一的策略，而是其策略空间上的一种概率分布）。ESS 虽然是一个来自生物学的概念，但是可以为人类行为提供一种有关稳定性的准则。

10.1.2 复制者动态

生物进化论用适应性的概念来描述种群体中个体的生殖能力：如果某一个体的适应性好于其他个体，那么它就具有较强的繁育后代的能力。复制者动态的概念与此相类似：种群体中高于平均支付水平的策略将被其他个体采纳，从而提高它们在种群体中的比例（Bowles，2004，p. 70）。

假设在一个无限大的种群体中，有策略 x 和策略 y，分别代表两种不同的习性。为简单起见，这里把种群体的大小规范化为 1。假设策略 x 和策略 y 在种群体中的比例（也就是出现频率）分别是 p（$0\leqslant p\leqslant 1$）和 $1-p$，个体间的两人对称博弈是随机进行的。下面的复制者动态方程可以用来描述该种群体构成比例在代际之间的变化（Taylor and Jonker，1978；Bowles，2004，p. 73）。

$$\Delta p = p' - p = p(1-p)(\pi_x - \pi_y) = p(\pi_x - \bar{\pi}) \tag{10.1}$$

式中 p 是当代种群体中采取策略 x 的比例，p' 是下一代种群体中采取策略 x 的比例；π_x 和 π_y 分别是策略 x 和策略 y 的期望支付，$\bar{\pi}=p\pi_x+(1-p)\pi_y$ 是种群体的平均期望支付。差异性（variance）$p(1-p)$ 反映了种群体的构成状况。当 $p=0$ 或 $p=1$ 时，种群体完全由一种类型的个体组成，差异性等于零；单纯的种群体发生变化的可能性最小。当 $p=1/2$ 时，种群体中两类个体平均分布，差异性取得最大值；这时种群体发生变化的可能性最大。

10.1.3 演化稳定状态

演化稳定状态（evolutionarily stable state）和演化稳定策略（ESS）是相互联系却又不同的两个概念。正如梅纳德·史密斯所说，如果一个种群体受到扰动，在扰动足够小的情况下，其遗传结构能够通过自然选择恢复原状，那么，该种群体就处于演化稳定状态（Maynard Smith，1982，p. 204）。演化稳定状态往往被作为复制者动态方程的解。

在实际应用中，稳态和静态这两个概念往往容易被混淆。这里借助力学的概念和方法，对动态、静态和稳态（其中又包括渐近稳态和中性稳态）加以比较和说明。在图 10.2 所示的四种状态中，每种状态都有一个球体和一个支撑面。不同条件会导致球体的不同状态。

（a）动态：支撑面是一个倾斜的平面，在重力和支撑力的共同作用下，球体沿着该斜面加速滚落下来。

(b) 不稳定的静态：球体处于凸面的顶端，重力和支撑力取得平衡，球体保持静止。然而，任何水平扰动都可能打破原有的平衡，使球体滚落下来。

(c) 中性稳定状态：支撑面是水平面，重力和支撑力取得平衡，球体保持静止。足够小的水平扰动可以使球体产生位移，但是在扰动消失后，球体不会进一步偏离原来的位置。

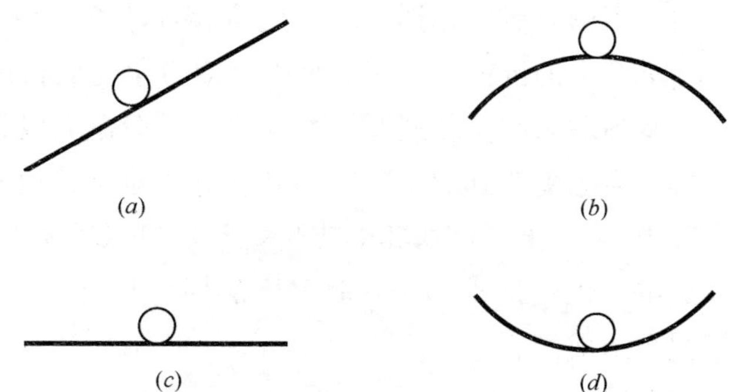

图 10.2　力学中的静态与稳态
(*a*) 动态；(*b*) 不稳定的静态；(*c*) 中性稳定状态；(*d*) 渐近稳定状态

(d) 渐近稳定状态：球体处于凹面的底部，重力和支撑力取得平衡，球体保持静止。足够小的水平扰动可以使球体产生位移，但是在扰动消失后，球体会自动恢复到原来的位置。显然，梅纳德·史密斯所说的演化稳定状态是渐进的稳定状态。

在演化博弈的语境中，静态是指种群体的构成比例（各种策略出现的频率）不随时间变化而变化。对于前面所提到的例子（无限大的种群体，两种策略 x 和 y）来说，这就意味着：

(1) 在连续函数的表达方式下，有 $\mathrm{d}p/\mathrm{d}t=0$（策略 x 的频率 p 对时间 t 的变化率为 0）；

(2) 在离散函数的表达方式下，有 $\Delta p=0$ 或者 $\pi_x=\bar{\pi}$。

应该强调指出的是，这里的研究对象是演化稳定状态。稳态属于静态，而静态不一定稳定。为了实现稳定状态，除了满足静态条件之外，还要满足稳态条件。对于前面所提到的例子来说，渐近稳态要求满足 $\mathrm{d}\Delta p/\mathrm{d}p<0$（$\Delta p$ 对 p 的变化率为负数，负反馈效应）——种群体的构成比例在受到足够小的扰动时会发生相应的变化，但是在扰动消失后会恢复到原来的状态；而中性稳态要求满足 $\mathrm{d}\Delta p/\mathrm{d}p=0$（$\Delta p$ 对 p 的变化率为 0）——种群体的构成比例在受到足够小的扰动时会发生相应的变化，但是在扰动消失后变化随即停止。

为了加深对演化稳定状态和 ESS 的理解，下面以鹰鸽博弈为例做具体的分析和解释。假设在一个无限大的种群体中，存在两种策略：H（Hawk，老鹰）与 D（Dove，鸽子）。老鹰所占比例是 p（$0\leqslant p\leqslant 1$）。如果所要分配的价值是 v，并且假设个体间的两人对称博弈❶是随机进行的，那么在种群体中将会发生以下三种情况：

❶ 在对称博弈中，一个参与人的支付矩阵是另一个参与人的支付矩阵的转置；这表明参与人是同质的。用一个参与人（比如说行参与人）的支付矩阵来表示对称博弈，是一种简洁的做法。

（1）当两只老鹰相遇时，它们会相互争夺。由于两者势均力敌，因此各有机会得到（$v-c$）/2的价值，其中c是因为双方争斗而付出的成本。

（2）当两只鸽子相遇时，两者会平均分配，各得到$v/2$的价值。

（3）当老鹰遇到鸽子时，前者会夺走全部价值v，后者的收益为0。

表10.1给出了该博弈的支付矩阵。可以证明，当所要分配的价值小于老鹰之间的争斗成本，也就是$v-c<0$时，鹰鸽博弈具有唯一的混合策略均衡；种群体由老鹰和鸽子混合组成。

鹰鸽博弈（行参与人的支付矩阵） **表10.1**

	H（鹰）	D（鸽）
H（鹰）	$(v-c)/2$，$(v-c)/2$	v，0
D（鸽）	0，v	$v/2$，$v/2$

（资料来源：Bowles，2004，p.79）

图10.3给出了行参与人的期望支付。策略H的期望支付曲线π_H和策略D的期望支付曲线π_D在$p=p^*$处相交。这个博弈有三个静态点：$p=0$、$p=1$和$p=p^*$。其中只有第三个静态点是稳定的，这是因为在前两个静态点，微小的扰动能够引发更大的偏离（正反馈效应，$d\Delta p/dp>0$），而在第三个静态点，负反馈效应（$d\Delta p/dp<0$）能够纠正微小扰动引发的偏离。

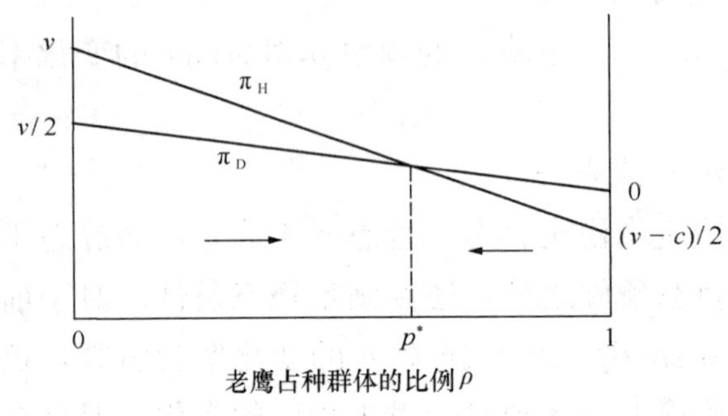

图10.3 鹰鸽博弈中行参与人的期望支付

（1）在$p=0$处，种群体的成员全部为鸽子。如果发生微小的扰动，会产生少量的老鹰。接下来，由于老鹰的期望支付大于鸽子的期望支付（π_H在π_D之上），老鹰在种群体中的比例p还会继续增加，一直到$p=p^*$，也就是$\pi_H=\pi_D$为止。图10.3中指向右方的箭头→反映了这种变化趋势。

（2）在$p=1$处，种群体的成员全部为老鹰。如果发生微小的扰动，会产生少量的鸽子。接下来，由于此时老鹰的期望支付小于鸽子的期望支付（π_H在π_D之下），鸽子在种群体中的比例还会继续增加，一直到$p=p^*$，也就是$\pi_H=\pi_D$为止。图10.3中指向左方的箭头←反映了这种变化趋势。

（3）在$p=p^*$处，种群体中老鹰所占比例为p^*，鸽子所占比例为$1-p^*$，如果发生微小的扰动，负反馈效应能够纠正微小扰动引发的偏离。图10.3中的两个箭头可以清楚地表明这种负反馈效应。尽管当$p=0$（全部是鸽子）时，平均支付将达到最大。但是，整个种群体由老鹰和鸽子混合组成，老鹰所占比例稳定在$p=p^*$。显然，这是一种演化稳定状态，相应的策略（种群体中采取老鹰策略的比例为p^*，采取鸽子策略

的比例为 $1-p^{*}$）是混合的演化稳定策略（ESS）。

10.2　建筑交易体制内生化

在现有的相关研究中，建筑交易体制多半是外生给定的。研究重点是建设项目的利益相关者在给定的建筑交易体制下的动态平衡关系。正如 Winch（2010，p. 21）所说："……游戏规则对体制内的行为者提供激励机制，……行为模式被制度化，它们又会通过结构化的过程反过来作用于行为者——游戏规则于是被看作是给定的、正规的和唯一的做事方式。"正因为如此，这些研究虽然揭示出建筑交易体制在变迁过程中所表现出的多样性、路径依赖性和循环反复性，却基本停留在"知其然，不知其所以然"的程度，不能进一步回答以下问题：

- 是什么造成了建筑交易体制的多样性？
- 为什么帕累托无效的建筑交易体制会长期存在？
- 建筑交易体制最有可能实现的方式是什么？

这些问题正是这一讲要研究解决的重点所在。

为了解释建筑交易体制演化过程的来龙去脉，需要将其内生化，也就是说，不把它看作是外生给定的参数，而是把它作为内生变量来处理。而内生化本身，又涉及制度理论和演化理论的一些基本问题。比如，制度的性质是什么——是博弈规则还是博弈的结果？规则是人为制定的还是"自然"制定的？等等。在第3讲3.1.1节（两种不同的制度观）中，对制度和博弈的关系问题已经有所讨论，因此，这里只是从制度演化的角度出发，对相关理论进行简要的梳理。

如前所述，以科斯和威廉姆森为代表的新（new）制度经济学（新古典学派）和以加尔布雷思为代表的"新"（neo-）制度经济学（演化学派）具有不同的制度观、方法论和价值判断。前者适用于制度的均衡分析，后者适用于制度的演化分析。有鉴于此，青木昌彦提出了两种不同的制度观，一是"作为博弈规则的制度"，二是"作为博弈内生结果的制度"（Aoki，2001）。根据第一种观点，制度变迁的原因是外生参数发生了变化。而根据第二种观点，制度可以看作是一种自我维持的共享信念系统；之所以发生制度变迁，是因为原有的均衡被打破，系统收敛到一个新的共享信念集合（Brousseau and Raynaud，2011）。任何事物都有前因后果，制度也不例外。实际上，不少文献都是同时从原因和效果两个方面研究制度以及制度变迁的相关问题。

在认知博弈论（epistemic game theory）领域，奥曼和布兰登伯格（Aumann and Brandenburger，1995）认为，文化信念是通过重复博弈产生的共同先验（common prior），共同的文化信念可以产生稳定一致的行为信念。美国分析哲学家塞尔（Searle，1995；2005）把制度归结为集体意向性（collective intentionality）。进一步，人们既可以把集体意向性看作是基因—文化共同演化的结果（Gintis，2009）；也可以根据族群选择理论（theory of group selection），把集体意向性归因于以下事实：具有较强合作模式的种群更适于生存（Wilson，1989）。反过来看，集体意向性本身又可以产生强制性的价值观和力量，如义务、责任和权利等。因此，有的作者把集体意向性称之为“族群脑”（group mind）（Aoki，2010）。

根据位势博弈理论（potential game theory），社会规范一方面可以看作是社会经济领域重复博弈的内生结果；另一方面可以引导理性的个体有效地协调信念，保持一致，形成所谓的“社会脑”（social brain）。社会规范一旦形成，当事人就可能将它作为一种“缺省策略”（default strategy）——人们在决策时会下意识地遵守某种社会规范，因此不用，实际上也不必老是精心考虑支付矩阵的内容及其对于利益最大化的影响（Yamagishi *et al.*，2008；Aoki，2010）。

威廉姆森提出的制度的层次结构包括内嵌性制度、基本制度环境、治理制度和短期的资源配置等四个层次（Williamson，2000）。建筑交易体制属于第二个层次，也就是基本制度环境的范畴。在将建筑交易体制内生化时，需要考虑三方面的因素。

首先是制度和博弈的关系问题。根据研究的目的，建筑交易体制可以从两方面来研究：既可以把它看作是外生给定的博弈规则，进而考察这些规则在实际中所发挥的作用以及产生的后果（后面的10.4节中列举的比较研究正是这么做的）；也可以把它看作是博弈的内生结果，并在此基础上探究建筑交易体制是如何产生的，又是如何发展变化的。由于这里所要研究的是制度的演进规律，因此应该把建筑交易体制看作是博弈的内生结果。此外，由于制度的演化在本质上是一种没有补偿，因而也没有一致意见的分散决策过程（Brousseau and Raynaud，2011），因此应该从“新”（neo-）制度经济学（演化学派）的角度出发，把建筑交易体制抽象为“当事人的未经协调的、带有偶然性的行动后果”（Bowles，2004，p. 57）。

其次是研究对象的问题。研究对象可以是个体，也可以是种群体。经典的非合作博弈的研究对象是贝叶斯理性的个体；研究重点是个体理性和个体的最优决策。由于这里所要研究的是制度的演进规律，因此需要从种群体而不是个体的角度来研究。应该看到，对个体的研究正是为了对总体的理解和把握。以失业问题为例，较之对某一个人的失业状况的研究，对全社会失业率的研究要重要得多（Bowles，2004，p. 58）。

最后是时间尺度的问题。研究尺度不仅涉及度量单位之间的换算，而且会影响到研究结果。以海岸线长度的测量为例，用一毫米长的尺子和十公里长的尺子作为测量单位，前者测得的数值要比后者大得多。因此，测量海岸线要用千米而不能用纳米做单位，测量物质的微观结构则正好相反（殷雅俊，2010）。与此相类似，在制度分析中也要十分重视制度的时间尺度问题。不同性质的制度需要采用不同的分析方法。由于这里所要研究的是基本制度环境的演化规律，因此应该采用较长的时间尺度——像威廉姆森所说的那样，在十年甚至百年的时间框架内考察建筑交易体制的变迁。

综合考虑以上因素，接下来的研究工作把建筑交易体制看作是当事人的未经协调的、带有偶然性的行动后果，并且在较长的时间框架内，从种群体的角度研究它的演化过程。

10.3　建筑交易体制变迁的贪婪者—分享者—中庸者博弈模型[1]

首先简要介绍已有的两个演化博弈模型，这是因为，后面将要建立的贪婪者—分享者—中庸者博弈模型是在这两个模型的基础上建立起来的。一是鹰—鸽—中庸者博弈模型，它是在经典的鹰鸽博弈中引入中庸者策略后形成的。在这个博弈中，中庸者策略是唯一的 ESS。由于中庸者策略的引入可以减少争斗性交往的次数，种群体的平均支付水平有所提高（Maynard Smith，1982，pp. 22—23）。二是掠夺者—分享者—惩罚者博弈模型，它被用来模拟人类历史上的第一次社会变革——从原始共产主义到奴隶社会——的演化过程。这个博弈有两种稳态均衡，其中一种是渐近稳定的点，另一种是中性稳定的线段（包含无数个点）（Bowles，2004，pp. 282—288）。下面对这二个模型进行改造和组合，并且根据建设项目和建筑市场的特点设置支付矩阵的内容，建立一个新的博弈模型。

10.3.1　构建模型

考虑一个种群体，其成员以从事建设项目为生。为简单起见，这里把种群体的大小规范化为 1，并假设成员之间的博弈是对称的。考虑到建设项目的复杂性，假设任何个体都不能单独完成项目的建设工作，因而不能从中获利。只有通过两个成员的合作，才能完成项目，从而得到 1 个单位的剩余。种群体的成员在建筑市场中随机游走，任何两个成员相遇时，他们可以根据各自的报价情况，决定是否合作。达成合作的前提条件是：两个成员对项目剩余的分配份额的报价之和不能超过 1。

这里的模型叫做贪婪者—分享者—中庸者博弈模型，是因为我们假设种群体中存在三种策略：G（grabbing，贪婪）、S（sharing，分享）和 B（bourgeois，中庸）。表 10.2 给出了该博弈中的行参与人的支付矩阵。下面对各种情况下的支付做一简要说明。

[1] 这一节的内容主要来自发表在 The Engineering Project Organization Journal 杂志的文章（Sha and Hua，2013）。为简单起见，这里省略了部分数学推导过程。感兴趣的读者可参考英文原文或《建设项目治理》一书（沙凯逊，2013）中的相关内容。

贪婪者—分享者—中庸者博弈（行参与人的支付矩阵）　　表 10.2

	G（贪婪者）	S（分享者）	B（中庸者）
G（贪婪者）	0	z	$z/2$
S（分享者）	$1-z$	1/2	$(3-2z)/4$
B（中庸者）	$(1-z)/2$	$(1+2z)/4$	1/2

顾名思义，贪婪者的报价 z 会超过 1/2，即 $1/2 < z < 1$。当两个贪婪者相遇，由于他们的报价之和超出了项目剩余，因此不可能达成合作协议，结果是两人的支付均为 0。当贪婪者遇到分享者时，假设后者可以接受前者的报价，贪婪者和分享者的支付分别是 z 和 $1-z$。当两个分享者相遇时，他们会平均分配项目剩余，两人的支付都是 1/2。

假设中庸者采取的是双重策略：如果是处于“在位”（先到）状态，采取贪婪策略 G；如果处于“进入”（后到）状态，则采取分享策略 S。例如，当中庸者遇到贪婪者时，中庸者会有一半的机会处于“在位”（先到）状态，他将采取贪婪策略 G，结果导致两人的支付均为 0。而在另一半时间里，中庸者处于“进入”（后到）状态，他将采取分享策略 S，向贪婪者让步，得到 $1-z$ 的支付。综合考虑这两种情况，中庸者遇到贪婪者时，中庸者的期望支付是 $(1-z)/2$；贪婪者的期望支付是 $z/2$。同样可以算出，当中庸者遇到分享者时，中庸者的期望支付是 $(1+2z)/4$；分享者的期望支付是 $(3-2z)/4$。

假设当两个中庸者相遇时，总有一个参与人处于“在位”（先到）状态，而另一参与人处于“进入”（后到）状态。第一个中庸者有一半的机会处于“在位”（先到）状态，他将采取贪婪策略 G；他所面对的是处于“进入”（后到）状态、采取分享策略 S 的中庸者，这时他的支付是 z。再来考虑另一半时间，这时第一个中庸者处于“进入”（后到）状态，他将采取分享策略 S；他所面对的是处于“在位”（先到）状态、采取贪婪策略 G 的中庸者，这时他的支付是 $1-z$。综合考虑这两种情况，两个中庸者相遇时的期望支付是 1/2。

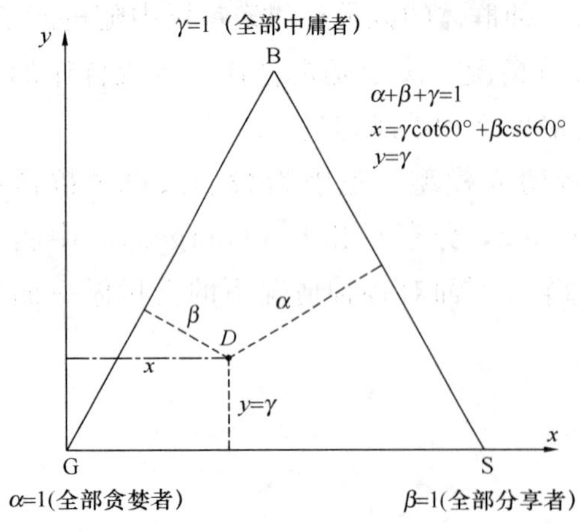

图 10.4　策略分布的状态空间：单纯形与直角坐标系

令 α、β 和 γ 分别代表贪婪者、分享者和中庸者在种群体中的比例。图 10.4 给出的单纯形可以表示三种策略分布的状态空间。单纯形的高为 1，在三个顶点处，种群体是完全同质的（所有个体都采取同样的策略）。D 是单纯形中的任意一点，从 D 点到三个边的垂直距离 α、β 和 γ 分别是相应策略的比例。由单纯形的性质容易得到 $\alpha+\beta+\gamma=1$。在随后的计算中涉及直角坐标系。以G点为原点的直角坐标系和单纯形之间存在以下的换算关系：$x=\gamma\cot 60°+\beta\csc 60°$ 和 $y=\gamma$。

给定博弈的支付矩阵（表10.2）和三种策略的比例α、β和γ，容易计算出贪婪者、分享者和中庸者的期望支付π^G、π^S和π^B以及种群体的平均支付$\bar{\pi}$。它们都是贪婪者报价z的函数。

10.3.2 确定静态点

在这个三人博弈中，静态点需要同时满足三种策略的静态条件，即$\Delta\alpha=\Delta\beta=\Delta\gamma=0$（策略比例不随时间的变化而变化，也就是对时间的变化率为0）。根据式（10.1），也就是复制者动态方程，可以求得三种策略的静态条件。图10.5给出了两种参数条件下的复制者动态。其中图10.5(*a*)中的贪婪者报价$z=0.65$，图10.5(*b*)中的$z=0.9$。通过计算可得到六条静态线，其中三条是单纯形的三个边（GB、BS和SG），另外三条是用MathCAD软件画出的曲线（$\Delta\alpha=0$、$\Delta\beta=0$和$\Delta\gamma=0$）。它们把单纯形划分为四个区域。单纯形内某一点处的三个箭头表示三种策略在该点处的动态特性。在每一条静态曲线的两侧，与这条静态曲线相应的策略比例表现出相反的变化趋势（负反馈）。例如，在图10.5(*a*)中，在静态曲线$\Delta\alpha=0$的左侧（区域Ⅰ、Ⅱ、Ⅳ），贪婪者的比例α是递减的（箭头垂直指向BS）；而在静态线$\Delta\alpha=0$的右侧（区域Ⅲ），α是递增的（箭头垂直背向BS）。

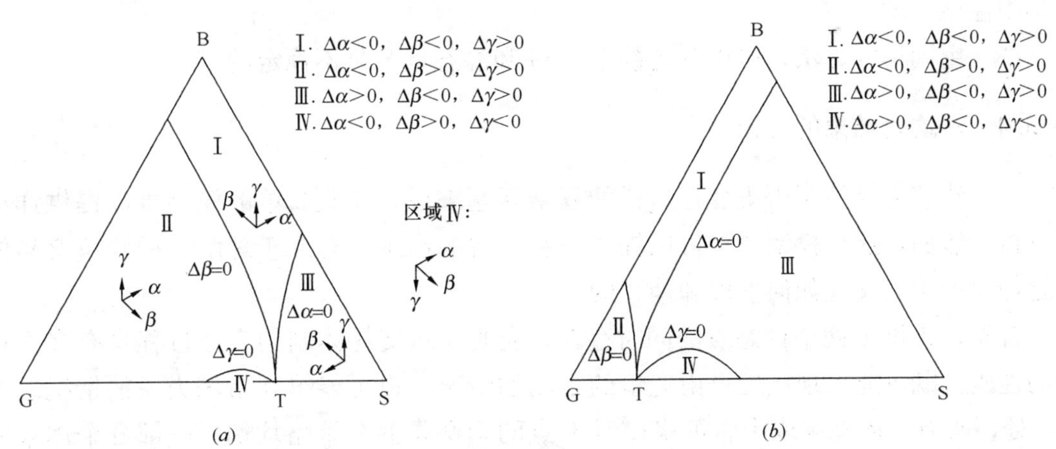

图10.5 贪婪者—分享者—中庸者博弈的复制者动态

（*a*）$z=0.65$；（*b*）$z=0.9$

于是可以得到四个静态点。显然，三个顶点G、S和B都是静态点。这是因为，在这三个点，种群体完全由一种类型的个体组成，差异性等于零；如果没有外界的扰动，种群体结构不会随时间的变化而变化。此外，三条静态曲线$\Delta\alpha=0$、$\Delta\beta=0$和$\Delta\gamma=0$的交点T也是静态点。MathCAD软件的计算结果表明，在T点处，三种策略的比例分别是$\alpha=2z-1$，$\beta=2(1-z)$和$\gamma=0$。

通过比较图 10.5(a)和图 10.5(b)容易看出，参数 z（贪婪者的报价）对静态曲线的分布，进而对静态点 T 的位置有较大影响：贪婪者的报价越高，静态点 T 离顶点 G（全部贪婪者）越近。此外，区域Ⅳ的位置也随参数 z 的变化而变化。在图 10.5(a)中，$z=0.65$，区域Ⅳ位于静态点 T 的左侧；而在图 10.5(b)中，$z=0.9$，区域Ⅳ位于静态点 T 的右侧。

10.3.3 检验静态点的稳定性

如前所述，对于给定种群体的某一策略比例 p（$0\leqslant p\leqslant 1$），实现渐近稳态的条件是 $\mathrm{d}\Delta p/\mathrm{d}p<0$。这个条件可以保证任何足够小的扰动不会使种群体的构成比例偏离原来的状态。对于贪婪者—分享者—中庸者博弈来说，渐近稳态要求同时满足以下三个条件：

$$\mathrm{d}\Delta\alpha/\mathrm{d}\alpha<0,\ \mathrm{d}\Delta\beta/\mathrm{d}\beta<0 \text{ 和 } \mathrm{d}\Delta\gamma/\mathrm{d}\gamma<0。$$

根据这三个条件，就可以对四个静态点 G、S、B 和 T 的稳定性进行判断和检验。

（1）在静态点 B 处，三种策略的比例分别是 $\gamma=1$ 和 $\alpha=\beta=0$，根据 MathCAD 软件的计算结果，我们有 $\mathrm{d}\Delta\alpha/\mathrm{d}\alpha<0$，$\mathrm{d}\Delta\beta/\mathrm{d}\beta<0$ 和 $\mathrm{d}\Delta\gamma/\mathrm{d}\gamma<0$，于是可以断定静态点 B 是渐近稳定的。

（2）在静态点 T 处，三种策略的比例分别是 $\alpha=2z-1$，$\beta=2(1-z)$ 和 $\gamma=0$，根据 MathCAD 软件的计算结果，我们有 $\mathrm{d}\Delta\alpha/\mathrm{d}\alpha<0$，$\mathrm{d}\Delta\beta/\mathrm{d}\beta<0$，和 $\mathrm{d}\Delta\gamma/\mathrm{d}\gamma=0$，于是可以断定静态点 T 对于贪婪者和分享者策略来说是渐近稳定的，而对于中庸者策略来说是中性稳定的。

（3）用同样的方法，可以判定静态点 G 和静态点 S 是不稳定的。

10.3.4 对均衡结果的讨论

对于建筑交易体制历史变迁这样的复杂问题来说，如此简单的模型难以提供详尽的分析。然而，这个模型毕竟可以提供一些有益的启示，有助于理解一种建筑交易体制是如何产生，又是如何发展和消亡的。

首先，B 和 T 两个稳态点的同时存在，表明建筑交易体制的变迁过程具有多重均衡的性质：既可能出现接近自由竞争的市场的情况，也可能出现市场失灵的情况。在 B 点处，所有个体都采取中庸策略；而 T 点的均衡是混合策略均衡——部分个体采取贪婪者策略，部分个体采取分享者策略。图 10.6 给出了平均支付水平的等值线。从中可以看出：

（1）单纯形的侧边 BS（没有贪婪者）和等值线重合，平均支付 $\bar{\pi}=0.5$，取得最大值。

（2）在 G 点处（全部贪婪者），平均支付 $\bar{\pi}=0$，取得最小值。

（3）其余的等值线都是曲线；平均支付 $0<\bar{\pi}<1$，在最大值和最小值之间。

如果说，S 点的均衡反映了自由竞争的市场条件，那么，B 点的均衡可以看作是一种“准市场”的状态[1]。T 点的均衡结果则有所不同。在 T 点处，平均支付 $\bar{\pi}=2z(1-z)<0.5$，它反映的是市场失灵的情况：激励不足导致较低的平均支付水平。这是一种帕累托无效的结果，除非出现某些“革命性”事件（即生物进化中的变异），否则，这种状态会长期存在。

其次，下面的分析可以说明，建筑交易体制的变迁过程是路径依赖的，并且对初始条件具有很强的敏感性。既然稳态点的数量不止一个，于是就会产生下面的问题：哪一个均衡状态出现的可能性更大？在不考虑非最优反应（non-best response）[2] 的情况下，对于这个问题的答案只能是：均衡结果取决于初始条件。如图 10.5 所示，单纯形内某一点处的箭头表示相应的策略在该点处的变化趋势。在没有非最优反应的情况下，种群体是在 B 点还是在 T 点实现稳定均衡，这取决于系统的初始状态。例如，如果初始状态是在单纯形的底边 GS，我们就可以预料到，系统将在 T 点实现均衡。如果初始状态是在单纯形的左侧边 GB 或右侧边 BS，可以预料到的均衡结果是 B 点。由于系统的动态演化过程十分复杂，数学解析的方法往往无能为力，可以通过动态模拟的方法来确定系统的均衡结果。“相对支付和”（relative payoff sum，RPS）的学习规则（Maynard Smith，1982，pp. 60—67）和基于智能体（agent-based）的方法（Bowles，2004，pp. 392—399）可以用来模拟系统的演化过程。在问题不是十分复杂的情况下，定性分析的方法也不失为一种简单有效的解决方案。根据以下两个理由，我们可以直观地判断，在多数情况下，建筑交易体制在 B 点而不是 T 点处实现均衡。

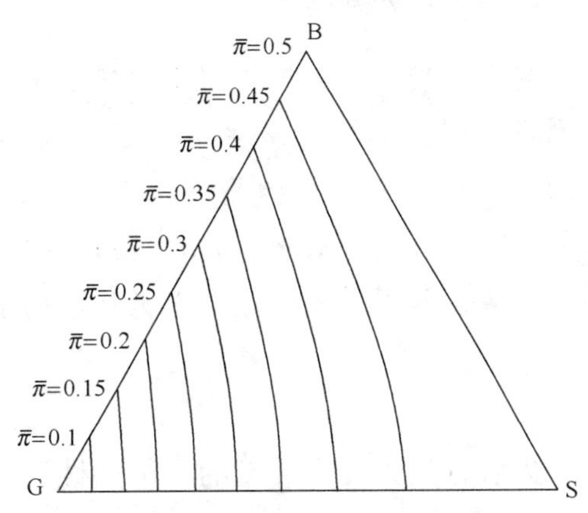

图 10.6　贪婪者—分享者—中庸者博弈平均支付水平的分布情况

（1）如图 10.5(a) 所示，在区域Ⅰ、区域Ⅱ和区域Ⅲ，中庸者的比例是递增的（箭头垂直背向底边）；只有在区域Ⅳ，是递减的（箭头垂直指向底边），而区域Ⅳ的面积要远远小于其他三个区域面积之和。因此，系统在底边实现均衡的机会较小，而 T 点正是落在底边之上。

---

[1] 策略 S 是无条件的分享——不管是“在位”还是“进入”，参与人都采取分享策略，而策略 B 是有条件的分享——如果“在位”，采取贪婪策略，如果“进入”，则采取分享策略。

[2] 所谓非最优反应，是指现有的博弈模型中没有明确考虑到的行动，也就是不按既有规则行事的情况。这些行动往往由处于不利地位的团体成员所发动。这种有意而非偶然的“革命性”事件，在制度变迁中具有重要的作用。例如，20 世纪早期，种族隔离制度在南非劳动力市场中形成了一种习俗。在这种习俗的支配下，白人雇主的最优反应是对黑人支付很少的工资；而黑人的最优反应是以低价提供劳动力。但是，从 20 世纪 70 年代开始，一些黑人不顾种族主义的高压，开始罢工。在 80 年代之后，参加罢工的黑人越来越多。黑人的非最优反应的行为最终改变了雇主的最优反应行为。不到十年的时间，整个种族隔离制度就分崩离析了（Bowles，2004，p. 371—372）。

（2）如前所述，在B点处，三种策略都是渐近稳定的；而在T点处，对于贪婪者和分享者来说是渐近稳定的，而对于中庸者来说是中性稳定的。因此，B点比T点具有更强的稳定性。实际上，现实社会中的许多现象可以印证上述论断。

背景资料：世界各地普遍采用的五五分成制（资料来源：Bowles，2004）

有研究表明，无论在印度的贫困地区西孟加拉州，还是在农业高度现代化的美国伊利诺伊州，佃户与地主之间五五分成的契约都是普遍采用的制度安排（Bowles，2004，p. 70）。有意思的是，在意大利语、法语和古梵语中，分成租佃这个词分别是*mezzadria*，*metayage*和*ardhika*，它们都有“二一添作五”的意思（Bowles，2004，p. 200）。这些例子表明，在人类社会的发展历程中，分享者策略是一种被广泛接受的生存策略。

最后，如果没有突发的“革命性”事件的发生，稳定均衡状态一旦形成就很难改变。“革命性”事件包括两种类型。一类是前面所说的非最优反应：系统中如果出现大量不按现有规则行事的个体，就会导致“革命”的发生。另一类则是现有体制的社会环境或文化基础发生的变化。这些外生的事件会带来两种结果：一是不同制度之间的竞争，例如社会主义与资本主义之间的较量。二是技术进步，例如蒸汽机技术、电气化和机械化，以及新时期发生的信息革命等。把这些“革命性”的因素引入博弈模型，就意味着支付矩阵的改变，这将打破原有的均衡，进而产生新的均衡结果。

10.3.5 小结

从不同的学派出发，建筑交易体制既可以看作是建筑市场中不同利益主体之间进行博弈的一整套规则，又可以看作是博弈的内生结果，是与工程质量低劣和腐败现象长期斗争的产物（沙凯逊、邓晓红，2001）。为了研究建筑交易体制的演化规律，我们将建筑交易体制内生化为建筑市场中各种参与人之间长期的、未经协调的、带有偶然性的行动后果。贪婪者—分享者—惩罚者模型是在高度抽象的基础上建立起来的，因而不可能详尽地说明问题。尽管如此，该模型还是有助于我们了解建筑交易体制演化的一些基本规律。

多重均衡和路径依赖可以用来解释建筑交易体制的多样性。建筑交易体制的多样性本身又意味着帕累托无效结果长期存在的可能性。每一种建筑交易体制，无论它是“好的”还是“坏的”，都有其存在的理由。在现实中，没有“最优的”，只有“最合适的”建筑交易体制。世界上的事物千差万别，因此，在借鉴国外经验时，不能采取削足适履的态度。

有意栽花花不开，无心插柳柳成荫。建筑交易体制的变革总是在“不经意”间发生，而那些精心策划的变革方案却往往难以实现。在建筑交易体制的变迁过程中，社会变革、战争和灾难等“革命性”事件往往发挥了十分重要的作用。例如，1666 年的伦敦大火使得雷恩（C. Wren）和霍克斯穆尔（N. Hawksmoor）等建筑师有机会去设计圣保罗大教堂这样宏伟壮丽的建筑，也促使英国制定了第一批建筑法规（Loosemore，2000）。再比如，美国基础设施建设的项目采购方式的三阶段变迁，就是以 20 世纪 30 年代的经济大萧条和第二次世界大战作为转折点（Piteroforte and Miller，2002）。然而，某一事件的“重大历史性”不可能仅仅由事件发生时那个偶然的、单独的日子所决定。历史性的事件是由事件背后长期的历史所决定的；既有赖于我们对其前因的追索，也有待于其后果在我们的对应行为中进一步展开（舒迟，2001）。

10.4　对建筑交易体制的比较研究

新旧世纪交替之际，建筑交易体制的比较研究成为一个受到普遍关注的问题。由于各国建筑业的内在矛盾以及世界经济全球化的外在压力，世界各国的建筑交易制度都发生了并正在发生重大变革。许多国家都从制度变迁的角度回顾和总结了本国建筑业发展的历史经验，并对新世纪的行业发展、制度建设等问题进行了广泛的讨论。在这种背景下，*Building Research and Information*（BRI）分别于 2000 年和 2002 年出了两期专刊。2000 年专刊的主题是“欧盟的建筑交易体制”（Construction Business System in European Union），介绍了欧盟五国建筑交易体制的历史沿革、各自的特点和最近几年所发生的变革（Winch，2000b，Campagnac，2000，Syben，2000，Brener and Kok，2000，Bologna and Nord，2000）。2002 年专刊的主题是“全球的建筑交易体制”（Global Construction Business System），其视野从欧洲扩展到全球，涉及美国（Pietroforte and Miller，2002）、日本（Reeves，2002）、新加坡（Dulaimi *et al.*，2002；Ofori，2002）、南非（Rwelamila，2002）和瑞典（Bröchner *et al.*，2002）等国家。

10.4.1　从欧盟五国看建筑交易体制的多样性[1]

欧洲是世界上最早形成建筑交易体制的地方。在这里，建筑交易体制的多样性得到了充分的体现。如表 10.3 所示，仅在欧盟，就存在三种类型的建筑交易体制：以英国为代表的盎格鲁—撒克逊型（Anglo—Saxon type），以德国和荷兰为代表的社团主义型（corporatist type）[2] 和以法国和意大利为代表的国家型（state type）。

---

[1] 这一节的内容主要来自发表在《建筑经济》杂志上的文章（沙凯逊，邓晓红，2001）。

[2] 社团主义（corporatism）又称为统合主义，在历史上是一种政治体制。在这种体制里，立法的权力交给了由工业、农业和职业团体所派出的代表。这些代表与一般的商业公司或法人组织并不相同。在多元制度里，众多团体必须经过民主竞争的过程才能取得权力，而在社团主义制度里，许多未经过选举的组织实体掌控了决策的过程。社团主义模式是不同于官僚模式和市场模式的另一种利益调整模式。该模式强调社会组织和团体的特定地位和作用。在议会的代表渠道之外，通过有组织的社团（如雇主联盟、同业公会、工会和职业团体等）取得正式资格而参与社会经济决策。

欧盟建筑交易体制的三种类型　　表 10.3

	盎格鲁—撒克逊型	社团主义型	国家型
代表国家	英国	德国、荷兰	法国、意大利
法律体系	不成文法	成文法	成文法
自由市场价值观	强	中等	弱
政府的调控作用	弱	中等	强
主要融资渠道	股市	银行	政府
对工人的保护	弱	强	强

尽管这些国家在地理位置、基本社会制度和生产力发展水平等方面都相近，但是，它们的建筑交易体制却存在较大差异。比如，在劳动力市场方面，单独的劳务承包方式在英国是合法的，而在德国和法国是非法的。因此，在英国，约有 45%的施工任务都是采用劳务承包方式完成的，而德国和法国的建筑企业不得不长期雇用大量的操作工人。又如，在法国和荷兰，城市规划具有法律效力，行政部门不得拒绝根据城市规划提出的建设项目申请；而在英国，对城市规划的解释和执行就有较大灵活性，在必要时甚至可以废止局部的城市规划。再如，申报建设项目时，法国的要求比较简单；而英国要求提供十分详细的资料。因此，完成大型基础设施建设项目的申报工作在法国平均需要 5 年，而在英国则需要 20 年的时间。此外，有关建筑物的结构安全性能、建筑物能耗等方面的法规，各国之间也不尽相同（Winch，2000a）。

这些国家建筑交易体制的变革不仅在内容上，而且在方向上都存在着差异。英国的变革重点在于推行公共项目的特许经营、私人融资和合伙制。法国和德国的变革使建筑企业，特别是大型建筑企业在决策链中的位置前移，在建筑市场中的作用得到增强。意大利则强调设计与施工的相互分离，致使建筑企业无法过多地介入建设项目的设计工作。荷兰变革的原因主要是来自欧盟的外部压力，建筑市场中的竞争仍在社团主义的框架中进行。

10.4.1.1　英国：从专业体制到合伙制与私人融资

英国是世界上最早采用总承包方式的国家。由于专业人士及其组织在传统的英国建筑市场中发挥着举足轻重的作用，所以这种体制被认为是一种专业体制（professional system)。建筑专业体制明确规定了建筑市场中各种参与人的权利、义务和责任，因而可以有效地保证工程质量。但是，这种制度在实践中也暴露出交易费用高、效率低下的弊端。它过分强调市场参与各方之间的对手关系，往往形成相互推卸责任而不是共担风险的局面。例如，设计方不仅要承担本身的设计责任，还要考虑承包商在施工中的机会主义行为倾向，往往造成过度设计。

英国建筑交易体制变革的重点是实行合伙制（partnering）与私人融资计划（PFI，

Private Finance Initiative)。合伙制可以有效地降低交易费用，例如，希斯罗快速铁路项目由于采用了合伙制，工料测量师的数目就比传统方式减少了一半。合伙制的实施不仅改善了建设项目参与各方的关系，还带来组织结构的变化。国防部的两个项目采用了合伙制，在组织设计时就改变了传统的做法，没有按照工作性质（即块块），而是按照施工工艺（即条条）进行组织设计。例如，负责建筑物立面的设计师和负责立面施工的承包商组合在一起，而不是和负责地基基础的设计师在一起工作。合伙制可分为单项目合伙制（single project partnering）和多项目合伙制（multi-project partnering)。显然，后一种方式的合作期限更长，合作关系更为紧密。

公共项目的特许经营（concession）被认为是 200 年来英国建筑业最具根本性的变革。特许经营是私人融资的一种形式，也可以看作合伙制的一种延伸。特许经营在法国已有 300 年的历史，而英国则是在英吉利海峡隧道工程中才首次采用这种方式。1994 年“设计—建设—融资—经营”（DBFO，Design Build Finance Operate）方法开始在公路建设项目中使用；1996 年公私合伙制计划公司（Public Private Partnership Program Ltd.，又叫 4P 公司）的成立，加快了 PFI 在地方政府建设项目中的普及。这些方法可以大规模动员私人投资，同时把设计、施工、经营、维护等各方面组合成为一个有机整体，最终取得缩短工期、减少交易费用的效果。到 21 世纪初，英国的许多公共交通、医院、学校、监狱等公共建设项目均采取 PFI 方式，私人融资量已达到 68.85 亿英镑（Winch，2000b)。

10.4.1.2　法国：专业人士与建筑企业之间的利益平衡

法国建筑交易体制的变革可以归因于 20 世纪 80 年代初的经济衰退。从 1981 至 1991 的十年间，法国的大型建筑企业在建筑市场中的作用显著增强，除了原来的施工领域之外，它们不仅涉足建设项目的规划、设计和物业管理，而且通过特许经营方式从事交通、通讯等基础设施的开发与经营。法国的公共工程管理法（LMOP，Law on the *Maitrise d' Ouvrage Publique*）正是在这种背景下制定的。LMOP 明确规定了“设计—施工”（*conception—construction*）的承包方式，鼓励大型建筑企业参与工程项目的设计工作。与此同时，BOT 方式也在法国得到广泛应用。

建筑交易体制变革所引发的有关各方的利益冲突，集中体现在大型建筑企业与专业人士，特别是建筑师之间的争论与抗衡。以建筑师为主的专业人士对 LMOP 做出强烈反应。由于在专业人士、建筑企业和业主之间没有形成共识，1985 年 7 月制定的 LMOP 迟迟不能颁布实施。1992 年以来，法国的许多大型建筑企业在房地产危机中蒙受重大损失，开始重新思考自己的战略定位。在这种情况下，LMOP 对“设计—施工”方式的应用做出了严格限制。几经修改的 LMOP 在 1993 年 12 月才得以颁布实施。虽然专业人士与建筑企业之间的利益较量还要一直进行下去，法国的大型建筑企业通过近 20 年的变革，在建筑市场中的作用已经明显增强（Campagnac，2000)。

10.4.1.3 德国：从面向业主需求到面向过程

建筑承发包条例（VOB，*Verdingsordnung für Bauleistungen*）是德国建筑交易体制的主要文件，已有七十年的历史。根据德国法律，公款投资建设项目以及政府投资额超过一半的私人建设项目必须按照 VOB 的规则进行招投标。VOB 不仅着眼于工程的质量、成本和效益，而且强调中小型企业平等参与竞争的机会。

在传统的交易体制中，业主及其代表建筑师占据了支配性地位。建筑师不仅负责确定建设项目的规模、形式、施工工艺和建筑材料，还要编制招标文件、施工计划、初步预算以及工期进度和组织计划。除此之外，建筑师还要协助业主进行招标。而处于决策链末端的承包商只是在上述一切都确定之后，才开始介入建设工程项目。承包商在建设项目中处于从属和被动的地位，不能有效地控制和规避风险。

德国的建筑交易体制改革的动力主要来自承包商。通过变革，承包商在决策链中位置的前移。承包商在决策链中的位置越靠前，在建设项目中能够发挥的作用就越大。根据承包商在决策链中的位置，项目承包可分为总承包（*Generalunternehmer*）、承担设计任务的总承包（*Generalübernehmer*）和项目开发商（*Projektentwickler*）等不同方式。在第一种方式中，承包商在详细设计完成后介入建设项目。在第二种方式中，承包商要承担起传统方式中建筑师的作用。而在最后一种方式中，承包商的位置移到了决策链的最前端。这种“从面向业主需求到面向过程”的变革引起德国建筑业的重组并形成新的格局：在国际或全德建筑市场中，大型企业将成为主导力量；中型企业将主要占有地方建筑市场；分包商的市场将被细化为若干领域，如混凝土工程、屋面防水工程、保温隔热工程、供热工程等等（Syben，2000）。

10.4.1.4 荷兰：竞争与社团主义的结合

以大公司、大工会等利益集团为基础的社团主义在荷兰经济中一直起着主导作用。1958 年颁布的经济竞争法和 1987 年颁布的建筑业竞争法规是荷兰建筑业的价格管理体制的法律基础。成立于 1963 年的建筑业价格管理合作组织（SPO）成员之间形成的卡特尔基本上控制了荷兰的建筑市场，1996 年荷兰建筑业只有 37%的产值是通过招投标实现的。

这种做法违背了欧共体关于建立一个基于竞争的共同市场的目标。1992 年欧盟责令 SPO 废止卡特尔协议，并对其课以相当于 2250 万欧元的罚款。迫于欧盟的压力，1998 年 1 月 1 日，荷兰政府颁布了新的经济竞争法，荷兰建筑业也相应地一再修改它的价格管理法规。然而，这种改革只是停留在“竞争+社团主义”的层面，也就是说，在社团主义的基础上适当扩大竞争的程度。研究与培训基金（O&O）可以从一个侧面反映出这种改革模式及其效果。长期以来，荷兰的建筑企业对研发活动和职工培训持消极态度，企业平均用于研发的资金只占其产值的 5‰。这是因为，由单个企业开展研发活动和职业培训是有风险的，例如，由某一企业出资培训的员工往往会被另一企业高薪聘请而跳槽，于是，“搭便车者”（free rider）就占了出资培训员工的企业的便宜。在O&O的框架下，建筑企业之间达成协议，为每一个员工缴纳一定的税金作为研发与培训基金，政府对此给予法律上的肯定。这样，研发活动和职业培训的成本和风险就可以由整个行业而不是由单个企业来承担，因而有力地促进了建筑企业的研发活动和职业培训（Brener and Kok，2000）。

10.4.1.5 意大利：增加透明度和竞争

由于缺乏透明度和严格的建设程序，改革前的意大利公款投资建设项目的管理体制已经成为一种产生腐败和丑闻的温床。意大利建筑交易体制的变革从加强立法入手。意大利政府先后颁布了1994年109号法、1995年215号法和1998年415号法等三项法令，其中，后两个法令是对第一个法令的补充和完善。这些法令以增加透明度和竞争为出发点，充分考虑了欧盟的有关规定，重新规范了公款投资项目的招标问题。

为强化公款投资项目的管理，新的法令规定大型公款投资项目必须按照“可行性研究—三年计划—分年度计划”的建设程序进行，每一步都要有相应的工程概（预）算及融资措施，建设程序一旦被批准确认就不能随意变动。新法令还明确规定了工程设计的三个阶段——初步设计、技术设计和详细设计阶段。设计任务不能分包，在施工过程中不得随意改动设计内容。30万欧元以上的新建项目必须通过招标进行。

新法令的一项重要内容是强调设计与施工的分离，不仅设计过程与施工过程要分离，设计人员与施工人员也要分离。这样做的目的主要是为了增加透明度，保证建设项目严格按照规定的程序进行。根据新法令，建筑企业无法过多地介入建设项目的设计工作，这是因为“设计—施工”（*appalto—concorso*）的承包方式被严格限制在一些特殊的建设项目。法令还要求必须有业主代表（*responsabile del procedimento*）参与公款投资项目管理的全过程，业主代表一般应从政府行政管理部门的技术人员中选派（Bologna and Nord，2000）。

尽管存在上述差异，欧盟五国建筑交易体制的变革还是有许多共同之处：

• 变革都是因为国内、国际建设市场竞争格局的变化所导致。

• 变革主要集中在公共项目的范畴，这是因为欧洲建筑业的总产值大约有一半是通过政府投资项目实现的。

• 为减少交易费用，在变革中出现了一些新的趋势。一是建立高信任关系的趋势，合伙制就是这种关系的典型代表。在这种关系下，为了取得共同的长远利益，建设项目实施各方均要克服短期行为。二是交易内部化（internalizing the transaction）的趋势，突出的例子是由政府部门设置的内部设计单位（in-house design services）。

• 新的制度安排都是通过立法实现的，并最终导致建筑业的重组。

• 一个国家的变革不是孤立进行的，各国之间是相互影响、相互制约的。

10.4.2 从日本看建筑交易体制变迁的路径依赖性[1]

所谓路径依赖，就是指制度变迁的最终结果往往与初始条件及偶然因素相关。这一点在日本建筑业表现得十分明显。在21世纪初，日本共有58万家建筑承包商，其中排名前20、前60和前100位的总承包商所占市场份额分别为16.3%、23.8%和26.9%。显然，超级总承包商在建筑市场中占据了支配地位。总承包商很少直接从事施工活动，施工任务几乎全部由分包商完成，总承包商委派项目经理对分包商进行管理。

在日本，总承包商的起源可以追溯到17世纪德川幕府时期。随着封建贵族大兴土木，行会体制初步形成，总承包商处在行会体制结构的最上层。明治维新之后的现代化进程推动了建筑业的发展，总承包商凭借其组织和管理方面的优势以及与政府官员之间的密切关系，进一步增强了在建筑业的地位。日本的传统文化强调人与人之间的长期合作。受传统观念和习惯的影响，多数分包商在与总承包商的博弈中选择了合作。分包商十分注重保持并发展与总承包商的长期业务联系。从整体上看，分包商在历史上一直处于从属地位。在调查中，有91.5%的专业分包商愿意和某一个总承包商保持长期稳定的合作关系。由专业分包商组成的“协力会”（*nakama*）是总承包商和分包商之间的联系纽带。大多数分包商都是“协力会”的成员；每个总承包商都有与自己长期合作的“协力会”。技术含量越低，专业分包商对总承包商的依赖程度越高。调查表明，81.7%的总承包商在脚手架工程中使用自己“协力会”的成员。而在钢结构工程中，这个比例只有26.4%。

在日本，私人项目和公共项目有不同的管理办法。私人项目主要采用总价包干（lump-sum）的合同形式，这种契约关系的基础是业主、总承包商和分包商之间在长期合作中形成的信任关系。根据公共会计法，公共项目必须进行选择性招标（selective tender），即邀请招标。公共项目交易体制的特点是：

• 根据官方价格指数确定的最高限价（ceiling price）。招投标过程中不对承包商的素质和技术能力等因素进行评估。承包商是否中标，完全取决于投标价格。

• 过大的甲方权力。这是导致行贿受贿、私下交易等腐败现象的重要原因。

• 有利于超级总承包商的资质等级制度。根据1949年颁布的建筑交易法，承包商分为五个资质等级。承包商的规模越大、年营业额越高，资质等级就越高，就越容易在大项目的竞争中取胜。

• 设计与施工相分离。

• 对新技术的限制条款。为防止个别承包商垄断建筑市场，在没有五家以上承包商同时提出使用的情况下，不允许某一个承包商在投标时独自提出使用某一项新技术

[1] 这一节的内容主要来自发表在《建筑经济》杂志上的文章（沙凯逊等，2003）

或新工艺。

• 严重的地方保护。鹿儿岛隧道的盾构工程是一个典型案例。这项总长度仅为 773 米的工程在地方官员的干预下被肢解为 11 段，有 19 家承包商参加竞标。最后，当地的 11 家承包商瓜分了这项工程，再转手分包给一家专业公司，形成 11 个总承包商对一个分包商的“倒挂分包”（upper subcontracting）。这种现象在公共项目中并不少见，比如，从事路面铺砌的大公司年营业额中的 40％—70％是通过这种“倒挂分包”方式实现的，而且这个比例还有上升的趋势（Reeves，2002）。

10.4.3　从美国看建筑交易体制变迁的循环往复性[1]

和其他制度一样，建筑交易体制的变迁是一个循环往复的螺旋式上升过程。美国的公共建设项目主要分布在基础设施领域，21 世纪初，美国基础设施的存量高达 7 万亿美元。在讨论建设交易体制变迁时，美国把基础设施建筑市场作为主要研究对象。在过去的 200 多年里，美国基础设施建设项目的采购方式经历了二维空间的三阶段变迁（Piteroforte and Miller，2002）。如图 10.7 所示，不同的融资方式与不同的一体化程度相组合，可得到不同的制度安排。图中列出的各种项目采购方式具有各自的优点和局限性，它们在不同的历史阶段发挥了不同的作用。

	设计与施工相分离	设计与施工合为一体	设计与施工、运营合为一体
政府直接投资	PP（并行承包）[2] DBB（设计–招标–施工）	TKY（交钥匙） DB（设计–施工）	Super–TKY（超级交钥匙） DBO（设计–施工–运营）
间接融资			BOT（建设–运营–转交） BOO（建设–拥有–运营） DBOT（设计–施工–运营–转交） BOOT（建设–拥有–运营–转交）

图 10.7　美国基础设施建设项目采购方式的变迁空间

（资料来源：Piteroforte and Miller，2002）

美国基础设施的项目采购方式的变迁大体上可分为三个阶段。第一阶段从独立起到“二战”结束。在独立初期，由于政府财力不足，向欧洲贷款也很困难，所以私人投资在基础设施建设中发挥了相当大的作用。通过特许经营方式进行的私人融资与政府财政拨款的直接融资并存，形成了双轨制。据统计，从 1789 年到 1933 年经济大萧条爆发之前这段时间，大约有 90％的基础设施是以设计—施工—运营三位一体的方式进行的，其中大约有 60％的项目依靠私人融资。这些项目兼有 DBO 和 BOT 的性质。

---

[1] 这一节的内容主要来自发表在《建筑经济》杂志上的文章（沙凯逊等，2003）

[2] PP（parallel prime）是美国在核电站等重大项目建设中常用的项目采购方式。在这种制度安排下，一个建设项目被分解为不同的部分，由两个或多个施工企业承包，这些承包商分别接受业主或项目管理委员会的直接管理，彼此之间不发生横向联系。

横贯美洲大陆的铁路和电报的特许经营是私人融资的典型案例。这种体制的效率高、交易成本低，但是设计与施工人员之间缺乏有效的相互监督和约束，再加上承包商自身设计力量的不足，工程质量难以得到保证。在1875年前的一段时间里，“豆腐渣”大坝、桥梁坍塌等恶性事故屡屡发生，平均每年有25座桥梁坍塌。针对这种情况，美国政府从1893年开始在联邦政府的公共项目中实行设计与施工分离（DBB）的项目采购方式，并在1926年的公共建筑法中作为强制执行的条款。

第二阶段从“二战”结束到20世纪80年代末。在这个时期美国的财力充足，政府有能力对公共项目直接投资。由于政府在法律和政策上的鼓励和支持，独立的专业设计人员自身实力有了很大提高。因此，这个阶段建设项目的采购方式以政府直接投资以及设计与施工的分离为主要特点，DBB成为基础设施建设的主要项目采购方式。这种方式对保证公共项目的质量发挥了很好的作用，但同时又逐渐衍生出庞大的官僚机构，使得效率降低，交易成本提高。此外，每年高达3500亿美元的基础设施维护管理费用也使政府背上不小的负担。

进入20世纪90年代以后，由于高新技术的发展和企业结构的变化，集设计与施工于一体的DB方式又重新受到重视。从1995年开始，以DB方式进行的项目每年以6%的速度递增。1999年对400家最大的承包商的统计表明，有62%的企业在建设项目中采用了DB方式。DBO和BOT等项目采购方式也在交通、污水处理等公共项目中重新得到广泛应用（Pietroforte and Miller，2002）。美国的经验再次印证了“天下大势，分久必合，合久必分”的道理。

10.5 我国的建筑交易体制：回顾与展望[1]

从严格意义上讲，在20世纪80年代之前我国没有建筑交易体制。在计划经济体制下，建筑业的独立地位和建筑产品的商品属性被抹杀。既然没有建筑市场和商品交易的概念，建筑交易体制也就无从谈起。1980年4月，邓小平关于建筑业和住宅问题的讲话迎来了建筑业的春天（杨慎，2010）：

> 要改变一个观念，就是认为建筑业是赔钱的。应该看到，建筑业是可以赚钱的，是可以为国家增加收入、增加积累的一个重要产业部门。要不然，就不能说明为什么资本主义国家把它当作经济的三大支柱之一。所以在长期规划中，必须把建筑业放在重要地位。

这个具有划时代意义的讲话在启动建筑业全面改革的同时，也为建筑交易体制注

[1] 这一节的内容主要来自发表在《建筑经济》杂志上的文章（沙凯逊，曾大林，张琳，2017；沙凯逊，张琳，房勤英，2017）。

入强劲的发展动力。经过三十多年的探索与努力，建筑业已经成为国民经济的支柱产业，具有中国特色的建筑交易体制框架也已初步成型。

10.5.1　从无到有的发展历程

图 10.8 给出了我国建筑交易体制发展的基本脉络。该体制的发展历程具有以下特点。一是自上而下的动力机制——这反映出对传统体制的“路径依赖”。首先，建筑业的改革是由政府发起的。具体来讲，是邓小平 1980 年 4 月的讲话拉开了建筑业改革的

阶段	主要事件
项目法施工和项目经理责任制	•1982年11月，鲁布革水电站开工。其中的引水隧洞工程首次利用世行贷款，采取国际招投标程序，授予外企承包权　取得了巨大成功，产生了“鲁布革冲击 ”。 •1987年9月，国务院召开全国施工会议，提出并推广鲁布革经验，推行项目法施工，把项目经理责任制作为工程项目管理的基本制度。
招标投标制	•1984年11月，国家计委和建设部联合印发《建设工程招标投标暂行规定》。 •1999年9月，《招标投标法》正式颁布，2000年1月施行。
工程监理制	•1988年7月，建设部颁发《关于开展建设监理工作的通知》，开展试点。 •1995年12月，建设部和国家计委联合颁布《工程建设监理规定》，1996年1月实施。 •1997年11月，《建筑法》正式颁布，其中第三十条规定“国家推行建筑工程监理制度”。 •2000年12月，建设部颁发《建设工程监理规范》（GB 50319–2000)，2001年5月实施。
合同管理制	•1991年，工商行政管理局和建设部联合制定《建设工程施工合同》（GF–91–0201），旨在推行建设项目合同管理制。 •1999年3月，《合同法》正式颁布。同年12月，建设部和工商行政管理局联合印发《建设工程施工合同（示范文本）》（GF–1999-0201），2013年4月升级为（GF–2013–0201）。
项目法人责任制	•1996年4月，国家计委印发《关于实行建设项目法人责任制的暂行规定》的通知，规定国有单位经营性基本建设大中型项目在建设阶段必须组建项目法人。项目法人可按《公司法》的规定设立有限责任公司（包括国有独资公司）和股份有限公司形式。
工程总承包和工程项目管理	•2002年8月，北京的LG大厦建设项目开工。该项目以扩大初步设计和技术规范、标准为基础进行招标，成为真正意义上的总承包工程。其成功经验产生了巨大影响，引发了所谓的“ LG冲击”。 •2003年2月，住建部颁发《关于培育发展工程总承包和工程项目管理企业的指导意见》。
代建制	•1993年，厦门市开始进行代建制试点工作。2001年7月，《厦门市重点工程建设项目代建管理暂行办法》明确提出代建制的定义及适用范围。 •2004年7月，国务院颁布《关于投资体制改革的决定》，规定对非经营性政府投资项目加快推行代建制 。
PPP	•2005年3月，住建部颁发《市政公用事业特许经营管理办法》。 •2013年12月，全国财政工作会议以 “政府和社会资本合作模式”的名义正式提出PPP。 •2014年9月，财政部发出《关于推广运用政府和社会资本合作模式有关问题的通知》，随后又相继颁布《政府和社会资本合作模式操作指南（试行）》等一系列文件。

图 10.8　我国建筑交易体制的发展脉络

大幕。如果没有这个讲话，我国建筑业恐怕还要在计划经济体制内徘徊一段时间。其次，在制度创新的每一个节点上，都是政府在扮演着推动者和决定者的角色。在改革的初期阶段，由政府主导的模式有其现实合理性，也取得了不错的成效。但是，从长远的角度来看，这种模式在变革动力的持续性方面存在较大的局限性。

二是由点到面的发展轨迹——这体现了"革命性"事件在制度变迁中的作用。"鲁布革冲击"之于我国的建筑交易体制，堪比安徽凤阳小岗村的"大包干"之于农村的经济体制改革。这些看似偶然的事件注定会因为它们在制度演进中的关键性作用而被载入史册。此外，从"LG 冲击"到工程总承包和工程项目管理的实施，从厦门的代建制试点到代建制的全面推行，这些变革也都是按照从个别到一般的逻辑展开的。

三是先易后难的推进策略——这符合渐进式改革的方法论。如何处理政府（计划）与市场的关系，是贯穿三十多年经济体制改革进程的核心问题。围绕这一问题，决策部门和理论界"摸着石头过河"，进行了艰苦曲折的探索。从第 1 讲的图 1.2 和这一讲的图 10.8 的比较中可以看出，建筑交易体制变迁和我国的市场化进程基本上保持同步。在计划经济体制"余威"的影响下，前期的变革重点是建设项目组织实施方式的科学化。在 1992 年中共十四大确立了"建立社会主义市场经济体制"的目标之后，改革的力度明显加大。在投资主体多元化、项目建设市场化的背景下，建设市场秩序的规范化成为后期变革的重点。与此同时，变革的难度也显著增加。

综上所述，我国的建筑交易体制是市场化改革的产物。它以发达国家的经验和国际惯例作为基本参照，同时又深受计划经济体制惯性作用和我国传统文化的影响，因而具有鲜明的中国特色和转型期的时代特征。例如，国际上通行的 PPP（public—private partnerships）在我国是以"政府和社会资本合作模式"的形式出现的。按照《政府和社会资本合作项目通用合同指南》的说明，"社会资本"是指"符合条件的国有企业、民营企业、外商投资企业、混合所有制企业，或其他投资、经营主体"。显然，政府与国有企业之间的合作不属于"公私合伙"的范畴。由此可见，此"PPP"（政府和社会资本合作模式）非彼 PPP（公私合伙制），两者不应混为一谈。再比如，工程监理制和代建制等制度的"中国特色"是如此鲜明，以至于我们在向国外同行介绍它们时找不出相应的国际通用词汇，不得不多费一些口舌。以工程监理制为例，一个可行的办法是先将其翻译成 *Jianli*，然后具体说明它的内涵[1]。这些特殊性为建筑交易体制研究提供了丰富的素材和独特的创新空间。

---

[1] 解释工作可分为三步。(1) 把"监理"(*Jianli*) 一词拆两个汉字"监"和"理"。(2) 分别解释这两个字的含义："监"(*Jian*) 意味着 supervision，monitoring，control，而"理"(*Li*) 的意思是 management，governance，handling。(3) 指出工程监理制的成败取决于"监"和"理"的平衡。这种方法在介绍我校校名时也取得很好的效果。一般我会先把"山东建筑大学"翻译成 Shandong *Jianzhu* University，然后用"ABC"来解释 *Jianzhu*——A，Architecture；B，Building；C，Construction。这样一来，外国朋友就能较好地理解汉语中"建筑"的含义了。

10.5.2　突出的矛盾和问题

我国的建筑交易体制虽然取得了长足的发展和明显的成效，但是从建筑企业、建设项目和建筑市场几个层面的实际情况来看，该体制在理论和实践两个层面上都还存在不少问题。首先是《建筑法》的局限性。我国的法律框架可分为法律、法规、规章制度、规范性文件等多个层次。《建筑法》是建设领域的综合性法律，属于较高的法律层次。然而，由于受当时主客观条件的限制，这部法律在 1997 年颁布之日就存在调整范围狭窄、与其法律地位不相称的问题。随着改革的深入进行，建筑市场环境、建设项目有关各方的利益格局等都发生了重大变化，《建筑法》的局限性愈加明显。虽然国家陆续出台一些层级较低的法规和文件以解燃眉之急，如《建设工程质量管理条例》（2000 年 1 月）、《建设工程勘察设计管理条例》（2000 年 9 月）和《建设工程安全生产管理条例》（2003 年 11 月）等，但是这些条例和法规并不能代替《建筑法》。此外，对设计方和施工方的规制多，而对建设单位的规制明显不足，这也是《建筑法》局限性的一个重要方面。

其次是国际惯例在我国的“水土不服”。这方面突出的例子是“最低价中标”。国际工程招投标一般采用最低价中标的评定办法。根据现有的法律，我国的建设工程招投标采用“经评估的最低价”，也就是“合理低价中标”[1]。然而在实际执行过程中，在“按国际惯例办事”的名义下，“合理低价中标”被理解为“最低价中标”。实践证明，全面放开国内建设工程招投标的价格管控的条件尚未成熟。“最低价中标”往往导致建设市场中的无序竞争，造成施工过程中的偷工减料和重大安全质量事故。

背景资料：最低价中标酿成的恶果（资料来源：朱树英，2016）

2009 年 6 月 27 日，在上海莲花河畔景苑小区施工现场一幢十三层楼房突然整体倒塌。调查结果表明，因合同约定的最低价包死不得调整，施工方为节约运输成本，把原本应该外运的土方堆放在大楼一侧，结果造成堆土高度严重超标，过大的水平力超出桩基的抗侧能力，最终导致楼房倾倒。上海市人大调研报告给出的结论是：废止最低价中标。

最后是制度的退化与失灵。这方面突出的例子是工程监理制和代建制。1984 年，我国在鲁布革水电站建设项目中首次利用世界银行贷款。世行贷款不仅带来了“菲迪克”（FIDIC）的管理模式，而且带来了“工程师”的概念。从此我国建筑业开始探索建立自己的“监理工程师”制度。1988 年发布的《关于开展建设监理工作的通知》是

[1] 《招标投标法》第四十一条规定：“中标人的投标应当符合下列条件之一：能够最大限度地满足招标文件中规定的各项综合评价标准；能够满足招标文件的实质性要求，并且经评审的投标价格最低；但是投标价格低于成本的除外。”

一个具有里程碑意义的文件。在此之后的二十多年的时间里，工程监理制取得了长足的发展，在“三控”（质量控制、工期控制、成本控制）、“两管”（合同管理、信息管理）、“一协调”（全面组织协调）等方面发挥了积极的作用，但是在实施过程中也出现了不少矛盾和问题。近年来，监理行业的发展之路越走越难，越走越窄，以至于不到“而立之年”就出现衰退的迹象。2014 年，深圳市决定在工程建设领域进行改革试点，首先对社会工程全部取消强制监理，然后将非强制监理范围逐步扩大到政府工程（俞小明，2014）。一石激起千层浪，“中国式监理向何处去”成为业界关注的话题。无独有偶，代建制也存在“未老先衰”的问题。我国在 2000 年前后开始试行代建制，旨在遏制政府工程领域的腐败，提高建设效率。但经过各地试行多年之后，代建制对政府工程建设的投资控制、质量控制以及工期控制三个主要绩效指标并没有显著改善。“三超工程”、“豆腐渣工程”以及“钓鱼工程”仍大量涌现，再加上近年来政府工程领域的腐败案件居高不下，代建制的必要性受到质疑（崔宏轶，2014）。

背景资料：监理之痛：监理人员因重大工程事故被判刑的典型案例

2000 年 10 月 25 日，南京电视台演播中心工程在施工中发生模板支撑系统整体坍塌事故，造成 6 人死亡。监理公司驻工地总监被判处有期徒刑五年。

2001 年 9 月 25 日，京福高速公路三明连接线匝道桥模板支架垮塌，造成 6 人死亡。现场监理工程师被判有期徒刑一年，缓刑一年，并处罚金人民币 2 万元。

2005 年 9 月 5 日，北京市西城区西西工程发生模板支撑体系坍塌事故，造成 8 人死亡。监理方北京希地环球建设工程顾问有限公司驻工地总监和监理员都受到有期徒刑三年缓刑三年的刑事处罚。

2007 年 8 月 13 日，湖南省湘西自治州凤凰县正在建设的堤溪沱江大桥发生坍塌事故，造成 64 人死亡。监理方湖南省金衢交通咨询监理有限公司的多名人员因涉嫌工程重大安全事故罪被移交司法机关处理并于次年获刑。

2009 年 6 月 27 日，上海莲花河畔景苑小区施工现场发生楼体坍塌事故，造成一名工人死亡。现场监理工程师被判有期徒刑三年。

2016 年 11 月 24 日，江西丰城发电厂冷却塔施工平台坍塌特别重大事故造成 74 人死亡。监理方上海斯耐迪工程咨询有限公司驻工地总监和安全副总监被依法刑事拘留。

“建筑业就像是一个长不大的孩子。”这是北方某城市一位建管局长的感叹。这位局长大学毕业后先是在当地建筑企业工作，后来被调到交通局工作了十几年，去年又回到建设管理部门担任领导工作。在经过一番调研之后，他发现建筑企业的生存状态和建设市场的基本格局都和当年相差无几，没有什么改善，于是发出了以上感叹。“长不大的孩子”这个命题说出了一个事实：我们的建筑交易体制在经历了早期的快速发展之后，现在似乎进入了一种低水平的均衡状态。

10.5.3　全面深化改革背景下的制度创新

改革进入了攻坚期，我国建筑业面临着巨大挑战。新老矛盾相互交织，许多问题积重难返。在此背景下，业内的有识之士提出了“建筑人之惑”：“建筑业是各行各业中最早进入市场经济的行业之一，为什么改革开放三十多年反而觉得路子越走越窄，甚至有些建筑企业到了举步维艰的地步?”（汪士和，2014）。在回答这个问题之前，不妨做一个横向比较，先看看电子商务行业的发展。

我国的电子商务自 1995 年开始起步，在不到二十年的时间里就按照“点—线—面—体”的逻辑，完成了“工具（百亿级）—渠道（千亿级）—基础设施（万亿级）—经济体（十万亿级）”的“三级跳”。由于电子商务的跨越式发展，我国在 2013 年超越美国，成为全球第一大网络零售市场（郝建彬，2015）。更为重要的是，电子商务正在深刻地改变着人们的生活方式、经济格局和社会面貌。突破 600 亿元的“双十一”单日交易额，遍及城乡的个人网店，无处不在的快递员，所有这一切都在彰显着这个新兴产业的生机和活力。电子商务的兴旺发达与建筑业的困难处境形成强烈的反差。对此人们不禁要问：这两个行业同样都在中国，它们的差距怎么就这么大呢？为什么电子商务行业能够做到后来居上，而最早进行市场化改革的建筑业却是“起了个大早，赶了个晚集”？下面就从制度演化的角度分析影响行业发展的主要因素。

第一个因素是对初始状态的敏感性。20 世纪 80 年代初，在“计划经济为主，市场调节为辅”的背景下启动的建筑业改革注定是一种自上而下的“强制性制度变迁”。这种模式的一个突出问题是重视解决眼前的紧迫性问题，忽视深层次的中长期问题；重视解决周期性矛盾，忽视结构性矛盾（迟福林，2011）。此外，政府主导的改革属于“自我革命”的范畴。一旦改革涉及改革者自身的利益，就会举步维艰。与建筑业的改革相比，电子商务发展的初始条件要好得多。20 世纪 90 年代中期，市场在资源配置中的“基础性作用”已经得到确认。电子商务在这时起步，可谓是恰逢其时。自下而上的市场自发性力量历史地成为行业发展的主要驱动力。不同的起点决定了不同的发展路径和动力机制，最终产生不同的结果。

第二个因素是路径依赖的作用。建筑业是受计划经济体制影响最大行业之一。时至今日，虽然市场经济展现出来的经济能量已经足以令人信服，但是传统体制的惯性仍然在起作用，不时对改革进程施加负面影响。这方面的一个突出例子是工程监理制在发展中遇到的问题。工程监理制是我国建筑业市场化改革进程中最早形成的制度之一，最早可以追溯到鲁布革项目。“监理工程师”这一称谓由 FIDIC 合同中的“工程师”衍生而来。我国是一个十分讲究“名正言顺”的国度。当时在“工程师”前面冠以“监理”两字，就是要和 FIDIC“工程师”保持一定距离。“监”字意味着监督、监控和监管；而“理”字则表示办理、管理和治理。在“有计划的商品经济”的语境中，

“监”字当头是题中应有之义。按理说，随着市场化改革的深入进展，监理工程师应该逐渐向 FIDIC“工程师”的角色靠拢；监理工作的重心也应该逐步从“监”字转到“理”字上来。实际情况却并非如此。2002 年旁站监理模式的推行更加突出了“监”的因素，使监理工程师和 FIDIC“工程师”渐行渐远。正是这种“逆市场化”的趋势使我国工程监理制的发展道路越走越窄。与建筑业相比，电子商务要幸运得多。它没有历史包袱，因而能够轻装前进，在市场化的道路上阔步前行。电子商务的基本经验是：尊重互联网创业者的首创精神，相信和依靠电子商务市场的自我管理与净化能力；秉持“先发展、后管理，在发展中逐步规范”的思路，致力于营造一个较为宽松的政策环境（郝建彬，2015）。这些经验值得建筑业认真思考和借鉴。

第三个因素是博弈结构的差异。博弈模型是对现实世界的理论抽象。从建设项目有关各方的关系来看，我国建筑市场的基本状态可以描述为：处于强势地位的甲方、处于弱势地位的乙方和有失公允的第三方（刘倩等，2008）。贪婪者—分享者—中庸者博弈模型就是根据建设市场的实际情况建立起来的；其中“贪婪者”策略是对公共项目业主行为的描述。而在电子商务领域，由于市场化程度较高，以强凌弱的行为较少发生。因此在相关的博弈模型中，可以把“贪婪者”策略排除在外。不同的支付矩阵导致不同的均衡结果。对贪婪者—分享者—中庸者博弈模型的分析表明，“贪婪者”的存在是帕累托无效结果长期存在的主要原因。要想走出这种低水平均衡，必须改变博弈的支付矩阵，也就是改变“贪婪者”的策略和行为。

分析至此，或许就可以找到“建筑人之惑”的答案。没错，建筑业是我国最早开始改革的行业之一。然而问题就出在这个“早”字上。在市场化改革目标尚未明确的情况下，初期的改革方案肯定是不彻底的，需要在后期逐步完善。但是，由于传统体制的强大惯性，再加上建筑市场中各方关系的不平衡，建筑业并没有按照预定的进程发展，而是进入了帕累托无效的均衡状态。换句话说，当前建筑业面临的诸多困难，在很大程度上都是因为改革不彻底造成的。要想使建筑业走出这种低水平的均衡状态，唯有坚持市场化改革的正确方向，坚持理论创新和制度创新，进一步加大改革的力度。

首先要转换动力机制，形成“有效市场”和“有为政府”的双轮驱动。政府主导的发展模式在我国经济快速增长中固然功不可没，但是政府对微观经济活动的过度干预和介入会扭曲政府与市场的关系，损害市场效率。此外，有些事情单靠行政手段是解决不了的。以农民工工资拖欠问题为例，虽然中央三令五申，各级政府高度重视，甚至总理亲自出面干预，结果也没能根治这一社会顽疾。因此，需要在制度创新上下功夫。在市场层面，要厘清政府和市场的角色和边界，捆绑政府的手，放开市场的腿。要通过权力清单明确政府该做什么，做到“法无授权不可为”；通过责任清单明确政府如何管市场，做到“法定责任必须为”。在项目层面，要对政府投资和非政府投资两种类型的建设项目采取“一手抓、一手放”的方针。前者有利于减少腐败行为和工程质量事故，后者有利于提高效率。在企业层面，要通过负面清单做到“法无禁止皆可为”，减轻负担，激发活力，强化企业的主体地位。

其次要改进方法论，实现“摸着石头过河”和顶层设计的有机结合和优势互补。在顶层设计中，要分清什么是主要矛盾，什么是矛盾的主要方面。一是要尽快完成《建筑法》的修订。在我国的建筑交易体制中，《建筑法》是个纲，纲举才能目张。要扩大《建筑法》的调整范围，从“狭义建筑业”扩展到“广义建筑业”。还要借修订《建筑法》的机会，对相关的法律、法规和政策文件进行全面审视和梳理，采取切实措施，研究和解决某些制度（如工程监理制、代建制等）的退化和失灵问题。二是要切实规范业主，特别是公共项目业主的行为。在建设市场的诸多矛盾中，建设项目各方的关系失衡是主要矛盾。在公共项目的诸多当事人中，政府业主是矛盾的主要方面。因此，规范公共项目业主行为应该作为顶层设计的一个重点。三是要下决心建立自己产业工人队伍。行业竞争力的提升最终取决于以人为本的良性循环。一个现代产业必须拥有一支高素质的产业工人队伍，否则就会成为无源之水、无本之木。要从理论和实践两方面对建筑企业管理层与作业层“两层分离”进行反思，总结劳务分包的利弊得失，下决心改变建筑业用工方式，建立新型产业工人队伍。

最后一点，也是最重要的一点是要转变思维方式，少一些监管思维，多一些治理思维。监管思维强调下级对上级的服从，强调令行禁止，其背后是“上智下愚”的价值判断，这种思维方式在国内外都有悠久的传统。治理思维则是现代化进程中“经理革命”的产物；这种思维方式重视当事人之间的策略性活动，承认“上有政策、下有对策”的事实，要求政策制定者在制定政策时尽量考虑可能出现的对策，通过适当的制度安排，激励人们有积极性去做正确的事情，并且把事情做好。当前，我国的改革已进入“深水区”，使所有人都受益的改革（帕累托改进）已经基本结束；剩下的改革都涉及利益的调整，必然会有人受益，也有人受损（卡尔多改进），都是些难啃的硬骨头（金社平，2016）。正是在这种背景下，“推进国家治理体系和治理能力现代化”被作为全面深化改革的总目标。前面的分析表明，我国建筑业走出低水平均衡状态的关键在于有效抑制“贪婪者”策略。实践证明，在这方面单靠政府监管是不行的。只有通过营造良好的制度环境，充分发挥市场（看不见的手）、政府（看得见的手）和建筑专业体制（第三只手）三方面的作用，才能促进建筑交易体制向有利的方向转变。

10.6　结　　论

在一个充满变化的世界里，唯一不变的事情就是“变化”。在建筑交易体制的演化过程中，均衡是相对的，变化是绝对的。从本质上看，现实世界是不均衡的。均衡经济学充其量是对现实世界的“接近”，而不是现实本身（宋小川，2003）。经济变化的原因是内生的，其动态过程本质上是非均衡和非线性的。建筑交易体制变迁的动力不在于无法解释的外部力量，而在于体制内部不均衡力量的相互作用。正因为如此，建筑交易体制表现出多样性和复杂性的特点。

博弈论模型的价值并不在于它解决具体问题的能力，而是在于它所提供的启示与洞察力。例如，经典的囚徒困境博弈模型，尽管十分简单，却揭示了一个深刻的道理：个人效用最大化行为未必导致社会福利最优。同样，这里的贪婪者—分享者—惩罚者博弈模型，一方面可以解释当前我国建筑市场失灵的现实，另一方面又可以帮助人们坚定市场化改革的方向。

制度的形成和发展有赖于文化的滋养。各种建筑交易体制无不打上历史、文化、社会和经济的烙印。西方在经济管理领域的先进经验，可分解为三个层面：科学性层面、技术性层面和文化性层面。如果说，这些先进经验在科学性层面和技术性层面具有国际化的特征，那么，在文化性层面，必须考虑本土化的问题，也就是如何适应所在国家和地区的文化传统的问题。

我国的建筑交易体制在市场化改革的背景下应运而生并且快速成型。从 20 世纪 80 年代中期算起，它现在已经进入“而立之年”。然而，从“而立”到“不惑”还有很长的路要走。从总体上看，我国的建筑交易体制仍处于其生命周期的初级阶段。前面提到的许多矛盾和问题都是结构性的；结构性的矛盾需要通过结构性改革来解决。结构性改革需要转换发展理念，涉及部门利益、地方利益和行业利益的深刻调整，因而注定是一项艰巨的任务。

“建筑人之惑”是对整个建筑业体制机制的一次深层次拷问。破解这个难题，不能就事论事，头痛医头，脚痛医脚，而是要坚持历史的、比较的和系统的立场和观点，从体制机制上找原因，从制度创新上找出路。在时间的维度上，历史的观点要求充分认识制度变迁的路径依赖性，瞻前顾后，认真总结历史经验，特别是改革开放以来的经验教训。在空间的维度上，比较的观点要求在学习和吸取国外经验的同时，充分认识不同文化对制度演进的影响。在关系的维度上，系统的观点要求充分考虑不同利益主体和要素之间的联系，具体来讲，就是要综合考虑建筑企业和建设项目之间，项目的甲方、乙方和第三方之间，以及体制、治理和管理三个层次之间的联系和相互影响关系。在这方面，第 5 讲提出的面向双重对象（建筑企业—建设项目）的三层次（建筑交易体制—治理—管理）分析框架或许是一个合适的工具。

参考文献

1. 迟福林（2011）把政府主导等同“中国模式”有可能耽误改革，光明日报，2011-10-2.
2. 崔宏轶（2014）委托人“理性”对激励约束机制的冲击：政府投资工程代建制改革困境研究，广州：中山大学出版社.
3. 郝建彬（2015）二十年：中国电子商务史话，互联网经济，(5)，90—97.
4. 亨德里克斯（2007）组织的经济学与管理学，中译本，胡雅梅，张学渊，曹利群译，北京：中国人民大学出版社.

5. 金社平（2016）全面深化改革三年了，人民日报，2016-11-14.
6. 刘倩，杨杰，沙凯逊（2008）建筑企业的盈利能力：调研与思考，建筑经济，（1），17—19.
7. 沙凯逊（2013）建设项目治理，北京：中国建筑工业出版社.
8. 沙凯逊，邓晓红（2001）欧盟建筑交易体制比较研究：启发与思考，建筑经济，（3），19—22.
9. 沙凯逊，宋涛，赵锦锴，殷涛（2003）从美日两国的历史经验看建筑交易体制创新，建筑经济，（3），10—12.
10. 沙凯逊，曾大林，张琳（2017）对我国建筑交易体制发展历程的回顾与反思，建筑经济，**38**（4），5—8.
11. 沙凯逊，张琳，房勤英（2017）全面深化改革背景下我国建筑业的制度创新，建筑经济，**38**（5），5—7.
12. 舒迟（2001）国际恐怖与国际政治，读书，（11），3—8.
13. 宋小川（2003）非均衡的经济动态模型，经济研究，（7），3—8.
14. 汪士和（2014）关于建筑业全面深化改革的思考，建筑，（2），6—11.
15. 杨慎（2010）《邓小平关于建筑业和住宅问题的谈话》发表纪实，中国发展观察，（7），36—37.
16. 殷雅俊（2010）超级分形雪花与埃舍尔的画作，水木清华，（7），47—49.
17. 俞小明（2014）对深圳市逐步取消强制监理制度的思考，建设监理，（5），5—6.
18. 朱树英（2016）低价中标 放开还是严控，建筑市场与招标投标，（1），22—24.
19. Aoki，M.（2001）*Towards a Comparative Institutional Analysis*，MIT Press，Cambridge.
20. Aoki，M.（2010）Between game theory and institutional studies：the dual-dualities of the institutional process，Available at SSRN：http://ssrn. com/abstract=1624003，(accessed 2 December 2014).
21. Aumann，R. J. and Brandenburger，A.（1995）Epistemic conditions for Nash equilibrium，*Econometrica*，**63**（5），1161—1180.
22. Bologna，R. and Nord，R. Del（2000）Effects of the law reforming public works contracts on the Italian building progress，*Building Research and Information*，**28**（2），109—18.
23. Bowles，S.（2004）*Microeconomics：Behavior，Institutions and Evolution*，Princeton University Press，Princeton.
24. Brener，W. and Kok，K.（2000）The Dutch construction industry：a combination of competition and corporatism，*Building Research and Information*，**28**（2），96—108.
25. Bröchner，J.，Josephson P. E. and Kadefors，A.（2002）Swedish construction culture，management and collaborative quality practice，*Building Research and Information*，**30**（6），392—400.
26. Brousseau，E. and Raynaud，E.（2011）'Climbing the hierarchical ladders of rules'：a life-cycle theory of institutional evolution，*Journal of Economic Behavior & Organization*，**79**（1—2），65—79.
27. Campagnac，E.（2000）The contracting system in the French construction industry：actors and institutions，Building Research and Information，**28**（2），131—40.
28. Dulaimi，M. F.，Ling，F. Y. Y.，Ofori，G. and Silva，N. D.（2002）Enhancing integration and innovation in construction，*Building Research and Information*，**30**（4），237—247.
29. Gintis，H.（2009）*The Bounds of Reason：Game Theory and the Unification of the Behavioral Sciences*，Princeton University Press，Princeton.
30. Loosemore，M.（2000）*Crisis Management in Construction Projects*，ASCE Press，Virginia.

31. Maynard Smith, J. (1982) *Evolution and the Theory of Games*, Cambridge University Press, Cambridge.

32. Maynard Smith, J. and Price, G. R. (1973) The logic of animal conflict, *Nature*, **246**, 15—18.

33. McKenzie, A. J. (2009) Evolutionary game theory, *The Stanford Encyclopedia of Philosophy*, Fall 2009 Edition, Zalta, E. N. (Ed.), URL = http://plato. tanford. edu/archives/fall2009/entries/game-evolutionary/.

34. Ofori, G. (2002) Singapore' s construction: moving towards a knowledge-based industry, *Building Research and Information*, **30** (6), 401—412.

35. Piteroforte, R. and Miller, J. B. (2002) Procurement methods for US infrastructure: historical perspective and recent trends, *Building Research and Information*, **30** (6), 425—434.

36. Reeves, K. (2002) Construction business system in Japan: general contractors and subcontractors, *Building Research and Information*, **30** (6), 413—424.

37. Rwelamila, P. D. (2002) Creating an effective construction industry strategy in South Africa, *Building Research and Information*, **30** (6), 435—4410.

38. Searle, J. R. (1995) *The Construction of Social Reality*, The Free Press, New York.

39. Searle, J. R. (2005) What is an institution? *Journal of Institutional Economics*, **1** (1), 1—22.

40. Sha, K. X. (2004) Construction business system in China: an institutional transformation perspective, *Building Research and Information*, **32** (6), 529—537.

41. Sha, K. X. and Hua, D. D. (2013) Historical dynamics of construction business systems: An institutional evolution perspective, *The Engineering Project Organization Journal*, **3** (4), 227—239.

42. Syben, G. (2000) Contractors take command: from a demand-based towards a procedure oriented model in German construction, *Building Research and Information*, **28** (2), 119—30.

43. Taylor, P. D. and Jonker, L. B. (1978). *Evolutionarily stable strategies and game dynamics*, Mathematical Biosciences, **40** (1-2), 145—156.

44. Williamson, O. E. (2000) The new institutional economics: taking stock, looking ahead, *Journal of Economic Literature*, **38** (3), 595—613.

45. Wilson, D. S. (1989) Levels of selection: an alternative to individualism in the human sciences, *Social Networks*, **11** (3), 257—272.

46. Winch, G. M. (2000a) Construction business systems in the European Union, *Building Research and Information*, **28** (2), 88—910.

47. Winch, G. M. (2000b) Institutional reform in British construction: partnering and private finance, *Building Research and Information*, **28** (2), 141—510.

48. Winch, G. M. (2010) *Managing Construction Projects: Information Processing Approach*, 2nd Edition, Wiley-Blackwell, Oxford.

49. Yamagishi, T., Hashimoto, H. and Schug, J. (2008). Preferences versus strategies as explanations for culture-specific behavior, *Psychological Science*, **19** (6), 578—83.

附录　近年来在国际刊物上发表的相关文章摘要

Vertical governance of construction projects: an information cost perspective

Kaixun Sha

Abstract: A research framework is developed to analyse the vertical governance, or transaction relationships between the client and its first-tier suppliers of construction projects in terms of project procurement route and payment terms. Starting from the particularity of the construction industry, reduced treatments that Williamson used in governance structure analysis are revised, and an assumption of ‘second-order transformation’ is proposed: as the information gap reaches a given level, and the proportion of specialized knowledge to deal with uncertainty exceeds a certain degree, the approach of selecting the governance structure of construction projects might deviate from the path anticipated by canonical theories. Both uncertainty and information cost are included in the analysis framework, and a principal—agent model is developed to analyse the procurement route and payment terms of construction projects. It is concluded that the information gap and the relative cost coefficient of information are decisive factors that determine the vertical governance structure of construction projects. They determine not only the time when ‘second-order transformation’ occurs, but also the distribution of ‘weak incentive regions’.

Keywords: Contracting, governance, information cost, project, transaction cost, uncertainty

此文发表在 *Construction Management and Economics* (CME), 2011, Vol. 29, No. 11, 1137—1147.

http://dx.doi.org/10.1080/01446193.2011.637939

Historical dynamics of construction business systems: an institutional evolution perspective

Kaixun Sha and Dongdong Hua

Abstract: As a kind of basic institutional environment, the construction business system provides an underlying platform of the interactions for stakeholders of construction projects and hence exerts a great influence on the building sector. Taking the view of 'the construction business system as a complex adaptive system', a research framework is developed with the aim of understanding how and why construction business systems emerge and evolve over time. The principles of evolutionarily stable strategy and replicator dynamic are briefly introduced. A three-strategy evolutionary game model is developed on the basis of a set of assumptions, with the distinctiveness of the construction industry fully taken into consideration. The model illustrates some characteristic outcomes: multiple equilibria, path dependence, original-state-sensitiveness, the long-term persistence of Pareto-inferior outcomes as well as proneness to the stable equilibrium characterized by more efficient negotiation and higher average payoff. It is expected that introducing 'revolutionary' events that are not explicitly modeled, such as non-best responses and exogenous changes, could break the existing equilibrium and bring about new equilibrium outcomes.

Keywords: Complexity, construction business system, equilibrium, evolution, game theory, modelling

此文发表在 *The Engineering Project Organization Journal*（EPOJ），2013，Vol. 3，No. 4，227—239.

http：//dx. doi. org/10. 1080/21573727. 2013. 822366

Relational contracting in China's building sector: potentialities and challenges

Kaixun Sha

Abstract: As an alternative way of governing construction projects, relational contracting (RC) can be understood as a historically and contextually embedded practice. This paper intends to examine the potentialities and challenges of RC implementation in China's building sector. Based on the review of law scholars' approach and new institutional economics approach to relational governance, RC in construction is conceptualized as an intentionally incomplete, largely self-enforcing arrangement that places emphasis on *ex post* 3Rs: renegotiation, realignment of the interests of contracting parties and restoration of the efficiency of the project. Two types of RC in construction, i. e., quasi RC such as design—bid—build and design—build procurement strategies and 'true' RC such as project partnering and framework agreements are distinguished from each other. The SWOT (strengths, weaknesses, opportunities, threats) method is used to assess both internal and external aspects of implementing RC in China's building sector. It is concluded that the successful application of RC is dependent on the maturity of the construction market, the improvement of professionalism in the building sector, and the alteration of attitude in the part of governments who are not only legislators and policy-makers, but also the largest construction clients.

Keywords: Construction project, relational governance, *ex post* renegotiation, SWOT method

此文发表在 *International Journal of Architecture, Engineering and Construction* (IJAEC), 2016, Vol. 5, No. 4, 207—216. DOI: 10.7492/IJAEC.2016.020

Professionalism in China's building sector: an economic governance perspective

Kaixun Sha

Abstract: As the third force beside markets and governments, professionalism emerged to protect the interests of civil society, and it has played a unique role in the building sector. By conceptualizing professionalism as a community-based governance structure, an economic governance perspective is adopted to examine professionalism in China's building sector. The development of professionalism in China's building sector is reviewed, and both its achievements and its weaknesses are assessed. Root-cause analysis reveals that the primary impediment to building professionalism is the imbalanced relationship between markets, governments and professionals. It is argued that the success of professionalism in China's building sector is dependent ultimately on whether the government can change its overly dominant role in the economy. To address the concern of creating an independent, vibrant professional culture that contributes to the long-term public interest, the following are recommended: separating professional associations and relevant bodies from government agencies completely; improving the administrative system for both practice qualification and market access; and increasing the proportion of non-government investments to change the imbalanced relationship between professionals and public clients.

Keywords: Built environment, construction industry, governance, integrity, professionalism, uncertainty, China

此文发表在 *Building Research and Information* (BRI), 2013, Vol. 41, No. 6, 742—751.

http://dx.doi.org/10.1080/09613218.2013.842459

Multi-level governance for building energy conservation in rural China

Kaixun Sha and Shaoyan Wu

Abstract: Under the city—countryside dual structure, the existing building governance system in China differentiates between urban and rural areas. When updating building regulations and related policies to meet challenges in the built environment, it is essential to develop different strategies for different locations according to local circumstances, requirements and capabilities. Based on two research projects, this article examines the mechanisms and strategies for promoting building energy conservation in rural China from the perspective of economic governance. The challenges and potentials of building energy conservation in rural China are analyzed. The essence of the governance paradigm is briefly reviewed. A three-level analysis framework is developed in which markets, governments and the third party (professionals and others) play complementary roles in regulating stakeholders' behaviour. A key question addressed is how to create a favourable institutional environment in which people are willing to do the right things. Different strategy portfolios are proposed for different levels, including technology strategy, financing strategy, as well as regulations and incentive policies. In conclusion, there is no 'best' but rather the 'most suitable' approach to building governance. In this light, the principle of discriminating alignment and the multilevel analysis approach provides conceptual insights.

Keywords: Economic incentives, energy conservation, flexibility, governance, regulation, China

此文发表在 *Building Research and Information* (BRI), 2016, Vol. 44, Nos. 5—6, 619—629.

http://dx. doi. org/10. 1080/09613218. 2016. 1152787

欲查看全文者请链接以下地址：https://www. researchgate. net/profile/Kaixun _ Sha/publications

后　记

本书的初衷是在《建设项目治理》（以下简称《治理》）一书的基础上，以“读者友好”（reader—friendly）的方式介绍近年来我在建设项目治理领域学习和研究的心得体会。所谓“读者友好”，就是要让读者易读易懂，易于掌握。因此在写作过程中，我不断用以下问题提醒自己：

- 对于所写的内容，你自己是否已经真正搞懂？
- 是否已经把自己想表达的意思清楚地表达出来？
- 对于这样的表达，一般的读者是否能够理解？
- 是否还有更简单或更清楚的表述方式？

就这样边写边问，原本以为可以在一年之内完成的工作计划，结果却用了三年的时间。进度虽慢，心里却比较踏实。

就表现形式而言，本书可以看作是《治理》的普及版。在《治理》一书中隐含了一个假设，即读者已经掌握了相应的经济学和数学知识。因此在《治理》中，形式化建模和解析方面的内容占了相当大的比重。本书放松了上述假设，省略了数学推导过程，力求以浅显易懂和直观形象的方式来说明问题。比如在介绍联盟博弈核仁解的概念时，我以“三妻分产”博弈为例，通过思想实验的方法来还原古代犹太人的推断过程。在单纯形中进行的“沙盘推演”的结果表明，“三妻分产”的分配方案是在一定的社会伦理法则支配下不断试错的结果；古代犹太人的观念“无意中”与两千多年后现代人的“最大最小原则”相吻合。我相信，这种方法有利于提高读者的阅读兴趣，并有助于他们对相关知识的理解和掌握。

就实际内容而言，本书又可以看作是《治理》的升级版。首先，本书增添了最近三年来的最新研究成果，涉及对项目和治理的再认识、共同代理理论、关系合同与非正式制度安排、建筑专业体制和行业自律等方面的内容。例如，本书的代序 Understanding construction project governance：an inter-organizational perspective 就是 2016 年发表的一篇文章。其次，本书用较大篇幅对一些基本概念和基本理论进行了比较系统深入的梳理和讨论，旨在确立正确的“项目观”，并且使治理摆脱管理的“阴影”，取得相对独立的地位。最后，本书的分析框架由《治理》的“一纲三目”扩展为“一纲五目”——“一纲”没有变，依然是基于博弈论的制度分析这条主线。“五目”是指后半部分所涉及的五个研究层次：（1）基于委托代理的建设项目垂直治理研究，（2）基于联盟博弈的建设项目水平治理研究，（3）基于共同代理的针对项目经理的治理研究，（4）建设项目治理中的非正式制度安排研究，涉及关系治理、建筑专业体制和行业自律，（5）基于演化博弈的建筑交易体制的变迁机理研究。此外，附录部分收录了几篇近年来在国际刊物上发表的文章摘要。

学而时习之，不亦说乎？诚哉斯言。有朋友问："你现在做什么？还在看书吗?"我答道："百无一用是书生，我除了看书还能做什么?"但转念一想，这样的回答未免有些消极。实际上，能静下心来读书学习，于人于己都是一件有益的事情。如果能够把经过消化吸收的读书心得传播出去，对他人或许可以提供一点有用的信息。再进一步，如果能够对相关领域的知识积累有些微贡献，岂不更好？对自己来说，让时光在没有压力的读写生活中逝去，实在是一种幸福。正如孔子所说，乐以忘忧，不知老之将至。最后借用一位诗人的话自勉：我有时间看书，没工夫去老。Just do it，and enjoy it. 没错，就这样做下去并尽情享受吧。